CHRONICLES

OF

THE PILGRIM FATHERS

OF

THE COLONY OF PLYMOUTH,

FROM 1602 TO 1625.

NOW FIRST COLLECTED FROM ORIGINAL RECORDS AND CONTEMPORANEOUS
PRINTED DOCUMENTS, AND ILLUSTRATED WITH NOTES.

By ALEXANDER YOUNG.

'Gentis cunabula nostræ.'
'The mother of us all.'

SECOND EDITION.

CLEARFIELD

Originally Published
Boston, Massachusetts
1844

Reprinted
Genealogical Publishing Co., Inc.
Baltimore, Maryland
1974

Reprinted for
Clearfield Company, Inc. by
Genealogical Publishing Co., Inc.
Baltimore, Maryland
1995, 2004

Library of Congress Cataloging in Publication Data

Young, Alexander, 1800-1854.
   Chronicles of the Pilgrim fathers of the colony of Plymouth, from 1602 to 1625.

   Reprint of the 2d ed. published in 1844 by C. C. Little and J. Brown, Boston.
   CONTENTS: Gov. Bradford's History of Plymouth colony.—Bradford's and Winslow's journal.—Cushman's discourse. [etc.]
   1. Massachusetts—History—Colonial period (New Plymouth)—Sources. 2. Pilgrim Fathers. I. Title.
F68.Y68 1974   974.4'02   74-830
ISBN 0-8063-0611-4

Reprinted from a volume in
the George Peabody Branch,
Enoch Pratt Free Library,
Baltimore, Maryland
1974

Made in the United States of America

TO

THE HONORABLE

WILLIAM PRESCOTT, LL.D.

IN TOKEN OF HIGH ESTEEM

AND SINCERE REGARD,

THIS VOLUME

IS RESPECTFULLY INSCRIBED

BY HIS OBLIGED FRIEND

AND PASTOR.

PREFACE.

THIS volume will be found to contain an authentic History of the Pilgrim Fathers who planted the Colony of Plymouth, from their origin in John Robinson's congregation in 1602, to his death in 1625, written by themselves. Some account of the nature of these Chronicles, and of the circumstances which led to their compilation in this form, may not be unacceptable to the reader.

It is well known to those who are familiar with the early history of New England, that William Bradford, the second governor of Plymouth, wrote a History of that People and Colony from 1602 to 1647, in 270 folio pages; which was used by Morton in compiling his Memorial, by Hutchinson in writing his History of Massachusetts, and by Prince in digesting his Annals of New England. The manuscript of this valuable work, being deposited with Prince's library in the tower of the Old South Church in this city, disappeared in the War of the Revolution, when that church was occupied by the British troops, and has long since been given up by our historians as lost. The most important part of this lost History I have had the good fortune to recover. On a visit at Plymouth, a few years since, I found in the records of the First Church a narrative, in the hand-writing of Secretary Morton, which, on comparing it with the large extracts in Hutchinson[1] and Prince,[2] I recognized as the identical History of Governor Bradford; a fact put beyond all doubt by a marginal note of Morton at the beginning of it, in which he says, "This was originally penned by Mr. William Bradford, governor of New Plymouth." This fact of the real authorship of the document seems to have escaped the observation of all who had preceded me in examining the records, such as Judge Davis, Mr. Bancroft, and even of Hazard, who attributes it expressly to Nathaniel Morton.[3] Hazard copied and printed the larger part of it, as a work of Morton's, in his valuable collection of State Papers, though in a very incomplete and inaccurate form, not being able always to decipher the cramped and abbreviated characters in which it is written, and being frequently obliged to leave blank spaces in his page.

[1] By comparing the second chapter in this volume with the first article in Hutchinson's Appendix, ii. 449–451, which he quotes from Bradford's MS., it will be found that they agree nearly word for word.

[2] The extracts in Prince are too numerous to be referred to; the principal are on pages 114, 120, 128, 130, 140–145, 147, 155, 160, of the octavo edition, printed in 1826.

[3] Hazard's State Papers, i. 340.

PREFACE. vii

By the favor of the Plymouth Church I was permitted to make a new transcript of this very important paper, the entire accuracy of which has been secured by its careful collation with another copy made by the Rev. William P. Lunt, of Quincy, who kindly favored me with the loan of it. The value of this document depends upon its authorship, and cannot be over-estimated. It takes precedence of every thing else relating to the Pilgrims, in time, authority, and interest. It will be found to contain a detailed history of their rise in the north of England, their persecutions there, their difficult and perilous escape into Holland, their residence in that hospitable land for twelve years, the causes which led to their emigration, and the means which they adopted to transport themselves to America.

The next document is Bradford's and Winslow's Journal of the first settlement of the Colony, containing a minute diary of events from the arrival of the Mayflower at Cape Cod, November 9, 1620, to the return of the Fortune, December 11, 1621. This document joins on to the former, making a continuous narrative. It was printed in London in 1622, with a Preface signed by G. MOURT, and has since been usually cited as Mourt's Relation. It will be seen from the notes on pages 113 and 115 of this volume, that Mourt was probably George Morton, the father of Nathaniel, the Secretary, then resident in England, that he had no hand in writing the Journal, but that it was actually written by Bradford and Winslow, a circumstance which gives to it new value and interest, and confers on it the highest authority. In 1625, this Relation was abridged by Purchas, and printed in the fourth volume of his Pilgrims. This abridgment, comprising only about half of the original, and abounding with errors, was reprinted in 1802 in the eighth volume of the Collections of the Massachusetts Historical Society. In 1822, after an interval of twenty years, the portions omitted by Purchas were reprinted in the nineteenth volume of the same Collections, from a manuscript copy of the original edition, made at Philadelphia. The transcriber, however, omitted some important passages, and committed many errors in copying. The parts of the work being thus disjointed, and printed in separate volumes, rendered the reading of it extremely difficult and repulsive. The present is the only correct and legible reprint that has been made since the appearance of the original in 1622.

The third paper is Robert Cushman's Discourse, delivered at Plymouth in November, 1621, reprinted from an old copy in the library of the American Antiquarian Society.

The fourth document is Edward Winslow's Relation, entitled "Good News from New England," which takes up the narrative where it was left off by the former Journal, and brings it down to September 10, 1623,

PREFACE. ix

This book was printed in London in 1624, was abridged by Purchas in the same way as the former Relation, was reprinted in the same fragmentary manner by the Massachusetts Historical Society in 1802, and the omissions in a separate volume in 1822. It is now reprinted for the first time entire, and in a legible form, from the original London edition, for which, as well as for the original of Bradford's and Winslow's Journal, I am indebted to the rich library of Harvard College.

Next in order is Edward Winslow's "Brief Narration of the true grounds or cause of the first planting of New England," which was printed at London in 1646, at the end of his Answer to Gorton. No copy of this rare book is known to exist in this country. The manuscript from which I print was kindly copied for me by the Rev. George E. Ellis, of Charlestown, from the printed volume in the British Museum. In this paper we have the original of Robinson's celebrated farewell address to the Pilgrims at Leyden, and several facts relating to them not recorded elsewhere.

The sixth paper is a Dialogue, written by Governor Bradford, which has never before appeared in print. A fragment of it, written with his own hand, I found among the manuscripts in the cabinet of the Massachusetts Historical Society; but the entire work I obtained from the records of the First Church in Plymouth, into which it was copied by Secretary Morton.

The next document is a Memoir of Elder Brewster, written by Governor Bradford as part of his History, and also copied by Morton into the Church records.

The volume closes with some letters of John Robinson, and of the Pilgrims at Leyden and Plymouth, procured from the records of the Plymouth Church and from Governor Bradford's Letter Book.

The value of these contemporaneous documents cannot be overstated. They are the earliest chronicles of New England. We have here the first book of our history, written by the actors themselves. We should esteem it a fortunate circumstance, a peculiar privilege, that we thus have the whole story of the origin of this earliest of our northern colonies in the very words of the first planters.[1] In authority and importance nothing can exceed them; and I feel that I have been engaged in a useful as well as interesting labor in collecting together and illustrating these scattered memorials of the Fathers. The notes will be found to be copious and various, touching upon all points, and in all cases referring to authorities from which the statements may be verified, and fuller information be obtained. Considering myself as engaged in erecting another monument to the memory of the Pilgrims, I have spared neither labor nor expense in endeavouring to render the work accurate and complete. If the

---

[1] " Quis est autem, quem non moveat clarissimis monumentis testata consignataque antiquitas?" CICERO *de Divinatione*, lib. i. 40.

reader shall derive from its perusal the same satisfaction which I have found in its compilation, I shall feel myself abundantly remunerated for this labor of love. Regarding these documents as the only authentic chronicles of those times, I have considered all deviations from them in subsequent writers as errors, and when they have fallen under my notice, I have not scrupled to point them out. In this I have no other object in view than historical accuracy; and accordingly for whatever errors I may have fallen into, I shall hold myself equally obnoxious to criticism.

The portrait of Governor Winslow at the beginning of the volume, so beautifully engraved by House, is an accurate copy of the original picture painted in London in 1651, in his 57th year. This picture, the only portrait that we have of any of the Pilgrims, has been handed down in the family ever since it was painted, one hundred and ninety years ago, and was kept till within a few years at the seat of the Winslows, in Marshfield. It is now the property of Mr. Isaac Winslow, of Boston, the only surviving male descendant of the Governor, bearing his name, by whose kindness I have been permitted to have it engraved, and who has deposited it, with other portraits of his ancestors, in the Hall of the Massachusetts Historical Society. The coat of arms was probably painted at the same time with the picture, and has always been an heirloom in the family. The facsimile of Winslow's signature was copied from a letter written by him to Governor Winthrop, from his seat at "Careswell, this 17th of the last month, 1639." The original is in the archives of the Massachusetts Historical Society, and it was printed by Hutchinson in his Collection of Original Papers, page 110.

The map of Plymouth, on page 160, is copied by permission, on an enlarged scale, from the accurate map of the State, now in preparation under the direction of Simeon Borden, Esq., and the map of Cape Cod, on page 116, is partly reduced from Major Graham's beautiful chart, and partly composed from recent surveys made for the State map. The engraving of the Mayflower on page 108 is copied from one of Sir Walter Raleigh's ships in De Bry, and is a correct representation of the vessels of that day. The chairs of Winslow, Carver, and Brewster, are faithfully drawn from the originals, the first of which is preserved in the Hall of the Massachusetts Historical Society, and the last two in the Pilgrim Hall, at Plymouth. The seal of the Colony is taken from the title-page of the Book of the General Laws of New Plymouth, printed in 1685. Judge Davis says, "it originated probably in Mr. Cushman's advice to Governor Bradford in a letter from England, Dec. 18, 1624: 'Make your corporation as formal as you can, under the name of the Society in Plymouth in New England.' Of this seal the Colony was deprived in the rapacious days of Andros. On a return to the old paths, the Governor was requested to procure its restoration. If this application were successful, the seal has since been lost."

In regard to the minuteness of some of the particulars recorded in the ensuing pages, no better apology can be offered than that of the Roman annalist: "Pleraque eorum quæ referam parva forsitan et levia memoratu videri, non nescius sum. Non tamen sine usu fuerit introspicere illa, primo adspectu levia, ex quis magnarum sæpe rerum motus oriuntur."[1]—"If any tax me for wasting paper with recording these small matters, such may consider that small commonwealths bring forth matters of small moment; the reading whereof yet is not to be despised by the judicious, because small things in the beginning of natural or politic bodies are as remarkable as greater in bodies full grown."[2]

BOSTON, JUNE 1, 1841.

[1] TACITUS, *Ann.* lib. iv. 32.
[2] DUDLEY's *Letter to the Countess of Lincoln.*

LIST OF THE ENGRAVINGS.

		PAGE
1.	PORTRAIT OF GOVERNOR WINSLOW	i
2.	THE MAYFLOWER	108
3.	MAP OF CAPE COD	116
4.	MAP OF PLYMOUTH BAY	160
5.	GOVERNOR WINSLOW'S CHAIR	238
6.	GOVERNOR CARVER'S CHAIR	458
7.	ELDER BREWSTER'S CHAIR	470
8.	SEAL OF PLYMOUTH COLONY	Back Title.

CONTENTS.

CHAP.		PAGE.
	Gov. Bradford's History of Plymouth Colony .	1
I.	The first beginnings of this church and people . .	19
II.	Their departure into Holland, and their troubles thereabout, with some of the many difficulties they found and met withal	25
III.	Their settling in Holland, and their manner of living and entertainment there	33
IV.	The reasons and causes of their removal from Holland	44
V.	The means they used for preparation to this weighty voyage	52
VI.	The conditions of their agreement with several merchant adventurers towards the voyage . . .	80
VII.	Their departure from Leyden, and embarkation from Delft-Haven	86
VIII.	The troubles that befell them on the coast of England, and in their voyage in coming over into New England, and their arrival at Cape Cod . . .	97
	Bradford's and Winslow's Journal . . .	109
IX.	The first planters' combination by entering into a body politic together; with their proceedings in discovery of a place for their settlement and habitation .	117
X.	Their landing and settling at New Plymouth . .	163
XI.	A Journey to Pokanoket, the habitation of the great king Massasoit; the message, and the answer and entertainment they received from him . . .	202
XII.	A Voyage to the kingdom of Nauset, to seek a boy that had lost himself in the woods; and the accidents that befell them in that voyage	214
XIII.	A Journey to the kingdom of Namaschet, in defence of the great king Massasoit against the Narragansetts, and to revenge the supposed death of Tisquantum .	219

CONTENTS.

CHAP.		PAGE.
XIV.	A Relation of their voyage to the Massachusetts, and what happened there	224
XV.	A Letter from Edward Winslow to a friend in England, setting forth a brief and true declaration of the worth of the Plantation at Plymouth; as also certain useful directions for such as intend a voyage into New England	230
XVI.	Robert Cushman's reasons and considerations touching the lawfulness of removing out of England into the parts of America	239
	CUSHMAN'S DISCOURSE	253
XVII.	The state of the Colony, and the need of public spirit in the Colonists	255
	WINSLOW'S RELATION	269
XVIII.	The first planters menaced by the Narragansetts, and their second voyage to the Massachusetts . .	280
XIX.	The planting of Weston's colony at Weymouth, and sundry excursions after corn . . .	296
XX.	Winslow's second journey to Pokanoket, to visit Massasoit in his sickness	313
XXI.	Standish's expedition against the Indians of Weymouth, and the breaking up of Weston's Colony at that place	327
XXII.	The first allotment of lands, and the distressed state of the Colony	346
XXIII.	The manners, customs, religious opinions and ceremonies of the Indians	354
XXIV.	The situation, climate, soil, and productions of New England	368
	WINSLOW'S BRIEF NARRATION	377
XXV.	The true grounds or cause of the first planting of New England	379
	GOV. BRADFORD'S DIALOGUE	409
XXVI.	A Dialogue, or the Sum of a Conference between some Young Men born in New England, and sundry Ancient Men that came out of Holland and Old England	414
	GOV. BRADFORD'S MEMOIR OF ELDER BREWSTER .	459
XXVII.	Memoir of Elder William Brewster . . .	461
XXVIII.	LETTERS	471

GOV. BRADFORD'S HISTORY

OF

PLYMOUTH COLONY.

MORTON'S PREFACE.

CHRISTIAN READER,

I HAVE looked at it as a duty incumbent on me to commit to writing the first beginnings and after progress of the Church of Christ at Plymouth in New England; forasmuch as I cannot understand that there is any thing particularly extant concerning it, and almost all the members of the said church, both elders and others, being deceased, by whom intelligence of matters in that behalf might be procured.[1] I dare not charge the reverend elders of that church who are gone to their rest, with any neglect on that behalf; for when they were in Holland, they were necessitated to defend the cause of Christ by writing against opposites of several sorts; so as such like employs, together with the constant and faithful discharge of the duties of their offices, probably took up the greatest part of their time; and since the church parted, and a considerable part thereof came unto this going down of the sun, it might be neglected partly on the account that divers writings, some whereof being put forth in print,

---

[1] In 1679, the year previous to the date of this Preface, twelve only were living of the hundred who came over in the Mayflower. See Hutchinson's History of Massachusetts, ii. 456.

did point at and in a great measure discriminate the affairs of the church; forasmuch as then the small commonwealth, in our first beginning at New Plymouth, consisted mostly of such as were members of the church which was first begun and afterwards carried on in Leyden, in Holland, for about the space of twelve years, and continued and carried on at Plymouth, in New England, a small part whereof remaineth until this day. If any thing was done on this kind by those worthy leaders, I suppose the blame is rather to be laid on those which had the first view of their studies, and had their books and writings in custody after their decease; for I am persuaded that such was their faithfulness and prudence, as that they did not wholly neglect this matter.[1]

Some years since it pleased God to put an impulse upon my spirit to do something in a historical way concerning New England, more especially with respect to the Colony of New Plymouth; which was entitled *New England's Memorial*;[2] in which I occasionally

---

[1] The records of John Robinson's church at Leyden contained, no doubt, some account of its origin and its memorable vicissitudes in England and Holland. These records, however, were probably lost when the remnants of that church were scattered after his death in 1625. The church at Plymouth had no settled pastor till 1629, and afterwards, for long intervals, was destitute of a regular ministry until 1669, when John Cotton, son of the famous John Cotton of Boston, was ordained. No records were kept by either of his three predecessors, Ralph Smith, Roger Williams, and John Reyner. The records of the church, previous to his settlement, are in the handwriting of Secretary Morton. MS. Records of Plymouth Ch. and Mass. Hist. Coll. iv. 107.

[2] This work was printed at Cambridge in 1669, in a small quarto volume, of 198 pages, and the expense was defrayed by a contribution in the several towns in the Colony. The greatest part of Morton's information was "borrowed," as he informs us, "from his much honored uncle, Mr. William Bradford, and such manuscripts as he left in his study." Prince, the New England annalist, whose copy of the first edition of the Memorial is now before me, enriched with his marginal notes and emendations, says that "Morton's History, from the beginning of the Plymouth people to the end of 1646, is chiefly Gov. Bradford's manuscript, abbre-

MORTON'S PREFACE. 5

took notice of God's great and gracious work in erecting so many churches of Christ in this wilderness. But it was judged by some that were judicious that I was too sparing and short in that behalf; the consideration whereof put me on thought of recollecting something more particularly relating to the church of Plymouth. But it pleased the Lord so to dispose, that having accomplished my desires, some time after the finishing of this work I was solicited to lend it to a reverend friend at Boston, where it was burned in the first fire that was so destructive at Boston, in the year 1667.[1] Yet, notwithstanding, I have, through the goodness of God, crowded through many difficulties to achieve it the second time; and, for that end, did once again repair to the study of my much honored uncle, William Bradford, Esquire, deceased,[2] for whose care and faithfulness in such like respects we stand bound; as firstly and mostly to the Lord, so seconda-

viated." In fact, Morton's chief merit is that of a diligent, but not always accurate copyist of his uncle's documents. He would have done a much greater service by causing Gov. Bradford's History to be printed entire. It is the loss of that work that now gives so much value to his extracts and compilations. The fifth edition of the Memorial, greatly enlarged by the valuable notes of the learned editor, Judge Davis, was printed at Boston in 1826, in an octavo volume of 480 pages. See Plymouth Colony Laws, p. 153, Morton's New England's Memorial, p. 10, Thacher's Hist. of Plymouth, p. 126, (second edition,) and Prince's Annals of New England, p. xx. (8vo ed. 1826.)

[1] This is unquestionably an error; it should be 1676. For the writer says he began this compilation after the publication of the Memorial in 1669; and the date of "the first fire that was so destructive at Boston" was Nov. 27, 1676. The reverend friend to whom the manuscript had been lent, was Increase Mather, whose church was destroyed by this fire, as well as his dwelling-house, and a part of his library. Increase Mather had married a daughter of John Cotton, of Boston; and her brother being at this time the minister of Plymouth, this circumstance probably led to an acquaintance between Mather and Secretary Morton. See Hubbard's Indian Wars, p. 194, Hutchinson's Hist. of Massachusetts, i. 349, Snow's History of Boston, p. 164, Mass. Hist. Coll. iv. 269, xvi. 648, and Cotton Mather's Memoirs of his Father, p. 79.

[2] Gov. Bradford died May 9, 1657, in his 69th year.

rily to him and his, whose labors in such respect might fitly have been published to the world, had they not been involved in and amongst particulars of other nature.

Gentle reader, I humbly crave thy patience, and acceptance of this small treatise, so as to read it over considerately; wherein so doing thou wilt discern much of the goodness, mercy, and power of God; who as at the first brought this fabric of the world out of the womb of nothing, hath brought so many famous churches of Christ out of so small beginnings; with many other useful considerations that thou mayest meet with in the serious perusal thereof. So leaving thee and this small work to the blessing of the only wise God,

I remain thine in Christ Jesus,
NATHANIEL MORTON.[1]

Plymouth, in New England, January 13th, 1680.

---

[1] Nathaniel Morton was the son of George Morton, who had married in England a sister of Gov. Bradford, and came over to Plymouth with his family in July, 1623, in the ship Anne. His father died in June, 1624, when Nathaniel was twelve years old. In 1645 he was chosen Secretary of the Colony Court, and continued in this office till his death, June 28, 1685, in his 73d year. His residence in Plymouth was by the side of Wellingsly Brook, half a mile south of the village. See Judge Davis's Preface to Morton's Memorial, pp. iv. and 101, and Mass. Hist. Coll. xiii. 178.

INTRODUCTION.

AN INTRODUCTION TO THE ECCLESIASTICAL HISTORY OF THE CHURCH OF CHRIST AT PLYMOUTH, IN NEW ENGLAND, AS FOLLOWETH.[1]

It is well known to the godly and judicious, how that ever since the first breaking out of the light of the Gospel in our honorable nation of England, — which was the first of nations whom the Lord adorned therewith, after that gross darkness of Popery, which had covered and overspread the Christian world, — what wars and oppositions ever since Satan hath raised, maintained, and continued against the saints from time to time, in one sort or other; sometimes by bloody death and cruel torments, otherwhiles imprisonments, banishments, and other hard usages; as being loth his kingdom should go down, the truth prevail, and the churches of God revert to their ancient purity, and recover their primitive order, liberty, and beauty. But when he could not prevail by these means against the main truths of the Gospel, but that they began to take footing in many places, being watered with the blood of the martyrs and blessed from heaven with a gracious

---

[1] This was originally penned by Mr. William Bradford, Governor of New Plymouth. — *Morton's Note.*

INTR. increase; he then began to take him to his ancient stratagems, used of old against the first Christians; that when by the bloody and barbarousness[1] of the heathen emperor he could not stop and subvert the course of the Gospel, but that it speedily overspread with a wonderful celerity to the then best known parts of the world, he then began to sow errors, heresies, and wonderful desertions amongst the professors themselves, working upon their pride and ambition, with other corrupt passions incident to all mortal men, yea to the saints themselves in some measure; by which woful effects followed, as not only bitter contentions and heart-burnings, schisms, with other horrible confusions, but Satan took occasion and advantage thereby to foist in a number of vile ceremonies, with many unprofitable canons and decrees, which have since been as snares to many peaceable poor souls even to this day; so, as in the ancient times the persecution by the heathen and their emperors was not greater than of the Christians, one against another, the Arians' and other their accomplices' against the orthodox and true Christians (as witnesseth Socrates in his second book, saith he) " was no less than that of old practised towards the Christians when they were compelled and drawn to sacrifice to idols; for many endured sundry kinds of torments, others racking, and dismembering of their joints, confiscating of their goods, some bereaved of their native soil, others departed this life under the hands of the tormentor, and some died in banishment, and never saw their country again."[2]

The like method Satan hath seemed to hold in these

---

[1] So in the MS.　　　　[2] Eccles. Hist. lib. ii. cap. 27.

latter times, since the truth began to spring and spread after the great defection made by Antichrist, the Man of Sin. For to let pass the many examples in sundry nations, in several places of the world, and instances of our own, whenas the old serpent could not prevail by those fiery flames, and other his cruel tragedies, which he by his instruments put in ure every where in the days of Queen Mary and before, he then began another kind of war, and went more closely to work, not only to oppugn, but even to ruinate and destroy the kingdom of Christ by more secret and subtle means, by kindling the flames of contention and sowing the seeds of discord and bitter enmity amongst the professors and seeming reformed themselves. For when he could not prevail by the former means against the principal doctrines of faith, he bent his force against the holy discipline and outward regiment of the kingdom of Christ, by which those holy doctrines should be confirmed, and true piety maintained amongst the saints and people of God.

Mr. Fox recordeth how that, besides those worthy martyrs and confessors which were burned in Queen Mary's days and otherwise tormented, many, both students and others, fled out of the land, to the number of eight hundred, and became several congregations at Wesel, Frankfort, Basle, Emden, Marburg, Strasburg, and Geneva, &c.[1] Amongst whom, especially those at Frankfort, began a bitter war of contention and persecution about the ceremonies and service book, and other popish and antichristian stuff, the plague of England to this day, which are like the high places in

---

[1] Fox, Acts and Monuments, iii. iii. 146, and Fuller's Ch. Hist. of 40. See also Strype's Memorials, Britain, ii. 405, (ed. 1837.)

INTR. Israel which the prophets cried out against, and were their ruin; which the better part sought, according to the purity of the Gospel, to root out and utterly destroy, and the other part, under veiled pretences, for their own ends and advancement, sought as stiffly to continue, maintain, and defend; as appeareth by the Discourse thereof published in print anno 1575, a book that deserves better to be known and considered than it is.[1] The one side labored to have the right worship of God and discipline of Christ established in the church according to the simplicity of the Gospel, without the mixture of men's inventions, and to have and to be ruled by the laws of God's word, dispensed in those offices and by those officers of pastors and teachers and elders, according to the Scriptures. The other party, though under many colors and pretences, endeavoured to have the episcopal dignity, after the popish manner, with their large power and jurisdiction, still retained, with all those courts, canons and ceremonies, together with all such livings, revenues, and subordinate officers, with other such means as formerly upheld their antichristian greatness, and enabled them with lordly and tyrannous power to persecute the poor servants of God.

---

[1] This work is entitled, "A Brief Discourse of the Troubles begun at Frankfort, in Germany, anno Domini 1554, about the Book of Common Prayer and Ceremonies, and continued by the Englishmen there to the end of Queen Mary's reign; in the which Discourse the gentle reader shall see the very original and beginning of all the contention that hath been, and what was the cause of the same. 1575." The place where it was printed is not mentioned. It was reprinted at London in 1642, and "humbly presented to the view and consideration of the most Honorable and High Court of Parliament, and the reverend divines of the intended ensuing Assembly." Hallam says, in his Constitutional History of England, i. 233, that "this tract is fairly and temperately written, though with an avowed bias towards the Puritan party. Whatever we read in any historian on the subject, is derived from this authority." Both editions of this rare book are in the Library of the Massachusetts Historical Society.

This contention was so great, as neither the honor of God, the common persecution, nor the mediation of Mr. Calvin and other worthies of the Lord in those places, could prevail with those thus episcopally minded; but they proceeded by all means to disturb the peace of this poor persecuted church, so far as to charge very unjustly and ungodlily (yet prelate like) some of their chief opposers with rebellion and high treason against the Emperor, and other such crimes.[1] And this contention died not with Queen Mary, nor was left beyond the seas. But at her death, these people returning into England, under gracious Queen Elizabeth, many of them preserved aspired to bishoprics and other promotions,[2] according to their aims and desires;

1558. Nov. 7.

---

[1] Calvin, in his letter of Jan. 20, 1555, addressed to John Knox and William Whittingham, at Frankfort, says, "In the liturgy of England I see that there were many tolerable foolish things; by these words I mean that there was not the *purity* which was to be desired. These vices, though they could not at the first day be amended, yet, seeing there was no manifest impiety, they were for a season to be tolerated. Therefore it was lawful to begin of such rudiments or abecedaries; but so that it behooved the learned, grave, and godly ministers of Christ to enterprise farther, and to set forth something more filed from rust, and *purer*. If godly religion had flourished till this day in England, there ought to have been a thing better corrected, and many things clean taken away. I cannot tell what they mean which so greatly delight in the leavings of popish dregs." Knox was soon after accused of treason before the magistrates of Frankfort by some of the opposite party, on the ground of certain passages in a book of his, entitled *An Admonition to Christ-* ians, in which he called the emperor of Germany "no less an enemy to Christ than was Nero;" in consequence of which he was obliged to leave the city. See Discourse of the Troubles of Frankfort, pp. 35 and 44, ed. of 1575, and Fuller's Ch. Hist. ii. 411.

[2] See in Prince's Annals, p. 288, a list of those who were thus promoted. It is a just remark of Hallam, Const. History of England, i. 238, that the objections to the church ceremonies and the clerical vestments "were by no means confined, as is perpetually insinuated, to a few discontented persons. The most eminent churchmen, such as Jewel, Grindal, Sandys, Nowell, were in favor of leaving off the surplice and what were called the popish ceremonies. The current opinion that these scruples were imbibed during the banishment of the reformers, must be received with great allowance. The dislike to some parts of the Anglican ritual had begun at home, it had broken out at Frankfort, it is displayed in all the early documents of Elizabeth's reign by the English divines,

INTR. so that inveterate hatred against the holy discipline of Christ in his church hath continued to this day; insomuch that, for fear it should prevail, all plots and devices have been used to keep it out, incensing the Queen and State against it as dangerous to her commonwealth; and that it was most needful for the fundamental points of religion should be preached in those ignorant and superstitious times, and to win the weak and ignorant, they might retain divers harmless ceremonies; and though it were to be wished that divers things were reformed, yet this was not a season for it; and many the like, to stop the mouths of the more godly, to bring them on to yield to one ceremony after another and one corruption after another; by these ways beguiling some and corrupting others, until at length they began to persecute all the zealous professors in the land, (although they knew little what this discipline meant), both by word and deed, if they would not submit to their ceremonies and become slaves to them and their popish trash, which have no ground in the word of God, but are relics of the Man of Sin. And the more the light of the Gospel grew, the more they urged their subscriptions to these corruptions, so as notwithstanding all their former pretences and fair colors, they whose eyes God had not justly blinded might easily see whereto these things tended. And to cast contempt the more upon the sincere servants of God, they opprobriously and most injuriously gave unto and imposed

1564. upon them that name of PURITANS,[1] which it is said the

far more warmly than by their Swiss correspondents. The queen alone was the cause of retaining those observances, to which the great separation from the Anglican establishment is ascribed." The most concise and accurate account of the origin and growth of Puritanism in England, will be found in Prince's Annals, p. 282—307.

[1] The era of the English Puritans properly begins in 1550, when

INTRODUCTION. 13

Novatians, out of pride, did assume and take unto themselves.[1] And lamentable it is to see the effects which have followed. Religion hath been disgraced, the godly grieved, afflicted, persecuted, and many exiled; sundry have lost their lives in prisons and other ways. On the other hand, sin hath been countenanced, ignorance, profaneness and atheism increased, the Papists encouraged to hope again for a day.

This made that holy man Mr. Perkins cry out in his Exhortation unto Repentance, on Zephaniah ii, " Religion," saith he, " hath been amongst us this thirty-

Hooper refused, for a time, to be consecrated in the ecclesiastical habits. But in the year 1564, " the English bishops," says Fuller, "conceiving themselves empowered by their canons, began to show their authority in urging the clergy of their respective dioceses to subscribe to the liturgy, ceremonies, and discipline of the Church; and such as refused the same were branded with the odious name of *Puritans*. We need not speak of the ancient *Cathari*, or primitive Puritans, sufficiently known by their heretical opinions. ' Puritan ' here was taken for the opposers of the hierarchy and church-service, as resenting of superstition. But profane mouths quickly improved this nickname, therewith on every occasion to abuse pious people; some of them so far from opposing the liturgy, that they endeavoured (according to the instructions thereof in the preparative to the Confession) ' to accompany the minister with a *pure* heart,' and labored (as it is in the Absolution) ' for a life *pure* and holy.' " An old writer of the Church of England, quoted by Prince, says, " they are called Puritans who would have the Church thoroughly reformed; that is, purged from all those inventions which have been brought into it since the age of the Apostles, and reduced entirely to the Scripture *purity*." See Fuller's Ch. Hist. ii. 331, 474; Strype's Annals, i. 459–463; Camden's Elizabeth, p. 107; Prince, pp. 100, 283; Neal's Puritans, i. 46, 72, 91. (4to ed.)

[1] " Novatus, a presbyter of the church of Rome, being puffed up with pride against those who in the times of persecution had lapsed through infirmity of mind, as if there were no further hope of salvation for them, although they performed all things appertaining to an unfeigned conversion and a sincere confession, constituted himself the ringleader of a peculiar sect, of those who by reason of their haughty minds styled themselves *Cathari*, that is, the *Pure*." Eusebius, Eccles. Hist. lib. vi. cap. 43. His excessive rigor towards the lapsed appears to have been the only heresy of Novatus; and it is quite as likely that the name of Puritan was fastened upon his followers in derision and reproach as that they assumed it of themselves; as we know was the case with the modern Quakers and Methodists. For an account of Novatus and his opinions, see Lardner's Credibility, part ii. ch. 47; Mosheim, de Rebus Christianorum ante Const. Magn. Comment. 512–527; Jackson's Novatian, Præf.

INTR. five years. But the more it is published, the more it is contemned and reproached of many, &c. Thus not profaneness nor wickedness, but religion itself is a by-word, a mocking-stock, and matter of reproach; so that in England at this day, the man or woman that begins to profess religion and to serve God, must resolve with himself to sustain mocks and injuries, even as though he lived amongst the enemies of religion; and this common experience hath been too apparent."[1]

But before I pass on, I cannot omit an observation worthy to be noted, which was observed by the author, viz. Mr. William Bradford, as followeth.

Saith he: Full little did I think that the downfall of the bishops, with their courts, canons, and ceremonies, had been so near when I first began this writing, which was about the year 1630, and so pieced at leisure times afterwards, or that I should have lived to have seen or heard of the same.[2] But it is the Lord's doing, and ought to be marvellous in our eyes. "Every plant which mine heavenly father hath not planted," saith our Saviour, "shall be rooted up."[3] "I have snared

Matt. xv. 13.

---

[1] Works, vol. iii. p. 421, ed. 1613. William Perkins lived in the reign of Elizabeth, was a fellow of Christ's College, Cambridge, and a Puritan Nonconformist. He was a strict Calvinist, and had a controversy with Arminius. His writings were held in high esteem by the fathers of New England. Fuller says, in his Life of him in the Holy State, that "he would pronounce the word *damn* with such an emphasis as left a doleful echo in his auditors' ears a good while after. And when catechist of Christ's College, in expounding the commandments, applied them so home, able almost to make his hearers' hearts fall down, and hairs to stand upright. But in his older age he altered his voice, and remitted much of his former rigidness, often professing that to preach mercy was the proper office of the ministers of the gospel."

[2] Charles I. was beheaded and the church establishment overthrown in 1649.

[3] The version of the Bible here quoted, and subsequently, is the one which was made by the English exiles at Geneva, in the reign of Queen Mary. It was first printed in 1560, and was so highly esteemed, particularly on account of its notes, that it passed through thirty editions. King James appears to have had a special dislike of it; for in the Conference at Hampton Court

thee, and thou art taken, O Babel, (bishops) and thou _{INTR.} wast not aware: thou art found and also caught, _{Jer. 1. 24.} because thou hast striven against the Lord." But will they needs strive against the truth, against the servants of the Lord, what! and against the Lord himself? Do they provoke the Lord to anger? Are they stronger _{1 Cor. x. 22.} than he? No, no, they have met with their match. Behold, I come against thee, O proud men, saith the _{Jer. l. 31.} Lord God of hosts; for thy day is coming, even the time that I will visit thee. May not the people of God now say, and these poor people among the rest, The Lord had brought forth our righteousness: come, let _{Jer. li. 10.} us declare in Zion the work of the Lord our God. Let all flesh be still before the Lord, for he is raised _{Zech. ii. 13.} up out of his holy place.[1]

This poor people may say among the thousands of Israel, When the Lord brought again the captivity of _{Psalm cxxv i. 1.} Zion, we were like them that dream. The Lord hath _{vs. 3} done great things for us, whereof we rejoice. They that sow in tears shall reap in joy. They went weep- _{vss. 5, 6.} ing and carried precious seed; but they shall return with joy, and bring their sheaves.

Do ye not now see the fruits of your labors, O all ye servants of the Lord that have suffered for his truth,

---

"he professed that he could never yet see a Bible well translated in English; but the worst of all his Majesty thought the Geneva to be." This opinion of the royal pedant would not lower it in the estimation of our fathers, who used it in England and Holland, and brought it with them to this country. King James's version, which was first printed in 1611, had hardly got into common use in England when they came over in 1620. See Strype's Annals, i. 229; Troubles at Frankfort, p. 192; Barlow's Sum and Substance of the Conference at Hampton Court, p. 46; Strype's Life of Abp. Parker, 205; Fuller's Ch. Hist. iii. 182, 247.

[1] This elevation of spirit was a considerable time after the first penning of these writings, but here entered because of the suitableness of the matter going before it. — *Morton's Note.*

and have been faithful witnesses of the same? And ye little handful amongst the rest, the least amongst the thousands of Israel? You have not had a seed-time, but many of you have seen a joyful harvest. Should ye not then rejoice, yea, again rejoice, and say, Hallelujah! salvation, and glory, and honor, and power, be to the Lord our God; for true and righteous are his judgments.

But thou wilt ask, What is the matter? What is done? — Why, art thou a stranger in Israel, that thou shouldst not know what is done? Are not those Jebusites overcome, that have vexed the people of Israel so long, even holding Jerusalem even until David's days, and been as thorns in their sides for many ages, and now began to scorn that not any David should meddle with them; they began to fortify their tower, as that of the old Babylonians. But these proud Anakims are now thrown down, and their glory laid in the dust. The tyrannous bishops are ejected, their courts dissolved, their canons forceless, their service-books cashiered, their ceremonies useless and despised, their plots for Popery prevented, and all their superstitions discarded, and returned to Rome, from whence they came; and the monuments of idolatry rooted out of the land, and the proud and profane supporters and cruel defenders of these, as bloody papists, wicked atheists, and their malignant consorts, marvellously overthrown. And are not these great things? Who can deny it?

But who hath done it? Even he that sitteth on the white horse, who is called Faithful and True, and judgeth and fighteth righteously, whose garments are dipped in blood, and his name was called The Word

INTRODUCTION. 17

of God; for he shall rule them with a rod of iron; for it is he that treadeth the wine-press of the fierceness and wrath of Almighty God; and he hath upon his garment and upon his thigh a name written, The King of Kings and Lord of Lords. Hallelujah! INTR.
vs. 15.

See how this holy man's spirit was elevated and his heart raised up in praising of the Lord in consideration of the downfall of the proud prelacy; as he and many more of the saints had good reason, who felt the smart of their bitter and cruel tyranny; who are, indeed, a limb of Antichrist. And if the generality of the saints had been thus sensible of this great and marvellous work of God, possibly that proud hierarchy had not got up so soon again as they have done, soon after this good man's departure out of this world.[1] Nevertheless, we doubt not but that God will bring them down in his good time. For undoubtedly all those that will not that the Lord Jesus should reign over them, but instead thereof exercise an usurped lordly power over the poor saints of God, shall be brought and slain before him, and (without repentance) shall, together with the beast and false prophet, be thrown into the lake burning with fire and brimstone. When Babylon cometh into remembrance before God, then shall the saints with the angel say, Thou art just and holy, because thou hast judged these things; for they, (viz. the whore of Rome and the prelates, their adherents,) have shed the blood of the saints. Give them blood to drink; for they are worthy. Rev.
xix. 20.

Rev.
xvi. 5.

vs. 6.

---

[1] Gov. Bradford died May 9, 1657. Charles II. was restored and Episcopacy reëstablished in 1660.

INTR. The exordium being concluded, I shall come more nearer my intended purpose, viz. in reference unto the Church of Christ at Plymouth in New England, first begun in Old England, and carried on in Holland and at Plymouth aforesaid.

CHAPTER I.

OF THE FIRST BEGINNINGS OF THIS CHURCH AND PEOPLE.

WHEN, by the travail and diligence of some godly and zealous preachers, and God's blessing on their labors, as in other places of the land, so in the north parts, many became enlightened by the word of God, and had their ignorance and sins discovered by the word of God's grace, and began, by his grace, to reform their lives and make conscience of their ways, the work of God was no sooner manifest in them, but presently they were both scoffed and scorned by the profane multitude, and the ministers urged with the yoke of subscription,[1] or else must be silenced ; and the poor people were so urged with apparitors and pursuivants and the Commission Courts,[2] as truly their

---

[1] Subscription to the book of common prayer, the rites and ceremonies, and all the thirty-nine articles. See Fuller, iii. 68 ; Prince, p. 99.

[2] This was the celebrated Court of High Commission, so called because it claimed a larger jurisdiction and higher powers than the ordinary courts of the bishops ; its jurisdiction extended over the whole kingdom. It was provided for by the Act of Supremacy, ¦passed in 1559, but did not go into full operation till 1584. It was an ecclesiastical court, consisting of forty-four persons, twelve of whom were bishops, many more privy counsellors, and the rest clergymen or civilians. Its spirit and mode of proceeding seem to have been derived from the Spanish Inquisition. The commissioners were empowered and directed to inquire of all heretical opinions, to punish all persons absent from church, to visit and reform all errors, heresies, and schisms, to deprive all persons of ecclesiastical livings who maintained any doctrine contrary to the thirty-nine articles, to examine all

affliction was not small. Which, notwithstanding, they bare sundry years with much patience, until they were occasioned, by the continuance and increase of these troubles, and other means which the Lord raised up in those days, to see further into these[1] things by the light of the word of God; how that[1] not only those base beggarly ceremonies were unlawful, but also that the lordly, tyrannous power of the prelates ought not to be submitted to, which those contrary to the freedom of the Gospel would load and burthen men's consciences with, and by their compulsive power make a profane mixture of persons and things in the worship of God; and that their offices and callings, courts and canons, &c. were unlawful and antichristian, being such as have no warrant in the word of God, but the same that were used in Popery, and still retained; of which a famous author thus writeth in his Dutch commentaries: —

1603.
April.
"At the coming of King James out of Scotland into England,[2] the new king," saith he, "found there estab-

suspected persons on their oaths, and to punish the refractory by excommunication, fine, or imprisonment, according to their discretion. They had full authority to command all sheriffs, justices, and other officers to apprehend and bring before them all persons that they should see fit. Pursuivants or messengers were sent to the houses of suspected persons with a citation for them to appear before the commissioners, when they were required to answer upon oath to a series of interrogatories, which as Lord Burleigh said, were "so curiously penned, so full of branches and circumstances, as he thought the inquisitors of Spain used not so many questions to trap their preys." See Strype's Annals, iii. 180; Neal's Puritans, i. 84, 274, 285; Hallam, i. 271.

[1] I have inserted the words *these* and *that* from Prince, who quotes this passage from Bradford's MS. See his Annals, p. 100.

[2] At the famous Conference at Hampton Court, held Jan. 14, 1604, James declared, "I will none of that liberty as to ceremonies; I will have one doctrine and one discipline, one religion in substance and ceremony. — I shall make them [the Puritans] conform themselves, or I will harry them out of the land, or else do worse. — If any would not be quiet, and show his obedience, he were worthy to be hanged." — In his speech at the opening of his first parliament, March 19, 1604, he "professed that the sect of Puri-

lished the reformed religion, according to the reformed religion of King Edward the Sixth, retaining or keeping still the spiritual state of the bishops, &c. after the old manner, much varying and differing from the Reformed Churches of Scotland, France, and the Netherlands, Emden, Geneva, &c., whose Reformation is cut or shapen much nearer the first churches, as it was used in the Apostles' times."¹

So many therefore of these professors as saw the evil of these things, in these parts, and whose hearts the Lord had touched with heavenly zeal for his truth, they shook off this yoke of antichristian bondage, and, as the Lord's free people, joined themselves, (by a 1602. covenant of the Lord,) into a church estate, in the fellowship of the Gospel, to walk in all his ways, made known, or to be made known unto them, according to their best endeavours, whatsoever it should cost them.²

tans or Novelists was not to be suffered in any well governed commonwealth." In a private letter written about the same time, he said, "I had rather live like a hermit in the forest, than be king over such a people as the pack of Puritans that overrules the lower house." He had previously written to his son in the *Basilicon Doron*, " Take heed, my son, to such Puritans, very pests in the church and commonwealth. I protest before the great God, that ye shall never find with any Highland or Border thieves greater ingratitude and more lies and vile perjuries than with these fanatic spirits." Barlow's Sum and Substance, pp. 71, 83, 92 ; Calderwood, Hist. Ch. Scotland, p. 478 ; Hallam, i. 419.

In conformity with these views, on the 5th of March, 1604, he issued a proclamation, that the same religion, with common prayer, and episcopal jurisdiction, shall fully and only be publicly exercised, in all respects, as in the reign of Queen Elizabeth, without hope of toleration of any other; and on the 6th of July he issued another proclamation in which he ordered the Puritan ministers either to conform before the last of November, or dispose of themselves and families some other way ; as being men unfit, for their obstinacy and contempt, to occupy such places. The consequence of this was, that before November of the next year more than three hundred ministers were ejected, silenced, or suspended, some of whom were imprisoned, and others driven into exile. Prince, pp. 107, 108, 110 ; Neal's Puritans, i. 432.

¹ The Reformed Churches shapen much nearer the primitive pattern than England ; for they cashiered the bishops, with their courts, canons and ceremonies at the first, and left them amongst the Popish trash, to which they appertain.—*Morton's Note.*

² Prince says, " Governor Brad-

CHAP. I.

And that it cost them much pains, trouble, sorrow, affliction, and persecution, and expense of their estates, &c. this ensuing history will declare.[1]

1606.

These people became two distinct bodies or churches, in regard of distance of place, and did congregate severally, for they were of several towns and villages, some in Nottinghamshire, some in Lincolnshire,[2] and some of Yorkshire, where they bordered nearest together. In the one of these churches, besides others of note, was Mr. John Smith,[3] a man of able gifts, and a good preacher, who afterwards was chosen their pastor. But these afterwards falling into some errors in the Low Countries, there for the most part buried themselves and their names.

But in this other church, which must be the subject of our discourse, besides other worthy men, was Mr. Richard Clifton, a grave and reverend preacher, who by his pains and diligence had done much good, and

---

ford's History takes no notice of the year of this federal incorporation; but Mr. Secretary Morton, in his Memorial, places it in 1602. And I suppose he had the account either from some other writings of Gov. Bradford, the Journals of Gov. Winslow, or from oral conference with them, or other of the first planters; with some of whom he was contemporary, and from whence, he tells us, he received his intelligence." Annals, p. 100.

[1] "These seem to be some of the first in England that were brave enough to improve the liberty wherewith the divine author of our religion has made us free, and observe his institutions as their only rule in church order, discipline, and worship." Prince, p. 100.

[2] I have substituted Lincolnshire for Lancashire, on the authority of Prince. This is most likely to be the correct reading, as Lincolnshire borders both on Nottinghamshire and Yorkshire, whilst Lancashire does not. Besides, Prince was remarkable for his accuracy, and is less likely to have made a mistake in deciphering and copying a word than Morton. He tells us, "In the passages relating to the Plymouth planters, I chiefly use Gov. Bradford's manuscript History of that Church and Colony, in folio; who was with them from their beginning to the end of his Narrative, which is now before me, and was never published." Annals, p. 99.

[3] Some account of Smith, Clifton, and Robinson, is contained in Gov. Bradford's Dialogue, in a subsequent part of this volume; where will also be found a more extended memoir of Elder Brewster, also written by Gov. Bradford.

under God had been a means of the conversion of many; and also that famous and worthy man, Mr. John Robinson, who afterwards was their pastor for many years, until the Lord took him away by death; and also Mr. William Brewster, a reverend man, who afterwards was chosen an elder of the church, and lived with them until old age and death.

But, after these things, they could not long continue in any peaceable manner, but were hunted and persecuted on every side, so as their former afflictions were but as molehills to mountains in comparison to these which now came upon them. For some were taken and clapped up in prisons, others had their houses beset and watched night and day, and hardly escaped their hands; and the most were fain to fly and leave their houses and habitations, and the means of their livelihood. Yet these, and many other sharper things which afterward befell them, were no other than they looked for, and therefore were the better prepared to bear them by the assistance of God's grace and spirit. Yet seeing themselves thus molested, and that there was no hope of their continuance there, by a joint consent they resolved to go into the Low Countries, where they heard was freedom of religion for all men,[1] as also how

---

[1] After the introduction of the Reformed religion into the Low Countries in 1573, the utmost religious freedom was allowed, all sects were tolerated, and an asylum was opened for fugitives from persecution from every land. See Grotius, Annals, p. 41; Brandt, i. 308; Strada, i. 457. This honorable peculiarity has often been made an occasion of reproach against the country. Thus Bishop Hall, in his letter to Smith and Robinson, Decade iii. Epist. 1, speaks of Amsterdam as "a common harbour of all opinions, of all heresies." Baylie, in his Dissuasive, p. 8, calls Holland "a cage for unclean birds." Owen Felltham, in his amusing description of the Low Countries, says that "all strange religions flock thither." Johnson, in his Wonderworking Providence, ch. 15, exclaims, "Ye Dutch, come out of your hodge-podge: the great mingle mangle of religion among you hath caused the churches of Christ to increase so little with you."

CHAP. I.

sundry from London and other parts of the land, that had been exiled and persecuted for the same cause, were gone thither, and lived at Amsterdam,[1] and in other places of the land.

1607. So after they had continued together about a year, and kept their meetings every Sabbath in one place or another, exercising the worship of God amongst themselves,[2] notwithstanding all the diligence and malice of their adversaries, they seeing they could no longer continue in that condition, they resolved to get over into Holland, as they could, which was in the year 1607 and 1608; of which more in that which followeth.

---

standing at a stay like corn among weeds." Beaumont and Fletcher, in their play, The Fair Maid of the Inn, introduce one of their characters as saying,

"I am a schoolmaster, Sir, and would fain
Confer with you about erecting four
New sects of religion at Amsterdam."

And Andrew Marvell, in his "Character of Holland," writes.

"Sure when religion did itself embark,
And from the east would westward steer its ark,
It struck; and splitting on this unknown ground,
Each one thence pillaged the first piece he found.
Hence Amsterdam, Turk, Christian, Pagan, Jew,
Staple of sects, and mint of schism, grew;
That bank of conscience, where not one so strange
Opinion, but finds credit and exchange.
In vain for catholics ourselves we bear;
The universal church is only there."

[1] The English church at Amsterdam was that of which Francis Johnson was pastor and Henry Ainsworth teacher, and which had been originally set up at London, in 1592, and soon afterwards removed to Holland. It came very near being torn in pieces at first by intestine divisions, but afterwards flourished under a succession of pastors for more than a century. In 1596 they published a "Confession of Faith of certain English people living in exile in the Low Countries," which was reprinted in 1604, in "An Apology or Defence of such true Christians as are commonly, but unjustly, called Brownists." This work has sometimes been confounded with John Robinson's "Just and Necessary Apology of certain Christians not less contumeliously than commonly called Brownsits or Barrowists," which was first published in 1619. Some account of Johnson and Ainsworth is contained in Bradford's Dialogue, in a subsequent part of this volume. See Brandt's History of the Reformation in the Low Countries, i. 479; Neal's Puritans, i. 363, 386; Prince, p. 303. Baylie's Dissuasive, p. 15.

[2] In Gov. Bradford's Memoir of Elder Brewster, it is stated that "they ordinarily met at his (Brewster's) house on the Lord's Day, which was within a manor of the bishop's; and with great love he entertained them when they came, making provision for them to his great charge, and continued to do so while they could stay in England."

CHAPTER II.

OF THEIR DEPARTURE INTO HOLLAND, AND THEIR TROUBLES THEREABOUT, WITH SOME OF THE MANY DIFFICULTIES THEY FOUND AND MET WITHAL.

BEING thus constrained to leave their native country, their lands and livings, and all their friends and familiar acquaintance, it was much, and thought marvellous by many. But to go into a country they knew not, but by hearsay, where they must learn a new language, and get their livings they knew not how, it being a dear place, and subject to the miseries of war,[1] it was by many thought an adventure almost desperate, a case intolerable, and a misery worse than death; especially seeing they were not acquainted with trades nor traffic, (by which the country doth subsist,) but had only been

---

[1] The Netherlands have, in every age, from the earliest times down to the last great conflict at Waterloo, been the battle-ground of Europe. Bishop Hall says in one of his epistles, "It were pity that your Holland should be still the amphitheatre of the world, on whose scaffolds all other nations should sit, and see variety of bloody shows, not without pity and horror." At this time Spain was waging that dreadful war with her revolted subjects of the United Provinces, which terminated in their independence. The best account of this war will be found in the contemporary historians, Bentivoglio, Della Guerra di Fiandra, parte iii. lib. viii. Strada, de Bello Belgico, and Grotius, Annales et Historiæ de Rebus Belgicis. See also Brandt's History of the Reformation in the Low Countries, Sir William Temple's Observations upon the United Provinces of the Netherlands, Watson's History of the Reign of Philip II. and III. and Grattan's History of the Netherlands, in Lardner's Cyclopedia.

used to a plain country life and the innocent trade of husbandry. But these things did not dismay them, (although they did sometimes trouble them,) for their desires were set on the ways of God, and to enjoy his ordinances. But they rested on his providence, and knew whom they had believed. Yet this was not all. For although they could not stay, yet were they not suffered to go; but the ports and havens were shut against them, so as they were fain to seek secret means of conveyance, and to fee the mariners, and give extraordinary rates for their passages. And yet were they oftentimes betrayed, many of them, and both they and their goods intercepted and surprised, and thereby put to great trouble and charge; of which I will give an instance or two, and omit the rest.

1607. There was a great company of them purposed to get passage at Boston, in Lincolnshire; and for that end had hired a ship wholly to themselves, and made agreement with the master to be ready at a certain day, and take them and their goods in at a convenient place, where they accordingly would all attend in readiness. So after long waiting and large expenses, though he kept not the day with them, yet he came at length, and took them in, in the night. And when he had them and their goods aboard, he betrayed them, having beforehand complotted with the searchers and other officers so to do; who took them and put them into open boats, and there rifled and ransacked them, searching them to their shirts for money, yea, even the women, further than became modesty; and then carried them back into the town, and made them a spectacle and wonderment to the multitude, which came flocking on all sides to behold them. Being thus by the catchpole officers rifled and stripped of their money, books, and much other goods, they were presented to the magistrates, and messengers sent to inform the Lords of the Council of them; and so they were committed to ward. Indeed, the magistrates used them courteously, and showed them what favor they could; but could not deliver them until order came from the Council table. But the issue was, that after a month's imprisonment the greatest part were dimissed, and sent to the places from whence they came; but seven [1] of the principal men [1] were still kept in prison, and bound over to the assizes.[2]

The next spring after, there was another attempt made, by some of these and others, to get over at another place; and it so fell out that they lighted of a Dutchman at Hull, having a ship of his own belonging

1608.

---

[1] The word in the MS. is *some;* but I have no doubt that *seven* was the original reading. Hutchinson, who quotes this passage at length from Bradford's History, reads it *seven;* and it will be seen by the next note that Morton himself, copying another manuscript of Gov. Bradford alluding to this same affair, mentions " the seven." The word *men* I have also restored from Hutchinson. See his History, ii. 450.

[2] Gov. Bradford says, in the memoir already referred to on page 24, that Elder Brewster " was the chief of those that were taken at Boston, in Lincolnshire, and suffered the greatest loss, and one of the seven that were kept longest in prison, and after bound over to the assizes." The books that were in the boats probably belonged to him, as we know that he had a considerable library, which he brought over with him to Plymouth. A catalogue of them is contained in his inventory, in the Records of the Old Colony.

The whole number of volumes was 275, of which 64 were in the learned languages. They were valued at £43. See Morton's Memorial, p. 221, and Mass. Hist. Coll. iv. 117.

Cotton Mather, in his Life of Gov. Bradford in the Magnalia, i. 102, states that he was one of those that were taken and imprisoned at Boston. He adds that " Mr. Bradford being a young man of about eighteen, was dismissed sooner than the rest, so that within a while he had opportunity with some others to get over to Zealand, through perils both by land and sea not inconsiderable; where he was not long ashore ere a viper seized on his hand, that is, an officer, who carried him unto the magistrates, unto whom an envious passenger had accused him as having fled out of England. When the magistrates understood the true cause of his coming thither, they were well satisfied with him; and so he repaired joyfully unto his brethren at Amsterdam."

CHAP.
II.

1608.

to Zealand. They made agreement with him, and acquainted him with their condition, hoping to find more faithfulness in him than in the former, of their own nation. He bade them not fear; for he would do well enough. He was by appointment to take them in between Grimsby[1] and Hull, where was a large common, a good way distant from any town. Now against the prefixed time, the women and children, with the goods, were sent to the place in a small bark, which they had hired for that end, and the men were to meet them by land. But it so fell out that they were there a day before the ship came; and the sea being rough, and the women very sick, prevailed with the seamen to put into a creek hard by, where they lay on ground at low water. The next morning the ship came; but they were fast, and could not stir until about noon. In the mean time, the shipmaster, perceiving how the matter was, sent his boat to be getting the men aboard, whom he saw walking about the shore. But after the first boat-full was got aboard, and she was ready to go for more, the master espied a great company, both horse and foot, with bills and guns and other weapons; for the country was raised to take them. The Dutchman seeing that, swore his country's oath, ("sacrament") and having the wind fair, weighed his anchor, hoisted sails, and away.

But the poor men which were got on board were in great distress for their wives and children, which they saw thus to be taken, and were left destitute of their helps, and themselves also not having a cloth to shift

[1] Grimsby is a sea-port town in Lincolnshire, near the mouth of the Humber. It was once rich and populous, and carried on a considerable foreign trade. See Camden's Britannia, p. 471, and Britton's Topographical Description of the County of Lincoln, p. 689.

A STORM AT SEA.

them with, more than they had on their backs, and some scarce a penny about them, all they had being on board the bark. It drew tears from their eyes, and any thing they had they would have given to have been on shore again. But all in vain; there was no remedy; they must thus sadly part; and afterwards endured a fearful storm at sea, being fourteen days or more before they arrived at their port; in seven whereof they neither saw sun, moon, nor stars, and were driven to the coast of Norway; the mariners themselves often despairing of life, and once with shrieks and cries gave over all, as if the ship had been foundered in the sea, and they sinking without recovery. But when man's hope and help wholly failed, the Lord's power and mercy appeared for their recovery; for the ship rose again, and gave the mariners courage again to manage her; and if modesty[1] would suffer me, I might declare with what fervent prayers they cried unto the Lord in this great distress, especially some of them, even without any great distraction. When the water ran into their very ears and mouths, and the mariners cried out, "We sink, we sink," they cried, if not with miraculous, yet with a great height of divine faith, "Yet, Lord, thou canst save; yet, Lord, thou canst save:" with such other expressions as I will forbear. Upon which the ship did not only recover, but shortly after the violence of the storm began to abate, and the Lord filled their afflicted minds with such comforts as every one cannot understand, and in the end brought them to their desired haven; where the people came flock-

---

[1] From this expression, as well as from the whole passage, there can hardly be a doubt that Bradford himself was in the vessel. The description is that of an eye-witness.

CHAP. II.
1608.

ing, admiring their deliverance, the storm having been so long and sore, in which much hurt had been done, as the master's friends had related unto him in their congratulations.[1]

But to return to the others where we left. The rest of the men that were in the greatest danger made shift to escape away before the troop could surprise them, those only staying that best might, to be assistant to the women. But pitiful it was to see the heavy case of these poor women in this distress; what weeping and crying on every side; some for their husbands that

---

[1] Cotton Mather, in the Magnalia, i. 101, 102, records this and the previous attempt to escape from England; but he perversely transposes their chronological order; the effect of which is to make it appear that Bradford was imprisoned in Boston after he had escaped to Holland. He did not derive his information from Bradford's original manuscript but from this copy of it in the records of Plymouth church, which he cursorily examined when on his visits to his uncle, John Cotton, the minister of that church.

Mather did not know how to use his valuable materials, and took no pains to ascertain his facts or verify his statements. One instance of his utter disregard of accuracy, even when it could be easily attained, will suffice. In his Life of his father, Increase Mather, he states, p. 24, that he married the *only* daughter of John Cotton; whilst in the Magnalia, i. 260, he asserts that Cotton had *three* daughters, two of whom were married. One would have thought that he might have taken the trouble to find the exact truth about such a simple fact as this, relating to his own mother. And yet Cotton Mather is universally cited by Europeans, as well as by our own countrymen, who undertake to write our history, not only as an authority, but as the highest authority. This has been the case from Neal and Robertson downwards. De Tocqueville, whose selection of authorities is in all other respects singularly judicious, puts the Magnalia at the head, calling it "the most valuable and important document on the history of New England;" and Grahame, whose excellent History of the United States evinces great discrimination, calls it "the most considerable of the early historical works, and the most interesting performance that the literature of New England has ever produced. The biographical portions, in particular," he adds, "possess the highest excellence, and are superior in dignity and interest to the compositions of Plutarch." It is quite time that it was generally understood that Cotton Mather is not to be relied upon as an authority for any fact, unsupported by other evidence. Mr. Savage, the learned editor of Winthrop's Journal, states the simple truth when he says, that "Cotton Mather has published more errors of carelessness than any other writer on the history of New England." De Tocqueville, Democracy in America, p. 424, Grahame, i. 415; Savage's Winthrop, ii. 24.

THE WOMEN LEFT BEHIND. 31

were carried away in the ship, as it was before related; others not knowing what should become of them and their little ones; others melted in tears, seeing their poor little ones hanging about them, crying for fear and quaking with cold. Being thus apprehended, they were hurried from one place to another, and from one justice to another, until, in the end, they knew not what to do with them. For to imprison so many women and innocent children for no other cause, many of them, but that they would[1] go with their husbands, seemed to be unreasonable, and all would cry out of them; and to send them home again was as difficult, for they alleged (as the truth was) they had no homes to go to, for they had sold or otherwise disposed of their houses and livings. To be short, after they had been thus turmoiled a good while, and conveyed from one constable to another, they were glad to be rid of them in the end upon any terms, for all were wearied and tired with them; though, in the mean time, the poor souls endured misery enough; and thus in the end necessity forced a way for them.

But that I be not tedious in these things, I will omit the rest, although I might relate other notable passages and troubles which they endured and underwent in these their wanderings and travels, both at land and sea.[2] But I haste to other things. Yet I may not omit the fruit that came hereby. For by these so

---

[1] I have here substituted *would*, which Hutchinson gives as the reading of Bradford's MS. for *must*, which is in Morton's copy. There can be no doubt as to which is the true reading.

[2] It is much to be regretted that the worthy Governor did not see fit to preserve the particulars of these perils and sufferings of his brethren. Could he have foreseen the deep interest which, two hundred years afterwards, would be felt in every thing relating to these poor exiles, he would not have failed to record the minutest occurrences

CHAP. II.
1608.

public troubles in so many eminent places [1] their cause became famous, and occasioned many to look into the same; and their godly carriage and christian behaviour was such as left a deep impression in the minds of many. And though some few shrunk at those first conflicts and sharp beginnings, (as it was no marvel,) yet many more came on with fresh courage, and greatly animated others; and in the end, notwithstanding all these storms of opposition, they all got over at length, some at one time and some at another, and met together again, according to their desires, with no small rejoicing.

in their history. But these humble and modest men did not suppose that posterity would be solicitous to know about their trials and persecutions. They were not aware that they were to be the germs of a great empire.

[1] Boston, Hull, and Grimsby.

CHAPTER III.

OF THEIR SETTLING IN HOLLAND, AND THEIR MANNER OF LIVING AND ENTERTAINMENT THERE.

BEING now come into the Low Countries, they saw many goodly and fortified cities, strongly walled, and guarded with troops of armed men. Also they heard a strange and uncouth language, and beheld the different manners and customs of the people, with their strange fashions and attires; all so far differing from that of their plain country villages, wherein they were bred and born and had so long lived, as it seemed they were come into a new world. But those were not the things they much looked on, or long took up their thoughts; for they had other work in hand, and another kind of war to wage and maintain. For though they saw fair and beautiful cities, flowing with abundance of all sorts of wealth and riches, yet it was not long before they saw the grim and griseled[1] face of poverty coming on them like an armed man, with whom they must buckle and encounter, and from whom they could not fly. But they were armed with faith and patience against him and all his encounters;

CHAP. III.

1608.

---

[1] Griseled, for grisly — frightful, hideous.

CHAP. III.

1608.

and though they were sometimes foiled, yet by God's assistance they prevailed and got the victory.

Now when Mr. Robinson, Mr. Brewster, and other principal members were come over, (for they were of the last, and stayed to help the weakest over before them,) such things were thought on as were necessary for their settling and best ordering of the church affairs. And when they had lived at Amsterdam about a year, Mr. Robinson, their pastor, and some others of best discerning, seeing how Mr. John Smith and his company was already fallen into contention with the church that was there before them, and no means they could use would do any good to cure the same; and also that the flames of contention were like to break out in that ancient church itself, (as afterwards lamentably came to pass); which things they prudently foreseeing, thought it was best to remove before they were any way engaged with the same;[1] though they well knew it would be much to the prejudice of their outward

---

[1] Neal, Hist. of New England, i. 76, falls into an error when he speaks of "the flames of contention having broken out in Mr. Smith's church." Belknap, Amer. Biog. ii. 157, follows it when he says, "these people (Smith and his congregation) fell into controversy, and were soon scattered;" and Francis Baylies, Memoir of Plymouth, i. 11, repeats it when he says, "some dissensions happening amongst them, (Smith's people) the church was dissolved." This error arises from their not being aware of, or not attending to, the fact of the existence of another congregation of Separatists at Amsterdam, which had been established many years before Smith settled there; who went over to Holland, as appears from page 22, only a short time before Robinson. The contention was not among the members of Smith's congregation, but between his church and "the church that was there before them," "that *ancient* church," namely Johnson's, mentioned in the note on page 24. Baylie, in his Dissuasive, p. 16, Hornius, Hist. Eccles. p. 232, and Neal, Hist. Puritans, i. 437, err in saying that Smith set up his church at Leyden; whereas it was to avoid him and his company that Robinson removed to that city. Cotton, in his Way of Cong. Churches, p. 7, says, "I understand by such as lived in those parts at that time, Smith lived at Amsterdam, and there died, and at Leyden in Holland he never came."

estate, both at present and, in likelihood, in the future; as indeed it proved to be.

For these and some other reasons they removed to Leyden,[1] a fair and beautiful city, and of a sweet situation, but made more famous by the university wherewith it is adorned, in which of late it had been by so many learned men;[2] but wanting that traffic by sea which Amsterdam enjoyed, it was not so beneficial for their outward means of living and estates. But being now here pitched, they fell to such trades and employments[3] as they best could, valuing peace and their spiritual comfort above any other riches whatsoever; and at length they came to raise a competent and comfortable living, and with hard and continual labor. Being thus settled, after many difficulties, they continued many years in a comfortable condition, enjoying much sweet and delightful society and spiritual comfort together, in the ways of God, under the able ministry

---

[1] "By several passages in Gov. Bradford's manuscript it seems as if they began to remove to Leyden at the end of 1608. Prince, p. 120. The distance from Amsterdam to Leyden is about 22 miles.

[2] The university of Leyden was established in 1575, the year after the memorable siege of that place. The Prince of Orange, wishing to reward the citizens for their constancy and valor, gave them the choice of two privileges — either an exemption from taxes, or a university; they chose the latter. It has been at times one of the most celebrated in Europe; and from its reputation the city itself was called the Athens of the West, and the North Star of Holland. Among its distinguished professors and scholars were Arminius, Episcopius, Grotius, Lipsius, Junius, Vossius, Descartes, Scaliger, Salmasius, and Booerhave. See Grotius, Annals, p. 266; Brandt, i. 312.

[3] Cotton Mather, in his Life of Gov. Bradford, in the Magnalia, i. 102, speaks of "the difficulties to which Bradford, when in Holland, stooped in learning and serving of a Frenchman at the working of silks;" and Belknap in his Amer. Biog. ii. 218, says that Bradford, "being under age, put himself as an apprentice to a French Protestant, who taught him the art of silkdying." Neither of them, however, refers to any authority for their statements. Brewster became a printer, as will be seen hereafter in Bradford's memoir of him. Many of the first colonists at Plymouth were weavers, from Yorkshire and Nottinghamshire, and brought over their looms with them. See Mass. Hist. Coll. xiii. 171.

CHAP.
III.

1609
to
1617.

and prudent government of Mr. John Robinson and Mr. William Brewster, who was an assistant unto him in the place of an elder, unto which he was now called and chosen by the church ; so as they grew in knowledge and other gifts and graces of the spirit of God ; and lived together in peace, and love, and holiness. And many came unto them from divers parts of England, so as they grew a great congregation.[1] And if at any time any differences did arise or offences broke out, (as it cannot be but that sometimes there will, even amongst the best of men), they were ever so met with and nipped in the head betimes, or otherwise so well composed, as still love, peace, and communion was continued, or else the church purged of those that were incurable and incorrigible, when, after much patience used, no other means would serve; which seldom comes to pass.

Yea, such was the mutual love and reciprocal respect that this worthy man had to his flock, and his flock to him, that it might be said of them, as it was once said[2] of that famous emperor, Marcus Aurelius, and the people of Rome, that it was hard to judge whether he delighted more in having such a people, or they in having

---

[1] It is impossible to ascertain the exact number of Robinson's congregation ; yet we may approximate to it. Gov. Bradford tells us, in his Dialogue, that in Johnson's church, "at Amsterdam, there were about three hundred communicants ; and for the church of Leyden, they were sometimes not much fewer in number." Edward Winslow says, in his Brief Narration, that "the difference of number was not great" between those who remained at Leyden and those who embarked for America. Now we know that 120 set sail from England in the Mayflower and Speedwell. Of these 100 arrived at Plymouth in the Mayflower in 1620 ; 36 came in the Fortune, in 1621 ; 60 in the Anne, in 1623 ; 35, with their families, in the Mayflower, in 1629 ; and 60 in 1630 in the Handmaid ; — making in all more than 300, including the "families." We have the names of those who came in the first three ships ; and also a list of the persons in the Colony in May, 1627. See Prince, pp. 264 and 343 ; Morton's Memorial, p. 381 ; Winthrop's Journal, i. 37, 378.

[2] Golden Book, &c. — *Morton's Note.*

such a pastor. His love was great towards them, and his care was always bent for their best good, both for soul and body. For, besides his singular abilities in divine things, wherein he excelled, he was able also to give direction in civil affairs,[1] and to foresee dangers and inconveniences; by which means he was very helpful to their outward estates; and so was every way as a common father unto them. And none did more offend him than those that were close and cleaving to themselves, and retired from the common good; as also such as would be stiff and rigid in matters of outward order, and inveigh against the evils of others, and yet be remiss in themselves, and not so careful to express a virtuous conversation. They, in like manner, had ever a reverent regard unto him, and had him in precious estimation, as his worth and wisdom did deserve; and although they esteemed him highly whilst he lived and labored amongst them, yet much more after his death,[2] when they came to feel the want of his help, and saw by woful experience what a treasure they had lost, to the grief of their hearts and wounding of their souls; yea, such a loss as they saw could not

---

[1] It has been the practice of the Independent or Congregational clergy, both in Old and New England, from the earliest times, to take an interest and part in public affairs. The prominent and efficient agency which they exercised in the infancy of our colonial settlements is well known; Cotton, Hooker, and Davenport shared at least an equal power with Winthrop, Haynes, and Eaton in moulding the civil polity of Massachusetts and Connecticut. The services of Increase Mather in obtaining the second charter of Massachusetts are recorded in her history; and the patriotic exertions of Mayhew, Chauncy, and Cooper, before and during the Revolution, will never be forgotten. The Congregational clergy were found, at that time, almost to a man, on the side of their country's independence; and they have ever been the earnest and consistent advocates of "liberty with order." See Hutchinson's Mass. i. 34, 419; Trumbull's Connecticut, i. 91, 99; Bacon's and Kingsley's Hist. Discourses at New Haven; Tudor's Life of Otis, pp. 140–155.

[2] Mr. Robinson died at Leyden, March 1st, 1625. He was about 50 years old. Prince, p. 237.

CHAP. III.

1609 to 1617.

be repaired; for it was hard for them to find such another leader and feeder in all respects, as the Taborites to find another Ziska.[1] And although they did not call themselves orphans, as the other did, after his death, yet they had cause as much to lament, in another regard, their present condition and after usage.

But to return. I know not but it may be spoken to the honor of God, and without prejudice to any, that such was the humble zeal and fervent love of this people (whilst they thus lived together) towards God and his ways, and the single-heartedness and sincere affection one towards another, that they came as near the primitive pattern of the first churches as any other church of these latter times have done, according to their rank and quality. But seeing it is not my purpose to treat of the several passages that befell this people whilst they thus lived in the Low Countries, (which might worthily require a large treatise of itself,) but to manifest something of their beginning and after progress in New England, which I principally scope and aim at; yet, because some of their adversaries did, upon the rumor of their removal, cast out slanders against them, as if that State had been weary of them, and had rather driven them out, (as the heathen histo-

---

[1] The burning of John Huss and Jerome of Prague by order of the Council of Constance, in 1415 and 1416, caused great indignation and excitement in Bohemia, their native country, which led to an open insurrection. The insurgents took up arms, and under the command of John Ziska, retired to a mountain ten miles from Prague, to which they gave the name of Mount Tabor, from the tent which they erected there for the celebration of the communion, and in allusion to the Mount of Transfiguration, on which the Apostle Peter wished to build tabernacles. Here they founded a city, to which also they gave the name of Tabor, and from it were themselves called *Taborites*. After the death of Ziska in 1424, his followers were inconsolable, and considering themselves deprived of a parent and protector, called themselves *Orphans*. See Gieseler's Eccles. Hist. iii. 359, and Encyc. Amer. articles *Ziska* and *Huss*.

ries did feign of Moses and the Israelites when they went out of Egypt,)[1] than it was their own free choice and motion, I will therefore mention a particular or two to show the contrary, and that good acceptation they had in the place.

And first, although it was low with many of them, yet their word would be taken amongst the Dutch when they wanted money, because they had found by experience how careful they were to keep their word,[2] and saw them so painful and diligent in their callings, that they strove to get their custom, and to employ them above others in their work, for their honesty and diligence.

Again; the magistrates of the city, about the time of their coming away, or a little before, in the public place of justice, gave this commendable testimony of them, in reproof of the Walloons,[3] who were of the French church in the city. " These English," said they, " have lived amongst us now this twelve years, and yet we never had any suit or accusation come

---

[1] It was a vulgar slander against the Jews, that they were expelled from Egypt on account of their having the leprosy. Tacitus says " A pestilential disease, disfiguring the race of men, and making the body an object of loathsome deformity, spread all over Egypt. Bocchoris, at that time the reigning monarch, consulted the oracle of Jupiter Hammon, and received for answer that the kingdom must be purified, by exterminating the infected multitude, as a race of men detested by the gods. After diligent search, the wretched sufferers were collected together, and in a wild and barren desert abandoned to their misery. In that distress, while the vulgar herd was sunk in deep despair, Moses, one of their number," &c. Josephus vindicates his countrymen from the same charge, as alleged by Manetho, Chæremon, and Lysimachus. See Tacitus, Hist. lib. v. 3, with the comments of Brotier and Oberlin, and Josephus against Apion, lib. 1. 26-35.

[2] A great honor to the Gospel.— *Morton's Note.*

[3] The Walloons are the inhabitants of the southern part of Belgium, bordering on France. Their language is a dialect differing from the French and German, as well as the Flemish, and is said to resemble the old French of the thirteenth century. See Grattan's Hist. of the Netherlands, p. 1.

CHAP. against any of¹ them. But your strifes and quarrels are continual," &c.

1612. In these times, also, were the great troubles raised by the Arminians;² who, as they greatly molested the whole State, so this city in particular, in which was the chief university; so as there were daily and hot disputes in the schools thereabouts. And as the students and other learned were divided in their opinions herein, so were the two professors or divinity readers themselves, the one daily teaching for it, and the other against it; which grew to that pass, that few of the disciples of the one would hear the other teach. But Mr. Robinson, although he taught thrice a week himself and wrote sundry books,³ besides, his manifold pains otherwise, yet he went constantly to hear their

---

¹ The words *any of* are inserted from Hutchinson, ii. 454. Morton himself has it so in the Memorial, p. 21.

² The fullest and best account of Arminianism, which Cotton Mather, (Magnalia, i. 46,) spitefully calls "that grand choke-weed of true Christianity," is contained in Brandt's History of the Reformation in the Low Countries. James Arminius, (Hermann), born at Oudewater in South Holland, in 1560, after having been fifteen years a minister at Amsterdam, was chosen professor of divinity at Leyden in 1603, and died Oct. 9; 1609, in his 49th year. The best Life of him is by Brandt. See also his Life by Nichols; Brandt's Hist. Ref. ii. 25–63; and Bayle, Dict. Hist. et Crit.

³ The following are the titles of the books which Robinson published after his arrival in Holland, and before the embarkation of the Pilgrims for America. 1. A Justification of Separation from the Church of England; against Mr. Richard Bernard his invective, intituled the Separatists' Scheme. By John Robinson. 1610. 2. Of Religious Communion, private and public. With the silencing of the clamors raised by Mr. Thomas Helwisse against our retaining the baptism received in England, and administering of baptism to infants. As also a survey of the confession of faith published in certain Conclusions by the remainders of Mr. Smith's company. By John Robinson. 1614. 3. Apologia Justa et Necessaria quorundam Christianorum, æque contumeliosè ac communiter dictorum Brownistarum sive Barrowistarum. Per Johannem Robinsonum, Anglo-Leidensem, suo et ecclesiæ nomine, cui præfigitur. 1619. This work was translated into English, and printed in 1644. The place where these books were printed is not mentioned on the title-page of either of them. It probably was Leyden, and Elder Brewster may have been the printer.

readings, and heard as well one as the other. By which means he was so well grounded in the controversy, and saw the force of all their arguments, and knew the shifts of the adversary; and being himself very able, none was fitter to buckle with them than himself, as appeared by sundry disputes; so as he began to be terrible to the Arminians; which made Episcopius,[1] the Arminian professor, to put forth his best strength, and set out sundry theses, which by public dispute he would defend against all men. Now Polyander,[1] the other professor, and the chief preachers of the city, desired Mr. Robinson to dispute against him. But he was loth, being a stranger. Yet the other did importune him, and told him that such was the ability and nimbleness of wit of the adversary, that the truth would suffer if he did not help them; so as he condescended, and prepared himself against the time. And when the time came, the Lord did so help him to defend the truth and foil his adversary, as he put him to an apparent nonplus in this great and public audience. And the like he did two or three times upon such like occasions; the which, as it caused many to praise God that the truth had so famous a victory, so it procured him much honor and respect from those learned men and others which loved the truth.[2]

1613.

---

[1] Simon Episcopius (Bisschop) and John Polyander were chosen professors of divinity in the university at Leyden in 1612. See Brandt, ii. 111; Limborch's Historia Vitæ Simonis Episcopii, p. 41; Calder's Memoirs of Episcopius, p. 128, and Bayle, Dict. Hist. et Crit.

[2] Winslow, in his Brief Narration, says, "Our pastor, Mr. Robinson, in the time when Arminianism prevailed so much, at the request of the most orthodox divines, as Polyander, Festus Hommius, &c. disputed daily against Episcopius (in the Academy at Leyden) and others, the grand champions of that error, and had as good respect amongst

CHAP. III.

1608 to 1620.

Yea, so far were they from being weary of him and his people, or desiring their absence, as that it was said by some, of no mean note, that were it not for giving offence to the State of England,[1] they would have preferred him otherwise, if he would, and allowed them some public favor. Yea, when there was speech of their removal into these parts, sundry of note and eminency of that nation would have had them come under them; and for that end made them large offers.[2]

Now although I might allege many particulars and examples of the like kind to show the untruth and unlikelihood of this slander, yet these shall suffice,

them as any of their own divines." I find, however, no account of this disputation in Brandt or in any of the biographers of Episcopius. Yet John Hoornbeek, a professor at Leyden, says in his Summa Controversiarum Religionis, p. 741, (published in 1658,) " Vir ille (Johannes Robinsonus) gratus nostris, dum vixit, fuit, et theologis Leidensibus familiaris ac honoratus. Scripsit præterea varia contra Arminianos: frequens quippe et acer erat Episcopii in Academiâ adversarius et opponens." Belknap judiciously remarks concerning this disputation, " It is usual, on such occasions, for the partisans on both sides to claim the victory for their respective champions. Whether it were so at this time cannot be determined, as we have no account of the controversy from the Arminian party." Amer. Biog. ii. 160.

[1] King James at this time exercised an unwarrantable influence in the Low Countries, both in civil and ecclesiastical affairs. He drove Vorstius from his professorship at Leyden for his heresies, and labored to procure his banishment; and prevented Ames from being elected to the same office. He seems to have kept an ambassador at the Hague chiefly to inform him of the progress of the theological disputes in that country. See Winwood's Memorials, iii. 293-6, 304, 310, 357. Sir Dudley Carleton's Letters, pp. 352, 373, 388, 435; Brandt, ii. 85, 97.

[2] Henry Hudson, in the employment of the Dutch East India Company, discovered the river called by his name, in 1609. On this ground the Dutch claimed the adjoining territory; a few huts were erected at New York and Albany in 1613 and 1615; but no colony was settled in the New Netherlands till 1623. The Dutch West India Company was incorporated in 1621 for this object; but individuals had for some years before been meditating colonization on the Hudson; and the offers to the Pilgrims probably came from them. See Hazard's State Papers, i. 121.

seeing it was believed of few, being only raised by the malice of some who labored their disgrace.[1]

[1] The English separatists in Holland attracted the notice of Cardinal Bentivoglio, who was the papal nuncio in that country from 1607 to 1616, though he misunderstood the cause of their leaving England, supposing it to be commerce, and not religion. He says, " I Puritani ancora vi son tolerati, che sono i più puri e più rigidi Calvinisti, i quali non vogliono riconoscere autorità alcuna ne' magistrati politici sopra il governo de' loro ministri heretici ; e sono quasi tutti de' Puritani d' Inghilterra, che per occasion di commercio frequentan l'Ollanda, e le altre Provincie Unite. —I Puritani Inglesi sono in Amsterdam quasi tutti per l'istesso rispetto ; e se ne trattengono alcuni medesimamente per occasione di mercantia nella città di Midelburgo in Zelanda. Per ogni parte dunque, e da tutti gli angoli, si può dire, delle Provincie Unite, s'odono i latrati, e gli urli di tanti infetti loro settarii." Relazione di Fiandra, parte ii. cap. ii.

CHAPTER IV.

SHOWING THE REASONS AND CAUSES OF THEIR REMOVAL.

CHAP. IV.

1609 to 1620.

1617.

AFTER they had lived in this city about eleven or twelve years, (which is the more observable, being the whole time of that famous truce between that State and the Spaniards,)[1] and sundry of them were taken away by death, and many others began to be well stricken in years, the grave mistress experience having taught them many things, these prudent governors, with sundry of the sagest members, began both deeply to apprehend their present dangers and wisely to foresee the future, and think of timely remedy. In the agitation of their thoughts and much discourse of particulars hereabout, they began to incline to this conclusion of removal to some other place; not out of any newfangledness, or other such like giddy humor, by which men are many times transported, to their great hurt and danger, but for sundry weighty and solid

---

[1] After the war had been raging for more than thirty years between Spain and the United Provinces, by the mediation of Henry IV. of France and James I. of England, a truce of twelve years was concluded on the 9th of April, 1609. See Bentivoglio, Della Guerra di Fiandra, parte iii. lib. viii., Opere Storiche, iv. 564 ; Grotius, p. 542, 569 ; Brandt, ii. 54 ; Watson's Philip III. p. 275 ; Grattan's Netherlands, p. 226.

reasons, the chief of which I will here recite and briefly touch.

1. And first, they found and saw by experience the hardness of the place and country to be such, as few in comparison would come to them, and fewer that would bide it out and continue with them. For many that came to them, and many more that desired to be with them, could not endure the great labor and hard fare, with other inconveniences, which they underwent and were contented with. But though they loved their persons, and approved their cause, and honored their sufferings, yet they left them as it were weeping, as Orpah did her mother-in-law Naomi, or as those Romans did Cato in Utica, who desired to be excused and borne with, though they could not all be Catos.[1] For many, though they desired to enjoy the ordinances of God in their purity, and the liberty of the Gospel with them, yet, alas, they admitted of bondage, with danger of conscience, rather than to endure these hardships; yea, some preferred and chose prisons in England rather than this liberty in Holland, with these afflictions. But it was thought, that if a better and easier place of living could be had, it would draw many and take away these discouragements; yea, their pastor would often say, that many of those that both writ and preached now against them, if they were in a place where they might have liberty, and live comfortably, they would then practise as they did.

CHAP. IV.

1617.

Ruth, i. 14.

[1] Plutarch says, in his Life of Cato the Younger, that the three hundred Roman citizens who were with him in Utica, intending to send messengers to Cæsar to intercede in their behalf, "implored him to trust them and make use of their services; but as they were no Catos, and had not Cato's dignity of mind, they hoped he would pity their weakness."

CHAP. IV.
1617.

2. They saw, that although the people generally bore all their difficulties very cheerfully and with a resolute courage, being in the best of their strength, yet old age began to come on some of them;[1] and their great and continual labors, with other crosses and sorrows, hastened it before the time; so as it was not only probably thought, but apparently seen, that within a few years more they were in danger to scatter by necessity pressing them, or sink under their burdens, or both; and therefore, according to the divine proverb, that "a wise man seeth the plague when it cometh, and hideth himself," so they, like skilful and beaten soldiers, were fearful either to be entrapped or surrounded by their enemies, so as they should neither be able to fight nor fly; and therefore thought it better to dislodge betimes to some place of better advantage and less danger, if any could be found.

Prov. xxii. 3.

3. As necessity was a taskmaster over them, so they were forced to be such not only to their servants, but in a sort to their dearest children; the which, as it did a little wound the tender hearts of many a loving father and mother, so it produced also many sad and sorrowful effects. For many of their children, that were of best dispositions and gracious inclinations, having learned to bear the yoke in their youth, and willing to bear part of their parents' burden, were oftentimes so oppressed with their heavy labors, that although their minds were free and willing, yet their bodies bowed under the weight of the same, and became decrepit in their early youth; the vigor of nature be-

---

[1] We know the age of but few of the Pilgrims. Carver was probably one of the oldest. In 1620 Elder Brewster was 56 years old, Robinson 45, Bradford 32, Edward Winslow 26, and John Howland 28.

THE REASONS FOR REMOVAL. 47

ing consumed in the very bud, as it were. But that which was more lamentable, and of all sorrows most heavy to be borne, was that many of their children, by these occasions, and the great licentiousness of youth in the country, and the manifold temptations of the place, were drawn away by evil examples unto extravagant and dangerous courses, getting the reins on their necks, and departing from their parents. Some became soldiers, others took them upon far voyages by sea, and other some worse courses tending to dissoluteness and the danger of their souls, to the great grief of their parents and dishonor of God; so that they saw their posterity would be in danger to degenerate and be corrupted.

CHAP. IV.

1617.

4. Lastly, (and which was not the least,) a great hope and inward zeal they had of laying some good foundation, or at least to make some way thereunto, for the propagating and advancing the Gospel of the kingdom of Christ in these remote parts of the world; yea, though they should be but as stepping-stones unto others for performing of so great a work.

These, and some other like reasons,[1] moved them

---

[1] Edward Winslow, in his Brief Narration, mentions three other reasons; first, their desire to live under the protection of England and to retain the language and the name of Englishmen; second, their inability to give their children such an education as they had themselves received; and third, their grief at the profanation of the sabbath in Holland. This violation of the sabbath attracted the attention of the Synod of Dort, which assembled in 1618. The Dutch ministers acknowledged the great difficulty they met with in withdrawing the people on Sundays from their sports or their ordinary work; and the English divines took notice of the great scandal which the neglect of the Lord's Day at Dort gave them, exhorting the Synod to interfere with the magistrates for preventing the opening of shops and the exercise of trade on Sundays. Sir Dudley Carleton, too, writing from the Hague July 22, 1619, says, "It falls out in these towns of Holland, that Sunday, which is elsewhere the day of rest, proves the day of labor, for they never knew yet how to observe the sabbath." See Brandt, iii. 28, 290; Hales's Letters

CHAP. IV.
1617.

to undertake this resolution of their removal, the which they afterward prosecuted with so great difficulties; as by the sequel will appear.

The place they had thoughts on were some of those unpeopled countries of America, which are fruitful and fit for habitation, being devoid of all civil inhabitants, where there are only salvage and brutish people, which range up and down little otherwise than the wild beasts. This proposition being made public, and coming to the scanning of all, it raised many variable opinions amongst men, and caused many fears and doubts amongst themselves. Some, from their reasons and hopes conceived, labored to stir up and encourage the rest to undertake and prosecute the same; others, again, out of their fears, objected against it, and

from the Synod of Dort, p. 8. (Glasgow, 1765); Carleton's Letters, p. 380.

These reasons for their removal, as stated by Bradford and Winslow, are sufficient, and are to be received as the true and sole reasons. Yet Douglass, in his Summary, i. 369, says, "Being of unsteady temper, they resolved to remove to some remote country in some wilderness, — as recluses." Chalmers, in his Political Annals, p. 85, says, "After twelve years' unmolested residence they became unhappy in their situation, because they foresaw the destruction of their society in the toleration they enjoyed; and determined to seek new adventures in America. — Continuing unhappy in a country where they were obscure and unpersecuted," &c. Robertson, in his History of America, book x. says, "They resided at Leyden for several years unmolested and obscure. But as their church received no increase, either by recruits from England or by proselytes gained in the country, they began to be afraid that all their high attainments in spiritual knowledge would be lost, if they remained longer in a strange land." And Burke, in his account of the European Settlements in America, says that "though in a country of the greatest religious freedom in the world, they did not find themselves better satisfied than they had been in England. They were tolerated indeed, but watched; their zeal began to have dangerous languors for want of opposition; and being without power or consequence, they grew tired of the indolent security of their sanctuary." These sneers are as contemptible as they are unjust. It is to be regretted that any respectable writer in this country should have incautiously given currency to such misrepresentations. Chief Justice Marshall perceived and corrected the error into which he had been led by following such unworthy authorities. Compare his Life of Washington, i. 90, (first ed.) with his History of the American Colonies, p. 78.

sought to divert from it, alleging many things, and those neither unreasonable nor unprobable; as that it was a great design, and subject to many inconceivable perils and dangers; as, besides the casualties of the seas, (which none can be freed from,) the length of the voyage was such as the weak bodies of men and women and such other persons, worn out with age and travail, (as many of them were,) could never be able to endure; and yet if they should, the miseries of the land which they should be exposed unto would be too hard to be borne, and likely, some or all of them, to consume and utterly to ruinate them.[1] For there they should be liable to famine, and nakedness, and the want, in a manner, of all things. The changing of the air, diet, and drinking of water would infect their bodies with sore sicknesses; and all those which should escape or overcome these difficulties should yet be in continual danger of the salvage people, who are cruel, barbarous, and treacherous, being most furious in their rage and merciless where they overcome, not being content only to kill and take away life, but delight to torment men in most bloody manner that may be, flaying men alive with the shells of fishes, cutting off the joints and members of others by piecemeals, and broiling them on the coals, and causing men to eat the collops of their flesh in their sight whilst they live; with other cruelties horrible to be related. And surely it could not be thought but the hearing of these things could not but move the bowels of men to grate

---

[1] " Immensus ultrà, utque sic dixerim, adversus oceanus raris ab orbe nostro navibus aditur? Quis porro, præter periculum horridi et ignoti maris, Asia, aut Africa aut Italiâ relictâ, Germaniam peteret, informem terris, asperam cœlo, tristem cultu aspectuque, nisi si patria sit?" Tacitus, Germania, ii.

CHAP. within them, and make the weak to quake and tremble. It was further objected, that it would require
IV.
1617. greater sums of money to furnish such a voyage and to fit them with necessaries, than their estates would amount to. And yet they must all as well look to be seconded with supplies, as presently to be transported. Also, the like precedents of ill success and lamentable miseries befallen others in the like designs,[1] were easy to be found, and not forgotten to be alleged; besides their own experience in their former troubles and hardships in their removal into Holland, and how hard a thing it was for them to live in that strange place, although it was a neighbour country, and a civil and rich commonwealth.

It was answered, that all great and honorable actions were accompanied with great difficulties, and must be both enterprised and overcome with answerable courages. It was granted the dangers were great, but not desperate, and the difficulties were many, but not invincible; for although there were many of them likely, yet they were not certain. It might be that some of the things feared might never befall them; others, by providence, care, and the use of good means, might in a great measure be prevented; and all of them through the help of God, by fortitude and patience, might either be borne or overcome. True it was that such attempts were not to be made and undertaken but upon good ground and reason, not rashly or lightly, as many have done for curiosity or

[1] The entire failure of the plantation at Sagadahoc, near the mouth of the Kennebec, in 1607, which was abandoned in less than a year, and the slow progress of the Virginia settlements, might well serve to discourage them from emigrating to America. See Gorges's Brief Narrative, in Mass. Hist. Coll. xxvi. 54—56, and Williamson's History of Maine, i. 197—203.

hope of gain, &c. But their condition was not ordi- CHAP. IV.
nary. Their ends were good and honorable, their
calling lawful and urgent, and therefore they might 1617.
expect a blessing of God in their proceeding; yea,
although they should lose their lives in this action, yet
they might have comfort in the same; and their endeavours would be honorable. They lived here but
as men in exile and in a poor condition; and as great
miseries might possibly befall them in this place; for
the twelve years of truce were now out,[1] and there
was nothing but beating of drums and preparing for
war, the events whereof are always uncertain. The
Spaniard might prove as cruel as the salvages of
America, and the famine and pestilence are sore
here as there, and liberty less to look out for remedy.

After many other particular things answered and
alleged on both sides, it was fully concluded by the
major part to put this design in execution, and to
prosecute it by the best means they could.

---

[1] The twelve years' truce, concluded April 9, 1609, expired in 1621, when the war was renewed. See Note on page 44.

CHAPTER V.

SHOWING WHAT MEANS THEY USED FOR PREPARATION TO THIS WEIGHTY VOYAGE.

CHAP. V.
1617.

AND first, after their humble prayers unto God for his direction and assistance, and a general conference held thereabouts, they consulted what particular place to pitch upon and prepare for. Some, and none of the meanest, had thoughts and were earnest for Guiana,[1] or some of those fertile places in those hot cli-

---

[1] Sir Walter Raleigh published in 1596 his "Discovery of Guiana," which he calls a mighty, rich and beautiful empire, directly east from Peru, towards the sea, lying under the equinoctial line. Its capital was "that great and golden city which the Spaniards call El Dorado, and the natives Manoa, and for greatness, riches, and excellent seat it far exceedeth any of the world." Having, in 1595, sailed up the Orinoco 400 miles in quest of it, he says, "On both sides of this river we passed the most beautiful country that ever mine eyes beheld; plains of twenty miles in length, the grass short and green, and in divers parts groves of trees by themselves, as if they had been by all the art and labor of the world so made of purpose; and still as we rowed, the deer came down feeding by the water's side, as if they had been used to a keeper's call. — I never saw a more beautiful country, nor more lively prospects, hills so raised here and there over the valleys, the river winding into divers branches, the plains adjoining without bush or stubble, all fair green grass, the deer crossing in every path, the birds towards the evening singing on every tree with a thousand several tunes, the air fresh, with a gentle easterly wind; and every stone that we stopped to take up promised either gold or silver by his complexion. — For health, good air, pleasure, and riches, I am resolved it cannot be equalled by any region either in the east or west." See Raleigh's Works, viii. 381, 398, 427, 442, 462. (Oxford ed.)

Chapman, too, the translator of

mates. Others were for some parts of Virginia,[1] where the English had already made entrance and beginning.

Those for Guiana alleged that the country was rich, fruitful, and blessed with a perpetual spring and a flourishing greenness; where vigorous nature brought forth all things in abundance and plenty, without any great labor or art of man; so as it must needs make the inhabitants rich, seeing less provision of clothing and other things would secure them than in more colder and less fruitful countries must be had. As also that the Spaniards, having much more than they could possess, had not yet planted there, nor any where very near the same.[2]

But to this it was answered, that out of question the country was both fruitful and pleasant, and might yield riches and maintenance to the possessors more easily than to others; yet, other things considered, it would not be so fit. And first, that such hot countries are subject to grievous diseases, and many noisome impediments, which other more temperate places are free from, and would not so well agree with our Eng-

---

Homer, in a poem on Guiana, written in 1595, thus celebrates the country:

"Guiana, whose rich feet are mines of gold,
Whose forehead knocks against the roof of stars,
Stands on her tiptoe at fair England looking,
Kissing her hand, bowing her mighty breast,
And every sign of all submission making,
To be the sister and the daughter both
Of our most sacred maid."

See Tytler's Life of Raleigh, p. 164; and Oldys's Life in Raleigh's Works, i. 215.

[1] The successful colonization of Virginia commenced in 1607, at Jamestown. See Stith's History of Virginia, p. 46; Grahame's History of the United States, i. 39.

[2] Although England and Spain were now at peace, and had been since 1604, and so continued till the rupture in 1624, yet the Pilgrims, from their long residence in Holland, had imbibed the national repugnance of the Dutch to their Spanish oppressors, a feeling which was long retained. In a letter written by the Plymouth colonists to the Dutch on Hudson's river in 1627, they speak of resisting "the pride of that common enemy, the Spaniards, from whose cruelty the Lord keep us both, and our native countries." See Mass. Hist. Coll. iii. 51, 52.

CHAP. V.

1617.
1565.
Sept. 21.

lish bodies. Again, if they should there live and do well, the jealous Spaniard would never suffer them long, but would displant and overthrow them, as he did the French in Florida,[1] who were settled further from his richest countries; and the sooner, because they should have none to protect them, and their own strength would be too small to resist so potent an enemy and so near a neighbour.

On the other hand, for Virginia it was objected, that if they lived amongst the English which were there planted, or so near them as to be under their government, they should be in as great danger to be troubled and persecuted for their cause of religion[2] as if they lived in England, and it might be worse; and if they lived too far off, they should neither have succour or defence from them.

And at length the conclusion was, to live in a distinct body by themselves, under the general government of Virginia;[3] and by their friends to sue to His

---

[1] See the account of the massacre of the Huguenots in Florida by the Spaniards, in Holmes's Annals, i. 86.

[2] Virginia had been colonized by persons belonging to the Church of England, and attached to its ceremonies and institutions. In the orders and instructions for the government of the colony, issued by King James under his sign manual and the privy seal of England, it was specially enjoined that "the word and service of God should be preached and used according to the rites and doctrines of the Church of England." See Stith's Virginia, p. 37, and Chalmers's Annals, p. 15.

[3] The Virginia Company was established in 1606. On the 10th of April of that year, King James, by letters patent, divided a strip of land, of 100 miles wide, along the Atlantic coast of North America, extending from the 34th to the 45th degree of north latitude — a territory which then went under the common name of Virginia — between two Companies, who were to colonize it. The First or Southern Colony was granted to certain knights, gentlemen, merchants, and adventurers of London, who were to colonize between the 34th and the 41st degrees. The Second, or Northern Colony, was granted to persons of like description in Bristol, Exeter, and Plymouth, who were to plant between the 38th and the 45th degrees. Each Company was to be under the government of a council of thirteen, and neither of them was to plant a colony within a hundred miles of a previous settle-

Majesty that he would be pleased to grant them free liberty, and freedom of religion. And that this may be obtained they were put in good hope by some great persons of good rank and quality that were made their friends.[1]

Whereupon two[2] were chosen and sent into England, at the charge of the rest, to solicit this matter; who found the Virginia Company very desirous to have them go thither,[3] and willing to grant them a patent, with as ample privileges as they had or could grant to any, and to give them the best furtherance they could; and some of the chief of the Company doubted not to obtain their suit of the king for liberty in religion, and to have it confirmed under the king's broad seal, according to their desires. But it proved a harder piece of work than they took it for. For although many means were used to bring it about, yet it could not be effected; for there were divers of good worth labored with the king

---

ment made by the other. The Second or Plymouth Company made the unsuccessful attempt in 1607 to establish a colony near the mouth of the Kennebec. The First or London Company was the one to which the agents of the Pilgrims applied, and which seems at this time to have appropriated to itself exclusively the title of the Virginia Company. Douglass, i. 370, 395, Moulton, History of New York, p. 356, and Grahame, i. 188, err in saying that they obtained a grant of land or a promise of a patent, from the *Plymouth* Company. See the Charter in Stith, App. p. 1, and in Hazard's State Papers, i. 50.

[1] Among others, no doubt, Sir Edwin Sandys, Sir Robert Naunton, and Sir John Wolstenholme, as will hereafter be seen.

[2] Robert Cushman and John Carver, as appears by the letter of Sir Edwin Sandys on page 58. The little that is known of Cushman and Carver will be found in Belknap, ii. 179, 267.

[3] Sir Ferdinando Gorges, one of the leaders of the Second or Plymouth Company, says "Before the unhappy controversy happened between those of Virginia and myself, they were forced, through the great charge they had been at, to hearken to any propositions that might give ease and furtherance to so hopeful a business. To that purpose, it was referred to their considerations how necessary it was that means might be used to draw into those enterprises some of those families that had retired themselves into Holland for scruple of conscience, giving them such freedom and liberty as might stand with their likings. This advice being hearkened unto, there were that undertook the putting it in practice, and accordingly brought it to effect so far forth," &c. See Gorges, in Mass. Hist. Coll. xxvi. 73.

to obtain it, amongst whom was one [1] of his chief Secretaries; and some other wrought with the Archbishop [2] to give way thereunto. But it proved all in vain. Yet thus far they prevailed in sounding His Majesty's mind, that he would connive at them, and not molest them, provided they carried themselves peaceably. But to allow or tolerate them by his public authority under his seal, they found it would not be granted.[3] And this was all that the chief of the Virginia Company, or any other of their best friends, could do in the case. Yet they persuaded them to go on, for they presumed they should not be troubled.[4] And with this answer the messengers returned, and signified what diligence had been used, and to what issue things were come.

But this made a damp in the business, and caused some distraction. For many were afraid that if they should unsettle themselves, put off their estates, and go upon these hopes, it might prove dangerous, and but

---

[1] Winslow, in his Brief Narration, says that the agents " got Sir Edwin Sandys, a religious gentleman then living, to stir in it, who procured Sir Robert Naunton, then principal Secretary of State to King James, to move his Majesty." Sir Robert Naunton was sworn the king's secretary. Jan. 8, 1618. He was the author of " *Fragmenta Regalia;* Observations on the late Queen Elizabeth, her Times and Favorites," "the fruit," as Fuller says, " of his younger years." Belknap, Am. Biog. ii. 170, and Baylies, Memoir of Plymouth Colony, i. 16, err in calling him *Norton.* See Fuller's Worthies of England, ii. 336, (4to ed.); Birch's Memoirs of Queen Elizabeth, i. 369.

[2] The See of Canterbury was at this time filled by Dr. George Abbot. He had been promoted to it from the bishopric of London, April 9, 1611, and on the 23d of June was sworn a member of the Privy Council. See an account of him, not a very favorable one, in Clarendon's History of the Rebellion, book i. under the year 1633, in which he died. He was too mild and tolerant for Clarendon. See also Wood's Athenæ Oxon. i. 561, (ed. Bliss,) and Neal's Puritans, i. 564.

[3] The word *granted* I have restored from Prince, p. 148.

Douglass, Summary, i. 369, and the authors of the Modern Universal History err in saying that the Pilgrims " obtained an instrument from James I. for the full exercise of their religion in any part of America."

[4] At the very time this negotiation was pending, King James issued a declaration, (May 24, 1618) in which he required the bishop of Lancashire to constrain all the Puritans within his diocess to conform, or to leave the country. Prince, p. 147.

a sandy foundation. Yea, it was thought they might better have presumed hereupon, without making any suit at all, than, having made it, to be thus rejected. But some of the chiefest thought otherwise, and that they might well proceed hereupon, and that the King's Majesty was willing enough to suffer them without molestation, though for other reasons he would not confirm it by any public act; and furthermore, if there was no security in this promise intimated, there would be no greater certainty in a further confirmation of the same. For if afterward there should be a purpose or desire to wrong them, though they had a seal as broad as the house-floor, it would not serve the turn, for there would be means enough found to recall or reverse it. And seeing, therefore, the course is probable, they must rest herein on God's providence, as they had done in other things.

Upon this resolution, other messengers [1] were despatched to end with the Virginia Company, as well as they could, and to procure a patent with as good and ample conditions as they might by any good means attain; as also to treat and conclude with such merchants and other friends as had manifested their forwardness to provoke to and adventure in this voyage. For which end they had instructions given them upon what conditions they should proceed with them; or else to conclude nothing without further advice. And here it will be requisite to insert a letter or two, that may give light to these proceedings.

---

[1] By Mr. Cushman's letter from London, of May 8, 1619, inserted on a following page, it appears that these messengers were Mr. Cushman himself and Mr. Brewster; not Mr. Bradford, as Prince says, page 151. Judge Davis follows Prince in this error, in his valuable edition of Morton's Memorial, p. 22. They were not despatched, it will be seen, till more than a year after the first agents were sent.

CHAP. V.
1617.
Nov. 12.

A Copy of a Letter from Sir Edwin Sandys,[1] *directed to Mr. John Robinson and Mr. William Brewster.*[2]

After my hearty salutations, — The agents of your congregation, Robert Cushman and John Carver,[3] have been in communication with divers select gentlemen of his Majesty's Council for Virginia; and by the writing of seven articles, subscribed[4] with your names, have given them that good degree of satisfaction which hath carried them on with a resolution to set forward your desire in the best sort that may be for your own and the public good; divers particulars whereof we leave to their faithful report, having carried themselves here with that good discretion as is both to their own and their credit from whom[5] they came. And whereas, being to treat for a multitude of people, they have requested further time to confer with them that are to be interested in this action about the several particulars which in the prosecution thereof will fall out considerable, it hath been very willingly assented unto; and so they do now return unto you.[6] If therefore it may

---

[1] This name is spelt Sands in the MS., which Stith says is "certainly wrong." See the Appendix to his History, p. 10, Note.

[2] This letter is contained in Hubbard's History of New England, in Mass. Hist. Coll. xv. 46, but very incorrectly transcribed. Prince says, in his Annals, pp. xxi. 232, that Hubbard "had never seen Gov. Bradford's History." But this I think a mistake, since Hubbard relates the whole history of this negotiation with the Virginia Company, which is not contained in Morton's Memorial, and which he could have got only from Bradford's original MS., or from Morton's copy of it in the records of the Plymouth Church. He gives passages of considerable length, which agree almost word for word with Bradford's History. Compare Hubbard, pp. 44 — 50.

[3] These were the agents that were first sent. See page 55.

[4] The word *subscribed* is inserted, from Prince, p. 142, and Hubbard, p. 46.

[5] I substitute *whom* for *whence*, on the authority of Prince, p. 142.

[6] From the expression, "they do *now* return unto you," it is evident that the agents must have returned to Leyden soon after this letter was written, of which they were undoubtedly the bearers, that is between Nov. 12, the date of the letter, and Dec. 15, the date of Robinson and Brewster's answer to it. Of course Prince, p. 148, and Davis

please God so to direct your desires as that on your
parts there fall out no just impediments, I trust by the
same direction it shall likewise appear that on our
parts all forwardness to set you forward shall be found
in the best sort which with reason may be expected.
And so I betake you with this design, (which I hope
verily is the work of God,) to the gracious protection
and blessing of the Highest.

Your very loving friend,
EDWIN SANDYS.[1]

London, November 12, 1617.

Their Answer was as followeth.

Right Worshipful,

Our humble duties remembered, in our own, our messengers' and our church's name, with all thankful acknowledgment of your singular love, expressing itself, as otherwise, so more especially in your great care and earnest endeavour of our good in this weighty business about Virginia, which the less able we are to

---

on Morton, p. 22, cannot be correct in stating that they returned in May, 1618. It appears from Robinson and Brewster's letter that Carver was sent a *second time* to the Council of Virginia, in Dec. 1617, attended by "a gentleman of the company." These agents may have returned to Leyden in May, 1618. Cushman and Brewster were afterwards sent in Feb. 1619, and returned late in the same year.

[1] Sir Edwin Sandys was one of the principal members of the Virginia Company. He was the son of Archbishop Sandys, and a favorite pupil of the judicious Hooker. In Parliament, he was "a member of great authority," according to Hume, and taking the popular side was in 1621 committed by James to the Tower for his free speech. Anthony Wood says he was "a person of great judgment and of a commanding pen, a solid statesman, ingenio et gravitate morum insignis." He was the author of "*Europæ Speculum;* or a View or Survey of the state of Religion in the western part of the World," and of a metrical version of the Book of Job, the Psalms of David, and other poetical parts of Holy Writ. He died in 1629. See Wood's Athenæ Oxonienses, ii. 472, (ed. Bliss); Walton's Lives, pp. 174, 178, 180, (Major's ed.); Hume's England, vi. 39, 97, (Pickering's ed.); Hallam's Const. Hist. of England, i. 495 — 499.

requite, we shall think ourselves the more bound to commend in our prayers unto God for recompense; whom as for the present you rightly behold in our endeavours, so shall we not be wanting on our parts, (the same God assisting us,) to return all answerable fruit and respect unto the labor of your love bestowed upon us. We have, with the best speed and consideration withal that we could, set down our requests in writing, subscribed, as you willed, with the hands of[1] the greatest part of our congregation, and have sent the same unto the Council[2] by our agent, a deacon of our church, John Carver, unto whom we have also requested a gentleman of our company to adjoin himself; to the care and discretion of which two we do refer the prosecuting of the business. Now we persuade ourselves, right worshipful, that we need not to provoke your godly and loving mind to any further or more tender care of us, since you have pleased so far to interest us in yourself, that, under God, above all persons and things in the world we rely upon you, expecting the care of your love, the counsel of your wisdom, and the help and countenance of your authority. Notwithstanding, for your encouragement in the work so far as probabilities may lead, we will not forbear to mention these instances of inducement.

1. We verily believe and trust the Lord is with us, unto whom and whose service we have given ourselves in many trials, and that he will graciously prosper our endeavours according to the simplicity of our hearts therein.

2. We are well weaned from the delicate milk of

---

[1] The words *the hands of* I restore from Prince, p. 142.

[2] The Council of the Virginia Company.

our mother country, and inured to the difficulties of a strange and hard land, which yet, in great part, we have by patience overcome.

1617.
Dec.
15.

3. The people are, for the body of them, industrious and frugal, we think we may safely say, as any company of people in the world.

4. We are knit together as a body in a more strict and sacred bond and covenant of the Lord, of the violation whereof we make great[1] conscience; and by virtue whereof we do hold ourselves straitly tied to all care of each other's good, and of the whole by every, and so mutual.

5. And lastly, it is not with us as with other men, whom small things can discourage, or small discontentments cause to wish themselves at home again. We know our entertainment in England and Holland. We shall much prejudice both our arts and means by removal; where, if we should be driven to return, we should not hope to recover our present helps and comforts, neither indeed look ever to attain the like in any other place during our lives, which are now drawing towards their periods.

These motives we have been bold to tender unto you, which you in your wisdom may also impart to any other our worshipful friends of the Council with you, of all whose godly dispositions and loving towards our despised persons we are most glad, and shall not fail by all good means to continue and increase the same. We shall not be further troublesome, but do, with the renewed remembrance of our humble duties to your worship, and (so far as in modesty we may be bold) to any other of our well-willers of the Council with

[1] The word *great* is restored from Prince, p. 143.

you, we take our leaves, committing your persons and counsels to the guidance and protection of the Almighty.

    Yours, much bounden in all duty,
       JOHN ROBINSON,
       WILLIAM BREWSTER.

Leyden, the 15th of December, 1617.

I found annexed unto the foregoing letters these following lines, written by Mr. Bradford with special reference unto the fourth particular on the other side written.[1]

O sacred bond! Whilst inviolably preserved, how sweet and precious were the fruits that flowed from the same. But when this fidelity decayed, then their ruin approached. Oh that these ancient members had not died or been dissipated, (if it had been the will of God,) or else that this holy care and constant faithfulness had still lived and remained with those that survived, that were in times afterwards added unto them. But, alas! that subtile serpent hath slily wound in himself, under fair pretences of necessity and the like, to untwist these sacred bonds and ties, and as it were insensibly, by degrees, to dissolve or in a great measure to weaken the same. I have been happy, in my first times, to see and with much comfort to enjoy the blessed fruits of this sweet communion. But it is now a part of my misery in old age to find and feel the decay and want thereof, in a great measure, and with grief and sorrow of heart to lament and bewail the same; and for others' warning and admonition, and my own humiliation, do I here note the same.

[1] On page 61.

Thus much by way of digression. For further light in these proceedings forenamed, see some other letters and notes, as followeth.

The Copy of a Letter sent to Sir John Wolstenholme.[1]

Right Worshipful,

With due acknowledgment of our thankfulness for your singular care and pains in the business of Virginia, for our and (we hope) the common good, we do remember our humble duties unto you, and have sent, as is desired, a further explanation of our judgments in the three points specified by some of His Majesty's honorable Privy Council. And although it be grievous unto us that such unjust insinuations are made against us, yet we are most glad of the occasion of making our just purgation unto the so honorable personages.

The Declarations we have sent enclosed; the one more brief and general, which we think the fitter to be presented; the other something more large, and in which we express some small accidental differences, which, if it seem good unto you and other of your worship's friends, you may send instead of the former. Our prayer unto God is, that your worship may see the fruit of your worthy endeavours, which on our part we shall not fail to further by all good means.

---

[1] It is Worsingham in the MS.; but this is an error. Prince. p. 144. and Hubbard, p. 47, write it Worstenholme. Sir John Wolstenholme was a wealthy merchant and a farmer of the customs, one of the principal members of the Virginia Company, and one of the Council established by the second charter. He died in 1639. In Hutchinson's Collection of papers, p. 383, there is a letter written to Mr. Edward Rawson, Secretary to the New England Plantations, by Sir John Wolstenholme, son of the individual in question, dated London, Feb. 1, 1663, in which he says, "I am a great well-wisher and good friend to your plantation, and so was my father before me, who died 24 years since." See Stith's Virginia, pp. 163, 167, 186, and App. p. 16.

CHAP. V.

1618. Jan. 27.

And so praying that you would, with all conveniency that may be, give us knowledge of the success of the business with His Majesty's Privy Council, and accordingly what your further pleasure is, either for our direction or furtherance in the same, so we rest

Your worship's, in all duty,

JOHN ROBINSON,
WILLIAM BREWSTER.

Leyden, January 27, 1617, old style.[1]

The first brief Note was this.

Touching the ecclesiastical ministry, namely, of pastors for teaching, elders for ruling, and deacons for distributing the church's contribution, as also for the two sacraments, baptism and the Lord's supper, we do wholly and in all points agree with the French Reformed Churches, according to their public Confession of Faith; though some small differences.

The oath of Supremacy we shall willingly take, if it be required of us, if that convenient satisfaction be not given by our taking the oath of Allegiance.[2]

JOHN ROBINSON,
WILLIAM BREWSTER.

---

[1] That is, Jan. 1618, new style. By the old style the year began March 25.

[2] In 1531, in the reign of Henry VIII. the king was declared " the supreme head of the Church of England," and all his majesty's subjects were required on oath to acknowledge his supremacy. In 1558, at the accession of Elizabeth, the Act of Supremacy, which had been repealed under Queen Mary, was restored, and all persons in office, civil or ecclesiastical, were required to take the oath. In 1605, in the reign of James, the oath of Allegiance was drawn up and appointed to be taken by all the king's subjects. This was an oath of "submission and obedience to the king as a temporal sovereign, independent of any other power upon earth." By the third charter of the Virginia Company, their Treasurer, or any two of the Council, were empowered to administer the oaths of Supremacy and Allegiance to all persons going to their Colony. See Burnet's History of the Reformation, ii. 387 (folio); Neal's Puritans, i. 8, 11, 84, 117, 440; Stith's App. p. 28; Hazard, i. 78.

The second was this.

Touching the ecclesiastical ministry, [as in the former, &c.] we agree, in all things, with the French Reformed Churches, according to their public Confession of Faith; though some small differences be to be found in our practices, not at all in the substance of the things, but only in some accidental circumstances: as

1. Their ministers do pray with their heads covered; we uncovered.

2. We choose none for governing elders but such as are able to teach; which ability they do not require.

3. Their elders and deacons are annual, or at the most for two or three years; ours perpetual.

4. Our elders do administer their office in admonitions and excommunications, for public scandals, publicly and before the congregation; theirs more privately and in their consistories.

5. We do administer baptism only to such infants as whereof the one parent, at the least, is of some church, which some of their churches do not observe; although in it our practice accords with their public Confession and the judgment of the most learned amongst them.

Other differences, worthy mentioning, we know none.

(Subscribed,)
JOHN ROBINSON,
WILLIAM BREWSTER.

Part of another Letter from him that delivered these.

London, Feb. 14, 1617.[1]

Your letter to Sir John Wolstenholme I delivered, almost as soon as I had it, to his own hands, and stayed with him the opening and reading thereof. There were two papers enclosed. He read them to himself, as also the letter; and in the reading he spake to me and said, "Who shall make them?" viz. the ministers. I answered his worship that the power of making was in the Church,[2] to be ordained by the imposition of hands by the fittest instruments they have. It must either be in the Church, or from the Pope; and the Pope is Antichrist. "Ho!" said Sir John, "what the Pope holds good, (as in the Trinity,) that we do well to assent to. But," said he, "we will not enter into dispute now;" and as for your letters, he would not show them at any hand, lest he should spoil all. He expected you should have been of the Archbishop's mind for the calling of ministers; but it seems you differed. I could have wished to have known the contents of your two enclosed, at which he stuck so much, especially the larger. I asked his worship what good news he had for me to write to-morrow. He

---

[1] That is, 1618, new style.

[2] That is, the congregation, each separate body of believers. This was Brownism; and it is Independency, or Congregationalism. The Cambridge Platform says, chaps. 8 and 9, "Calling unto office is by the church. — Officers are to be called by such churches whereunto they are to minister. — The choice of church officers belongeth not to the civil magistrates, as such, or diocesan bishops, or patrons. — In churhes where there are no elders, imposition of hands may be performed by some of the brethren, orderly chosen by the church thereunto. For if the people may elect officers, which is the greater, and wherein the substance of the office doth consist, they may much more (occasion and need so requiring) impose hands in ordination, which is less, and but the accomplishment of the other." It was practised upon at the first ordination in America, at Salem, in 1629. See Morton's Memorial, p. 146.

told me, "Very[1] good news; for both the King's Majesty and the bishops have consented." He said he would go to Mr. Chancellor, Sir Fulke Greville,[2] as this day, and next week I should know more. I met with Sir Edwin Sandys on Wednesday night. He wished me to be at the Virginia Court[3] the next Wednesday, where I purpose to be. Thus loth to be troublesome at present, I hope to have something next week of certainty concerning you. I commit you to the Lord.

Yours,

S. B.

1618.
Feb.
14.

These things being long in agitation, and messengers passing to and again about them, after all their hopes they were long delayed by many obstacles that fell in the way. For at the return of these messengers into England, they found things far otherwise than they expected. For the Virginia Council was now so disturbed with factions and quarrels amongst

[1] The word *very* is restored from Prince, p. 145.
[2] Sir Fulke Greville was appointed chancellor of the exchequer, and sworn of the Privy Council Oct. 1, 1614. On the 9th of Jan. 1621, he was raised to the peerage by the title of Lord Brooke, of Beauchamp's Court. He wrote a Life of Sir Philip Sidney, and "The First Five Years of King James," which is contained in the Harleian Miscellany, vii. 407,(Park's ed.) On his tomb-stone in Warwick Church, he had inscribed this brief but noble epitaph : " Fulke Greville, servant to Queen Elizabeth, counsellor to King James, and friend to Sir Philip Sidney." See Wood's Athenæ Oxon. ii. 430 ; Fuller's Worthies, ii. 415 ; Birch's Queen Elizabeth, i. 178 ; Naunton's Fragmenta Regalia, p. 112, (ed. 1824) ; Walpole, Royal and Noble Authors, ii. 220.
[3] By the third charter of Virginia it was provided that "the Company shall and may once every week, or oftener, at their pleasure, hold and keep a court and assembly for despatching all casual matters of less consequence and weight concerning the plantation ; and for all affairs of government trade, and disposal of lands, there shall be held every year four great and general courts," at which all officers were to be chosen, and all laws and ordinances enacted. See Stith, App. 26, and Hazard, i. 76.

CHAP. themselves, as no business could well go forward; the
V. which may the better appear in one of the messen-
1619. gers' letters, as followeth.

To his Loving Friends.

May 8.
I had thought long since to have writ unto you; but could not effect that which I aimed at, neither can yet set things as I wished. Yet, notwithstanding, I doubt not but Mr. Brewster hath written to Mr. Robinson; but I think myself bound also to do something, lest I be thought to neglect you.

The main hindrance of our proceedings in the Virginia business is the dissensions and factions, as they term it, amongst the Council and Company of Virginia, which are such as that ever since we came up no business could by them be despatched. The occasion of this trouble amongst them is, that a while since Sir Thomas Smith,[1] repining at his many offices and troubles, wished the Company of Virginia to ease him of his office in being treasurer and governor of the
April 28.
Virginia Company. Whereupon the Company took occasion to dismiss him, and chose Sir Edwin Sandys[2]

---

[1] Sir Thomas Smith was the first treasurer and governor of the Virginia Company, and continued in office till superseded by Sir Edwin Sandys. He had the chief management of their affairs, and presided in all the meetings of the Council and Company. He was a London merchant, of great wealth and influence, governor of the East India and Muscovy Companies, and of the company associated for the discovery of the north-west passage. In 1604 he was sent ambassador from King James to the Emperor of Russia. He was also one of the assignees of Sir Walter Raleigh's patent, and thus became interested in the colony of Virginia. See Belknap, ii. 9 — 19; Stith, pp. 42, 158.

[2] Sir Edwin Sandys was elected April 28, 1619. Stith says that "he was a person of excellent understanding and judgment, of great industry, vigor and resolution, and indefatigable in his application to the business of the company and colony." His election was brought about by the Earl of Warwick's (Lord Rich) hostility to Sir Thomas Smith. Sandys was very ob

treasurer and governor of the Company, he having sixty voices, Sir John Wolstenholme sixteen voices, and Alderman Johnson[1] twenty-four. But Sir Thomas Smith, when he saw some part of his honor lost, was very angry, and raised a faction to cavil and contend about the election, and sought to tax Sir Edwin with many things that might both disgrace him and also put him by his office of governor. In which contentions they yet stick, and are not fit nor ready to intermeddle in any business; and what issue things will come to, I know not, nor are we yet certain. It is most like Sir Edwin will carry it away; and if he do, things will go well in Virginia; if otherwise, they will go ill enough always. We hope in two or three Court days things will settle. Mean space I think to go down into Kent, and come up again about fourteen days or three weeks hence; except either by these aforesaid contentions,[2] or by the ill tidings from Virginia, we be wholly discouraged; of which tidings as followeth.

Capt. Argall[3] is come home this week. He, upon

noxious to King James, on account of his political principles. The king said, "he knew him to be a man of exorbitant ambition." Accordingly, when the year for which he was chosen, had expired, James objected to his re-election, and in a furious passion exclaimed, "Choose the devil, if you will, but not Sir Edwin Sandys." To get out of the difficulty, the Company chose the Earl of Southampton treasurer, and Sandys deputy. See Stith, 159, 178, 181; Burk, i. 322; Short Collection, pp. 6, 8, 19.

[1] Alderman Johnson was at this time the deputy treasurer of the Company. See Stith, p. 150.

[2] For an account of the contentions in the Virginia Company, see Stith's Virginia, pp. v. 158, 180.

Stith had in his possession copies of the records of the Company, from April 28, 1619, to June 7, 1624. See also a declaration made by the Council of Virginia, in 1623, entitled "The Company's Chief Root of the Differences and Discontents," in the Appendix to Burk's History of Virginia, i. 316; and "A Short Collection of the most remarkable passages from the original to the dissolution of the Virginia Company. London, 1651." (4to. pp. 20.)

[3] Sir Samuel Argall was a kinsman of Sir Thomas Smith, and a favorite of the Earl of Warwick, who procured his election as deputy governor of the Virginia Colony in the beginning of 1617. He arrived in Virginia in May; but his admin-

CHAP. V.

1619.
May 8.

notice of the intent of the Council, came away before Sir George Yeardley[1] came there, and so there is no small dissension. But his tidings is ill, although his person be welcome. He saith Mr. Blackwell's ship came not there until March; but going towards winter they had still northwest winds, which carried them to the southward beyond their course; and the master of the ship and some six of the mariners dying, it seemed they could not find the Bay, till after long seeking and beating about. Mr. Blackwell is dead, and Mr. Maggner, the captain. Yea, there are dead, he saith, a hundred and thirty persons, one and another, in the ship. It is said there was in all a hundred and eighty persons in the ship, so as they were packed together like herrings. They had amongst them a flux and also want of fresh water; so as it is here rather wondered that so many are alive, than that so many are dead. The merchants here say it was Mr. Blackwell's fault to pack so many in the ship; yea, and there was great murmuring and repining amongst them, and upbraiding of Mr. Blackwell for his dealing and disposing of them, when they saw how he had disposed of them, and how he insulted over them. Yea, the streets of Gravesend rang of their extreme quarrelling, crying out one of another, "Thou hast brought me to this. I may thank thee for this." Heavy news it is,

istration was so tyrannical and oppressive, that he was displaced the next year, and sailed for England in April, 1619. See his Life in Belknap, ii. 51—63; Stith, pp. 145, 149; Burk, i. 317—322; Smith's General History of Virginia, ii. 33. (8vo ed. Richmond, 1819.)

[1] Sir George Yeardley was chosen governor of the colony early in 1619, and was empowered to investigate the charges against Argall on the spot. But the Earl of Warwick having sent over a small bark, to inform him of what was preparing against him, and to bring him away, Yeardley did not arrive in Virginia till ten or twelve days after Argall's escape. See Belknap, ii. 61—72; Stith, p. 157; Burk, p. 322; Smith, ii. 37.

and I would be glad to hear how far it will discourage. I see none here discouraged much, but rather desire to learn to beware by other men's harms, and to amend that wherein they have failed; as we desire to serve one another in love, so take heed of being enthralled by other imperious persons, especially if they be discerned to have an eye to themselves. It doth often trouble me to think that in this business we are to learn, and none to teach. But better so than to depend upon such teachers as Mr. Blackwell was. Such a stratagem he made for Mr. Johnson and his people at Emden; much was their subversion. But though he then cleanlily yet unhonestly plucked his neck out of the collar, yet at last his foot is caught.

Here are no letters come. The ship Captain Argall came in is yet in the west parts. All that we hear is but his report. It seemeth he came away secretly. The ship that Mr. Blackwell went in will be here shortly. It is as Mr. Robinson once said; he thought we should hear no good of them.

Mr. Brewster is not well at this time. Whether he will go back to you or go into the north, I yet know not. For myself, I hope to see an end of this business ere I come, though I am sorry to be thus from you. If things had gone roundly forward, I should have been with you within this fourteen days. I pray God direct us, and give us that spirit which is fitting for such a business.

Thus having summarily pointed at things which Mr. Brewster, I think, hath more largely writ of to Mr. Robinson, I leave you to the Lord's protection.

Yours, in all readiness, &c.
ROBERT CUSHMAN.

London, May the 8th, 1619.

CHAP. V.
1619.

A word or two, by way of digression, touching this Mr. Blackwell. He was an elder of the church of Amsterdam, a man well known of most of them. He declined from the truth with Mr. Johnson and the rest, and went with him when they departed asunder in that woful manner which brought so great dishonor to God, scandal to the truth, and outward ruin to themselves, in this world. But I hope, notwithstanding, through the mercies of the Lord, their souls are now at rest with God, in the heavens, and that they are arrived in the haven of happiness, though some of their bodies were thus buried in the terrible seas, and others sunk under the burden of bitter afflictions. He, with some others, had prepared for to go to Virginia; and he with sundry godly citizens being at a private meeting (I take it, at a Fast,) in London, being discovered, many of them were apprehended, whereof Mr. Blackwell was one. But he so glossed with the bishops, and either dissembled or flatly denied the truth which formerly he had maintained; and not only so, but unworthily betrayed and accused another godly man who had escaped, that so he might slip his own neck out of the collar, and to obtain his own freedom brought others into bonds. Whereupon he so won the bishops' favor, (but lost the Lord's,) as he was not only dismissed, but in open court the Archbishop gave him great applause and his solemn blessing to proceed in his voyage. But if such events follow the bishops' blessing, happy are they that miss the same. It is much better to keep a good conscience and have the Lord's blessing, whether in life or death. But see how that man, apprehended by Mr. Blackwell's means, writes to a friend of his.

Right dear friend and christian brother, Mr. Carver, I salute you and yours in the Lord.

Sir, as for my own present condition, I doubt not but you well understand it by our brother Masterson,[1] who should have tasted of the same cup, had his place of residence and his person been as well known as myself. Somewhat I have written to Mr. Cushman how the matter still continues. I have petitioned twice to Mr. sheriff, and once to my Lord Cook,[2] and have used such reasons to move them to pity, that if they were not overruled by some others, I suppose I should have soon gained my liberty; — as that I was a man living by my credit, in debt to divers in our city, living in more than ordinary charges in a close and tedious prison; besides great rents abroad, all my business lying still, my own servant lying lame in the country, my wife being also great with child: and yet no answer until the Lords of His Majesty's Council gave consent. Howbeit, Mr. Blackwell, a man as deep in this action as I, was delivered at a cheaper rate with a great deal less ado, yea, with an addition of the Archbishop's blessing. I am sorry for Mr. Blackwell's weakness. I wish it may prove no worse; but yet he and some others of them were not sorry, but thought it was for the best that I was nominated; not because the Lord sanctifies evil to good, but that the action

---

[1] Richard Masterson was one of Robinson's church, and his name is subscribed, with others, to a letter written from Leyden to Bradford and Brewster, Nov. 30, 1625, nine months after their pastor's death. On his coming over to Plymouth, he was chosen a deacon of the church. In the church records he is described as "a holy man and an experienced saint, having been officious with part of his estate for public good, and a man of ability, as a second Stephen, to defend the truth by sound argument, grounded on the Scriptures of truth." See Mass. Hist. Coll. iii. 44.

[2] This was the eminent lawyer, whose name is commonly spelt Coke. See an account of him in Fuller's Worthies, ii. 128, and in Lardner's Cab. Cyc. vi. 1 — 43.

was good, yea, for the best. One reason I well remember he used was, because this trouble would increase the Virginia plantation; that now people began more generally to incline to go; and if he had not nominated some such as I, he had not been free, being it was known that many citizens, besides themselves, were there. I expect an answer shortly what they intend concerning me. I purpose to write to some other of you, by whom you shall know the certainty.

Thus not having further at present to acquaint you withal, commending myself to your prayers I cease, and commit you and us all to the Lord.

Your friend and brother, in bonds,

SABIN STARSMORE.[1]

From my Chamber in Wood-street Counter,[2] Sept. 4th, 1618.

But thus much by the way which may be of good use. I have been the larger in these things, that the rising generation may seriously take notice of the many difficulties their poor leaders underwent in the first enterprises towards coming into New England.

But at last, after all these things, and their long attendance, they had a patent granted them, and confirmed under the Company's seal.[3] But these divisions

---

[1] There was a Mr. ' Staismore among the associates of Henry Jacob, who, after having conferred with Mr. Robinson, in Leyden, laid the foundation of an Independent or Congregational Church in England in the year 1616. See Neal's Puritans, i. 476. Some further account of Jacob will be given hereafter in a Note to Bradford's Dialogue.

[2] The Compter in Wood Street, erected in 1555, was one of the prison-houses pertaining to the sheriffs of London. Stow's Survey of London, p. 394, (folio.)

[3] Morton says, in his Memorial, p. 22, that they "obtained letters patent for the northern parts of Virginia, of King James, of famous memory." He confounds the king with the Virginia Company. Dudley makes the same mistake in his Letter to the Countess of Lincoln, in Mass. Hist. Coll. viii. 37. Oldmixon, i. 29, errs in saying that

and distractions had shaken off many of their pretended friends, and disappointed them of many of their hoped for and proffered means. By the advice of some friends this patent was not taken in the name of any of their own company,[1] but in the name of Mr. John Wincob,[2] a religious gentleman, then belonging to the Countess of Lincoln,[3] who intended to go with them. But God so disposed as he never went, nor they never

---

"Mr. Brewster made an agreement with the Company for a large tract of land in the southwest parts of New England," an error into which he was led by Cotton Mather, i. 47. The Virginia Company could grant no patent for lands north of the 40th degree. The authors of the Modern Universal History, xxxix. 272, err in stating that "their intention was to have made a settlement under the sanction of Gosnold's patent." Gosnold had no patent. Dunlap, Hist. of New York, i. 43, and Hugh Murray, Hist. of Discoveries in North America, i. 245, err in asserting that the agents of the Pilgrims negotiated with the *Plymouth* Company. See p. 55, note.

[1] The word *company* I restore from Hubbard, p. 47.

[2] Nothing is known of John Wincob. Baylies, in his Memoir of Plymouth, i. 17, errs in calling his Christian name *Jacob*. It was probably to avoid notoriety and escape suspicion, that the patent was taken out in the name of an obscure individual, rather than in the name of the Earl of Lincoln, whose grandfather, Henry, had been one of the Council of the Virginia Company, established by its second charter in 1609. I suppose that in consequence of the Leyden people being out of the realm, the patent would not be granted in any of their names. See Stith, App. p. 16; Collins's Peerage, ii. 162.

[3] The Countess of Lincoln here mentioned was Elizabeth, the daughter of Sir Henry Knevet, and the dowager of Thomas, the third earl of that noble house, who died Jan. 15, 1619. Arthur Collins calls her "a lady of great piety and virtue," and Cotton Mather speaks of the family as "religious," and "the best family of any nobleman then in England." She was the mother of eighteen children, and wrote a book, printed at Oxford in 1621, entitled, "The Countess of Lincoln's Nursery," on the duty of mothers nursing their own children. This family had a more intimate connexion with the New England settlements, and must have felt a deeper interest in their success, than any other noble house in England. Two of the first magistrates, or assistants, of the Massachusetts Colony had lived many years in the family as stewards, a capacity which Wincob also may have sustained. Frances, a daughter of the Countess, married John, son and heir to Sir Ferdinando Gorges, who took so active a part in the attempts to colonize New England. Two other daughters, Susan and Arbella, married two other of the principal colonists of Massachusetts, John Humfrey and Isaac Johnson, and came over with their husbands to America. The lady Arbella died at the end of August, 1630, about six weeks after her arrival. "She came from a paradise of plenty and pleasure, in the family of a noble earldom, into a wilderness of wants, and took New England in her way to heaven." Like the Spanish lady

CHAP. V.
1619.

made use of this patent, which had cost them so much labor and charge ; as by the sequel will appear.[1] This patent being sent over for them to view and consider,[2] as also the passages about the propositions between them and such merchants and friends as should either go or adventure with them, and especially with them on whom they did chiefly depend for shipping and means, whose proffers had been large, they were requested to fit and prepare themselves with all speed.

A right emblem it may be of the uncertain things of this world, that when men have toiled themselves, they vanish into smoke.

---

mentioned by Peter Martyr, " perceiving her husband now furnishing himself to depart to the unknown coasts of the new world, and those large tracts of land and sea, she spake these words unto him : Whithersoever your fatal destiny shall drive you, either by the furious waves of the great ocean, or by the manifold and horrible dangers of the land, I will surely bear you company. There can no peril chance to me so terrible, nor any kind of death so cruel, that shall not be much easier for me to abide, than to live so far separate from you." Her husband survived her only a month :

" He tried
To live without her, liked it not, and died."

The "right honorable and approved virtuous lady, Bridget, Countess of Lincoln," to whom Dudley addressed his letter of March 12, 1631, was the wife of Theophilus, the son of the Countess mentioned in the text, and the daughter of Viscount Saye and Sele. See Collins's Peerage, ii. 163 ; Burke's Peerage, CLINTON and NEWCASTLE ; Walpole's Royal and Noble Authors, ii. 272 ; Savage's Winthrop, i. 34 ;

Hutchinson's Mass. i. 15, 17 ; Mather's Magnalia, i. 71, 126 ; Mass. Hist. Coll. viii. 36, 40 ; Eden's translation of Peter Martyr's Decades, p. 84, (ed. 1577.)

[1] The whole of this paragraph is contained, almost word for word, in Hubbard's History, p. 47, which is conclusive proof that he had seen Bradford's History. See Note [2] on page 58. — Hubbard says, p. 50, " that a patent, as is afore said, was obtained, is published in print, and affirmed by such as yet survive of the first planters ; but where it is, or how it came to be lost, is not known to any that belong to the said colony." Hubbard wrote his History before 1682. See Mass. Hist. Coll. xv. p. iii. — Grahame, i. 410, errs in asserting that Hubbard's History has never been published ; and also in stating that Gov. Bradford's History of Plymouth Colony has been published.

[2] Prince, p. 155, quoting from Gov. Bradford's MS. history, inserts after consider, " with several proposals for their transmigration, made by Mr. Thomas Weston, of London, merchant, and other friends and merchants as should either," &c.

THE PILGRIMS KEEP A FAST.

Upon a receipt of these things by one of their messengers, they had a solemn meeting and a day of humiliation, to seek the Lord for his direction. And their pastor took this text. "And David's men said unto him, See, we be afraid here in Judah. How much more, if we come to Keilah, against the host of the Philistines. Then David asked counsel of the Lord again." From which text he taught many things very aptly, and befitting their present occasion and condition, to strengthen them against their fears and perplexities, and encouraging them in their resolutions: [and then conclude how many and who should prepare to go first;[1] for all that were willing could not get ready quickly. The greater number being to stay, require their pastor to tarry with them; their elder, Mr. Brewster, to go with the other; those who go first to be an absolute church[2] of themselves, as well as those that stay; with this proviso, that as any go over or return, they shall be reputed as members, without further dismission or testimonial; and those who tarry, to follow the rest as soon as they can.

CHAP. V.
1620.
1 Sam. xxiii. 3, 4.

---

[1] Winslow, in his Brief Narration says, "the youngest and strongest part to go; and they that went should freely offer themselves."

[2] The Church at Plymouth thus became the First Independent or Congregational Church in America. Of course the statement of Holmes in his accurate Annals of America, i. 160, that "the adventurers and their brethren remaining in Holland were to continue to be *one* church," is incorrect; and the position of Upham, in his eloquent Century Lecture, at Salem in 1829, that the first church in Salem is "the First American Congregational Church," cannot be maintained. Even if the first colonists had not been "an *absolute* church of themselves," yet before the formation of Higginson's church at Salem, a majority of the Leyden congregation had actually arrived at Plymouth, as appears from the note on page 36. Nor is there any ground for Palfrey's intimation, in his Centennial Discourse at Barnstable, p. 9, that "the first church in Barnstable is the representative of the first Congregational Church established in England," since it appears from p. 21-24, of this volume, that the exception, on the presumed absence of which he builds this opinion, was an actual fact, namely, that "Robinson's church now surviving in that of Plymouth,

CHAP. V.
1620.

Mr. Weston[1] coming to Leyden, the people agree with him on articles both for shipping and money to assist in their transportation ; then send Mr. Carver and Cushman to England to receive the money and provide for the voyage ; Mr. Cushman at London, Mr. Carver at Southampton. Those who are to go first prepare with speed, sell their estates, put their money into the common stock to be disposed by their managers for making general provisions. There was also one Mr. Martin[2] chosen in England to join with Mr. Carver and Cushman. He came from Billerica, in Essex ; from which county came several others, as also from London and other places, to go with them.][3]

In the foregoing five Chapters the reader may take a view of some of the many difficulties our blessed predecessors went through in their first achievement of this weighty enterprise of removal of our Church into these American parts. The immediate following relations in Mr Bradford's book, out of which divers of these matters are recollected, do more especially con-

was organized on Congregational principles before he left the mother country for Holland." With the History of Gov. Bradford to support her claims, the First Church at Plymouth cannot recognise the pretensions of any other American church to priority of existence.

[1] Thomas Weston was one of the most active of the merchant adventurers, and Hubbard says, p. 72, that he had disbursed £500 to advance the interest of Plymouth colony. Edward Winslow says, in 1622, "he formerly deserved well of us," and Bradford, in 1623, that he "becomes our enemy on all occasions." He employed several vessels in trade and fishing on the coast of New England. His unsuc-cessful attempt to establish a rival colony at Wessagussett, now Weymouth, will be related hereafter. He visited Plymouth twice in 1623, and again in 1624, and then sailed for Virginia. He died at Bristol, (Eng.) in the time of the civil war. See Prince, pp. 216, 222, 224 ; Morton's Memorial, p. 105.

[2] This was undoubtedly Mr. Christopher Martin, who, with his wife and two children, came over in the Mayflower. His name stands the ninth in the subscription to the Compact signed at Cape Cod, Nov. 11, 1620, and he died Jan. 8, 1621.

[3] The passage included in brackets is taken from Prince, p. 156, who copied it from Bradford's MS.

cern the conditions of their agreement with several merchant adventurers towards the voyage, &c. as also several letters sent to and fro from friend to friend relating to the premises, which are not so pertinent to the nature of this small History. Wherefore I shall here omit to insert them,[1] judging them not so suitable to my present purpose; and here also cease to follow the foregoing method by way of Chapters.[2]

---

[1] It is much to be regretted that Morton did not see fit to copy these letters. It will be seen, a few pages further on, that he again testifies that "their transactings with the merchant adventurers were penned at large in Mr. Bradford's book." Though omitted in this copy, "the Conditions" were fortunately preserved from oblivion by Hubbard, and we are thus enabled to present them in the next Chapter. They are undoubtedly the most valuable portion of Hubbard's History, and their existence in it puts it beyond a doubt that he had both seen and used Bradford's MS. notwithstanding Prince's assertion to the contrary. See Note[2] on page 58.

[2] For the sake of uniformity I have taken the liberty still "to follow the foregoing method by way of chapters," and the rather as I find that Morton has preserved in his Memorial, pp. 30, 37, and 67, the original titles of three of Gov. Bradford's chapters.

CHAPTER VI.

THE CONDITIONS OF THEIR AGREEMENT WITH SEVERAL MERCHANT ADVENTURERS TOWARDS THE VOYAGE.

CHAP. VI.

1620.

[About this time they were informed by Mr. Weston and others, that sundry honorable lords and worthy gentlemen had obtained a large patent from the King for the more northerly part of America, distinct from the Virginia patent, and wholly excluded from their government, and to be called by another name, viz. NEW ENGLAND.[1] Unto which Mr. Weston and the chiefest of them began to incline, thinking it was best for them to go thither; as for other reasons, so chiefly

---

[1] On the 23d of July, 1620, King James gave a warrant to his solicitor, Sir Thomas Coventry, to prepare a new patent for the incorporation of the adventurers to the northern colony of Virginia, between 40 and 48 degrees north, which patent the king signed on Nov. 3, styling them "The Council established at Plymouth, in the county of Devon, for the planting, ruling, ordering, and governing of New England, in America," which is the great civil basis of all the future patents and plantations, that divide this country. Prince, p. 160. See the patent in Hazard, i. 104; and the warrant in Mass. Hist. Coll. xxvi. 64.

The name of New England was first given, in 1614, by the famous Capt. John Smith, to North Virginia, lying between the degrees of 41 and 45. In that year he ranged along the coast, from the Penobscot to Cape Cod, in a small boat, with eight men. "I took the description" he says "of the coast as well by map as writing, and called it New England. At my humble suit, Charles, Prince of Wales, was pleased to confirm it by that title." Smith, in Mass. Hist. Coll. xxiii. 20. This map was published with his "Description of New England," in 1616. They are both reprinted in Mass. Hist Coll. xxiii. 1, and xxvi. 95 — 140.

for the hope of present profit, to be made by fishing[1] on that coast. But in all business the active part is most difficult, especially when there are many agents that may be concerned. So it was found in them; for some of them who should have gone in England, fell off, and would not go. Other merchants and friends, that proffered to adventure their money, withdrew and pretended many excuses; some disliking they went not to Guiana; others would do nothing unless they went to Virginia; and many who were most relied on refused to adventure if they went thither. In the midst of these difficulties, they of Leyden were driven to great straits; but at the length, the generality was swayed to the better opinion. Howbeit, the patent for the northern part of the country not being fully settled at that time, they resolved to adventure with that patent they had, intending for some place more southward than that they fell upon in their voyage, at Cape Cod, as may appear afterwards.

The CONDITIONS, on which those of Leyden engaged with the merchants, the adventurers,[2] were hard

---

[1] Edward Winslow says, in his Brief Narration, that on King James asking the agents of the Pilgrims "what profits might arise in the part they intended, it was answered, Fishing."

I know not what authority Hutchinson had for asserting, ii. 472, that "their views when they left England were rather to establish a *factory* than a colony. They had no notion of cultivating any more ground than would afford their own necessary provisions, but proposed that their chief secular employment should be commerce with the natives." This seems inconsistent with the views with which they left Holland; and the simple fact of their bringing their wives and children with them is conclusive evidence that they came to establish a permanent colony, in which the several occupations of farming, fishing, and trading, would each have its proper place.

[2] Little is known of these merchant adventurers. Capt. John Smith, a good authority in such matters, writing in 1624, says that "the adventurers which raised the stock to begin and supply this plantation, were about seventy, some gentlemen, some merchants, some handicraftsmen, some adventuring great sums, some small, as their estates and affection served. These dwell most about London. They

enough at the first for the poor people, that were to adventure their persons as well as their estates. Yet were their agents forced to change one or two of them, to satisfy the merchants, who were not willing to be concerned with them; although the altering them without their knowledge or consent was very distasteful to them, and became the occasion of some contention amongst them afterwards. They are these that follow.

1. The adventurers and planters do agree, that every person that goeth, being sixteen years old and upward, be rated at ten pounds, and that ten pounds be accounted a single share.

2. That he that goeth in person, and furnisheth himself out with ten pounds, either in money or other provisions, be accounted as having twenty pounds in stock, and in the division shall receive a double share.

3. The persons transported and the adventurers shall continue their joint stock and partnership the space of seven years, except some unexpected impediments do cause the whole Company to agree otherwise; during which time all profits and benefits that are gotten by trade, traffic, trucking, working, fishing, or any other means, of any other person or persons, shall remain still in the common stock until the division.

4. That at their coming there they shall choose out such a number of fit persons as may furnish their ships

---

are not a corporation, but knit together by a voluntary combination in a society without constraint or penalty, aiming to do good and to plant religion." Smith's Gen. Hist. of Virginia, ii. 251. Some of these merchants, as appears from the Correspondence with them preserved by Gov. Bradford, were very friendly to the Colony, and a few came over and settled in it. Others were unreasonable, clamorous, and hostile. Their names in 1626 are preserved. See Mass. Hist. Coll. iii. 27 — 34, 48.

and boats for fishing upon the sea; employing the rest in their several faculties upon the land, as building houses, tilling and planting the ground, and making such commodities as shall be most useful for the Colony.

5. That at the end of the seven years, the capital and the profits, viz. the houses, lands, goods, and chattels, be equally divided among the adventurers. If any debt or detriment concerning this adventure [1]

6. Whosoever cometh to the Colony hereafter, or putteth any thing into the stock, shall at the end of the seven years be allowed proportionally to the time of his so doing.

7. He that shall carry his wife, or children, or servants, shall be allowed for every person, now aged sixteen years and upward, a single share in the division; or if he provide them necessaries, a double share; or if they be between ten years old and sixteen, then two of them to be reckoned for a person, both in transportation and division.

8. That such children that now go and are under the age of ten years, have no other share in the division than fifty acres of unmanured land.

9. That such persons as die before the seven years be expired, their executors to have their parts or share at the division, proportionably to the time of their life in the Colony.

10. That all such persons as are of the Colony are to have meat, drink, and apparel, and all provisions, out of the common stock and goods of the said Colony.

---

[1] Here something seems to be wanting, of the nature of a new article or condition, which cannot now be supplied. This hiatus might, possibly, be filled up from the MS. copy of Hubbard in England. See Mass. Hist. Coll. xiii. 286 — 290.

CHAP. VI.
1620.

The difference between the conditions thus expressed and the former, before their alteration, stood in these two points; first, that the houses and lands improved, especially gardens and home-fields, should remain undivided, wholly to the planters, at the seven years' end; secondly, that the planters should have two days in the week for their own private employment, for the comfort of themselves and their families, especially such as had them to take care for.[1]

The altering of those two conditions was very afflictive to the minds of such as were concerned in the voyage. But Mr. Cushman, their principal agent, answered the complaints peremptorily, that unless they had so ordered the conditions, the whole design would have fallen to the ground; and necessity, they said,

---

[1] Robertson says, in his History of America, book x., "Under the influence of this wild notion — that the Scriptures contain a complete system not only of spiritual instruction, but of civil wisdom and polity — the colonists of New Plymouth, in imitation of the primitive Christians, threw all their property into a common stock." This misrepresentation, which he professes to derive from Chalmers, p. 90, and Douglass, p. 370, (though there is nothing in either of them to sanction the statement,) is repeated substantially by Grahame, i. 194, and verbally by Murray, Hist. of North America, i. 246. It is to be regretted that credit and countenance should have been given to such an imputation on the good sense of the Pilgrims, by so respectable an American writer as Chief Justice Marshall, in his Life of Washington, i. 93, (first ed.) and in his History of the American Colonies, p. 81.

There is no foundation for this charge. The Plymouth people were not "misguided by their religious theories," nor influenced by an "imitation of the primitive Christians," in forming their joint stock company. They entered into this hard and disadvantageous engagement with the merchant adventurers not voluntarily, but of necessity, in order to obtain shipping for transporting themselves to America; and they put their own little property into a common fund in order to purchase provisions for the voyage. It was a partnership that was instituted, not a community of goods, as that phrase is commonly understood. They dissolved this partnership, and set up for themselves, as soon as they were able; as will be seen hereafter.

The charge is destitute of foundation even in regard to the primitive Christians. "Nothing like a community of goods," says Milman, "ever appears to have prevailed in the Christian community. Mosheim appears to me to have proved this point conclusively." See Milman's History of Christianity, i. 389, and Mosheim's Dissertation "De verâ naturâ communionis bonorum in ecclesiâ Hierosolymitanâ." Diss. ii. 1 — 53.

having no law, they were constrained to be silent. The poor planters met with much difficulty both before and after the expiring of the seven years, and found much trouble in making up accounts with the adventurers about the division; at which time, though those that adventured their money were no great gainers, yet those that adventured their lives in carrying on the business of the Plantation were by much the greatest sufferers.][1]

1620.

[Mr. Robinson writes to Mr. Carver, and complains of Mr. Weston's neglect in getting shipping in England; for want of which they are in a piteous case at Leyden. And S. F., E. W., W. B., and J. A.[2] write from Leyden to Mr. Carver and Cushman, that the coming of Mr. Nash[3] and their pilot is a great encouragement to them.

June 4.

10.

Mr. Cushman, in a letter from London to Mr. Carver at Southampton, says that Mr. Crabe, a minister, had promised to go, but is much opposed, and like to fail; and in a letter to the people at Leyden, that he had hired another pilot, one Mr. Clark,[4] who went last year to Virginia; that he is getting a ship, hopes he shall make all ready at London in fourteen days, and would have Mr. Reynolds tarry in Holland, and bring the ship[5] there to Southampton.][6]

10.

---

[1] The passage within brackets is taken from Hubbard's History. It is impossible to say where he obtained it, except from Bradford's MS. It is to be found nowhere else, and is essential to the completeness of the History. I have taken care to collate Hubbard's MS. which is in the archives of the Massachusetts Historical Society.

[2] These doubtless are the initials of Samuel Fuller, Edward Winslow, William Bradford, and Isaac Allerton.

[3] The name of Thomas Nash is subscribed, with others, to a letter written at Leyden Nov. 30, 1625, addressed to Bradford and Brewster. See Mass. Hist. Coll. iii. 44.

[4] Clark, as will be seen hereafter, was master's mate on board the Mayflower.

[5] The small ship, called the Speedwell, of which Reynolds was captain.

[6] These last two paragraphs are taken from Prince, p. 158, who copied them from Bradford's MS.

CHAPTER VII.

OF THEIR DEPARTURE FROM LEYDEN, AND EMBARKATION FROM DELFT-HAVEN.

CHAP. VII.
1620.

AFTER such travail and turmoils[1] and debates which they went through, things were gotten ready for their departure from Leyden. A small ship was provided in Holland, of about sixty tons, which was intended, as to serve to transport some of them over the seas, so to stay in the country and to tend upon fishing and such other affairs as might be for the good and benefit of the whole, when they should come to the place intended.[2] Another was hired at London, of burden about ninescore, and all other things got in a readiness.

---

[1] "Much of their troubles respecting this matter is not expressed in this book." — *Morton's Note.*

[2] This vessel was less than the average size of the fishing-smacks that go to the Grand Bank. This seems a frail bark in which to cross a stormy ocean of three thousand miles in extent. Yet it should be remembered, that two of the ships of Columbus on his first daring and perilous voyage of discovery were light vessels, without decks, little superior to the small craft that ply on our rivers and along our coasts. Peter Martyr d'Anghiera, the contemporary of Columbus, and the first writer who mentions the discovery of America, says "Ex regio fisco destinata sunt tria navigia; unum onerarium cavatum, alia duo levia mercatoria, sine caveis quæ ab Hispanis caravelæ vocantur." De Orbe Novo, dec. i. cap. i. (p. 2, ed. 1587.) "At the length three ships were appointed him at the king's charges; of the which one was a great carrack with decks, and the other two light merchant ships without decks, which the Spaniards call caravels." (Eden's trans. p. 8, ed. 1577.) Frobisher's fleet consisted of two barks of twenty-five tons each, and a pinnace of ten tons, when he sailed in 1576, to discover a north-west passage to the Indies. Sir Francis Drake, too, embarked on his voyage for circumnavigating the globe, in 1577, with five vessels, of which the largest was of one hundred, and the smallest of fifteen tons.

So being ready to depart, they had a day of solemn humiliation, their pastor taking his text from Ezra the viiith, 21. "And there, at the river, by Ahava, I proclaimed a fast, that we might humble ourselves before our God, and seek of him a right way for us, and for our children, and for all our substance." Upon which he spent a good part of the day very profitably, and suitably to their present occasion.[1] The rest of the time was spent in pouring out prayers to the Lord with great fervency, mixed with abundance of tears. And the time being come that they must depart, they were accompanied with the most of their brethren out of the city unto a town sundry miles off, called Delft-Haven,[2] where the ship lay ready to receive them. So they left that goodly and pleasant city, which had been their resting-place near twelve years. But they knew they were PILGRIMS,[3] and looked not much on those things, but lifted up their eyes to heaven, their dearest country, and quieted their spirits.

CHAP. VII.

1620.

July 21.

Heb. xi. 13.

The bark in which Sir Humphrey Gilbert perished was of ten tons only. The Little James, which the Company sent over to Plymouth in July 1623, was a pinnace of only forty-four tons. See Navarrete, Coleccion de Viages, ii. p. 11, Doc. Diplom. 7 ; Irving's Life of Columbus, i. 113, iii. 303 — 306 ; Kippis's Biog. Britann. v. 345 ; Aikin's Gen. Biog. iii. 449, iv. 249 ; Prince, p. 220. — Mather, i. 47, is inaccurate in stating that the Speedwell was *hired*, in which error he is followed by the authors of the Mod. Univ. Hist. xxxix. 272. — In a vessel of the same name, of fifty tons, Martin Pring had in 1603 coasted along the shores of New England. See Prince, p. 102 ; Belknap. ii. 124.

[1] Edward Winslow, who was present, has preserved a portion of Robinson's farewell discourse. It will be found in his Brief Narration, in a subsequent part of this volume ; but it ought to be read in this connexion.

[2] Delft-Haven is a commodious port on the north side of the Meuse, two miles south-west from Rotterdam, eight miles from Delft, and about fourteen miles south of Leyden.

[3] "I think I may with singular propriety call their lives *a pilgrimage*. Most of them left England about the year 1609, after the truce with the Spaniards, young men between twenty and thirty years of age. They spent near twelve years, strangers among the Dutch, first at Amsterdam, afterwards at Leyden. After having arrived to the meridian of life, the declining part was to

THE SAD PARTING AT DELFT-HAVEN.

CHAP. VII.

1620.

July 22.

When they came to the place, they found the ship and all things ready; and such of their friends as could not come with them, followed after them; and sundry also came from Amsterdam[1] to see them shipped, and to take their leave of them. That night was spent with little sleep by the most, but with friendly entertainment[2] and Christian discourse, and other real expressions of true Christian love. The next day, the wind being fair, they went on board, and their friends with them; when truly doleful was the sight of that sad and mournful parting; to see what sighs and sobs and prayers did sound amongst them; what tears did gush from every eye, and pithy speeches pierced each other's heart; that sundry of the Dutch strangers, that stood on the quay as spectators, could not refrain from tears. Yet comfortable and sweet it was to see such lively and true expressions of dear and unfeigned love. But the tide, which stays for no man, calling them away, that were thus loth to depart, their reverend pastor, falling down on his knees, and they all with him, with watery cheeks commended them, with most fervent prayers, to the Lord and his blessing; and then, with mutual embraces and many tears, they took their leaves of one another, which proved to be their last leave to many of them.[3]

Thus hoisting sail, with a prosperous wind,[4] they

---

be spent in another world, among savages, of whom every European must have received a most unfavorable, if not formidable idea. 'Tantum religio potuit suadere.'" — Hutchinson, Hist. Mass. ii. 452.

The term PILGRIMS belongs exclusively to the *Plymouth* colonists.

[1] The distance from Amsterdam to Delft-Haven is about 36 miles.

[2] Prince, p. 159, reads *entertaining*.

[3] This scene is the subject of one of the great national pictures in the rotunda of the capitol at Washington. It was painted by Robert W. Weir, Esq.

[4] Edward Winslow says, in his Brief Narration, "We gave them a volley of small shot and three pieces of ordnance."

came in a short time to Southampton,[1] where they found the bigger ship come from London,[2] lying ready with all the rest of their company. After a joyful welcome and mutual congratulation, with other friendly entertainments, they fell to parley about their proceedings. [Seven hundred pounds sterling are laid out at Southampton, and they carry about seventeen hundred pounds venture with them; and Mr. Weston comes thither from London to see them despatched.][3]

A brief Letter written by Mr. John Robinson to Mr. John Carver, at their parting aforesaid, in which the tender love and godly care of a true pastor appears.

My Dear Brother,

I received enclosed your last letter and note of information, which I shall carefully keep and make use of, as there shall be occasion. I have a true feeling of your perplexity of mind and toil of body; but I hope that you, having always been able so plentifully to administer comfort unto others in their trials, are so well furnished for yourself, as that far greater difficulties than you have yet undergone (though I conceive them to be great enough) cannot oppress you, though they press you, as the Apostle speaketh. "The spirit of a man (sustained by the Spirit of God) will sustain

---

[1] Southampton is a seaport in Hampshire, situated at the head of an estuary, running up from the isle of Wight, called the Southampton Water. It was the rendezvous of seven of Winthrop's fleet in March, 1630, when he was preparing to transport his colony to Massachusetts Bay. See Savage's Winthrop, i. 2, 366.

[2] After London, Prince, p. 160, inserts from Gov. Bradford's MS., "Mr. Jones master, with the rest of the company, who had been waiting there with Mr. Cushman seven days."

[3] The sentence in brackets is from Prince, p. 160, who quotes Bradford's MS.

his infirmity." I doubt not so will yours; and the better much, when you shall enjoy the presence and help of so many godly and wise brethren, for the bearing of part of your burden; who also will not admit into their hearts the least thought of suspicion of any the least negligence, at least presumption, to have been in you, whatsoever they think in others.[1] Now what shall I say or write unto you and your good wife, my loving sister? Even only this; I desire, and always shall, mercy and blessing unto you from the Lord, as unto my own soul; and assure yourself that my heart is with you, and that I will not foreslow[2] my bodily coming at the first opportunity. I have written a large letter to the whole, and am sorry I shall not rather speak than write to them; and the more, considering the want of a preacher,[3] which I shall also make some spur to my hastening towards you. I do ever commend my best affection unto you; which if I thought you made any doubt of, I would express in more, and the same more ample and full words. And the Lord, in whom you trust, and whom you serve ever in this business and journey, guide you with his hand, protect you with his wing, and show you and us his salvation in the end, and bring us, in the mean

---

[1] This sentence indicates the great confidence reposed in Carver by the Church. His being sent as their first and principal agent to England, shows that he was a leading and trusted man among the Pilgrims, a fact which is confirmed by the circumstance of his being selected by Robinson as the individual to whom to address this parting letter. Some passages in it seem to betoken that the burden of government was expected to rest on him, as it afterwards turned out. See Hutchinson, ii. 456.

[2] Foreslow,—delay.

[3] It appears from page 85, that "Mr. Crabe, a minister, had promised to go." They suffered much afterward for want of a regular pastor.

while, together in the place desired (if such be his good will) for his Christ's sake. Amen.

Yours,
JOHN ROBINSON.

July 27th, 1620.

This was the last letter that Mr. Carver lived to see from him.[1]

At their parting, Mr. Robinson[2] writ a letter to the whole company, which, although it hath already been printed, yet I thought good here likewise to insert it.[3]

Loving Christian Friends,

I do heartily and in the Lord salute you, as being those with whom I am present in my best affections, and most earnest longings after you, though I be constrained for a while to be bodily absent from you. I say constrained, God knowing how willingly, and much rather than otherwise, I would have borne my part with you in this first brunt, were I not by strong necessity held back for the present. Make account of me, in the mean while, as of a man divided in myself with great pain, and as (natural bonds set aside) having my better part with you. And though I doubt not but in your godly wisdom you both foresee and resolve upon that which concerneth your present state and condition, both severally and jointly, yet have I thought it but my duty to add some further spur of provoca-

---

[1] Carver died in April, 1621.
[2] Oldmixon, i. 29, errs in saying that "Mr. Robinson did not *live* to go in person" with the first colonists. He lived till 1625.
[3] It was printed in 1622, in the Relation, or Journal, sent over by the Plymouth colonists in Dec. 1621, and in 1669, in Morton's New England's Memorial. There are some variations in the text of these several copies. It is not in Neal's New England, as stated by Prince, p. 160.

CHAP. VII.

1620. July.

tion to them, that run well already; if not because you need it, yet because I owe it in love and duty.

And first, as we are daily to renew our repentance with our God, especially for our sins known, and generally for our unknown sins and trespasses, so doth the Lord call us in a singular manner, upon occasions of such difficulty and danger as lieth upon you, to a both more narrow search and careful reformation of our ways in his sight; lest he calling to remembrance our sins forgotten by us or unrepented of, take advantage against us, and in judgment leave us for the same to be swallowed up in one danger or other. Whereas, on the contrary, sin being taken away by earnest repentance, and the pardon thereof from the Lord sealed up unto a man's conscience by his Spirit, great shall be his security and peace in all dangers, sweet his comforts in all distresses, with happy deliverance from all evil, whether in life or in death.

Now next after this heavenly peace with God and our own consciences, we are carefully to provide for peace with all men, what in us lieth, especially with our associates; and for that end, watchfulness must be had, that we neither at all in ourselves do give, no, nor easily take offence, being given by others. Wo be unto the world for offences; for although it be necessary (considering the malice of Satan and man's cor-

Matt. xviii. 7.

ruption) that offences come, yet wo unto that man, or woman either, by whom the offence cometh, saith

1 Cor. ix. 15.

Christ. And if offences in the unseasonable use of things in themselves indifferent be more to be feared than death itself, as the Apostle teacheth, how much more in things simply evil, in which neither honor of God nor love of man is thought worthy to be regarded.

Neither yet is it sufficient that we keep ourselves, by the grace of God, from giving offence, except withal we be armed against the taking of them, when they be given by others. For how unperfect and lame is the work of grace in that person who wants charity to cover a multitude of offences,[1] as the Scripture speaks. Neither are you to be exhorted to this grace only upon the common grounds of Christianity, which are, that persons ready to take offence, either want charity to cover offences,[1] or wisdom duly to weigh human frailties, or, lastly, are gross though close hypocrites, as Christ our Lord teacheth; as indeed, in my own experience, few or none have been found which sooner give offence, than such as easily take it; neither have they ever proved sound and profitable members in societies, which have nourished this touchy humor. But, besides these, there are divers motives provoking you, above others, to great care and conscience this way. As first, you are many of you strangers, as to the persons, so to the infirmities one of another, and so stand in need of more watchfulness this way; lest, when such things fall out in men and women as you suspected not, you be inordinately affected with them; which doth require at your hands much wisdom and charity, for the covering and preventing of incident offences that way. And lastly, your intended course of civil community will minister continual occasion of

CHAP. VII.

1620. July.

Matt. vii. 1-5.

---

[1] The passage between [1] and [1] is omitted in Morton's copy, in the Church Records, but is restored from his Memorial, p. 26. It is also contained in the Relation or Journal mentioned in the Note on page 91. The cause of this accidental omission is evident enough — the recurrence of the word *offences* — the eye of the transcriber glancing over the intervening words. This is what the critics call an ὁμοιοτέλευτον. See Le Clerc's Ars Critica, ii. 49. Michaelis, Introd. N. T. i. 271, (Marsh's ed.); Wetstein, N. T. ii. 863.

CHAP. VII.

1620. July.

offence, and will be as fuel for that fire, except you diligently quench it with brotherly forbearance. And if taking of offence causelessly or easily at men's doings be so carefully to be avoided, how much more heed is to be taken that we take not offence at God himself; which yet we certainly do, so oft as we do murmur at his providence in our crosses, or bear impatiently such afflictions as wherewith he pleaseth to visit us. Store we up therefore patience against the evil day; without which we take offence at the Lord himself in his holy and just works.

A fourth thing there is carefully to be provided for, to wit, that with your common employments you join common affections, truly bent upon the general good; avoiding, as a deadly plague of your both common and special comfort, all retiredness of mind for proper advantage, and all singularly affected any manner of way. Let every man repress in himself, and the whole body in each person, as so many rebels against the common good, all private respects of men's selves, not sorting with the general conveniency. And as men are careful not to have a new house shaken with any violence before it be well settled, and the parts firmly knit, so be you, I beseech you, brethren, much more careful that the house of God, which you are, and are to be, be not shaken with unnecessary novelties, or other oppositions, at the first settling thereof.[1]

---

[1] " Plutarch," says Jeremy Taylor, " compares a new marriage to a vessel before the hoops are on." " Therefore " Plutarch adds, " it behooves those people who are newly married to avoid the first occasions of discord and dissension; considering that vessels newly formed are subject to be bruised and put out of shape by many slight accidents; but when the materials come once to be settled and hardened by time, nor fire nor sword will hardly prejudice the solid substance." See Plutarch's Morals, iii. 17, (ed. 1694); Taylor's Works, v. 260, (Heber's ed.)

Lastly, whereas you are to become a body politic, using amongst yourselves civil government, and are not furnished with any persons of special eminency above the rest to be chosen by you into office of government, let your wisdom and godliness appear not only in choosing such persons as do entirely love and will diligently promote the common good, but also in yielding unto them all due honor and obedience in their lawful administrations, not beholding in them the ordinariness of their persons, but God's ordinance for your good; nor being like the foolish multitude, who more honor the gay coat than either the virtuous mind of the man, or glorious ordinance of the Lord. But you know better things, and that the image of the Lord's power and authority, which the magistrate beareth, is honorable, in how mean persons soever. And this duty you both may the more willingly and ought the more conscionably to perform, because you are, at least for the present, to have only them for your ordinary governors which yourselves shall make choice of for that work.

Sundry other things of importance I could put you in mind of, and of those before mentioned in more words. But I will not so far wrong your godly minds as to think you heedless of these things; there being also divers among you so well able to admonish both themselves and others of what concerneth them. These few things, therefore, and the same in few words, I do earnestly commend unto your care and conscience, joining therewith my daily, incessant prayers unto the Lord, that He who hath made the heavens and the earth, the sea and all rivers of waters, and whose providence is over all his works, especially over all his dear children, for good, would so guide and guard you in your ways, as inwardly by his Spirit, so outwardly by the hand of his power, as that both you, and we also, for and with you, may have after matter of praising his name all the days of your and our lives. Fare you well in Him in whom you trust, and in whom I rest

An unfeigned well-wisher of your

Happy success is this hopeful voyage,

JOHN ROBINSON.

This letter, though large, being so fruitful in itself and suitable to their occasions, I thought meet to insert in this place.[1]

---

[1] There is no date to this letter; but it was writen about the same time as the one to Carver, since in that letter Robinson says, "I have written a large letter to the whole."

CHAPTER VIII.

OF THE TROUBLES THAT BEFELL THE FIRST PLANTERS UPON THE COAST OF ENGLAND, AND IN THEIR VOYAGE IN COMING OVER INTO NEW ENGLAND, AND THEIR ARRIVAL AT CAPE COD, ALIAS CAPE JAMES.

ALL things being got ready, and every business despatched, the company was called together, and this letter read amongst them; which had good acception with all, and after fruit with many. Then they ordered and distributed their company for either ship, as they conceived for the best, and chose a governor and two or three assistants for each ship, to order the people by the way, and to see to the disposing of their provisions, and such like affairs; all which was not only with the liking of the masters of the ships, but according to their desires.

Which being done, they set sail[1] from thence about the fifth of August.[2] [But, alas, the best enterprises

---

[1] Smith, in his New England's Trials, printed in 1622, and Purchas, in his Pilgrims, iv. 1840, printed in 1625, say they sailed "with about 120 persons."

[2] "But what befell them further upon the coast of England, will appear in the book entitled New England's Memorial, page 31; and likewise of the voyage, and how they passed the sea, and of their safe arrival at Cape Cod, see New England's Memorial, page 33." *Morton's Note.*

CHAP. VIII.
1620.
Aug. 13.
Aug. 21.

meet oftentimes with many discouragements. For they had not sailed far, before Mr. Reynolds, the master of the lesser ship, complained that he found his ship so leaky, as he durst not put further to sea. On which they were forced to put in at Dartmouth, Mr. Jones, the master of the biggest ship, likewise putting in there with him; and the said lesser ship was searched, and mended, and judged sufficient for the voyage by the workmen that mended her. On which both the said ships put to sea the second time. But they had not sailed above a hundred leagues, ere the said Reynolds again complained of his ship being so leaky as that he feared he should founder in the sea if he held on; and then both ships bore up again, and went in at Plymouth.[1] But being there searched again, no great matter appeared, but it was judged to be the general weakness of the ship.

But the true reason of the retarding and delaying of matters was not as yet discerned. The one of them respecting the ship, (as afterwards was found,) was that she was overmasted; which when she came to her trim in that respect, she did well, and made divers profitable and successful voyages. But secondly, and more especially by the deceit of the master and his company, who were hired to stay a whole

As this account of the voyage is substantially Bradford's, as appears from comparing it with the extracts from his MS. in Prince, and as Morton refers to his Memorial merely to save the labor of copying, and would undoubtedly have inserted it had he caused his uncle's History to be printed, I have deemed it proper to make it a part of the narrative; enclosing it, however, in brackets to distinguish it from what is contained in the Church records.

[1] Grahame, i. 190, errs in saying that "the emigrants were at first driven back by a *storm*, which *destroyed one* of their vessels;" and Gorges is wrong in stating that they sailed in *three* ships, "whereof *two* proved unserviceable, and so were left behind." See Mass. Hist. Coll. xxvi. 73.

year in the country; but now fancying dislike, and fearing want of victuals, they plotted this stratagem to free themselves, as afterwards was known, and by some of them confessed. For they apprehended that the greater ship being of force, and in whom most of the provisions were bestowed, that she should retain enough for herself, whatsoever became of them and the passengers. But so strong was self-love and deceit in this man, as he forgot all duty and former kindness, and dealt thus falsely with them.

These things thus falling out, it was resolved by the whole to dismiss the lesser ship and part of the company with her, and that the other part of the company should proceed in the bigger ship.[1] Which when they had ordered matters in reference thereunto, they made another sad parting, the one ship, viz. the lesser, going back for London, and the other, viz. the MAYFLOWER,[2] Mr. Jones being master, proceeding on in the intended voyage.

---

[1] Neal, in his History of New England, i. 86, says, "Mr. Cushman and his family, with some others, that were more *fearful*, went ashore, and did not proceed on the voyage." Baylies, too, in his Memoir of Plymouth, i. 25. says, "about twenty of the passengers were *discouraged*, and would not reimbark. There is no ground for such an imputation on the courage or perseverance of any of the emigrants. The dismissal of a part was a matter of necessity, as the Mayflower could not carry the whole. Bradford, as quoted by Prince, p. 161, says, "they *agree* to dismiss her, (the Speedwell,) and those who are willing, to return to London, though this was very grievous and discouraging; Mr. Cushman and family returning with them." In the text, too, which is virtually Bradford's, we are told, "it was resolved by the *whole* to dismiss the lesser ship and part of the company with her." It was the captain and crew of the Speedwell that were unwilling to go, not his passengers; and the error seems to have arisen from considering the word *company*, in the passage "by the deceit of the master and his company," as meaning the emigrants instead of the sailors; in which latter sense it is constantly used at the present day by merchants and seamen. — Smith and Purchas say they discharge twenty of their passengers.

[2] The Mayflower is a ship of renown in the history of the colonization of New England. She was one of the five vessels which in

CHAP.
VIII.

1620.
Sept.
6.

These troubles being blown over, and now all being compact together in one ship, they put to sea again with a prosperous wind.[1] But after they had enjoyed fair winds for a season, they met with many contrary winds and fierce storms, with which their ship was shrewdly shaken, and her upper works made very leaky; and one of the main beams of the midships was bowed and cracked,[2] which put them to some fear that she would not be able to perform the voyage; on which the principal of the seamen and passengers had serious consultation what to do, whether to return or hold on. But the ship proving strong under water, by a screw[3] the said beam was brought into his place again; which being done, and well secured by the carpenter, they resolved to hold their voyage.[4] And so, after many boisterous storms, in which they could bear no sail, but were forced to lie at hull many days together,[5] after long beating at

---

1629 conveyed Higginson's com-company to Salem, and also one of the fleet which in 1630 brought over Winthrop and his Colony to Massachusetts Bay. See Savage's Winthrop, i. 2; Hutchinson's Collection of Papers, p. 33; Hazard, i. 278.

[1] With 100 persons, besides the crew of the vessel, according to Smith and Purchas — which corresponds exactly to the number that arrived at Cape Cod, according to Gov. Bradford's list, preserved by Prince, p. 172. — Neal, Hist. N. E. i. 87, Douglass, i. 370, Robertson, History of America, book x., and Marshall, Life of Washington, i. 91, and again Hist. Amer. Col. p. 80, err in crowding the whole 120 into the ship. Oldmixon, i. 30, who generally outdoes all others in his blunders, magnifies the number to 150.

[2] Prince, p. 161, reads this word *wracked* in Bradford's MS.

[3] Prince, p. 161, quotes Bradford's MS. as saying, "a passenger having brought a great iron screw from Holland."

[4] "Nov. 6, dies at sea William Butten, a youth, and servant to Samuel Fuller, being the only passenger who dies on the voyage." Bradford, in Prince, p. 161. One child was born, and called Oceanus, the son of Stephen Hopkins. Bradford, in Prince, p. 172.

[5] On Nov. 3, about a week before their arrival at Cape Cod, King James had signed the patent for the incorporation of the adventurers to the Northern Colony of Virginia, or New England. The Pilgrims, however, did not hear of this till the arrival of the next ship, the Fortune, in Nov. 1621. See Note on page 80, and Prince, p. 180.

THEY FALL IN WITH CAPE COD.

sea, they fell in with the land called CAPE COD;[1] the which being made, and certainly known to be it, they were not a little joyful.

After some little deliberation had amongst themselves with the master of the ship, they tacked about to stand to the southward to find some place about Hudson's river (according to their first intentions) for their habitations.[2] But they had not sailed that course

CHAP. VIII.

1620. Nov. 9.

---

[1] CAPE COD, the most remarkable feature in the configuration of the New England coast, and the first spot in it ever pressed by the footsteps of Englishmen, was discovered May 15, 1602, by Bartholomew Gosnold, who gave it the name on account of the abundance of cod which he caught in its neighbourhood. John Brereton, who was one of the companions of Gosnold, and wrote a Journal of the voyage, says, they first made land May 14, in lat. 43°, and "about three of the clock the same day in the afternoon we weighed, and standing southerly off into the sea the rest of that day and the night following, with a fresh gale of wind, in the morning we found ourselves embayed with a mighty headland.—At length we perceived this headland to be parcel of the main.—In five or six hours we pestered our ship so with codfish, that we threw numbers of them overboard again.—We sailed round about this headland almost all the points of the compass, the shore very bold, the land somewhat low, full of goodly woods, but in some places plain." Henry Hudson, Aug. 3, 1609, saw land in 41° 43′, and sailing north, anchored at the north end of this headland. Five of his men went on shore and "found goodly grapes and rose trees, and brought them aboard with them." Supposing it to be an island, and that he was its first discoverer, he called it New Holland. In a Dutch map, printed at Amsterdam in 1659, by Nicholas John Vischer, the whole Cape is called Nieuw Hollant, and the northern extremity is called Staaten Hoeck, State Point, or Witte Hoeck, White Point, probably from the white sand hills. The French called it, for the same reason, Cap Blanc. Capt. John Smith, who surveyed the coast in 1614, says, "Cape Cod is a headland of high hills of sand, overgrown with shrubby pines, hursts, and such trash, but an excellent harbour for all weathers. This Cape is made by the main sea, on the one side, and a great bay on the other, in form of a sickle. On it doth inhabit the people of Pawmet." Charles, Prince of Wales, altered its name to Cape James, in honor of his father. But the original name could not be so easily supplanted; "a name," says Cotton Mather, "which I suppose it will never lose till shoals of codfish be seen swimming on its highest hills." See Purchas's Pilgrims, iv. 1647; iii. 587; De Laet, Indiæ Occidentalis Descriptio, p. 70; Moulton's N. Y. p. 206; N. Y. Hist. Coll. i. 121; Mass. Hist. Coll. xxvi. 119; Mather's Magnalia, i. 43. Brereton's Journal is printed entire in the Mass. Hist. Coll. xxviii. 83.

[2] There can be no doubt that the Pilgrims intended to settle in the neighbourhood of Hudson's river. This is evident from the early narratives written by Bradford and Winslow. As their patent from the Virginia Company did not authorize them to plant themselves north of the 40th degree, they probably de-

CHAP. VIII.

1620.
Nov. 9.

above half a day before they fell amongst perilous shoals and breakers,[1] and they were so far entangled therewith as they conceived themselves in great danger; and the wind shrinking upon them withal, they signed to settle south of the Hudson, somewhere in New Jersey. But head winds, the shoals and breakers of Cape Cod, and the lateness of the season, conspired to prevent their original purpose. As Belknap says, ii. 188, "having been so long at sea, the sight of any land was welcome to women and children; the new danger was formidable; and the eagerness of the passengers to be set on shore was irresistible."

Morton, in his Memorial, gives another account of the matter. He says, p. 34, "Their putting into this place, (Cape Cod harbour,) was partly by reason of a storm, by which they were forced in, but more especially by the fraudulency and contrivance of Mr. Jones, the master of the ship; for their intention, as is before noted, and his engagement, was to Hudson's river. But some of the Dutch having notice of their intentions, and having thoughts about the same time of erecting a plantation there likewise, they fraudulently hired the said Jones, by delays while they were in England, and now under pretence of the danger of the shoals, &c. to disappoint them in their going thither." He adds, in a note, "Of this plot betwixt the Dutch and Mr. Jones I have had late and certain intelligence." But the contemporary narratives, written by Bradford and Winslow, say not a word about this treachery of the captain; nor does Bradford's History, as quoted by Prince, p. 162, who is therefore obliged to derive this statement from Morton. Morton is the first to mention it, and he does it in a book printed in 1669, half a century after the event is said to have occurred. He says, it is true, that he "had *late* and certain intelligence of this plot." If it had been *early* intelligence, it would have been more certain. But Morton was only eleven years old when he came over with his father to Plymouth in 1623; and in 1669, when he published his book, most of the first comers were dead, who could have furnished *credible* information on this point. They had died, and "given no sign"—not even lisped a syllable of complaint against the master of the Mayflower. It was too late then to get *certain* intelligence of a fact that had slumbered for fifty years, and which, if well founded, would from the first landing have been notorious, and had a place in every account that was written of the Colony. The silence of Bradford and Winslow seems conclusive on the point.— Yet this story has been repeated from Morton in an endless series by Hubbard, Mather, Prince, Neal, Hutchinson, Belknap, Holmes, Baylies, and Grahame, down to the present time. Moulton, in his unfinished but valuable History of New York, p. 355, was the first to question it. — I know not why Oldmixon, i. 29, and Grahame, i. 190, call Jones *a Dutchman.*

[1] The Mayflower probably made the Cape towards its northern extremity. The perilous shoals and breakers, among which she became entangled after sailing above half a day south, (or south-south-west, as the contemporary account states, in Bradford's Journal,) were undoubtedly those which lie off the southeastern extremity of the Cape, near Monamoy Point. The Pollock Rip, the most considerable of these. corresponds to the "roaring" shoals mentioned by Bradford, in Prince,

resolved to bear up again for the Cape aforesaid. The next day, by God's providence, they got into the Cape harbour.]¹

Being now passed the vast ocean and a sea of troubles, before their preparation unto further proceedings, as to seek out a place for habitation, &c. they fell down upon their knees and blessed the Lord, the

CHAP. VIII.

1620.
Nov. 11.

---

p. 162. She may also have encountered the Great and Little Round Shoals. It is not likely that she sailed far enough south to fall in with the Bass Rip or the Great Rip. Before she could reach these, the current and the flood tide probably drove her in between Monamoy Point and Nantucket. Had the wind permitted her to pursue a southern course, she might, in a few hours, have found an opening, and passed safely to the westward.

Gabriel Archer, in his Relation of Gosnold's voyage, in Purchas, iv. 1648, says, " We trended the coast southerly ; twelve leagues from Cape Cod (Provincetown) we descried a point, with some breach (breaker) a good distance off, and keeping our luff to double it, we came on the sudden into shoal water ; yet well quitted ourselves thereof. This breach we called Tucker's Terror, upon his expressed fear. The point we named Point Care." Tucker's Terror is no doubt the Pollock Rip, and Point Care is Monamoy Point. Robert Juet, Hudson's mate, in his account of their voyage, after stating that they first made the land at the south-eastern point of the Cape, says, " We found a flood come from the south-east, and an ebb from the north-west, with a very strong stream, and a great hurling and noises." This too was the Pollock Rip. Smith says, " Towards the south and south-west of this Cape is found a long and dangerous shoal of sands and rocks ; but so far as I encircled it, I found thirty fathom water aboard the shore, which makes me think there is a channel about this shoal." This also must have been the Pollock Rip. See Purchas, iii. 587 ; N. Y. Hist. Coll. i. 121 ; Mass. Hist. Coll. xxvi. 119, xxviii. 74.

¹ " Let us go up in imagination to yonder hill, and look out upon the November scene. That single dark speck, just discernible through the perspective glass, on the waste of waters, is the fated vessel. The storm moans through her tattered canvass, as she creeps, almost sinking, to her anchorage in Provincetown harbour ; and there she lies with all her treasures, not of silver and gold, (for of these she has none,) but of courage, of patience, of zeal, of high spiritual daring. So often as I dwell in imagination on this scene ; when I consider the condition of the Mayflower, utterly incapable as she was of living through another gale ; when I survey the terrible front presented by our coast to the navigator, who, unacquainted with its channels and roadsteads, should approach it in the stormy season, I dare not call it a mere piece of good fortune, that the general north and south wall of the shore of New England should be broken by this extraordinary projection of the Cape, running out into the ocean a hundred miles, as if on purpose to receive and encircle the precious vessel. As I now see her, freighted with the destinies of a continent, barely

CHAP. VIII.

1620. Nov.

God of heaven, who had brought them over the vast and furious ocean, and delivered them from all perils and miseries thereof, again to set their feet on the firm and stable earth, their proper element. And no marvel if they were thus joyful, seeing wise Seneca was so affected with sailing a few miles on the coast of his own Italy, as he affirms he had rather remain twenty years in his way by land, than pass by sea to any place in a short time; so tedious and dreadful was the same to him.[1]

But here I cannot but stay and make a pause, and stand half amazed at these poor people's condition; and so I think will the reader too, when he well considers the same. For having passed through many troubles, both before and upon the voyage, as aforesaid, they had now no friends to welcome them, nor inns to entertain and refresh them, no houses, much less towns, to repair unto to seek for succour.[2] It is

---

escaped from the perils of the deep, approaching the shore precisely where the broad sweep of this most remarkable headland presents almost the only point at which for hundreds of miles she could with any ease have made a harbour, and this perhaps the very best on the seaboard, I feel my spirit raised above the sphere of mere natural agencies. I see the mountains of New England rising from their rocky thrones. They rush forward into the ocean, settling down as they advance; and there they range themselves a mighty bulwark around the heaven-directed vessel. Yes, the everlasting God himself stretches out the arm of his mercy and his power in substantial manifestation, and gathers the meek company of his worshippers as in the hollow of his hand." Edward Everett's Address at the Cape Cod Centennial Celebration at Barnstable, Sept. 3, 1839, p. 45.

[1] Seneca says, in his 53d Epistle, that he set out to sail only from Parthenope (Naples) to Puteoli, (Pozzuoli,) and to get thither the sooner, launched out into the deep in a direct course to Nesis, (Nisida,) without coasting along the shore. This beautiful letter, which is well worth reading, may be found in Thomas Morrell's translation of the Epistles, i. 184, (London, 1786, 2 vols. 4to.)

[2] "The nearest plantation to them is a French one at Port Royal, who have another at Canada; and the only English ones are at Virginia, Bermudas, and Newfoundland; the nearest of these about five hundred miles off, and every one incapable of helping them." Prince, p. 180.

recorded in Scripture as a mercy to the Apostle and his shipwrecked company, that "the barbarians showed them no small kindness" in refreshing them. But these salvage barbarians, when they met with them, (as after will appear,) were readier to fill their sides full of arrows, than otherwise. And for the season, it was winter;[1] and they that know the winters of that country, know them to be sharp and violent, and subject to violent storms, dangerous to travel to known places, much more to search out unknown coasts. Besides, what could they see but a hideous and desolate wilderness, full of wild beasts and wild men? and what multitudes there might be of them they knew not. Neither could they, as it were, go up to the top of Pisgah, to view from this wilderness a more goodly country[2] to feed their hopes. For which way soever they turned their eyes (save upward to the heavens) they could have little solace or content in respect of any outward objects. For summer being done, all things stand for them to look

CHAP. VIII.

1620. Nov.

Acts xxviii. 2.

---

[1] Grahame says, i. 191, that "the intense severity of their first winter in America painfully convinced the settlers that a more unfavorable season of the year could not have been selected for the plantation of their colony." But it was not the season which they selected. They sailed from England at a very proper and favorable time, in the beginning of August, and might reasonably expect to arrive on the American coast by the middle of September, in ample season to build their houses and provide for the winter. But being obliged to put back twice, and then meeting with head winds, and having a boisterous passage of sixty-four days, they lost two months, and arrived just as the winter set in. The winter was more severe than they had been accustomed to, but it was unusually mild for this country and climate. Dudley says, in his Letter to the Countess of Lincoln, written in 1631, that the Plymouth colonists "were favored with a calm winter, such as was never seen here since." See Mass. Hist. Coll. viii. 37. Wood, too, who was here in 1633, and published his New England's Prospect in 1634, says, p. 5, (ed. 1764,) that "the year of New Plymouth men's arrival was no winter in comparison."

[2] In the MS. the word is *company*, manifestly an error of the pen. Morton, copying the same passage into his Memorial, p. 35, reads it *country*, as in the text.

CHAP. VIII.
1620. Nov.

upon with a weather-beaten face; and the whole country being full of woods and thickets, represented a wild and salvage hue. If they looked behind them, there was the mighty ocean which they had passed, and was now as a main bar and gulf to separate them from all the civil parts of the world. If it be said they had a ship to succour them, it is true; but what heard they daily from the master and company but that with speed they should look out a place with their shallop, where they would be at some near distance; for the season was such as he would not stir from thence until a safe harbour was discovered by them, where they would be and he might go without danger; and that victuals consumed apace, but he must and would keep sufficient for himself and company for their return. Yea, it was muttered by some, that if they got not a place in time, they would turn them and their goods on shore, and leave them. Let it be also considered what weak hopes of supply and succour they left behind them, that might bear up their minds in this sad condition and trials they were under, and they could not but be very small. It is true, indeed, the affections and love of their brethren at Leyden were cordial and entire; but they had little power to help them, or themselves; and how the case stood between them and the merchants at their coming away, hath already been declared. What could now sustain them but the spirit of God and his grace?[1]

[1] "Divers attempts had been made to settle this rough and northern country; first by the French, who would fain account it a part of Canada; and then by the English; and both from mere secular views. But such a train of crosses accompanied the designs of both these nations, that they seem to give it over as not worth the planting: till a pious people of England, not allowed to worship their Maker according to his institutions only, without the mixture of huma-

May not and ought not the children of these fathers rightly say, "Our fathers were Englishmen, which came over this great ocean, and were ready to perish in this wilderness. But they cried unto the Lord, and he heard their voice, and looked on their adversity." And let them therefore praise the Lord because he is good, and his mercies endure forever. Yea, let them which have been thus redeemed of the Lord show how he hath delivered them from the hand of the oppressor. When they wandered in the desert wilderness, out of the way, and found no city to dwell in, both hungry and thirsty, their soul was overwhelmed in them. Let them confess before the Lord his loving kindness and his wonderful works before the children of men.[1]

Of the troubles that befell them after their arrival,

---

monies, are spirited to attempt the settlement, that they might enjoy a worship purely scriptural, and leave the same to their posterity." Prince, p. 98.

"Whether Britain would have had any colonies in America, if religion had not been the grand inducement, is doubtful. One hundred and twenty years had passed, from the discovery of the northern continent by the Cabots, without any successful attempt. After repeated attempts had failed, it seems less probable that any should undertake in such an affair, than it would have been if no attempt had been made." Hutchinson's Mass. i. 3.

[1] Milton, in his treatise on Reformation in England, written in 1641, thus alludes to the persecution and exile of our New England fathers. "What numbers of faithful and freeborn Englishmen and good Christians, have been constrained to forsake their dearest home, their friends and kindred, whom nothing but the wide ocean, and the savage deserts of America, could hide and shelter from the fury of the bishops. O if we could but see the shape of our dear mother England, as poets are wont to give a personal form to what they please, how would she appear, think ye, but in a mourning weed, with ashes upon her head, and tears abundantly flowing from her eyes, to behold so many of her children exposed at once, and thrust from things of dearest necessity, because their conscience could not assent to things which the bishops thought indifferent? Let the astrologer be dismayed at the portentous blaze of comets, and impressions in the air, as foretelling troubles and changes to states; I shall believe there cannot be a more ill-boding sign to a nation, (God turn the omen from us!) then when the inhabitants, to avoid insufferable grievances at home, are enforced by heaps to forsake their native country." Prose Works, i. 37, (Symmons's ed.)

CHAP. VIII.
1620.
Nov.

with sundry other particulars concerning their transactings with the merchants adventurers, and many other passages not so pertinent to this present discourse, I shall refer the reader to *New England's Memorial*, and unto Mr. Bradford's book, where they are at large penned to his plentiful satisfaction.[1]

[1] Here we take leave of Morton's copy of Gov. Bradford's History. As the rest of it is lost, except the few scattered passages preserved by Prince and Hutchinson, and as we have a Journal of " the troubles that befell them after their arrival," written at the time, and chiefly, as I conceive, by Gov. Bradford, and much more copious and minute than the account in Morton's Memorial, the narrative will proceed in the words of that Journal.

BRADFORD'S AND WINSLOW'S

JOURNAL.

"RELATION or Iournall of the beginning and proceedings of the English Plantation setled at *Plimoth* in NEW-ENGLAND, by certaine English Adventurers both Merchants and others.

With their difficult passage, their safe arriuall, their ioyfull building of, and comfortable planting themselues in the now well defended Towne of NEW PLIMOTH.

As also a Relation of foure seuerall discoueries since made by some of the same English Planters there resident.

I. In a iourney to *Packanokick*, the habitation of the Indians greatest King Massasoyt; as also their message, the answer and entertainment they had of him.

II. In a voyage made by ten of them to the Kingdome of *Nawset*, to seeke a boy that had lost himselfe in the woods: with such accidents as befell them in that voyage.

III. In their iourney to the Kingdome of *Namaschet*, in defence of their greatest King *Massasoyt*, against the *Narrohiggonsets*, and to reuenge the supposed death of their Interpreter *Tisquantum*.

IIII. Their voyage to the *Massachusets*, and their entertainment there.

With an answer to all such objections as are any way made against the lawfulnesse of English plantations in those parts.

LONDON. Printed for *Iohn Bellamie*, and are to be sold at his shop at the two Greyhounds in Cornhill neere the Royall Exchange. 1622." sm. 4to.

TO THE READER.

COURTEOUS READER,

BE entreated to make a favorable construction of my forwardness in publishing these ensuing discourses. The desire of carrying the Gospel of Christ into those foreign parts, amongst those people that as yet have had no knowledge nor taste of God, as also to procure unto themselves and others a quiet and comfortable habitation, were, amongst other things, the inducements unto these undertakers of the then hopeful, and now experimentally known good enterprise for plantation in New England, to set afoot and prosecute the same. And though it fared with them, as it is common to the most actions of this nature, that the first attempts prove difficult, as the sequel more at large expresseth, yet it hath pleased God, even beyond our expectation in so short a time, to give hope of letting some of them see (though some he hath taken out of this vale of tears)[1] some grounds of hope of the accomplishment of both those ends by them at first propounded.

---

[1] The writer studiously suppresses the discouraging fact that more than half of the first Colonists had already perished.

GEORGE MORTON'S PREFACE.

And as myself then much desired, and shortly hope to effect, if the Lord will, the putting to of my shoulder in this hopeful business, and in the mean time these Relations coming to my hand from my both known and faithful friends, on whose writings I do much rely, I thought it not amiss to make them more general, hoping of a cheerful proceeding both of adventurers and planters; entreating that the example of the honorable Virginia and Bermudas[1] Companies, encountering with so many disasters, and that for divers years together with an unwearied resolution, the good effects whereof are now eminent, may prevail as a spur of preparation also touching this no less hopeful[2] country, though yet an infant, the extent and commodities whereof are as yet not fully known: after time will unfold more. Such as desire to take knowledge of things, may inform themselves by this ensuing treatise, and, if they please also by such as have been there a first and second time.[3] My hearty prayer to God is that the event of his and all other honorable and honest undertakings, may be for the furtherance of the kingdom of Christ, the enlarging of the bounds of our sovereign lord King James, and the good and profit of those

---

[1] By the third patent of the Virginia Company, granted in 1612, the Bermudas, and all islands within three hundred leagues of the coast, were included within the limits of their jurisdiction. These islands they sold to 120 of their own members, who became a distinct corporation, under the name of the Somer Islands Company. See Stith's Virginia, p. 127, App. 24.

[2] After the failure of Popham's colony at Sagadahoc in 1608, North Virginia or New England had been branded as "a cold, barren, mountainous, rocky desert," and had been abandoned as "uninhabitable by Englishmen." See Gorges in Mass. Hist. Coll. xxvi. 56; and Capt. John Smith in his Gen. Hist. ii. 174.

[3] Cushman had just returned from Plymouth, and Clark and Coppin, the mates or pilots of the Mayflower, had been on the coast twice.

who, either by purse or person or both, are agents in the same. So I take leave, and rest

Thy friend,

G. MOURT.[1]

[1] Who was G. Mourt? From his Preface it is evident that he was a person in England interested in the success of the Plymouth Colony, identifying himself with it, as appears from the expression, "even beyond *our* expectation," having "much desired" to embark with the first colonists, and intending soon to go over and join them. It is also evident that he had familiar and friendly relations with some of them, ("these Relations coming to my hand from my both known and faithful friends,") and that he was one in whom they reposed such entire confidence as to send to him their first despatches of letters and journals.

The only individual answering to this description that I can ascertain, is George Morton, who had married a sister of Gov. Bradford, and came over to Plymouth in July, 1623, in the first ship that sailed for the Colony after this Journal was printed. He is represented in the Memorial, p. 101, as "very faithful in whatsoever public employment he was betrusted withal, and an unfeigned well-willer and promoter of the common good and growth of the plantation of New Plymouth." Mourt may have been written designedly for Morton, from a disinclination on his part to have his name appear publicly in print, or it may have been a mistake of the printer, the final letters, from some flourish of the pen or otherwise, not being distinctly legible. Several other typographical errors, more important and palpable than this, occur in the Journal. It will be seen hereafter that Carver's name was printed Leaver, and Williams, by a flourish of the pen, was converted into Williamson.

Prince, p. 132, errs in saying that this Journal was *published* by Mourt; and his editor, p. 439, (ed. 1826,) errs in stating that Prince had only Purchas's abridgment of it. He had the entire work, on the title-page of which it is stated that it was "printed for John Bellamy," who continued for at least twenty-five years from that time (1622,) to be the principal publisher of books relating to New England.

TO HIS MUCH RESPECTED FRIEND, MR. I. P.[1]

GOOD FRIEND,

As we cannot but account it an extraordinary blessing of God in directing our course for these parts, after we came out of our native country,—for that we had the happiness to be possessed of the comforts we receive by the benefit of one of the most pleasant, most healthful, and most fruitful parts of the world,— so must we acknowledge the same blessing to be multiplied upon our whole company, for that we obtained the honor to receive allowance and approbation of our free possession and enjoying thereof, under the authority of those thrice honored persons, The President and Council for the Affairs of New England;[2] by whose bounty and grace, in that behalf, all of us are tied to dedicate our best service unto them, as those, under his Majesty, that we owe it unto; whose noble endea-

---

[1] These are probably the initials of John Pierce, in whose name their second patent was taken. See Prince, p. 204.

[2] The Pilgrims, by coming so far north, had got beyond the limits of the Virginia Company, and accordingly their patent was of no value. On the return of the Mayflower in May, 1621, the merchant adventurers applied, in their behalf, to the President and Council of New England, for a grant of the territory on which they had unintentionally settled. This, it seems, was readily accorded. — The President and Council put forth in 1622, "A Brief Relation of the Discovery and Plantation of New England," which is reprinted in the Mass. Hist. Coll. xix. 1—25.

vours in these their actions the God of heaven and earth multiply to his glory and their own eternal comforts.

As for this poor Relation, I pray you to accept it as being writ by the several actors themselves,[1] after their plain and rude manner. Therefore doubt nothing of the truth thereof. If it be defective in any thing, it is their ignorance, that are better acquainted with planting than writing. If it satisfy those that are well affected to the business, it is all I care for. Sure I am the place we are in, and the hopes that are apparent, cannot but suffice any that will not desire more than enough. Neither is there want of

---

[1] This constitutes its great value, and confers on it the highest authority. George Morton, in his Preface, alludes to the same fact. Edward Winslow, in a postscript to his "Good News from New England," printed in 1624, states that this Relation was "gathered by the inhabitants of this present plantation at Plymouth, in New England," and in the body of his work alludes to "former letters written by myself and others, which came to the press against my will and knowledge." The Journal, too, directly and by implication, repeatedly testifies to the same point. Under Dec. 6, in mentioning their third excursion, it says, "the narrative of which discovery follows, penned by one of the company."

I do not hesitate to ascribe this Journal to Bradford and Winslow, chiefly to the former. They were among the most active and efficient leaders of the Pilgrims; and one or the other of them went on almost every expedition here recorded, and were therefore cognizant of the facts as eye-witnesses. They were also the only practised writers among them. We are not aware that any of the other colonists were accustomed to writing; at least none of their writings have come down to us. Standish, though "the best linguist among them," in the Indian dialects, was more expert with the sword than the pen; and Elder Brewster, then fifty-six years old, was prevented by his office, if not by his age, from going on any of the excursions, and was therefore not competent to write the journal of them. Carver had the weight of government on his shoulders, which would leave little time for writing; he died too in April, five months after their arrival at the Cape. Allerton, Fuller, and Hopkins, are the only other persons likely to have had any hand in writing the Journal; and the part they contributed to it, if any, would probably be confined to furnishing the rough sketches of such expeditions as those to Nauset, Namaschet, and Massachusetts, in which Bradford and Winslow may not have been personally engaged. The style, too, seems to correspond, in its plainness and directness, with that of Bradford, in his History.

aught among us but company to enjoy the blessings so plentifully bestowed upon the inhabitants that are here. While I was a writing this, I had almost forgot that I had but the recommendation of the Relation itself to your further consideration, and therefore I will end without saying more, save that I shall always rest

Yours, in the way of friendship,
R. G.[1]

From Plymouth, in New England.

---

[1] Who was R. G.? At the time this Journal was sent over from Plymouth, in Dec. 1621, the only person there whose initials were R. G. was Richard Gardiner. He was one of the signers of the Compact on board the Mayflower, as will be seen hereafter. In that list it is apparent that the 41 names are, for the most part, subscribed in the order of the reputed rank of the signers. The two last, Dotey and Leister, were servants; the two next preceding, Allerton and English, were seamen; then comes Richard Gardiner. Now it is very unlikely that such an obscure person as this, No. 37, of whom nothing is known, whose name does not appear in the assignment of the lands in 1623, nor in the division of the cattle in 1627, and occurs no where subsequently in the records of the Colony, should be selected and deputed by the leading men in it to endorse "the recommendation" of their Journal. Such a person, even had he been chosen for this purpose, would not have presumed to speak of his superiors as having written their narrative "after their plain and rude manner," and apologize for "their ignorance," by saying they were "better acquainted with planting than writing." Such language would be used only by one of their compeers.

Nor could R. G. have been Richard Greene, as is suggested in Mass. Hist. Coll. xxvii. 298, 300; since Greene did not arrive at Plymouth till July, 1622, and this Relation was sent to England in Dec. 1621. See note [1] on page 236, and pages 296 and 299.

R. G. (or R. C. as I think it should be,) was Robert Cushman, their active and efficient agent, who being prevented from coming over in the Mayflower, came in Nov. 1621, in the Fortune, and returned in her the next month. Cushman brought the intelligence that a charter had been procured for them by the merchant adventurers from the President and Council of New England, "better than their former, and with less limitation." It was very natural, under these circumstances, that the leading colonists should request him to write a letter in their behalf, enclosing a copy of their Journal, to Pierce, in whose name the charter had been taken; and it was no less natural, that in writing it, he should render a deserved tribute of acknowledgment to the Company, for their "bounty and grace" in allowing them the free possession and enjoyment of the land on which they had involuntarily settled. See Prince, p. 198.

This letter of Cushman is followed in the original by Robinson's parting Letter of Advice, which has already been printed on page 91.

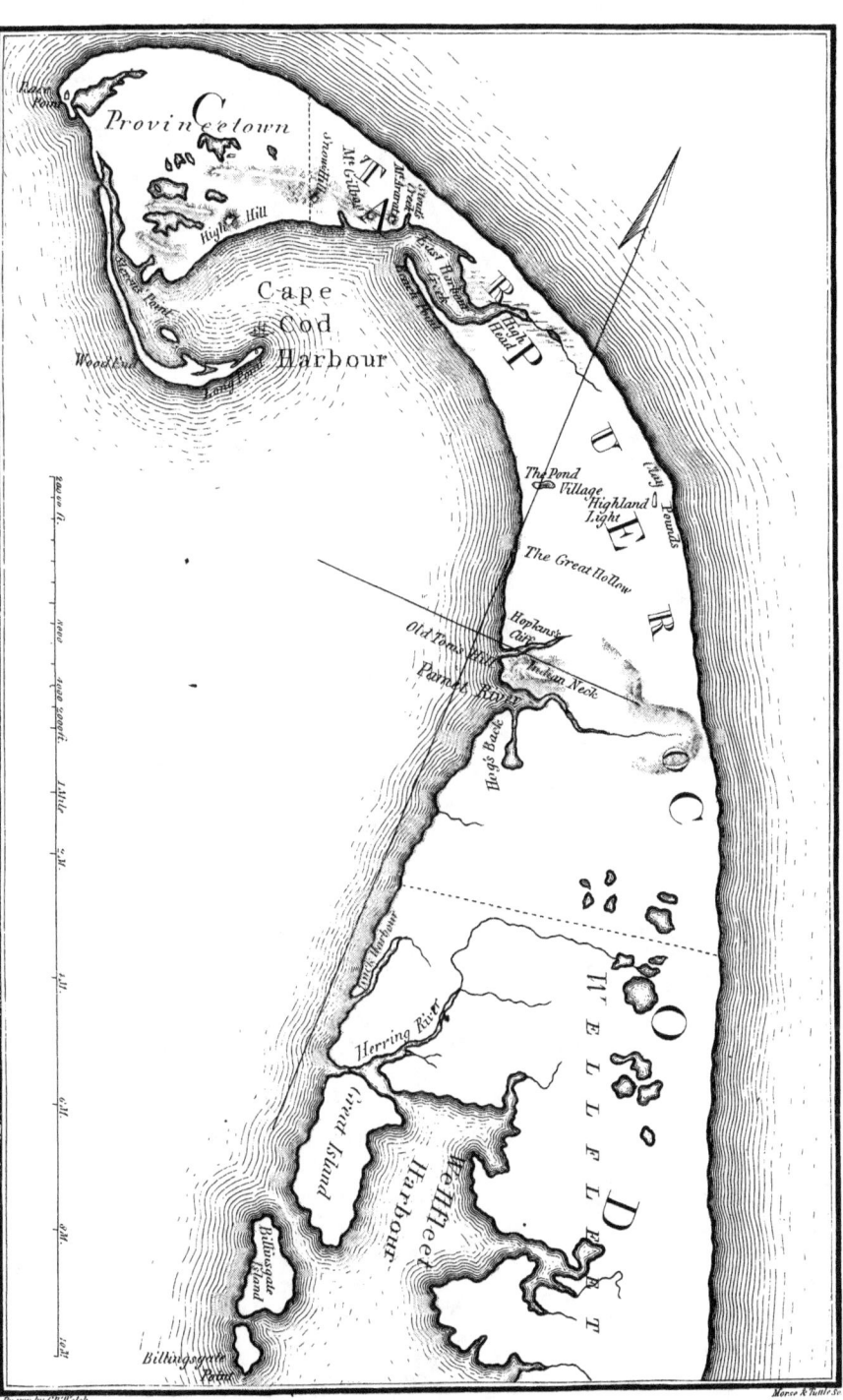

CHAPTER IX.

OF THE FIRST PLANTERS' COMBINATION BY ENTERING INTO A BODY POLITIC TOGETHER; WITH THEIR PROCEEDINGS IN DISCOVERY OF A PLACE FOR THEIR SETTLEMENT AND HABITATION.

WEDNESDAY, the 6th of September, the wind coming east-north-east, a fine small gale, we loosed from Plymouth, having been kindly entertained and courteously used by divers friends there dwelling; and after many difficulties in boisterous storms, at length, by God's providence, upon the 9th of November following, by break of the day, we espied land, which we deemed to be Cape Cod, and so afterward it proved. And the appearance of it much comforted us, especially seeing so goodly a land, and wooded to the brink of the sea. It caused us to rejoice together, and praise God that had given us once again to see land. And thus we made our course south-south-west, purposing to go to a river ten leagues to the south of the Cape.[1] But at night the wind being contrary, we put round again for the bay of Cape Cod; and upon the 11th of November we came to an anchor

CHAP. IX.

1620. Sept. 6.

Nov. 9.

Nov. 11.

---

[1] This river was the Hudson. Little was known at that time about distances on this unsurveyed coast. *Ten* may possibly be an error of the press.

CAPE COD WELL WOODED.

CHAP. IX.
1620.
Nov. 11.

in the bay,[1] which is a good harbour and pleasant bay, circled round, except in the entrance, which is about four miles over from land to land,[2] compassed about to the very sea with oaks, pines, juniper, sassafras, and other sweet wood.[3] It is a harbour wherein a thousand sail of ships may safely ride.[4] There we relieved our-

---

[1] That is, in Cape Cod or Provincetown harbour.

[2] This is just the distance from Long Point to the nearest land in Truro.

[3] Few trees are now left round Cape Cod harbour. That they were once common, appears from the name *Wood End*, given to a part of the coast, and from the stumps that are still found along the shore, particularly at the west end of the harbour, below the present high water mark, just above what is called "*the rising*." There is quite a grove of pines, called Mayo's Wood, near Snow's hill, at the eastern end of the village. There are dwarf oaks, too, growing on High Hill. The young trees would thrive if they were enclosed and protected from the cows, who now get part of their living by browsing on them. There are a few sassafras bushes, but no juniper. The juniper was probably the red cedar. Josselyn, in his New England's Rarities, published in 1672, says, page 49, "Cardan says juniper is cedar in hot countries, and juniper in cold countries; it is here very dwarfish and shrubby, growing for the most part by the sea-side." And Wood, in his New England's Prospect, printed in 1634, says, p. 19, "the cedar tree is a tree of no great growth, not bearing above a foot and a half at the most, neither is it very high. This wood is of color red and white, like yew, smelling as sweet as juniper." In 1740 there was a number of oaks in the woods northwest of East Harbour.

[4] Cape Cod harbour is formed by the spiral bending of the land, from Pamet river to Long Point, nearly round every point of the compass; it is completely land-locked. "It is one of the finest harbours for ships of war on the whole of our Atlantic coast. The width, and freedom from obstructions of every kind, at its entrance, and the extent of searoom upon the bay side, make it accessible to vessels of the largest class in almost all winds. This advantage, its capacity, depth of water, excellent anchorage, and the complete shelter it affords from all winds, render it one of the most valuable ship harbours upon our coast, whether considered in a commercial or military point of view." See Major J. D. Graham's Report, pp. 2 and 13, No. 121 of Executive Documents of the 25th Congress, 2d Sess. 1837–8, vol. 5. — Major Graham was employed by the government of the United States, during portions of the years 1833, 1834, and 1835, assisted by seven engineers, to survey the extremity of Cape Cod, including the townships of Provincetown and Truro, with their sea-coast, and the harbour of Cape Cod. This survey was executed with the greatest accuracy and precision, and a large and beautiful map, on a scale of six inches to a mile, was projected from it and published by order of Congress in 1838. It was republished in 1841, on a reduced scale of three inches to a mile, by I. W. P. Lewis, civil engineer. It is very desirable that the whole Cape should be surveyed in the same manner.

ABUNDANCE OF WHALES.

selves with wood and water, and refreshed our people, while our shallop was fitted to coast the bay, to search for a habitation. There was the greatest store of fowl[1] that ever we saw.

And every day we saw whales[2] playing hard by us; of which in that place, if we had instruments and means to take them, we might have made a very rich return; which, to our great grief, we wanted. Our master and his mate, and others experienced in fishing, professed we might have made three or four thousand pounds' worth of oil. They preferred it before Greenland whale-fishing, and purpose the next winter to fish for whale here. For cod we assayed, but found none; there is good store, no doubt, in their season.[3] Neither got we any fish all the time we lay there, but some few little ones on the shore. We found great muscles,[4] and very fat and full of sea-pearl; but we could not eat them, for they made us all sick that did

CHAP. IX.

1620.
Nov.
11.

---

[1] Sea fowls come in late in the autumn and remain during the winter. They were formerly plentiful on the shores; but they have been so frequently molested, that their numbers are much reduced.

[2] Whales are frequently seen in Barnstable Bay and on the outside of the Cape, and are killed by boats from Provincetown. Occasionally, though more rarely of late, they come into the harbour; at the beginning of the present century, two or three whales, producing about a hundred barrels of oil, were annually caught; the last that was killed in the harbour was in Dec. 1840, a hump-back, that made fifty barrels of oil. The appearance of a whale in the harbour is the signal for a general stir among the hundred graceful five-hand boats that line the circling shore of this beautiful bay. The American whale fishery commenced at Cape Cod, where it was carried on entirely in boats, which put off whenever a signal was given by persons on the look out from an elevated station, that a whale was seen to blow. In 1690 " one Ichabod Paddock" went from the Cape to Nantucket to teach the inhabitants of that isle the art and mystery of catching whales. See Mass. Hist. Coll. iii. 157.

[3] This is a little remarkable; for cod are caught at the Cape as early as November. They probably fished only in the harbour. The best season is in February and March, when they are caught in great plenty between Race Point and Wood End. It was May when Gosnold found them in such abundance.

[4] Though muscles are found in Cape Cod harbour, yet the sea clam seems to be meant, as it frequently produces on the stomach the effects

CHAP. IX.
1620.

eat, as well sailors as passengers. They caused to cast and scour; but they were soon well again.

The bay is so round and circling, that before we could come to anchor,[1] we went round all the points of the compass. We could not come near the shore by three quarters of an English mile, because of shallow water;[2] which was a great prejudice to us; for our people, going on shore, were forced to wade a bowshot or two in going a land, which caused many to get colds and coughs; for it was many times freezing cold weather.

Nov. 11.

This day, before we came to harbour, observing some not well affected to unity and concord, but gave some appearance of faction, it was thought good there should be an association and agreement, that we should combine together in one body,[3] and to submit to such government and governors as we should by

---

here described. F.—The notes to which this letter is annexed were written by the Rev. James Freeman, D.D., of Boston. His father being a native of Truro, Dr. Freeman frequently visited the Cape, and became strongly attached to it. He wrote a very minute and accurate topographical account of it, which may be found in the Mass. Hist. Coll. vol. viii. His papers are signed *r. s.* denoting his office of Recording Secretary of the Mass. Hist. Society; a Society which, in its 28 volumes, has accomplished more than any other literary or scientific association in America.

[1] The Mayflower anchored "within less than a furlong" of the end of Long Point, two miles from the present village of Provincetown. The shore is here very bold, and the water deep. See p. 150.

[2] At the head of the harbour, towards Wood End, and at East Harbour, the flats extend three quarters of a mile from the shore. They also lie all along the shore in front of the town, but do not extend so far from the land. At low water it is very shallow, and it is still necessary to wade a considerable distance, to get into a boat, as the writer knows by experience.

[3] Here, for the first time in the world's history, the philosophical fiction of a social compact was realized in practice. And yet it seems to me that a great deal more has been discerned in this document than the signers contemplated. It is evident, from page 95, that when they left Holland, they expected "to become a body politic, using amongst themselves civil government, and to choose their own rulers from among themselves." Their purpose in drawing up and signing this compact was simply, as they state, to restrain certain of their number, who had manifested an unruly and factious disposition. This was the whole philosophy of the instrument,

common consent agree to make and choose, and set our hands to this that follows, word for word.

In the name of God, Amen. We, whose names are underwritten, the loyal subjects of our dread sovereign lord, King James, by the grace of God, of Great Britain, France, and Ireland king, defender of the faith, &c., having undertaken, for the glory of God, and advancement of the Christian faith, and honor of our king and country, a voyage to plant the first colony in the northern parts of Virginia, do, by these presents, solemnly and mutually, in the presence of God and one of another, covenant and combine ourselves together into a civil body politic, for our better ordering and preservation, and furtherance of the ends aforesaid; and by virtue hereof to enact, constitute and frame such just and equal laws, ordinances, acts, constitutions, and offices, from time to time, as shall be thought most meet and convenient for the general good of the colony; unto which we promise all due submission and obedience. In witness whereof we have hereunder subscribed our names, at Cape Cod, the 11th of November, in the year of the reign of our sovereign lord, King James, of England, France and Ireland the eighteenth, and of Scotland the fifty-fourth, anno Domini 1620.

[Mr. John Carver †	8	John Alden	1
William Bradford †	2	Mr. Samuel Fuller	2
Mr. Edward Winslow †	5	* Mr. Christopher Martin †	4
Mr. William Brewster †	6	* Mr. William Mullins †	5
Mr. Isaac Allerton †	6	* Mr. William White †	5
Capt. Miles Standish †	2	Mr Richard Warren	1

whatever may since have been discovered and deduced from it by astute civilians, philosophical historians, and imaginative orators. "One great reason of this covenant," as Hutchinson says, ii. 458, "seems to have been of a mere moral nature, that they might remove all scruples of inflicting necessary punishments, even capital ones, seeing all had voluntarily subjected themselves to them."

THE LANDING AT CAPE COD.

CHAP. IX.
1 6 2 0.
Nov. 11.

John Howland		* John Goodman	1
Mr. Stephen Hopkins †	8	* Degory Priest	1
* Edward Tilly †	4	* Thomas Williams	1
* John Tilly †	3	Gilbert Winslow	1
Francis Cook	2	* Edmund Margeson	1
* Thomas Rogers	2	Peter Brown	1
* Thomas Tinker †	3	* Richard Britterige	1
* John Ridgdale †	2	George Soule	
* Edward Fuller †	3	* Richard Clarke	1
* John Turner	3	Richard Gardiner	1
Francis Eaton †	3	* John Allerton	1
* James Chilton †	3	* Thomas English	1
* John Crackston	2	Edward Dotey	
John Billington †	4	Edward Leister	
* Moses Fletcher	1		101] [1]

The same day, so soon as we could, we set ashore fifteen or sixteen men, well armed, with some to fetch wood, for we had none left; as also to see what the land was, and what inhabitants they could meet with.

---

[1] I have inserted this list from Prince, who found it at the end of Gov. Bradford's MS. From modesty, Bradford omits the title of Mr. to his own name. The figures denote the number in each family. Those with an asterisk (*) prefixed to their names, 21 in number, died before the end of March. Those with an obelisk (†) affixed, 18, brought their wives with them. Three, Samuel Fuller, Richard Warren, and Francis Cook, left their wives for the present either in Holland or England. They came in the Anne. Some left behind them part, and others all their children, who afterwards came over. John Howland was of Carver's family, George Soule of Edward Winslow's, and Dotey and Leister of Hopkins's family. Martin, Warren, Hopkins, Billington, Dotey, Leister, and probably some others, joined them in England. John Allerton and English were seamen. The list includes the child that was born at sea, and the servant who died; the latter ought not to have been counted. The number *living* at the signing of the compact was therefore only 100. See Prince, p. 172.

"So there were just 101, (no, 100,) who sailed from Plymouth in England, and just as many arrived in Cape Cod harbour. And this is the solitary number, who, for an undefiled conscience and the love of pure Christianity, first left their native and pleasant land, and encountered all the toils and hazards of the tumultuous ocean, in search of some uncultivated region in North Virginia, where they might quietly enjoy their religious liberties and transmit them to posterity." Prince, p. 173.

"These were the founders of the Colony of New Plymouth. The settlement of this colony occasioned the settlement of Massachusetts Bay, which was the source of all the other colonies of New England. Virginia was in a dying state, and seemed to revive and flourish from the example of New England. I am not preserving from oblivion the names of heroes whose chief merit is the overthrow of cities, provinces, and empires, but the names of the founders of a flourishing town and colony, if not of the whole British empire in America." Hutchinson, ii. 462.

THE SOIL OF CAPE COD.

They found it to be a small neck of land;[1] on this side where we lay, is the bay,[2] and the further side the sea;[3] the ground or earth sand hills, much like the downs[4] in Holland, but much better; the crust of the earth, a spit's depth,[5] excellent black earth; all

CHAP. IX.

1620. Nov. 11.

The same day " they choose Mr. John Carver, a pious and well approved gentleman, their governor for the first year." Bradford, in Prince, p. 162.

[1] The men appear to have been landed on Long Point, which tradition says has been diminished in its length, breadth, and height. F.

[2] By the bay is intended the harbour. Plymouth harbour is afterwards called a bay; and the same name is given to the harbour of Cummaquid, or Barnstable. F.

[3] That is, Barnstable bay. F.

[4] Gosnold, on landing at Cape Cod, in 1602, found "the sand by the shore somewhat deep." Smith, too, calls it " a headland of high hills of sand." The downs, or *dunes*, along the coast of Holland, are formed by the wind blowing up the sands of the sea-shore. To check the dispersion of the sand, the dunes are sowed regularly every year with a species of reed grass (*arundo arenaria*.) In a short time the roots spread and combine so as to hold the sand fast together. Linnæus, in his journey to the islands of Oëland and Gothland, in the Baltic, pointed out to the natives the advantage of planting the seareed grass to arrest the sand and form soil on the shores, to which it is extremely well adapted by the length of its roots. A similar practice has within a few years been adopted at Cape Cod, under the direction and at the expense of the general government. Large tracts of white sand at Provincetown have been planted with the beach grass (*psamma arenaria*.) The grass, during the spring and summer, grows about two feet and a half. If surrounded by naked beach, the storms of autumn and winter heap up the sand on all sides, and cause it to rise nearly to the top of the plant. In the ensuing spring the grass sprouts anew; is again covered with sand in the winter; and thus a hill or ridge continues to ascend as long as there is a sufficient base to support it, or till the surrounding sand, being also covered with beach grass, will no longer yield to the force of the wind. See Purchas, iv. 1648; Mass. Hist. Coll. xxvi. 119, viii. 110; Bigelow's Plants of Boston and its Vicinity, p. 40; Pulteney's General View of the Writings of Linnæus, p. 35.

[5] The depth of a spade. F. " A spade's depth thrown out in digging is still called *a spit*." Richardson's Dict. art. *Spade*.

Some persons may smile at reading of " a spade's depth of excellent black earth " at the extremity of Cape Cod. And yet, even now, after the woods are cut down, and free scope is given to the winds to scatter the sands over the vegetable mould of centuries, there is, at High head, in Truro, within four miles of Long Point, where the Mayflower was anchored, an "excellent black earth" more than a foot in depth, which for years, without manure, has produced 50 to 60 bushels of corn to the acre. It is based on an old Indian clambed, in which I observed the shells of the oyster, the scallop, the quahaug, the sea clam, and the common clam. This rich soil is on the property of James Small, whose hospitable dwelling is near the Highland Light.

CHAP. IX.

1620.
Nov. 11.

wooded[1] with oaks, pines, sassafras, juniper, birch, holly, vines, some ash, walnut;[2] the wood for the most part open and without underwood,[3] fit either to go or ride in. At night our people returned, but found not any person, nor habitation; and laded their boat with juniper,[4] which smelled very sweet and strong, and of which we burnt the most part of the time we lay there.

[1] See note [3] on page 118.

[2] There are three kinds of oak on the Cape, the red oak, (*quercus rubra*,) the black oak, (*quercus tinctoria*,) and the white oak, (*quercus alba*.) The frames of the oldest buildings there are made of white oak, which is one of the most durable kinds of timber. The pine is the pitch pine, (*pinus rigida*); the birch is the white birch, (*betula populifolia*); the holly is the American holly, an evergreen, (*ilex opaca*); the ash is the white ash, (*fraxinus Americana*,) and the walnut is the white walnut, (*juglans tomentosa*.)

[3] "The salvages are accustomed to set fire to the country in all places where they come, and to burn it twice a year, viz. at the spring, and the fall of the leaf. The reason that moves them to do so is because it would otherwise be so overgrown with underweeds, that it would be all a coppice wood, and the people would not be able in any wise to pass through the country out of a beaten path. This custom of firing the country is the means to make it passable, and by that means the trees grow here and there, as in our parks, and makes the country very beautiful and commodious." Morton's New English Canaan, ch. 18, (printed in 1632. Morton was here in 1622 and 1625.) "Whereas it is generally conceived that the woods grow so thick that there is no more clear ground than is hewed out by labor of men, it is nothing so; in many places, divers acres being clear, so that one may ride a hunting in most places of the land. There is no underwood, saving in swamps and low grounds; for it being the custom of the Indians to burn the woods in November, when the grass is withered, and leaves dried, it consumes all the underwood and rubbish, which otherwise would overgrow the country, making it impassable, and spoil their much affected hunting. So that by this means, in these places where the Indians inhabit, there is scarce a bush or bramble, or any cumbersome underwood to be seen in the more champaign ground." Wood's New England's Prospect, ch. 5. (Wood was here in 1633.) The woods in some parts of Wellfleet and Eastham are now entirely free from underwood, as in the time of the Pilgrims.

[4] The juniper was no doubt the red cedar, or savin, (*juniperus Virginiana*,) an evergreen which is still common on the Cape. It resembles very much the *juniperus sabina*, or common savin of Europe, which bears the juniper berries. The taste of the leaves in the two species is nearly the same. The wood of the red cedar is odorous, and the leaves, when bruised, emit a resinous, aromatic odor. It burns freely on account of its resinous qualities. Morton says, "Of cedar there is abundance; and this wood was such as Solomon used for the building of that glorious temple of Hierusalem. This wood cuts red."

THE FIRST EXCURSION UP THE CAPE. 125

Monday,[1] the 13th of November, we unshipped our shallop, and drew her on land, to mend and repair her, having been forced to cut her down in bestowing her betwixt the decks, and she was much opened with the people's lying in her; which kept us long there, for it was sixteen or seventeen days before the carpenter had finished her. Our people went on shore to refresh themselves, and our women to wash, as they had great need. But whilst we lay thus still, hoping our shallop would be ready in five or six days, at the furthest, (but our carpenter made slow work of it, so that) some of our people, impatient of delay, desired for our better furtherance to travel by land into the country, (which was not without appearance of danger, not having the shallop with them, nor means to carry provision but on their backs,) to see whether it might be fit for us to seat in or no; and the rather, because, as we sailed into the harbour, there seemed to be a river[2] opening itself into the main land. The willingness of the persons was liked, but the thing itself, in regard to the danger, was rather permitted than approved; and so with cautions, directions, and instructions, sixteen men were set out, with every man his musket,[3] sword, and corslet, under the conduct of Captain Miles Standish;[4] unto whom was

CHAP.
IX.

1620.
Nov.
13.

See Michaux's Sylva Americana, iii. 221, and Bigelow's Medical Botany, iii. 49.

[1] It would seem that the day before, being Sunday, they remained quietly on board.

[2] Pamet river. Winslow spells it Paomet, and Capt. Smith Pawmet. It is pronounced as if spelt Parmit.

[3] Their guns were matchlocks, as appears from their having " five or six inches of match burning," Nov. 16, and from their " lighting all their matches," Nov. 30. Even as late as 1687, match-locks were used instead of flint-locks in the regiments of the Duke of Brunswick. See Beckmann's History of Inventions, iii. 440.

[4] MILES STANDISH appears now in these Chronicles for the first time, as the military leader of the Pilgrims. His name has not been

CAPTAIN MILES STANDISH.

CHAP. IX.

1620.
Nov.

adjoined, for counsel and advice, William Bradford,[1] Stephen Hopkins,[2] and Edward Tilley.

mentioned in Gov. Bradford's History. He took no part in the negotiations with the Virginia Company or with the merchant adventurers. He was not one of Robinson's church before it left England; but serving in the Low Countries, in the forces sent over by Queen Elizabeth to aid the Dutch against the Spaniards, he fell in, as Winslow did, with Robinson and his congregation, liked them and their principles, and though not a member of their church, either voluntarily, or at their request, embarked with them for America. Morton, p. 262, says that he was " a gentleman, born in Lancashire, and was heir apparent unto a great estate of lands and livings, surreptitiously detained from him, his great grandfather being a second or younger brother from the house of Standish." This is not improbable. There are at this time in England two ancient families of the name, one of Standish Hall, and the other of Duxbury Park, both in Lancashire, who trace their descent from a common ancestor, Ralph de Standish, living in 1221. There seems always to have been a military spirit in the family. Froissart, relating in his Chronicles the memorable meeting between Richard II. and Wat Tyler, says that after the rebel was struck from his horse by William Walworth, " then a squyer of the kynges alyted, called John Standysshe, and he drewe out his sworde, and put into Wat Tyler's belye, and so he dyed." For this act Standish was knighted. In 1415, another Sir John Standish fought at the battle of Agincourt. From his giving the name of Duxbury to the town where he settled, near Plymouth, and calling his eldest son Alexander, (a common name in the Standish family,) I have no doubt that Miles was a scion from this ancient and warlike stock, which he did not dishonor. Whilst writing this note, I observe in the journals of the day, the death (Dec. 7, 1840, at Cadiz,) of "Frank Hall Standish, Esq. of Duxbury Hall, Lancashire."—The Plymouth soldier was a man of small stature, but of such an active and daring spirit that he spread terror through all the Indian tribes from Massachusetts Bay to Martha's Vineyard, and from Cape Cod harbour to Narraganset. In the autumn of 1625 he went to England, as an agent of the colony, and returned in the spring of 1626. In 1630 he removed to Duxbury, which was undoubtedly so called after the family seat of his ancestors. He had six children, and four sons, Alexander, Miles, Josiah, and Charles, survived him, whose numerous descendants are to be found in several towns in Plymouth county, in Connecticut, and in the State of New York. He lived and died at the foot of Captain's Hill, in Duxbury, so called after him, a monumental landmark that will hand his name down to the latest times. He was an assistant in 1633, and was repeatedly reëlected to this office. He died in 1656, but his age is unknown.—Smith, in his Hist. of N. Jersey, p. 18, commits a singular error in saying that "about the year 1620 the Plymouth Company sent a fresh recruit from England under the command of Capt. Standish." See Belknap, Am. Biog. ii. 310; Mass. Hist. Coll. xviii. 121, xx. 58—61; Hutchinson's Mass. ii. 461; Mitchell's Hist. of Bridgewater, p. 307; Burke's Hist. of the Commoners of Great Britain, ii. 64, and iv. 642.

[1] Winslow not being one of the party, I consider Bradford the sole author of this part of the Journal.

[2] STEPHEN HOPKINS, whose name stands the 14th in order among the signers of the Compact, with the

FIRST SIGHT OF THE INDIANS.

Wednesday, the 15th of November, they were set ashore;[1] and when they had ordered themselves in the order of a single file, and marched about the space of a mile by the sea, they espied five or six people, with a dog, coming towards them, who were savages; who, when they saw them, ran into the wood,[2] and whistled the dog after them, &c. First they supposed them to be Master Jones, the master, and some of his men, for they were ashore and knew of their coming; but after they knew them to be Indians, they marched after them into the woods, lest other of the Indians should lie in ambush. But when the Indians saw our men following them, they ran away with might and main; and our men turned out of the wood after them, for it was the way they intended to go, but they could not come near them. They followed them that night about ten miles[3] by

CHAP. IX.

1620.
Nov.
15.

honorable prefix of Mr., seems to have been a person of some consideration among the Pilgrims. From the same list it appears that he brought two servants or laborers with him, Dotey and Leister. It has already been mentioned, p. 100, that he had a son born on the voyage, named Oceanus. His wife's name was Elizabeth, and her three other children were Giles, Caleb, and Deborah. We are told further on in this Journal, under Dec. 6, that he joined the emigrants in England, not having been one of Robinson's congregation at Leyden. He went on two at least of the three excursions from Cape Cod harbour, and on the present occasion in the capacity of a counsellor. He was generally deputed to accompany Standish, and from this it may be inferred that he was somewhat of a military man, at least more so than the others; or it may be, his coolness was deemed important to temper the ardor of the captain. Thus he was adjoined to Standish Feb. 17, 1621, to meet the two Indians who showed themselves on Watson's hill; and March 16, Samoset was lodged for safe keeping at his house. He was also Winslow's companion on his visit to Massasoit at Pokanoket in July. He was an assistant to the governor of Plymouth from 1633 to 1636, and seems to have been much employed in public affairs. Nothing more is known about him, except that he was alive in 1643. See Mass. Hist. Coll. xiii. 184.

[1] The men were probably set ashore at Long Point.
[2] Probably at Wood End.
[3] After keeping along the shore for a mile, they turned in to the left after the Indians, and probably pursued them circuitously among the hills back of the village. As they were travelling on foot in the sands, the distance is probably overrated.

CHAP. IX.
1620.

the trace of their footings, and saw how they had come the same way they went, and at a turning perceived how they ran up a hill,[1] to see whether they followed them. At length night came upon them, and they were constrained to take up their lodging.[2] So they set forth three sentinels; and the rest, some kindled a fire, and others fetched wood, and there held our[3] rendezvous that night.

Nov. 16.

In the morning, so soon as we could see the trace, we proceeded on our journey, and had the track until we had compassed the head of a long creek;[4] and there they took into another wood, and we after them, supposing to find some of their dwellings. But we marched through boughs and bushes, and under hills and valleys,[5] which tore our very armor in pieces, and yet could meet with none of them, nor their houses, nor find any fresh water, which we greatly desired and stood in need of; for we brought neither beer nor water with us, and our victuals was only biscuit and Holland cheese, and a little bottle of aqua-vitæ, so as we were sore athirst. About ten o'clock

---

[1] Perhaps Snow's hill; or, it may be, Mt. Gilboa or Mt. Ararat.

[2] Probably near Stout's Creek, opposite Beach Point. Stout's Creek is a small branch of East Harbour Creek. Many years ago there was a body of salt marsh on it, and it then deserved the name of a creek. But the marsh was long since destroyed; and the creek scarcely exists, appearing only like a small depression in the sand, and being entirely dry at half tide. One of the life-boats provided by the Humane Society of Massachusetts, at the expense of the State, is stationed on the outer shore of the Cape, opposite Stout's Creek. Graham puts the creek down on his chart, but omits the name. See Mass. Hist. Coll. iii. 198; viii. 111.

[3] The writer of course was one of the party — undoubtedly Bradford.

[4] East Harbour Creek, a distance of about three miles and a half. F. The entrance into East Harbour is at the extremity of Beach Point. It is very shoal, both at its entrance and within it, having only one to three feet at ordinary low water. No other use is made of it as a harbour than to moor or lay up the small craft belonging to this place, in the winter season, to protect them from the ice. See Major Graham's Report, p. 13.

[5] Excepting the trees and bushes, which have disappeared, this is an exact description of that part of Truro, called East Harbour. F.

we came into a deep valley,[1] full of brush, wood-gaile,[2] and long grass, through which we found little paths or tracks; and there we saw a deer, and found springs of fresh water,[3] of which we were heartily glad, and sat us down and drunk our first New England water, with as much delight as ever we drunk drink in all our lives.[4]

CHAP. IX.

1620. Nov. 16.

When we had refreshed ourselves, we directed our course full south,[5] that we might come to the shore, which within a short while after we did, and there

[1] In this valley is the small village of East Harbour. It is going to decay, and probably will not long exist. F. — There are now four or five houses remaining. An old gentleman, resident in the valley, told me on the spot in Aug. 1840, that he recollected when there were seventeen houses there.

[2] The wood-gaile was probably what is called the sweet gale, or Dutch myrtle, (*myrica gale.*) See Bigelow's Plants of Boston and its vicinity, p. 393, (3d ed.)

[3] In the midst of the valley above mentioned is a swamp called Dyer's Swamp. Around it was formerly a number of springs of fresh water; and a few still remain, though probably before another century is closed, they will be choked with sand, as many of them already have been. F. — There is now in the valley a hollow overgrown with bushes; but in Aug. 1840, I could find no springs round it, and the oldest inhabitant recollected none.

[4] The water and air of New England have always been justly famous. Brereton, who accompanied Gosnold in 1602, speaks of the "many springs of excellent sweet water" which he found on the Elizabeth islands. Capt. John Smith, in his Description of New England says, "The waters are most pure, proceeding from the entrails of rocky mountains." Higginson, in his New England's Plantation, remarks that "the country is full of dainty springs," and that "a sup of New England's air is better than a whole draught of Old England's ale." Morton, in his New English Canaan, ch. 8, says "and for the water, therein it excelleth Canaan by much; for the land is so apt for fountains, a man cannot dig amiss. Therefore if the Abrahams and Lots of our times come thither, there needs be no contention for wells. In the delicacy of waters, and the conveniency of them, Canaan came not near this country." Wood, in his New England's Prospect, ch. 5, says "The country is as well watered as any land under the sun; every family or every two families having a spring of sweet water betwixt them. It is thought there can be no better water in the world. These springs be not only within land, but likewise bordering on the sea-coast, so that sometimes the tides overflow some of them." It is well known that the first settlement of Boston was determined by its abundance of "sweet and pleasant springs." See Mass. Hist. Coll. xxvi. 120, i. 120, 121, xii. 88, xx. 173, 175; Snow's History of Boston, p. 31. — The water of Truro is still excellent, whilst that of Provincetown is poor.

[5] The course from Dyer's Swamp to the Pond is south. F.

CHAP IX.
1620.
Nov. 16.

made a fire, that they in the ship might see where we were, as we had direction; and so marched on towards this supposed river. And as we went, in another valley we found a fine clear pond of fresh water, being about a musket shot broad, and twice as long.[1] There grew also many small vines, and fowl and deer[2] haunted there. There grew much sassafras.[3] From thence we went on, and found much plain ground,[4] about fifty acres, fit for the plough, and some signs where the

[1] Pond Village, which was formerly the principal village in Truro, but of late years exceeded by Pamet, takes its name from this pond. It is situated about a mile south of the village of East Harbour. The high and steep banks on the bay are here intersected by a valley which runs directly from the shore, and soon divides itself into two branches. In this valley the houses stand, and are defended from the winds, whilst the entrance of it affords a convenient landing place. The pond begins near the western shore, and extends east. About a mile east of it, on the Clay Pounds, stands the Highland or Cape Cod light-house. The pond is not now more than half-a-musket shot broad, though it is quite as long as it is here represented. In Aug. 1840, I found the upper or eastern part of it overgrown with flags and bushes. It was no doubt formerly much larger, and has been gradually filling up. Many of our swamps were originally ponds of water.

[2] Deer were seen near this pond by persons living at the beginning of the present century. F.

[3] This is the third time the sassafras has been mentioned. On the first discovery of America, great medicinal virtues were ascribed to the bark and roots of this tree, and ship-loads of it were exported to Europe. Monardes, a Spanish physician of Seville, who published in 1574, his second part of his "Historia medicinal de las cosas que se traen de nuestras Indias Occidentales que sirven en medicina," after mentioning its great efficacy in dropsies, agues, liver-complaints, &c. ends with exclaiming, fol. 62, "Bendito nuestro Señor, que nos dio este tan excelentissimo arbol, llamado sassafras, que tan grandes virtudes y tan maravillosos efectos, como avemos dicho, tiene, y mas los que el tiempo nos enseñara, que es descubridor de todas las cosas." The roots were sold in England at three shillings a pound in Gosnold's time, (1602,) who partly loaded his vessel with it from one of the Elizabeth islands. Brereton, the journalist of that voyage, speaks of "sassafras trees, great plenty, all the island over, a tree of high price and profit;" and Archer, another of the voyagers, says that "the powder of sassafras in twelve hours cured one of our company that had taken a great surfeit by eating the bellies of dog-fish, a very delicious meat." See Purchas, iv. 1646, 1649, 1653; Mass. Hist. Coll. xxiii. 257; Michaux's Sylva Americana, ii. 144; Bigelow's Medical Botany, ii. 142, and Plants of Boston and its Vicinity, p. 170. For the use of Monardes, and of "Frampton's Ioyfull Newes out of the New-found Worlde," which is nothing but a translation of it, printed at London in 1596, I am indebted to the rich library of Harvard College. — Sassafras is still found on Cape Cod, but in a dwarfish form.

[4] The land on the south side of the Pond is an elevated plain. F.

Indians had formerly planted their corn.[1] After this, some thought it best, for nearness of the river, to go down and travel on the sea sands, by which means some of our men were tired, and lagged behind. So we stayed and gathered them up, and struck into the land again;[2] where we found a little path to certain heaps of sand, one whereof was covered with old

---

[1] "The Indian corn (*zea mays*) called by the Mexicans *tlaölli* by the Haytians *maize*, and by the Massachusetts Indians *eachimmineash*, is found everywhere on the continent from Patagonia to Canada, and next to rice and wheat, is the most valuable of grains. There can hardly be a doubt that it is a native of America, unknown before the discovery of Columbus. The adventurers who first penetrated into Mexico and Peru found it everywhere cultivated, and in common use as an article of food among the aborigines. Its culture did not attract notice in Europe till after the voyage of Columbus, nor is it described in any work prior to the end of the 15th century. It was unknown to the ancient Greek and Roman writers, the passages in their works which have been supposed to refer to it being more applicable to other grains, such as the *holcus sorghum*. It is not mentioned by the earlier travellers who visited China, India, and other parts of Asia and Africa, and who were very minute in describing the productions of the countries which they visited. Acosta, in his Natural and Moral History of the Indies, (published in 1596,) says, lib. iv. ch. 16. "In our discourse on plants we will begin with those which are proper and peculiar to the Indies. As wheat is the most common grain for the use of man in the regions of the old world, so in the new found world the most common grain is *mays*, the which is found almost in all the kingdoms of the West Indies. I do not think that this mays is any thing inferior to our wheat, in strength nor substance. To conclude, God hath imparted to every region what is needful. To this continent he hath given wheat, which is the chief nourishment of man; and to the Indians he hath given mays, which hath the second place to wheat, for the nourishment of men and beasts." The maize is correctly figured in Oviedo's General and Natural History of the Indies, in Ramusio, Delle Navigationi et Viaggi, iii. fol. 131. See Hernandez, Historia Plantarum Novæ Hispaniæ, lib. vi. cap. 44; Lamarck's Botany, in the Encyclopédie Méthodique, xxxvi. 680, Planches, 749; and Winthrop's Description of Maize in the London Phil. Trans. xi. 1065.
—The principal argument against the American origin of maize is that it has never been found growing wild in any part of this continent. This statement, however, is disputed. Cobbett, in his Essay on Corn, ch. 2, maintains that "the cultivation of Indian corn is as old as the world itself," and draws his chief arguments from the following passages of Scripture— Matt. xii. 1; 2 Kings, iv. 2; Job xxiv. 24; Lev. ii. 14; xxiii. 14; Deut. xxiii. 24, 25; Gen. xli. 5, which he thinks are applicable to maize, but not to wheat.

[2] Probably at the Great Hollow. F. A mile south of the Pond village, the bank on the bay is intersected by another valley called the Great Hollow. This valley and another near it, towards the northeast, called the Great Swamp, contain several houses. The Great Hollow is separated from the Pond

CHAP. IX.
1620.
Nov. 16.

mats, and had a wooden thing, like a mortar, whelmed on the top of it, and an earthen pot laid in a little hole at the end thereof. We, musing what it might be, digged and found a bow, and, as we thought, arrows, but they were rotten. We supposed there were many other things; but because we deemed them graves, we put in the bow again, and made it up as it was, and left the rest untouched, because we thought it would be odious unto them to ransack their sepulchres.

We went on further and found new stubble, of which they had gotten corn this year, and many walnut trees [1] full of nuts, and great store of strawberries,[2] and some vines.[3] Passing thus a field or two, which were not

village by a high hill, which commands an extensive prospect of the ocean, Cape Cod harbour, and the opposite shore, as far as the broad bluff of Manomet, in Plymouth, and the high lands of Marshfield.

[1] T. Morton says, ch. 2, "Of walnut trees there is infinite store, and there are four sorts; it is an excellent wood, for many uses approved." Wood says, ch. 5. "The walnut tree is something different from the English walnut, and bears a very good nut, something smaller, but nothing inferior in sweetness and goodness to the English nut, having no bitter peel." And Josselyn says, p. 50, "The nuts of the walnut differ much from ours in Europe, they being smooth, much like a nutmeg in shape, and not much bigger; some three-cornered, all of them but thinly replenished with kernels."

[2] "There is strawberries," says Wood, "in abundance, very large ones, some being two inches about; one may gather half a bushel in a forenoon." Roger Williams, in his Key into the Language of America, ch. 16, says "This berry is the wonder of all the fruits, growing naturally in those parts. In some places where the natives have planted, I have many times seen as many as would fill a good ship within a few miles' compass." See Mass. Hist. Coll. iii. 221. "The common wild strawberry, (*fragaria Virginiana,*)" says Bigelow, Plants of Boston, p. 215, "is a very delicious fruit, and when cultivated is inferior to few imported species. The berries ripen early, are of a light scarlet color, exquisitely flavored, but more soft and perishable than the other kinds."

[3] "Vines there are that bear grapes of three colors, white, black, and red. The country is so apt for vines that, but for the fire at the spring of the year, the vines would so overspread the land, that one should not be able to pass for them. The fruit is as big, of some, as a musket ball, and is excellent in taste." T. Morton, ch. 2. "The vines afford great store of grapes, which are very big, both for the grape and cluster, sweet and good. These be of two sorts, red and white. There is likewise a smaller kind of grape, which groweth in the islands, which is sooner ripe, and more delectable." Wood, ch. 5.

great, we came to another,[1] which had also been new gotten, and there we found where a house had been, and four or five old planks laid together.[2] Also we found a great kettle, which had been some ship's kettle, and brought out of Europe. There was also a heap of sand,[3] made like the former, — but it was newly done, we might see how they had paddled it with their hands, — which we digged up, and in it we found a little old basket, full of fair Indian corn ; and digged further, and found a fine great new basket, full of very fair corn of this year, with some six and thirty goodly ears of corn, some yellow, and some red, and others mixed with blue,[4] which was a very goodly sight. The basket was round, and narrow at the top. It held about three or four bushels, which was as much as two of us could lift up from the ground, and was very handsomely and cunningly made.[5] But whilst

CHAP. IX.

1620.
Nov.
16.

---

[1] From the Great Hollow the sixteen adventurers travelled south to the hill which terminates in Hopkins's Cliff (or Uncle Sam's hill, as it is now vulgarly called.) This they called Cornhill. The Indians formerly dwelt in great numbers on this hill ; and the shells, deposited by them on it, are still ploughed up in abundance. Hopkins's Cliff is between the Great Hollow and Hopkins's Creek, or Pamet little river, as it is now called.

[2] This was probably the remains of a hut built by some shipwrecked sailors.

[3] "Their barns are holes made in the earth, that will hold a hogshead of corn apiece. In these, when their corn is out of the husk, and well dried, they lay their store in great baskets, with mats under, about the sides, and on the top ; and putting it into the place made for it, they cover it with earth, and in this manner it is preserved from destruction or putrefaction, to be used in case of necessity, and not else." T. Morton. ch. 13. "Their corn being ripe, they gather it, and dry it hard in the sun, convey it to their barns, which be great holes digged in the ground, in form of a brass pot, ceiled with rinds of trees, wherein they put their corn." Wood, ch. 20.

[4] This corn of mixed colors on the same cob, yellow, red, and blue, is still common at Truro.

[5] "In summer they gather flags, of which they make mats for houses, and hemp and rushes, with dying stuff, of which they make curious baskets, with intermixed colors, and portraitures of antique imagery. These baskets be of all sizes, from a quart to a quarter, in which they carry their luggage." Wood, ch. 30. "Instead of shelves, they have several baskets, wherein they put all their household stuff.

we were busy about these things, we set our men sentinel in a round ring, all but two or three, which digged up the corn. We were in suspense what to do with it and the kettle; and at length, after much consultation, we concluded to take the kettle, and as much of the corn as we could carry away with us; and when our shallop came, if we could find any of the people, and come to parley with them, we would give them the kettle again, and satisfy them for their corn.[1] So we took all the ears, and put a good deal of the loose corn in the kettle, for two men to bring away on a staff. Besides, they that could put any into their pockets, filled the same. The rest we buried again; for we were so laden with armor[2] that we could carry no more.

Not far from this place we found the remainder of an old fort or palisado, which, as we conceived, had been made by some Christians.[3] This was also hard by that place which we thought had been a river; unto which we went, and found it so to be, dividing itself into two arms by a high bank,[4] standing right

They have some great bags or sacks, made of hemp, which will hold five or six bushels." Roger Williams, in Mass. Hist. Coll. iii. 212.

[1] It will be seen that within eight months they scrupulously fulfilled this their honest intention, and gave the owners of the corn " full content." The censure of Baylies, i. 54, on their conduct as " inexcusable," and as " compromising their consciences," might as well have been spared. See p. 204.

[2] It is worthy of notice that the Pilgrims were cased in *armor*. See pages 125 and 128. One of their corslets would be a far more precious relic than a cuirass from the field of Waterloo. One of Standish's grandsons is said to have been in possession of his coat of mail. His sword and that of Carver and Brewster, are in the cabinet of the Massachusetts Historical Society. Some doubt however is thrown on this point from the circumstance that the Pilgrim Society of Plymouth have also in their possession " the identical sword-blade used by Miles Standish." See Belknap's Am. Biog. ii. 216, 336; Thacher's History of Plymouth, p. 258, second edition.

[3] Perhaps by the same persons who owned the kettle and built the hut. See p. 133.

[4] Bradford, in his History, as quoted by Prince, p. 163, says " a high cliff of sand at the entrance."

PAMET RIVER.   135

by the cut or mouth, which came from the sea. That which was next unto us was the less.¹ The other arm² was more than twice as big, and not unlike to be a harbour for ships; but whether it be a fresh river, or only an indraught of the sea, we had no time to discover; for we had commandment to be out but two days. Here also we saw two canoes;³ the one

CHAP.
IX.

1620.
Nov.
16.

This is an accurate description of the entrance of Pamet river. The high bank of sand, is called Old Tom's hill, after an Indian chief, who in former times had its seat on its summit, and who received this name from the first English settlers. It is the termination of a neck of land situated between the two creeks, called Indian Neck, it having been reserved to the Indians on the first settlement of Truro, about the year 1700. Prince, p. 163, has fallen into a great mistake in supposing that Barnstable harbour was the place here described. The description does not suit the harbour of Barnstable, or any other creek or inlet in the bay, except Pamet harbour; and, as Belknap rightly observes, (Am. Biog. ii. 196,) neither the time nor distance can agree with Prince's conjecture. Barnstable is fifty miles from Cape Cod harbour by land; a distance which could not have been travelled, and back again, in three short days of November. F.

¹ The smallest creek, which was next to the travellers, is called Hopkins's Creek, or Pamet little river. There is on it a body of salt marsh, which runs half way across the township of Truro. The depth of water in this creek, when the tide is in, is five feet. F.

² Pamet river, which is a creek forced into the land from the bay, and extends almost across the township, being separated from the ocean by nothing but a narrow beach and embankment, which the water has been known to break over. The creek runs through a body of salt marsh. The mouth of it lies nearly south-east from Cape Cod harbour, nine miles distant. It is about a mile south of the Great Hollow, and is a little to the north of what is called the shoal ground, without Billingsgate Point. The part of Truro, south of Pamet river, on the bay, is called Hog's Back. See Mass. Hist. Coll. iii. 196.

³ "Of the birch bark the salvages of the northern parts make them delicate canoes, so light that two men will transport one of them over land whither they list, and one of them will transport ten or twelve salvages by water at a time." T. Morton, ch. 2. "Their canoes are made either of pine trees, which, before they were acquainted with English tools, they burned hollow, scraping them smooth with clam shells and oyster shells, cutting their outsides with stone hatchets; these boats be not above a foot and a half or two foot wide, and twenty foot long. Their other canoes be made of thin birch rinds, close ribbed on the inside with broad thin hoops, like the hoops of a tub; these are made very light; a man may carry one of them a mile; being made purposely to carry from river to river, and bay to bay, to shorten land passages. In these cockling fly-boats, wherein an Englishman can scarce sit without a fearful tottering, they will venture to sea, when an English shallop dare not bare a knot of sail, scudding over the overgrown waves as fast as a wind-driven ship, being driven by their paddles; being much

on the one side, the other on the other side.[1] We could not believe it was a canoe, till we came near it. So we returned, leaving the further discovery hereof to our shallop, and came that night back again to the fresh water pond; and there we made our rendezvous that night, making a great fire, and a barricado to windward of us, and kept good watch with three sentinels all night, every one standing when his turn came, while five or six inches of match[2] was burning. It proved a very rainy night.

In the morning, we took our kettle and sunk it in the pond, and trimmed our muskets, for few of them would go off because of the wet; and so coasted the wood[3] again to come home, in which we were shrewdly puzzled, and lost our way. As we wandered we came to a tree, where a young sprit[4] was bowed down over a bow, and some acorns strewed underneath. Stephen Hopkins said, it had been to catch some deer. So as we were looking at it, William Bradford being in the rear, when he came looked also upon it, and as he went about, it gave a sudden jerk up, and he was immediately caught by the leg.[5] It was a very pretty

---

like battledoors; if a cross wave (which is seldom) turn her keel upside down, they by swimming free her, and scramble into her again." Wood, ch. 17.

[1] That is, of the bank, in the two arms of the creek.

[2] This proves that their guns were matchlocks. See p. 125.

[3] The wood was terminated by the Pond, by the side of which they travelled, and then through a valley, which is continued from it, east, toward the ocean. F.

[4] A sapling, a young tree.

[5] Wood says, ch. 15, "their deer-traps are springs made of young trees and smooth wrought cords; so strong as it will toss a horse if he be caught in it. An English mare, being strayed from her owner, and grown wild by her long sojourning in the woods, ranging up and down with the wild crew, stumbled into one of these traps, which stopped her speed, hanging her, like Mahomet's coffin, betwixt earth and heaven. In these traps deer, moose, bears, wolves, cats and foxes are often caught." "The salvages" says T. Morton, ch. 5, "take the deer in traps made of their natural hemp, which they place in the earth, where they fell

device, made with a rope of their own making, and having a noose as artificially made as any roper[1] in England can make, and as like ours as can be; which we brought away with us. In the end we got out of the wood, and were fallen about a mile too high above the creek;[2] where we saw three bucks,[3] but we had rather have had one of them. We also did spring three couple of partridges;[4] and as we came along by the creek, we saw great flocks of wild geese and ducks,[5] but they were very fearful of us. So we marched some while in the woods, some while on the sands, and other while in the water up to the knees; till at length we came near the ship;[6] and then we shot off our pieces, and the long boat came to fetch us. Master Jones and Master Carver being on the shore, with many of our people, came to meet us. And thus we came both weary and welcome home;[7] and delivered in our corn into the store to be kept for seed, for we knew not how to come by any, and therefore were very glad, purposing, so soon as we could meet with any of the inhabitants of that place, to make them large satisfaction. This was our first discovery, whilst our shallop was in repairing.

Our people did make things as fitting as they could,

CHAP. IX.

1620. Nov. 17.

a tree for browse; and when he rounds the tree for the browse, if he tread on the trap, he is horsed up by the leg, by means of a pole that starts up and catcheth him."
[1] Ropemaker.
[2] This brought them out about a mile east of High Head, and about two miles north-west of the Highland Light.
[3] See page 130.
[4] The partridge, (*perdrix Virginiana*,) or quail, as it is called in New England, is still found in Truro.

[5] Probably the Canada goose, (*anser Canadensis*,) and the dusky duck, (*anas obscura*).
[6] After going about a mile east, they compassed the head of East Harbour Creek, and went down on the north side of it. They then waded through Stout's Creek, and also through Mill Creek, near Gull Hill, and passed on to the end of Long Point, near which the ship lay. See note [1] on page 120.
[7] They had been absent three days.

CHAP. IX.
1620.

Nov. 27.

and time would, in seeking out wood, and helving of tools, and sawing of timber, to build a new shallop. But the discommodiousness of the harbour did much hinder us; for we could neither go to nor come from the shore but at high water, which was much to our hindrance and hurt; for oftentimes they waded to the middle of the thigh, and oft to the knees, to go and come from land.[1] Some did it necessarily, and some for their own pleasure; but it brought to the most, if not to all, coughs and colds, (the weather proving suddenly cold and stormy,) which afterwards turned to the scurvy, whereof many died.

When our shallop was fit, (indeed before she was fully fitted, for there was two days' work after bestowed on her,) there was appointed some four and twenty men of our own, and armed, then to go and make a more full discovery of the rivers before mentioned. Master Jones was desirous to go with us, and we took such of his sailors as he thought useful for us; so as we were in all about four and thirty men.[2] We made Master Jones our leader; for we thought it best herein to gratify his kindness and forwardness.[3] When we were set forth,[4] it proved rough weather and cross winds; so as we were constrained, some in the shallop, and others in the long boat, to row to the nearest shore the wind would suffer them to go unto, and then to wade out above the knees. The wind was so strong as the shallop could not keep the water, but was forced to harbour there[5] that night. But we marched

---

[1] See note [2] on page 120.
[2] Of course they had ten of Jones's crew.
[3] This shows that they could have harboured no suspicion that Jones had betrayed and wronged them. See note [1] on page 102.
[4] This was ten days after their return from their first excursion.
[5] In East Harbour. The men who marched *several* miles, and

six or seven miles further, and appointed the shallop to come to us as soon as they could. It blowed and did snow all that day and night, and froze withal. Some of our people that are dead took the original of their death here.[1]

The next day, about eleven o'clock, our shallop came to us, and we shipped ourselves; and the wind being good, we sailed to the river we formerly discovered, which we named *Cold Harbour;* to which when we came, we found it not navigable for ships; yet we thought it might be a good harbour for boats, for it flows there twelve foot at high water.[2] We landed our men between the two creeks,[3] and marched some four or five miles[4] by the greater of them, and the shallop followed us. At length night grew on, and our men were tired with marching up and down the steep hills and deep valleys,[5] which lay half a foot thick with snow. Master Jones, wearied with marching, was desirous we should take up our lodging, though some of us would have marched further. So we made there our rendezvous for that night under a few pine trees; and as it fell out, we got three fat geese,[6]

what they supposed to be *six* or *seven* miles farther, were landed on Beach Point, which forms this harbour. F.
[1] See pages 120 and 138.
[2] The mouth of Pamet river is twelve feet deep at high water. Thence the water gradually decreases to five feet, which is the depth at the lower bridge. This is to be understood of the lowest tides, during the summer. F.
[3] The men were landed at the foot of Old Tom's hill. F.
[4] From Old Tom's hill to the head of Pamet river the distance is about three miles and a half, as the hills run, or three miles in a

straight line. The tradition is, that Pamet river was formerly deeper than it is at present, and therefore the shallop might easily follow them. F.
[5] This is an exact description of the land on Pamet river. F. Truro is composed of hills and narrow circular valleys. There are also some long valleys, running at right angles with the shore. The tops of some of the hills spread out into a plain.
[6] "There are three kinds of goose, the gray goose, the white goose, and the brant." Josselyn, p. 9. "There are geese of three sorts, viz. brant geese, which are

CHAP. IX.
1620.

and six ducks[1] to our supper, which we eat with soldiers' stomachs, for we had eaten little all that day. Our resolution was, next morning to go up to the head of this river, for we supposed it would prove fresh water.

Nov. 29.

But in the morning our resolution held not, because many liked not the hilliness of the soil and badness of the harbour. So we turned towards the other creek, that we might go over and look for the rest of the corn that we left behind when we were here before. When we came to the creek, we saw the canoe lie on the dry ground, and a flock of geese in the river, at which one made a shot and killed a couple of them; and we launched the canoe and fetched them, and when we had done, she carried us over by seven or eight at once. This done, we marched to the place where we had the corn formerly, which place we called *Cornhill*; and digged and found the rest, of which

pied, and white geese which are bigger, and gray geese which are as big and bigger than the tame geese of England, with black legs, black bills, heads and necks black; the flesh far more excellent than the geese of England, wild or tame. There is of them great abundance; I have had often a thousand before the mouth of my gun." T. Morton, ch. 4. "The geese of the country be of three sorts; first a brant goose, which is a goose almost like the wild goose of England. The second kind is a white goose, almost as big as an English tame goose; these come in great flocks about Michaelmas; sometimes there will be two or three thousand in a flock; those continue six weeks and so fly to the southward, returning in March, and staying six weeks more, returning to the northward. The third kind of goose is a great gray goose, with a black neck and a black and white head, strong of flight, and these be a great deal bigger than the ordinary geese of England; most of these geese remain with us from Michaelmas to April. They feed on the sea, upon the grass in bays at low water, and gravel, and in the woods of acorns, having, as other fowl have, their pass and repass to the northward and southward." Wood, ch. 8.

[1] "Ducks there are of three kinds, pied ducks, gray ducks, and black ducks, in great abundance; they are bigger bodied than the tame ducks of England. T. Morton, ch. 4. "The ducks of the country be very large ones, and in great abundance. So there is of teal likewise. If I should tell you how some have killed a hundred geese in a week, fifty ducks at a shot, forty teal at another, it may be counted almost impossible, though nothing more certain." Wood, ch. 8.

we were very glad. We also digged in a place a little further off, and found a bottle of oil. We went to another place, which we had seen before, and digged and found more corn, viz. two or three baskets full of Indian wheat, and a bag of beans, with a good many of fair wheat [1] ears. Whilst some of us were digging up this, some others found another heap of corn, which they digged up also; so as we had in all about ten bushels, which will serve us sufficiently for seed. And sure it was God's good providence that we found this corn, for else we know not how we should have done; for we knew not how we should find or meet with any of the Indians, except it be to do us a mischief. Also, we had never in all likelihood seen a grain of it, if we had not made our first journey; for the ground was now covered with snow, and so hard frozen that we were fain with our curtlaxes [2] and short swords to hew and carve the ground a foot deep, and then wrest it up with levers, for we had forgot to bring other tools. Whilst we were in this employment, foul weather being towards, Master Jones was earnest to go aboard; but sundry of us desired to make further discovery, and to find out the Indians' habitations. So we sent home with him our weakest people, and some that were sick, and all the corn; and eighteen of us stayed still and lodged there that night, and desired that the shallop might return to us next day, and bring us some mattocks and spades with them.

The next morning, we followed certain beaten paths and tracks of the Indians into the woods, supposing they would have led us into some town or houses. After we had gone a while, we light upon a very

---

[1] Indian corn is still meant. F. [2] Cutlasses.

broad beaten path, well nigh two foot broad. Then we lighted all our matches,[1] and prepared ourselves, concluding that we were near their dwellings. But, in the end, we found it to be only a path[2] made to drive deer in, when the Indians hunt, as we supposed.

When we had marched five or six miles into the woods, and could find no signs of any people, we returned again another way; and as we came into the plain ground, we found a place like a grave, but it was much bigger and longer than any we had yet seen. It was also covered with boards, so as we mused what it should be, and resolved to dig it up; where we found first a mat, and under that a fair bow, and then[3] another mat, and under that a board about three quarters[4] long, finely carved and painted; with three tines or broaches[5] on the top, like a crown. Also between the mats we found bowls, trays, dishes, and such like trinkets. At length we came to a fair new mat, and under that two bundles, the one bigger, the other less. We opened the greater, and found in it a great quantity of fine and perfect red powder, and in it the bones and skull of a man. The skull had fine yellow hair still on it, and some of the flesh unconsumed. There was bound up with it a knife, a packneedle, and two or three old iron things. It was bound up in a sailor's

---

[1] See note [3] on page 125.

[2] "The Indians," says Wood, ch. 15, "have other devices to kill their game, as sometimes hedges a mile or two miles long, being a mile wide at one end, and made narrower and narrower by degrees, leaving only a gap of six foot long, over against which, in the day time, they lie lurking to shoot the deer which come through that narrow gut; in the night, at the gut of this hedge, they set deer traps." See the description of them on page 136.

[3] In the original *there* — undoubtedly a typographical error.

[4] Of a yard.

[5] Tines, prongs; broaches, spits. Tines is a word still in common use in the interior of New England; e. g. the tines of a pitchfork. See Ray's North Country Words, p. 20.

AN EMBALMED BODY.   143

canvass cassock and a pair of cloth breeches.¹ The strong, but no offensive smell; it was as fine as any flour. We opened the less bundle likewise, and found of the same powder in it, and the bones and head of a little child. About the legs and other parts of it was bound strings and bracelets of fine white beads.² There was also by it a little bow, about three quarters long, and some other odd knacks.³ We brought sundry of the prettiest things away with us, and covered the corpse up again. After this we digged in sundry like places, but found no more corn, nor any thing else but graves.

There was variety of opinions amongst us about the embalmed person. Some thought it was an Indian lord and king. Others said, the Indians have all black hair, and never any was seen with brown or yellow hair. Some thought it was a Christian of some special note, which had died amongst them, and they thus buried him to honor him. Others thought they had killed him, and did it in triumph over him.

Whilst we were thus ranging and searching, two of the sailors which were newly come on the shore,⁴ by chance espied two houses, which had been lately dwelt in, but the people were gone. They having their

---

¹ See pages 133 and 134.
² Wampom, made of the periwinkle. F.
³ "It is their custom," says Wood, ch. 19, "to bury with their deceased friends their bows and arrows, and good store of their wampompeag." Morton says, ch. 17, that "in the grave of the more noble they put a plank in the bottom for the corpse to be laid upon, and on each side a plank, and a plank upon the top, in the form of a chest, before they cover the place with earth." And Roger Williams says, ch. 32, "After the dead is laid in the grave, sometimes, in some parts, some goods are cast in with them; and upon the grave is spread the mat that the party died on, and the dish he ate in."
⁴ Having come from the ship in the shallop when she returned after carrying Jones on board.

CHAP.
IX.

1620.
Nov.
30.

CHAP. IX.
1620.
Nov. 30.

pieces, and hearing nobody, entered the houses, and took out some things, and durst not stay, but came again and told us. So some seven or eight of us went with them, and found how we had gone within a flight shot of them before. The houses [1] were made with long young sapling trees bended, and both ends stuck into the ground. They were made round, like unto an arbour, and covered down to the ground with thick and well wrought mats; and the door was not over a yard high, made of a mat to open. The chimney was a wide open hole in the top; for which they had a mat to cover it close when they pleased. One might stand and go upright in them. In the midst of them were four little trunches [2] knocked into the ground, and small sticks laid over, on which they hung their pots, and what they had to seethe. Round about the fire they lay on mats, which are their beds. The houses were double mattted; for as they were matted without, so were they within, with newer and fairer mats. In the houses we found wooden bowls, trays, and dishes, earthen pots,[3] hand-baskets made of crab-shells wrought together; also an English pail or bucket;[4] it wanted a bail, but it had two iron ears. There was also baskets of sundry sorts, bigger and some lesser, finer and some coarser. Some were curiously

---

[1] For the description of the Indian wigwams, see Roger Williams's Key, ch. 6; Wood's New England's Prospect, ch. 20; Morton's New English Canaan, ch. 4, and Gookin's Historical Collections of the Indians in New England, ch. 3, sec. 4, in Mass. Hist. Coll. i. 149.

[2] Truncheons, sticks.

[3] "They have dainty wooden bowls of maple, of high price amongst them." T. Morton, ch. 12. "Their household stuff is but little and mean. The pots they seethe their food in are made of clay or earth, almost in the form of an egg, the top taken off. Their dishes and spoons and ladles are made of wood, very smooth and artificial, and of a sort of wood not subject to split." Gookin, ch. 3, sec. 6.

[4] This probably belonged to the persons who built the hut and owned the kettle, mentioned on page 133.

wrought with black and white in pretty works, and sundry other of their household stuff.¹ We found also two or three deer's heads, one whereof had been newly killed, for it was still fresh. There was also a company of deer's feet stuck up in the houses, harts' horns, and eagles' claws, and sundry such like things there was; also two or three baskets full of parched acorns,² pieces of fish, and a piece of a broiled herring. We found also a little silk grass, and a little tobacco seed, with some other seeds which we knew not. Without was sundry bundles of flags, and sedge, bulrushes, and other stuff to make mats.³ There was thrust into a hollow tree two or three pieces of venison; but we thought it fitter for the dogs than for us. Some of the best things we took away with us, and left the houses standing still as they were.

So it growing towards night, and the tide almost spent, we hasted with our things down to the shallop, and got aboard that night, intending to have brought some beads and other things to have left in the houses, in sign of peace, and that we meant to truck with them; but it was not done by means of our hasty coming away from Cape Cod. But so soon as we

---

¹ "Some of their baskets are made of rushes, some of bents, others of maize husks, others of a kind of *silk grass*, others of a kind of wild hemp, and some of barks of trees; many of them very neat and artificial, with the portraitures of birds, beasts, fishes and flowers upon them in colors." Gookin, ch. 3, sec. 6.

² "They also dry acorns; and in case of want of corn, by much boiling they make a good dish of them; yea, sometimes in plenty of corn, do they eat these acorns for a novelty." Williams's Key, ch. 16. "They mix with their pottage, several sorts of nuts or masts, as oak acorns, chestnuts, walnuts; these husked, and dried, and powdered, they thicken their pottage therewith." Gookin, ch. 3, sec. 5.

³ "They make mats of several sorts, for covering their houses and doors, and to sleep and sit upon. The meaner sort of wigwams are covered with mats made of a kind of bulrush." Gookin, ch. 3, sec. 4 and 6.

CHAP. IX.
1620.
Dec.

can meet conveniently with them, we will give them full satisfaction.[1] Thus much of our second discovery.

Having thus discovered this place, it was controversal[2] amongst us what to do touching our abode and settling there.[3]

Some thought it best, for many reasons, to abide there. As first, that there was a convenient harbour for boats, though not for ships. Secondly, good corn-ground ready to our hands, as we saw by experience in the goodly corn it yielded, which would again agree with the ground and be natural seed for the same. Thirdly, Cape Cod was like to be a place of good fishing; for we saw daily great whales, of the best kind for oil and bone, come close aboard our ship, and, in fair weather, swim and play about us.[4] There was once one, when the sun shone warm, came and lay above water, as if she had been dead, for a good while together, within half a musket shot of the ship; at which two were prepared to shoot, to see whether she would stir or no. He that gave fire first, his musket flew in pieces, both stock and barrel; yet, thanks be to God, neither he nor any man else was hurt with it, though many were there about. But when the whale saw her time, she gave a snuff, and away. Fourthly, the place was likely to be healthful, secure, and defensible.

But the last and especial reason was, that now the heart of winter and unseasonable weather was come upon us, so that we could not go upon coasting and discovery without danger of losing men and boat, upon

---

[1] See page 137 and note [1] on page 134.
[2] Controverted, says Morton, in his Memorial, page 42.
[3] That is, at Pamet river.
[4] See note [2] on page 119.

which would follow the overthrow of all, especially considering what variable winds and sudden storms do there arise. Also, cold and wet lodging had so tainted our people, (for scarce any of us were free from vehement coughs,) as if they should continue long in that estate, it would endanger the lives of many, and breed diseases and infection amongst us. Again, we had yet some beer, butter, flesh, and other such victuals left, which would quickly be all gone; and then we should have nothing to comfort us in the great labor and toil we were likely to undergo at the first. It was also conceived, whilst we had competent victuals, that the ship would stay with us; but when that grew low, they would be gone, and let us shift as we could.

Others, again, urged greatly the going to Anguum, or Angoum,[1] a place twenty leagues off to the northwards, which they had heard to be an excellent harbour for ships, better ground, and better fishing. Secondly, for any thing we knew, there might be hard by us a far better seat; and it should be a great hindrance to seat where[2] we should remove again. Thirdly, the water was but in ponds; and it was thought there would be none in summer, or very little. Fourthly, the water there must be fetched up a steep hill.[3]

But to omit many reasons and replies used hereabouts, it was in the end concluded to make some

---

[1] Agawam, Ipswich; Smith calls it Augoam. Little was known at this time of Massachusetts Bay, or the distances from one place to another; that little was derived from Smith's map and Description of New England. See Mass. Hist. Coll. xxiii. 1, and xxvi. 118.

[2] Perhaps an error for *whence*.

[3] I suppose they contemplated building their town, for protection against the Indians, on the high bank, called Old Tom's hill, near the entrance of Pamet river. This hill is still very steep. There is a well now in front of it on the shore, where vessels water. The Pilgrims seemed to have relied on running streams, and never thought of sinking wells.

CHAP. IX.
1620.

discovery within the bay; but in no case so far as Angoum. Besides, Robert Coppin, our pilot,[1] made relation of a great navigable river and good harbour in the other head-land of the bay,[2] almost right over against Cape Cod, being, in[3] a right line, not much above eight leagues distant, in which he had been once; and because that one of the wild men with whom they had some trucking stole a harping iron[4] from them, they called it *Thievish Harbour*. And beyond that place they were enjoined not to go. Whereupon a company was chosen to go out upon a third discovery. Whilst some were employed in this discovery, it pleased God that Mistress White was brought a bed of a son, which was called Peregrine.[5]

Dec. 5.

The 5th day we, through God's mercy, escaped a great danger by the foolishness of a boy, one of Fran-

---

[1] Coppin was second mate of the Mayflower.

[2] The other headland of the bay was Manomet Point, and the river was probably the North river, in Scituate.

[3] The word *in* I insert from Morton, p. 43.

[4] A harpoon.

[5] In the Boston News Letter, of July 31, 1704, the 15th No. of the first newspaper printed in New England, is the following article of intelligence. "Marshfield, July 22, Captain Peregrine White, of this town, aged 83 years and eight months, died here the 20th inst. He was vigorous and of a comely aspect to the last; was the son of William White and Susanna his wife, born on board the Mayflower, Capt Jones commander, in Cape Cod harbour, Nov. 1620, the first Englishman born in New England." In the records of Plymouth Colony is the following entry under Oct. 1665, when Thomas Prince was governor. "In reference unto the request of the King's commissioners in behalf of Lieut. Peregrine White, desiring that the Court would accommodate him with a portion of land, in respect that he was the first of the English that was born in these parts; and in answer unto his own petition preferred to this Court respecting the premises, the Court have granted unto him 200 acres of land, lying and being at the path that goes from Bridgewater to the Bay, adjoining to the Bay line." A list of his descendants, some of whom are still living, may be seen in Thacher's Plymouth, p. 23.

"Dec. 4, dies Edward Thomson, servant of Mr. White, the first that dies since their arrival. Dec. 6, dies Jasper, a boy of Mr. Carver's. Dec. 7, Dorothy, wife to Mr. William Bradford, (drowned.) Dec. 8, James Chilton." Gov. Bradford, in Prince, p. 165. Prince had Bradford's pocket-book, which contained a register of deaths, births, and marriages, from Nov. 6, 1620, to the end of March, 1621.

THE THIRD EXPEDITION. 149

cis Billington's sons,[1] who, in his father's absence, had got gunpowder, and had shot off a piece or two, and made squibs; and there being a fowling-piece charged in his father's cabin, shot her off in the cabin; there being a little barrel of powder half full, scattered in and about the cabin, the fire being within four foot of the bed between the decks, and many flints and iron things about the cabin, and many people about the fire; and yet, by God's mercy, no harm done.

Wednesday, the 6th of December, it was resolved our discoverers should set forth, for the day before was too foul weather, — and so they did, though it was well o'er the day ere all things could be ready. So ten of our men were appointed who were of themselves willing to undertake it, to wit, Captain Standish, Master Carver, William Bradford, Edward Winsloe, John Tilley, Edward Tilley, John Houland,[2] and

---

[1] Billington was not one of the Leyden church, but slipped in among the Pilgrims in England. His accession was of no benefit to the colony. He was a mischievous and troublesome fellow. The first offence in the settlement was committed by him. In March, 1621, he was "convented before the whole company for contempt of the Captain's (Standish) lawful commands, with opprobrious speeches, for which he was adjudged to have his neck and heels tied together." Gov. Bradford, in a letter to Cushman, written June 9, 1625, says, "Billington still rails against you, and threatens to arrest you, I know not wherefore. He is a knave, and so will live and die." The prophecy was fulfilled, for he was hung in Oct. 1630, for waylaying and shooting a young man, named John Newcomen. Gov. Bradford says, in his History, "The said Billington was one of the profanest among us.

He came from London, and I know not by what friends shuffled into our company." John, his eldest son, who probably fired the powder, was a young scape-grace, who the next summer wandered off down the Cape as far as Eastham, causing great anxiety to the infant colony, and putting them to the trouble of sending an expedition after him. Francis, the other son, was the discoverer of Billington sea, which will immortalize the name. The mother's name was Helen. See Prince, pp. 189, 192, and 319. Mass. Hist. Coll. iii. 37; Hutchinson's Mass. ii. 464; Hubbard's New England, p. 101.

[2] JOHN HOWLAND, the 13th signer of the Compact, is counted as belonging to Carver's family, whose daughter Elizabeth he married. The Plymouth Colony records say that "he was an ancient professor of the ways of Christ; one of the first comers, and proved a useful

CHAP. IX.
1620.

three of London,[1] Richard Warren,[2] Steeven Hopkins, and Edward Dotte, and two of our[3] seamen, John Alderton and Thomas English. Of the ship's company there went two of the master's mates, Master Clarke and Master Coppin, the master gunner, and three sailors.[4] The narration of which discovery follows, penned by one[5] of the company.

Dec. 6.

Wednesday, the 6th of December, we set out, being very cold and hard weather. We were a long while, after we launched from the ship, before we could get clear of a sandy point,[6] which lay within less than a furlong of the same. In which time two were very sick,

---

instrument of good, and was the last of the male survivors of those who came over in the Mayflower in 1620, and whose place of abode was Plymouth." John Alden, of Duxbury, outlived him 15 years. The last survivor of the Mayflower was Mary Cushman, daughter of Isaac Allerton, who was alive in 1698. Howland died in 1672 at Rocky Nook, in Kingston, aged 80. He had four sons and six daughters, some of whose descendants are still living in the Old Colony and in Rhode Island. A genealogy of the family, written by one of them, the venerable John Howland, President of the R. I. Historical Society, is inserted in Thacher's Plymouth, p. 129. See Farmer's Genealogical Register of the First Settlers of New England, App. art. *Howland;* Mitchell's Bridgewater, p. 379; Hutchinson's Mass. ii. 456, 462.

[1] They were therefore not members of Robinson's congregation at Leyden. See p. 78, and note [1] on p. 122 of this volume.

[2] RICHARD WARREN, the 12th signer of the Compact, with the honorable prefix of Mr. is mentioned by Bradford as a most useful man, during the short time he lived, bearing a deep share in the difficulties and troubles of the plantation. He died in 1628. His widow, Elizabeth, survived him about 45 years, dying in 1673, at the age of 90. They had two sons and five daughters. His descendants perpetuate the name in Plymouth, New Bedford, Lowell, Boston, New York, and elsewhere. At the partition of the lands in 1623, Richard Warren's lot was assigned him near Eel river. The farm has continued in the possession of his posterity till within a few years. See Hutchinson's Mass. ii. 462; Morton's Memorial, p. 135; Thacher's Plymouth, p. 71.

[3] They were not a part of the Mayflower's crew, but were intended to remain in the country and to manage the Speedwell, had she come over. Their occupation at present, I suppose, was to take charge of the shallop, until another small vessel should be sent over; which took place in Aug. 1623, when a pinnace of 44 tons, called the Little James, arrived.

[4] There were 18 in all; among whom were 12 out of the 41 signers of the Compact.

[5] I take it to be Bradford. See note [1] on page 115.

[6] The end of Long Point. F.

and Edward Tilley had like to have sounded[1] with cold. The gunner also was sick unto death (but hope of trucking made him to go,) and so remained all that day and the next night. At length we got clear of the sandy point, and got up our sails, and within an hour or two we got under the weather shore,[2] and then had smoother water and better sailing. But it was very cold; for the water froze on our clothes, and made them many times like coats of iron.

CHAP. IX.

1620. Dec. 6.

We sailed six or seven leagues by the shore, but saw neither river nor creek. At length we met with a tongue of land, being flat off from the shore, with a sandy point.[3] We bore up to gain the point, and found there a fair income or road of a bay, being a league over at the narrowest, and some two or three in length; but we made right over to the land before us, and left the discovery of this income till the next day. As we drew near to the shore,[4] we espied some ten or twelve Indians very busy about a black thing, — what it was we could not tell, — till afterwards they saw us, and ran to and fro, as if they had been carrying something away. We landed a league or two from them,[5] and had much ado to put ashore any where, it

---

[1] Swooned. Nothing further is known of Edward Tilley than that he brought his wife with him, and had two other individuals in his family, probably his children, and died before the end of March. John Tilley, who was also one of this exploring party, was probably a brother of Edward. He also brought his wife and one other person, most likely a child, and died before the end of March. The name does not appear in the division of the lands in 1623, nor of the cattle in 1627.

[2] The shore of Truro.

[3] Billingsgate Point. This point then joined the land north of it; but it is now an island, having been cut off by a ditch many years since; and being constantly washed by the tide, there is now a passage for small light vessels to pass at full sea. Wellfleet bay is, as here described, a league over at the narrowest and two or three in length. The distance from Long Point to Billingsgate Point is seven leagues. See Mass. Hist. Coll. iv. 41.

[4] In Eastham, north of Great pond.

[5] South.

CHAP. IX.
1620.

lay so full of flat sands.[1] When we came to shore, we made us a barricado, and got firewood, and set out sentinels, and betook us to our lodging, such as it was. We saw the smoke of the fire which the savages made that night about four or five miles from us.

Dec. 7.

In the morning we divided our company, some eight in the shallop, and the rest on the shore went to discover this place. But we found it only to be a bay,[2] without either river or creek coming into it. Yet we deemed it to be as good a harbour as Cape Cod; for they that sounded it found a ship might ride in five fathom water. We on the land found it to be a level[3] soil, though none of the fruitfullest. We saw two becks[4] of fresh water, which were the first running streams that we saw in the country; but one might stride over them. We found also a great fish, called a grampus,[5] dead on the sands. They in the shallop

---

[1] A sandy flat, a mile wide, extends along the western shore of Eastham, from Dennis to the bounds of Wellfleet. It is left dry about three hours, and may easily be crossed by horses and carriages. See Mass. Hist. Coll. viii. 155.

[2] Wellfleet harbour, which is large, indented within with creeks, where vessels of 70 or 80 tons may lie. Large ships may lie safe in what is called the Deep Hole, near the town. There are five and a half fathom of water in the harbour. See Mass. Hist. Coll. iii. 117.

[3] The land in Eastham is a level plain.

[4] Becks — rivulets, small brooks. See Ray's North Country Words, pp. 17 and 99. One of these no doubt was Indian brook, which forms the boundary between Eastham and Wellfleet, and runs into the harbour of Silver Springs. The spring from which it issues has a white sand at the bottom, resembling that metal. The other was probably Cook's brook, in Eastham, three quarters of a mile south of Indian brook, or possibly Snow's brook a mile further south. See Mass Hist. Coll. iv. 41, and viii. 155.

[5] The grampus, (*grand-poisson*, Fr., *grapois*, Norm., *delphinus orca*,) is the largest and most remarkable species of the genus Phocæna, of the cetaceous order of Mammalia. It is a large animal, half the size of the Greenland fullgrown whale, being often seen from 25 to 30 feet in length and 10 or 12 in circumference. The color is black above, suddenly giving place to white on the sides, which is continued over the abdomen. Individuals of this species are sometimes thrown ashore on the Cape, 20 feet long, and having four inches of blubber. See Jardine's Naturalist's Library, Mammalia, vi. 228 — 232; Shaw's Zoölogy, Mammalia, vol. ii. part ii. p. 513; Josselyn, p. 26.

found two of them also in the bottom of the bay, dead in like sort. They were cast up at high water, and could not get off for the frost and ice. They were some five or six paces long, and about two inches thick of fat, and fleshed like a swine. They would have yielded a great deal of oil, if there had been time and means to have taken it. So we finding nothing for our turn, both we and our shallop returned.

We then directed our course along the sea sands to the place where we first saw the Indians.[1] When we were there, we saw it was also a grampus which they were cutting up. They cut it into long rands[2] or pieces, about an ell long and two handfull broad. We found here and there a piece scattered by the way, as it seemed for haste. This place the most were minded we should call the *Grampus Bay*,[3] because we found so many of them there. We followed the track of the Indians' bare feet a good way on the sands. At length we saw where they struck into the woods by the side of a pond.[4] As we went to view the place, one said he thought he saw an Indian house among the trees; so went up to see. And here we and the shallop lost sight one of another till night, it being now about nine or ten o'clock. So we light on a path, but saw no house, and followed a great way into the woods. At length we found where corn had been set, but not that year. Anon, we found a great burying place, one part whereof was encompassed with a large palisado, like a

---

[1] They went back, north, towards Wellfleet harbour.
[2] Rands — strips.
[3] Wellfleet harbour.
[4] Great pond, in Eastham, north of which they landed. F. This pond is a quarter of a mile from the shore. A narrow neck, about forty feet wide, separates it from Long pond; the distance of which from Mill pond, connected with the northern arm of Nauset harbour, is not more than a furlong. A canal might thus be easily cut, connecting the bay with the ocean. See Mass. Hist. Coll. viii. 156.

church-yard, with young spires,[1] four or five yards long, set as close one by another as they could, two or three foot in the ground. Within it was full of graves, some bigger and some less. Some were also paled about; and others had like an Indian house[2] made over them, but not matted. Those graves were more sumptuous than those at *Cornhill*; yet we digged none of them up, but only viewed them and went our way. Without the palisado were graves also, but not so costly. From this place we went and found more corn-ground, but not of this year. As we ranged, we light on four or five Indian houses, which had been lately dwelt in; but they were uncovered, and had no mats about them; else they were like those we found at *Cornhill*,[3] but had not been so lately dwelt in. There was nothing left but two or three pieces of old mats, and a little sedge. Also, a little further, we found two baskets full of parched acorns[4] hid in the ground, which we supposed had been corn when we began to dig the same; we cast earth thereon again, and went our way. All this while we saw no people.

We went ranging up and down till the sun began to draw low, and then we hasted out of the woods, that we might come to our shallop; which, when we were out of the woods, we espied a great way off, and called them to come unto us; the which they did as soon as they could, for it was not yet high water. They were exceeding glad to see us, for they feared

---

[1] Spires — twisted or wreathed boughs.

[2] "Over the grave of the more noble they erect something in form of a hearse-cloth." T. Morton, ch. 17. The Pilgrims, on their first visit to Massachusetts Bay, in Sept. 1621, saw the grave of Nanepashemet, the deceased king, surrounded by a palisado, and over it "the frame of a house, wherein, being dead, he lay buried." See page 142.

[3] See page 144.

[4] See note[2] on page 145.

A MIDNIGHT ALARM.

because they had not seen us in so long a time, thinking we would have kept by the shore side. So being both weary and faint, — for we had eaten nothing all that day, — we fell to make our rendezvous and get firewood, which always costs us a great deal of labor. By that time we had done, and our shallop come to us,[1] it was within night; and we fed upon such victuals as we had, and betook us to our rest, after we had set out our watch. About midnight we heard a great and hideous cry; and our sentinels called, "*Arm! Arm!*" So we bestirred ourselves, and shot off a couple of muskets, and the noise ceased. We concluded that it was a company of wolves or foxes; for one[2] told us he had heard such a noise in Newfoundland.[3]

---

[1] It appears from Gov. Bradford's MS. History, quoted by Prince, p. 165, that the shallop coasted along the shore, south, and that towards night, the people on land met it at a creek. This Morton, in his Memorial, p. 44, conjectures to be Namskeket, which is the dividing line between Orleans and Brewster. But it may with more probability be concluded that it was Great Meadow creek, in Eastham. If the travellers had gone as far as Namskeket, they must have crossed Great Meadow creek, then, half a mile south, Boat Meadow creek, then, half a mile further south, Rock Harbour creek, and then, a mile southwest, Little Namskeket creek; or they must have passed round their heads, which, at a time when the country was covered with a forest very difficult to be penetrated, would have been no easy task. Namskeket creek was best known to the first settlers of Plymouth; and this appears to have been the cause of Morton's supposition. F. See Mass. Hist. Coll. viii. 155, 188.

[2] Probably either Clark or Coppin, the mates of the Mayflower, who had been on the coast before. See pp. 85 and 148.

[3] Newfoundland was *not* discovered in 1497 by Sebastian Cabot. See Biddle's Life of Cabot, book i. ch. 6. Captain Richard Whitbourne, who wrote a book, printed in London in 1622, entitled "A Discourse and Discovery of Newfound-land," says that he was first there in 1582, and again in 1586, "at which time Sir Humfrey Gilbert, a Devonshire knight, came thither with two good ships and a pinnace, and brought with him a large patent from the late most renowned Queen Elizabeth, and in her name took possession of that country, in the harbour of St. John's, whereof I was an eye-witness." Whitbourne was at Newfoundland again in 1588, 1611, 1614, 1615, and 1618. Clark or Coppin may have gone in one of his ships. Whitbourne says, p. 8, "In divers parts of the country there are many foxes, wolves, and bears. In 1615, three several times the wolves and

CHAP. IX.

1620.
Dec. 8.

About five o'clock in the morning we began to be stirring; and two or three, which doubted whether their pieces would go off or no, made trial of them and shot them off, but thought nothing at all. After prayer[1] we prepared ourselves for breakfast, and for a journey; and it being now the twilight in the morning, it was thought meet to carry the things down to the shallop. Some said it was not best to carry the armor[2] down. Others said, they would be readier. Two or three said, they would not carry theirs till they went themselves, but mistrusting nothing at all. As it fell out, the water not being high enough, they laid the things down upon the shore, and came up to breakfast. Anon, all upon a sudden, we heard a great and strange cry, which we knew to be the same voices, though they varied their notes. One of our company, being abroad, came running in, and cried, "They are men! Indians! Indians!" and withal their arrows came flying amongst us. Our men ran out with all speed to recover their arms; as by the good providence of God they did. In the mean time, Captain Miles Standish, having a snaphance[3] ready, made a shot; and after

---

beasts of the country came down to the sea-side, near to 48 persons of my company, who were laboring about their fish, howling and making a noise." Whitbourne's book was published by royal authority, and distributed throughout the several parishes of the kingdom. A contribution too was ordered by the Privy Council to be taken in the parish churches to defray the expense of the printing, and as "some reward to him for his great charge, travails, and divers losses at sea."

[1] This incidental remark shows the religious character of the Pilgrims. No dangers or hardships were permitted to interfere with their stated devotions.

[2] See note [2] on page 134.

[3] A snaphance is a musket with a flint-lock. In 1643 the householders at Plymouth were "ordered to be furnished with approved arms, viz. muskets with snaphance, or matchlocks with match calivers, and carbines, which are allowed, and also fowling-pieces." At the time of Philip's war, in 1674, snaphances were rare, yet a few of them were used. See Mass. Hist. Coll. xiii. 183, and Haven's Centennial Address at Dedham, p. 61.

Meyrick, in his Critical Inquiry into Ancient Armour, iii. 88, points

him another. After they two had shot, other two of us were ready; but he wished us not to shoot till we could take aim, for we knew not what need we should have; and there were four only of us which had their arms there ready, and stood before the open side of our barricado, which was first assaulted. They thought it best to defend it, lest the enemy should take it and our stuff; and so have the more vantage against us. Our care was no less for the shallop; but we hoped all the rest would defend it. We called unto them to know how it was with them; and they answered "Well! Well!" every one, and "Be of good courage!" We heard three of their pieces go off, and the rest called for a firebrand to light their matches.[1] One took a log out of the fire on his shoulder and went and carried it unto them; which was thought did not a little discourage our enemies. The cry of our enemies[2] was dreadful, especially when our men ran out to recover their arms. Their note was after this manner, "*Woach, woach, ha ha hach woach.*" Our men were no sooner come to their arms, but the enemy was ready to assault them.

There was a lusty man, and no whit less valiant, who was thought to be their captain, stood behind a tree within half a musket shot of us, and there let his arrows fly at us. He was seen to shoot three arrows, which were all avoided; for he at whom the first arrow was aimed, saw it, and stooped down, and it

out a difference between the firelock and the snaphance, and quotes a document which "prefers the firelock," but "if they cannot be procured, snaphances will do." The difference seems to be that in the snaphance a movable hammer was placed beyond the pan, and separate from its cover; whilst in the firelock the hammer is affixed to the pan, supplying the place of its cover, and opening at the percussion of the cock.

[1] See note [3] on page 125.
[2] These were the Nauset Indians, as will appear hereafter.

CHAP. IX.
1620.
Dec. 8.

flew over him. The rest were avoided also. He stood three shots of a musket. At length, one took, as he said, full aim at him; after which he gave an extraordinary cry, and away they went all.[1] We followed them about a quarter of a mile; but we left six to keep our shallop, for we were very careful of our business. Then we shouted all together two several times, and shot off a couple of muskets, and so returned. This we did that they might see we were not afraid of them, nor discouraged.

Thus it pleased God to vanquish our enemies and give us deliverance. By their noise we could not guess that they were less than thirty or forty, though some thought that they were many more. Yet, in the dark of the morning, we could not so well discern them among the trees, as they could see us by our fire-side. We took up eighteen of their arrows, which we have sent to England by Master Jones;[2] some whereof were headed with brass, others with harts' horn, and others with eagles' claws. Many more no doubt were shot, for these we found were almost covered with leaves; yet, by the especial providence of God, none of them either hit or hurt us, though many came close by us and on every side of us, and some coats which hung up in our barricado were shot through and through.

---

[1] Johnson, in his Wonder-working Providence, ch. 8, says that "one Captain Miles Standish, having his fowling-piece in readiness, presented full at them. His shot, being directed by the provident hand of the most high God, struck the stoutest sachem among them on the right arm, it being bent over his shoulder to reach an arrow forth his quiver." We know not what authority Johnson had for this statement. In the same chapter he says, "Of Plymouth plantation the author purposes not to speak particularly, being prevented by the honored Mr. Winslow, who was an eye-witness of the work." Edward Johnson lived at Woburn, in Massachusetts, and his book was printed in London in 1654. See Mass. Hist. Coll. xii 49, 67.

[2] On the return of the Mayflower in April, 1621.

So after we had given God thanks for our deliverance, we took our shallop and went on our journey, and called this place *The First Encounter*. From hence we intended to have sailed to the aforesaid *Thievish Harbour*, if we found no convenient harbour by the way.[1] Having the wind good, we sailed all that day along the coast about fifteen leagues;[2] but saw neither river nor creek[3] to put into. After we had sailed an hour or two, it began to snow and rain, and to be bad weather. About the midst of the afternoon the wind increased, and the seas began to be very rough; and the hinges of the rudder broke, so that we could steer no longer with it, but two men, with much ado, were fain to serve with a couple of oars. The seas were grown so great that we were much troubled and in great danger; and night grew on. Anon, Master Coppin bade us be of good cheer; he saw the harbour. As we drew near, the gale being stiff, and we bearing great sail to get in, split our mast in three pieces, and were like to have cast away our shallop.[4] Yet, by God's mercy, recovering our-

---

[1] Gov. Bradford, in his History, as quoted by Prince, p. 166, says, "They hasten on to a port which Mr. Coppin, their pilot, assures them is a good one, which he had been in, and they might reach before night." Coppin might have been on the coast before, either with Smith or Hunt, in 1614.

[2] The distance along the coast from Eastham to the high bluff of Manomet, in Plymouth, is about 45 miles or 15 leagues.

[3] The snow-storm, which began "after they had sailed an hour or two," prevented their seeing Sandy Neck, and led them to overshoot Barnstable harbour. Had it not been for this, it is highly probable that they would have entered and made their settlement there.

[4] Bradford says, in his History, "The pilot, being deceived, cries out, 'Lord be merciful! my eyes never saw this place before!' And he and the mate would have run her ashore in a cove full of breakers, before the wind; but a steersman calling to the rowers, 'About with her, or we are cast away,' they get her about immediately, and Providence showing a fair sound before them, they get under the lee of a small rise of land; but are divided about going ashore, lest they fall into the midst of savages. Some, therefore, keep the boat, but others being so wet,

CHAP. IX.

1620. Dec. 8.

selves, we had the flood with us, and struck into the harbour.

Now he that thought that had been the place, was deceived, it being a place where not any of us had been before; and coming into the harbour, he that was our pilot did bear up northward, which if we had continued, we had been cast away.[1] Yet still the Lord kept us, and we bare up for an island[2] before us; and recovering of that island, being compassed about with many rocks, and dark night growing upon us, it pleased the Divine Providence that we fell upon a place of sandy ground, where our shallop did ride safe and secure all that night; and coming upon a strange island, kept our watch all night in the rain upon that island.[3]

cold, and feeble, cannot bear it, but venture ashore, and with great difficulty kindle a fire; and after midnight, the wind shifting to the northwest, and freezing hard, the rest are glad to get to them, and here stay the night." See Prince, p. 166.

[1] The cove where they were in danger lies between the Gurnet Head and Saquish Point, at the entrance of Plymouth harbour.

[2] Clark's island just within the entrance of Plymouth harbour, and so called after the mate of the Mayflower, who is said to have been the first to step ashore on it. It is sheltered from the ocean by Salt-house beach, contains about eighty acres of fertile land, and is called by Gov. Hutchinson, i. 360, "one of the best islands in New England." It was neither sold nor allotted in any of the early divisions of the lands, but was reserved for the benefit of the poor of the town, to furnish them with wood, and with pasture for their cattle. Previous to 1638 the "Court granted that Clark's island, the Eel river beach, Saquish, and the Gurnet's Nose, shall be and remain unto the town of Plymouth, with the woods, thereupon." In 1690, Clark's island was sold to Samuel Lucas, Elkanah Watson, and George Morton. The Watson family have been in possession of this island for half a century, and one of them, Edward Watson, now resides on it. See Mass. Hist. Coll. xiii. 162, 181; Thacher's Plymouth, pp. 82, 153, 158, 330.

One of the oldest grave-stones on the burial hill in Plymouth, is that of a Thomas Clark, who died March 24, 1697, aged 98. He came in the Anne, in 1623. Some have thought that this was the mate of the Mayflower. But it is not known that his name was Thomas, nor is there any evidence that he ever returned to this country. See Thacher's Plymouth, 168.

[3] Bradford adds, in his History, "In the morning they find the place to be a small island, secure from Indians. And this being the last day of the week, they here dry their stuff, fix their pieces, rest themselves, return God thanks for their many deliverances; and here the next day keep their Christian Sabbath." Prince, p. 167.

And in the morning we marched about it, and found no inhabitants at all; and here we made our rendezvous all that day, being Saturday, 10th[1] of December. On the Sabbath day we rested; and on Monday we sounded the harbour, and found it a very good harbour for our shipping. We marched also into the land,[2]

CHAP. IX.

1620. Dec. 9—11

---

[1] This is an error. Saturday was the 9th; for on page 163 the next Saturday is called the 16th, and by Allestree's Almanac for 1620, I find that the 9th of December fell on a Saturday.

[2] This is the ever-memorable day of the Landing of the Fathers at Plymouth. "The place of the landing is satisfactorily ascertained. Unquestionable tradition had declared that it was on a large rock at the foot of a cliff near the termination of the north street leading to the water. In the year 1774 an attempt was made to remove this rock (over which a wharf had been built) to a more central situation. The rock was split in the operation. The upper part, weighing several tons, was removed, and now stands in front of the Pilgrim Hall, enclosed by a very appropriate iron railing, of an elliptical form. It is regarded by the inhabitants and by visiters as a precious memorial of that interesting event; the arrival of the first planters of New England at their place of settlement. The 22d of December, corresponding to the 11th, old style, has long been observed at Plymouth in commemoration of the landing of the Fathers. It has there universally the familiar and endearing appellation of *Forefathers' Day.*" See Morton's Memorial, p. 48, and Thacher's Plymouth, pp. 29, 199.

President Dwight, of Yale College, says, " Plymouth was the first town built in New England by civilized men; and those by whom it was built were inferior in worth to no body of men whose names are recorded in history during the last 1700 years. A kind of venerableness, arising from these facts, attaches to this town, which may be termed a prejudice. Still, it has its foundation in the nature of man, and will never be eradicated either by philosophy or ridicule. No New Englander, who is willing to indulge his native feelings, can stand upon the rock where our ancestors set the first foot after their arrival on the American shore, without experiencing emotions very different from those which are excited by any common object of the same nature. No New Englander could be willing to have that rock buried and forgotten. Let him reason as much, as coldly, and as ingeniously as he pleases, he will still regard that spot with emotions wholly different from those which are excited by other places of equal or even superior importance." Travels through New England, ii. 110.

De Tocqueville, in the second chapter of his work on America, says, " Ce rocher est devenu un objet de vénération aux Etats Unis. J'en ai vu des fragmens conservés avec soin dans plusieurs villes de l'Union. Ceci ne montre-t-il pas bien clairement que la puissance et la grandeur de l'homme est tout entière dans son ame ? Voici une pierre que les pieds de quelques misérables touchent un instant, et cette pierre devient célèbre; elle attire les regards d'un grand peuple; on en vénère les debris, on s'en partage au loin la poussière. Qu'est devenu le seuil de tant de palais ? Qui s'en inquiète ? " —

CHAP. and found divers cornfields, and little running brooks,
IX. a place very good for situation. So we returned to
1620. our ship¹ again with good news to the rest of our
Dec.
13. people, which did much comfort their hearts.

"This rock has become an object of veneration in the United States. I have seen bits of it carefully preserved in several towns of the Union. Does not this sufficiently show that all human power and greatness is in the soul of man? Here is a stone which the feet of a few outcasts pressed for an instant; and this stone becomes famous; it is treasured by a great nation; its very dust is shared as a relic. And what has become of the gateways of a thousand palaces? Who cares for them?"—Reeves's Trans.

[1] They left the Mayflower in Cape Cod harbour, December 6, and were three days in getting to Plymouth. They probably started on their return to the ship on the 12th, and striking across the bay, a distance of 25 miles, reached her on the 13th. They found that the day after their leaving the vessel, December 7, Dorothy, the wife of William Bradford, who was one of the party in the shallop, fell overboard, and was drowned. See Prince, p. 165.

CHAPTER X.

OF THEIR LANDING AND SETTLING AT NEW PLYMOUTH.

On the 15th day we weighed anchor to go to the place we had discovered; and coming within two leagues of the land, we could not fetch the harbour, but were fain to put round[1] again towards Cape Cod, our course lying west, and the wind was at northwest. But it pleased God that the next day, being Saturday the 16th day, the wind came fair, and we put to sea again, and came safely into a safe harbour; and within half an hour the wind changed, so as if we had been letted but a little, we had gone back to Cape Cod.

This harbour is a bay greater than Cape Cod, compassed with a goodly land; and in the bay two fine islands,[2] uninhabited, wherein are nothing but woods,

---

[1] In the original, *roome;* manifestly an error of the press.

[2] Clark's island is now the only island in Plymouth harbour. It has sometimes been supposed that a shoal, called Brown's island, which lies near the entrance of the harbour, about half a mile east by north of Beach point, was above water at the time the Pilgrims arrived. Gov. Winthrop, in his History of New England, i. 169, has the following record: October 6, 1635, two shallops going, laden with goods, to Connecticut, were taken with an easterly storm, and cast away upon Brown's island, near the Gurnet's Nose, and the men all drowned." Dr. Freeman, in his note on this place, considers this passage as confirming the supposition. But Morton, in recording the same event in his Memorial, p. 182, says, the night being dark and stormy, they ran upon a skirt of a *flat* that lieth near

CHAP. X.
1620.

oaks, pines, walnuts, beech, sassafras, vines, and other trees[1] which we know not. This bay is a most hopeful place; innumerable store of fowl,[2] and excellent good; and cannot but be of fish in their seasons; skate, cod, turbot,[3] and herring, we have tasted of; abundance of muscles, the greatest and best that ever we saw; crabs and lobsters,[4] in their time, infinite. It is in fashion like a sickle, or fish-hook.[5]

Dec. 18.

Monday, the 18th day, we went a land,[6] manned

the mouth of the harbour." This seems conclusive of the point that Brown's island was then under water. The other island I suppose was Saquish, which, although a peninsula, very much resembles an island, and may very naturally have been mistaken for one; or at that time the water may have flowed across the narrow neck which now unites it with the Gurnet, and completely isolated it. Oldmixon, i. 30, commits an egregious blunder when he states, that "the harbour (Plymouth) was a bay larger than Cape Cod, and two fine islands, Rhode Island and Elizabeth Island, in it!"

[1] The only forest trees now on Clark's island are three red cedars, which appear to be very old, and are decaying. This wood was the original growth of the island, a tree which loves the vicinity of rocks, which abound here. A few years since, the present proprietor of the island, whilst digging out some large roots on its margin, found a number of acorns four feet beneath the surface. Blackberry vines are still found there. On Saquish there is one solitary tree, which has weathered the storms of ages. In 1815 there were two. In earlier times the town forbade felling trees at Saquish within 40 feet of the bank. See Mass. Hist. Coll. xiii. 182.

[2] Wild fowl are yet abundant in Plymouth harbour.

[3] Skate and cod are still caught here. The European turbot, it is well known, is not found in our waters. The first settlers probably gave this name to the flounder or small halibut. See Storer's Report on the Fishes of Massachusetts, pp. 140, 145, 146. Higginson, in his New England's Plantation, enumerates the turbot among other fish. T. Morton, in his New English Canaan, ch. vii. says, "there is a large-sized fish, called halibut, or turbot; some are taken so big that two men have much ado to haul them into the boat." Wood, ch. ix. says, "the halibut is not much unlike a plaice or turbot, some being two yards long, and one wide, and a foot thick." And Josselyn, p. 26, says, "some will have the halibut and turbot all one; others distinguish them; there is no question to be made of it but that they are distinct kinds of fish." The turbot and plaice are very much alike in appearance. See the figures of them in Yarrell's British Fishes, i. 209, 233.

[4] There are muscles in Plymouth, but generally small, and clams; the Journal probably refers to the latter. Crabs and lobsters are very abundant in the summer season.

[5] The form of Plymouth Bay, which includes Kingston and Duxbury harbours, is accurately described.

[6] The words "in the long-boat" seem to be omitted.

THE TREES AND PLANTS OF PLYMOUTH. 165

with the master of the ship and three or four of the sailors. We marched along the coast in the woods some seven or eight miles,¹ but saw not an Indian nor an Indian house ; only we found where formerly had been some inhabitants, and where they had planted their corn. We found not any navigable river, but four or five small running brooks² of very sweet fresh water, that all run into the sea. The land for the crust of the earth is, a spit's depth,³ excellent black mould, and fat in some places ;⁴ two or three great oaks, but not very thick, pines, walnuts, beech, ash, birch, hazel, holly, asp, sassafras in abundance, and vines⁵ every where, cherry trees, plum trees, and many others which we know not.⁶ Many kinds of herbs we found here in winter, as strawberry leaves innumerable, sorrel, yarrow, carvel, brooklime, liverwort, water-

CHAP. X.

1 6 2 0.
Dec.
18.

---

¹ Whichever way the travellers went, they could not have walked seven miles ; because northwest, at the distance of four miles, they would have come to Jones's river in Kingston, and southeast, at the distance of three miles, to Eel river. These rivers, though not large, cannot be denominated brooks. F.
² North of the village, towards Kingston, there are five brooks, which were named by the original planters First Brook, Second Brook, &c. in order, beginning from the town. Half a mile south of the village is Wellingsly Brook, by the side of which dwelt Secretary Morton. Double Brook, or Shingle Brook of the first settlers, runs northerly by the post road to Sandwich, and unites with Eel river. Beaver Dam Brook is in the village of Manomet Ponds. Indian Brook is still further south on the shore. See Mass. Hist. Coll. xiii. 178, and Thacher's Plymouth, p. 322.
³ See note ⁵ on page 123.

⁴ This is an exact description of a strip of land, between the hills and the sea-shore, where the gardens now are. The soil too is good on Clark's Island, Saquish, and the Gurnet.
⁵ The wild grape, both white and red, the blackberry and the raspberry, are found here now.
⁶ All the trees here enumerated are now found in Plymouth. The asp, or aspen, was probably our native poplar. The beach, about three miles long, which lies in front of the village, extending from Eel river, N. N. West, and protecting the harbour, was originally well wooded. Towards the northern part, till 1770, it was quite thickly covered with trees. The inner side of the beach was covered with plum and wild-cherry trees, and the swamp with large pitch pine and beech wood. Beech plums, wild gooseberries, and white grapes were found here in great quantities in their proper season. See a list of the trees, in Mass. Hist. Coll.

CHAP. X.

1620.

cresses, great store of leeks and onions,[1] and an excellent strong kind of flax and hemp.[2] Here is sand, gravel, and excellent clay, no better in the world, excellent for pots, and will wash like soap, and great store of stone,[3] though somewhat soft, and the best water[4] that ever we drunk ; and the brooks now begin to be full of fish.[5] That night, many being weary with marching, we went aboard again.

Dec. 19.

The next morning, being Tuesday, the 19th of December, we went again to discover further ; some went on land, and some in the shallop. The land we found as the former day we did ; and we found a creek, and went up three English miles, a very pleasant river[6] at full sea. A bark of thirty tons may go up ; but at low water scarce our shallop could pass. This place we had a great liking to plant in, but that it was so far from our fishing, our principal profit, and so encompassed with woods, that we should be in much danger of the salvages ; and our number being so little, and so much ground to clear ; so as we thought good to

---

xiii. 165, 172, 206 ; Thacher's Plymouth, p. 328.

[1] These were probably the *allium Canadense.*

[2] The Indian hemp (*apocynum cannabinum.*) Wood says, ch. 5, " This land likewise affords hemp and flax naturally;" and Captain John Smith mentions " a kind or two of flax, wherewith they make nets, lines and ropes, both small and great, very strong for their quantities." T. Morton too, says, ch. 2, " there is hemp, that naturally groweth, finer than our hemp of England." See Mass. Hist. Coll. xxvi. 120.

[3] The sand, gravel and clay are aptly described. There is not much stone at Plymouth, except a few bowlders of sienite.

[4] Plymouth is abundantly supplied with springs and brooks of excellent water. F. See p. 129.

[5] Some years since, before the Town Brook was obstructed, tomcods were abundant in December ; eels and smelts enter the brooks in autumn.

[6] This was Jones's river, in Kingston, so called, it is supposed, by the Pilgrims, in compliment to the Captain of the Mayflower; which they would not have done had they entertained any doubt of his fidelity. Jones's river parish was set off from Plymouth in 1717, and incorporated in 1726, as the town of Kingston. See note [2] on p. 138, and Mass. Hist. Coll. xiii. 208 and 217.

quit and[1] clear that place till we were of more strength. Some of us, having a good mind, for safety, to plant in the greater isle, we crossed the bay, which is there five or six miles over, and found the isle about a mile and a half or two miles about,[2] all wooded, and no fresh water but two or three pits, that we doubted of fresh water in summer, and so full of wood as we could hardly clear so much as to serve us for corn. Besides, we judged it cold for our corn, and some part very rocky; yet divers thought of it as a place defensible, and of great security. That night we returned again a shipboard, with resolution the next morning to settle on some of those places.

So in the morning, after we had called on God for direction, we came to this resolution, to go presently ashore again, and to take a better view of two places which we thought most fitting for us; for we could not now take time for further search or consideration, our victuals being much spent, especially our beer, and it being now the 19th of December. After our landing and viewing of the places, so well as we could, we came to a conclusion, by most voices, to set on the main land, on the first place, on a high ground,[3] where there is a great deal of land cleared, and hath been planted with corn three or four years ago; and there is a very sweet brook[4] runs under the hill side, and many delicate springs of as good water as can be drunk, and where we may harbour our shallops and boats exceeding well; and in this brook much good

---

[1] I think the word *not* is here accidentally omitted.
[2] See note [1] on page 160.
[3] On the bank, facing the harbour.
[4] Now called Town brook. It issues from a pond called Billington Sea. F.

CHAP. X.

1620.

fish in their seasons; on the further side of the river also much corn-ground cleared.¹ In one field is a great hill,² on which we point to make a platform, and plant our ordnance, which will command all round about. From thence we may see into the bay, and far into the sea; and we may see thence Cape Cod.³ Our greatest labor will be fetching of our wood, which is half a quarter of an English mile; but there is enough so far off. What people inhabit here we yet know not, for as yet we have seen none. So there we made our rendezvous, and a place for some of our people, about twenty, resolving in the morning to come all ashore and to build houses.

Dec. 21.

But the next morning, being Thursday, the 21st of December, it was stormy and wet, that we could not go ashore; and those that remained there all night could do nothing, but were wet, not having daylight enough to make them a sufficient court of guard, to keep them dry. All that night it blew and rained extremely. It was so tempestuous that the shallop could not go on land so soon as was meet, for they had no victuals on land. About eleven o'clock the shallop went off with much ado with provision, but could not return, it blew so strong; and was such foul weather that we were forced to let fall our anchor, and ride with three anchors ahead.⁴

Dec. 22.

Friday, the 22d, the storm still continued, that we

---

¹ On the spot now called the Training Green.

² The Burial Hill, rising 165 feet above the level of the sea, and covering about eight acres. The view from this eminence, embracing the harbour, the beach, the Gurnet, Manomet Point, Clark's island, Saquish, Captain's Hill in Duxbury, and the shores of the bay for miles around, is unrivalled by any sea-view in the country.

³ In a clear day the white sand hills of Provincetown may be distinctly seen from this hill.

⁴ "Dec. 21, dies Richard Britterige, the first who dies in this harbour." Bradford, in Prince, p. 168.

could not get a land, nor they come to us aboard. This morning goodwife Alderton[1] was delivered of a son, but dead born.

Saturday, the 23d, so many of us as could went on shore, felled and carried timber, to provide themselves stuff for building.

Sunday, the 24th, our people on shore heard a cry of some savages, as they thought, which caused an alarm and to stand on their guard, expecting an assault; but all was quiet.[2]

Monday, the 25th day, we went on shore, some to fell timber, some to saw, some to rive, and some to carry;[3] so no man rested all that day. But, towards night, some, as they were at work, heard a noise of some Indians, which caused us all to go to our muskets; but we heard no further. So we came aboard again, and left some twenty to keep the court of guard. That night we had a sore storm of wind and rain.

Monday, the 25th, being Christmas day, we began to drink water aboard. But at night the master caused us to have some beer; and so on board we had divers times now and then some beer, but on shore none at all.

Tuesday, the 26th, it was foul weather, that we could not go ashore.

Wednesday, the 27th, we went to work again.

Thursday, the 28th of December, so many as could went to work on the hill, where we purposed to build

---

[1] This was the second child born. Its father was Isaac Allerton. The mother, named Mary, died Feb. 25.

[2] "Dec. 24, this day dies Solomon Martin, the sixth and last who dies this month." Bradford, in Prince, p. 168. He must have been a son of Christopher Martin.

[3] Bradford adds in his History, "They begin to erect the first house about twenty foot square, for their common use, to receive them and their goods." See Prince, p. 168.

CHAP. X.

1620.

our platform for our ordnance,[1] and which doth command all the plain and the bay, and from whence we may see far into the sea,[2] and might be easier impaled, having two rows of houses and a fair street. So in the afternoon we went to measure out the grounds, and first we took notice how many families there were, willing all single men that had no wives to join with some family, as they thought fit, that so we might build fewer houses; which was done, and we reduced them to nineteen families. To greater families we allotted larger plots;[3] to every person half a pole in breadth, and three in length; and so lots were cast where every man should lie; which was done, and staked out. We thought this proportion was large enough at the first, for houses and gardens to impale them round, considering the weakness of our people, many of them growing ill with colds; for our former discoveries in frost and storms, and the wading at Cape Cod had brought much weakness amongst us, which increased so every day more and more, and after was the cause of many of their deaths.

Dec. 29. 30.

Friday and Saturday we fitted ourselves for our labor; but our people on shore were much troubled and discouraged with rain and wet that day, being very stormy and cold. We saw great smokes of fire made by the Indians, about six or seven miles from us, as we conjectured.[4]

---

[1] Vestiges of this fortification are still visible on the Burial hill. See Holmes's Annals, i. 163.

[2] I think there is something omitted here. The house-lots were not laid out on the hill, but in front of it, on Leyden-street, which runs from the Town Square to Water-street.

[3] The single lots were 8 1-4 feet front by 49 1-2 in depth.

[4] "Here," says Prince, p. 169, "Governor Bradford ends his First Book, containing ten Chapters, in fifty-three pages folio." I conceive that much of this Relation is in substance, and often in language, Gov. Bradford's History.

STANDISH GOES IN SEARCH OF THE INDIANS. 171

Monday, the 1st of January, we went betimes to work. We were much hindered in lying so far off from the land, and fain to go as the tide served, that we lost much time; for our ship drew so much water that she lay a mile and almost a half off,[1] though a ship of seventy or eighty tons at high water may come to the shore.

Wednesday, the 3d of January, some of our people being abroad to get and gather thatch, they saw great fires of the Indians; and were at their corn-fields, yet saw none of the savages, nor had seen any of them since we came to this bay.

Thursday, the 4th of January, Captain Miles Standish, with four or five more, went to see if they could meet with any of the savages in that place where the fires were made. They went to some of their houses, but not lately inhabited; yet could they not meet with any. As they came home, they shot at an eagle and killed her, which was excellent meat; it was hardly to be discerned from mutton.

Friday, the 5th of January, one of the sailors found alive upon the shore a herring, which the master had to his supper; which put us in hope of fish, but as yet we had got but one cod; we wanted small hooks.[2]

Saturday, the 6th of January, Master Marten was very sick, and, to our judgment, no hope of life. So Master Carver was sent for to come aboard to speak

CHAP. X.

1621. Jan. 1.

3.

4.

5.

6.

---

[1] Being a vessel of 180 tons, she probably anchored in the Cow Yard, an anchorage near Clark's island, which takes its name from a cow whale which once came into it, and was there killed. See Mass. Hist. Coll. xiii. 182, and Thacher's Plymouth, p. 331.

"The year begins with the death of Degory Priest." Bradford, in Prince, p. 182.

[2] This was a singular oversight. If they had had fish-hooks, they could hardly have suffered so much for want of food. Winslow, in his Good News from New England, says they wanted "fit and strong seines and other netting."

CHAP. X.

1621.
Jan.
8.

with him about his accounts; who came the next morning.

Monday, the 8th of January, was a very fair day, and we went betimes to work. Master Jones sent the shallop, as he had formerly done, to see where fish could be got. They had a great storm at sea, and were in some danger. At night they returned with three great seals,[1] and an excellent good cod, which did assure us that we should have plenty of fish shortly.

This day Francis Billington, having the week before seen from the top of a tree on a high hill a great sea,[2] as he thought, went with one of the master's mates to see it. They went three miles and then came to a great water, divided into two great lakes; the bigger of them five or six miles in circuit, and in it an isle of a cable length square; the other three miles in compass, in their estimation. They are fine fresh water, full of fish and fowl. A brook[3] issues from it; it will be an excellent place for us in time. They found seven or eight Indian houses, but not lately inhabited.

---

[1] Seals still haunt the harbour of Plymouth and the Bay of Cape Cod.

[2] The beautiful pond, so accurately described in the text, bears the appropriate name of Billington Sea. In the first century it was called Fresh Lake. It is about two miles southwest from the town, proving that the distances in this Relation are overstated; and in it are two small islands. It is now, as at first, embosomed in a wilderness of woods. The eagle still sails over it, and builds in the branches of the surrounding forest. Here the loon cries, and leaves her eggs on the shore of the smaller island. Here too the beautiful wood-duck finds a sequestered retreat; and the fallow deer, mindful of their ancient haunts, still resort to it to drink and to browse on its margin. See page 149, and Mass. Hist. Coll. xiii. 181, and Thacher's Plymouth, p. 320.

[3] Town Brook. It passes through the town, and empties into the harbour a little south of Forefathers' rock. It has proved an "excellent place" indeed, its stream supplying an unfailing water power for numerous manufactories. In 1636, it was "concluded upon by the Court, that Mr. John Jenney shall have liberty to erect a mill for grinding and beating of corn upon the brook of Plymouth." Before the brook was so much impeded by dams, vast quantities of alewives passed up through it annually to Billington Sea. In a single season 800 barrels have been taken. See Thacher's Plymouth, p. 321, 332; Plymouth Colony Laws, p. 56.

When they saw the houses, they were in some fear; for they were but two persons, and one piece.¹

Tuesday, the 9th of January, was a reasonable fair day; and we went to labor that day in the building of our town, in two rows of houses, for more safety.² We divided by lot the plot of ground whereon to build our town, after the proportion formerly allotted. We agreed that every man should build his own house, thinking by that course men would make more haste than working in common.³ The common house,⁴ in which for the first we made our rendezvous, being near finished, wanted only covering, it being about twenty foot square. Some should make mortar, and some gather thatch; so that in four days half of it was thatched. Frost and foul weather hindered us much.⁵

¹ "Jan. 8, this day dies Mr. Christopher Martin." Bradford, in Prince, p. 182. He was the ninth signer of the Compact, and one of the few distinguished with the title of Mr. He was not one of the Leyden church, but came from Billerica, in Essex, and was associated with Cushman and Carver to provide means for the voyage. He brought his wife and two children, with him, one of whom, Solomon, died Dec. 24. See pages 78 and 169.

² The houses were built on each side of Leyden street, which extends from the First Church to the harbour. The first entry in the records of Plymouth Colony is an incomplete list of "The Meersteads and Garden-plotes of those which came first, layed out, 1620." Edward Winslow, in his Letter at the end of this Relation, says, "We have built seven dwelling-houses, and four for the use of the plantation." The highway led to the Town Brook.

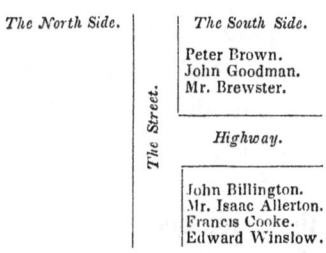

See Hazard's State Papers, i. 100.
³ See note ¹ on page 84.
⁴ On the spot where it is supposed the common house stood, in digging a cellar, in 1801, there were discovered sundry tools and a plate of iron, seven feet below the surface of the ground. F.
⁵ Providentially it was a very mild winter. See page 105. The ice often remains in the harbour from Christmas to March; but at this time it appears not to have been frozen. In Dec. of 1831 and 1834 the harbour and shores were an expanse of ice and snow, and the thermometer several degrees

CHAP. X.

This time of the year seldom could we work half the week.

1621. Jan. 11.

Thursday, the 11th, William Bradford being at work, (for it was a fair day,) was vehemently taken with a grief and pain, and so shot to his huckle-bone,[1] it was doubted that he would have instantly died. He got cold in the former discoveries, especially the last; and felt some pain in his ankles by times; but he grew a little better towards night, and in time, through God's mercy in the use of means, recovered.

12.

Friday the 12th we went to work; but about noon it began to rain, that it forced us to give over work.

This day two of our people put us in great sorrow and care. There was four sent to gather and cut thatch in the morning; and two of them, John Goodman and Peter Browne,[2] having cut thatch all the forenoon, went to a further place, and willed the other two to bind up that which was cut, and to follow them. So they did, being about a mile and a half from our plantation. But when the two came after, they could not find them, nor hear any thing of them at all, though they hallooed and shouted as loud as they could. So they returned to the company, and told them of it. Whereupon Master Carver,[3] and three or four more

below zero. Had it been so when the Pilgrims landed, they must have perished from cold. See Mass. Hist. Coll. xiii. 196, and Thacher's Plymouth, p. 27.

[1] Hip-bone.

[2] Goodman and Brown both had lots assigned them in Leyden-street, in 1620. Nothing more is known of Goodman, except that he died before the end of March. Brown had also an acre assigned him in the division of the lands in 1623, and a share in the division of the cattle in 1627, with Martha and Mary Brown, the former of whom was probably his wife, and the latter his daughter.

[3] In the original, *Leaver;* unquestionably a typographical error. There is no such name as Leaver among the signers of the Compact, and it is not at all probable that one of the ship's crew would be distinguished by the title of Mr. or be sent on such an errand. This error escaped the acute observation of Prince, who copies the

went to seek them; but could hear nothing of them. So they returning, sent more; but that night they could hear nothing at all of them. The next day they armed ten or twelve men out, verily thinking the Indians had surprised them. They went seeking seven or eight miles; but could neither see nor hear any thing at all. So they returned, with much discomfort to us all.

CHAP.
X.

1621.
Jan.
12.

These two that were missed at dinner time, took their meat in their hands, and would go walk and refresh themselves. So going a little off, they find a lake of water,[1] and having a great mastiff bitch with them and a spaniel, by the water side they found a great deer.[2] The dogs chased him; and they followed so far as they lost themselves, and they could not find the way back. They wandered all that afternoon, being wet; and at night it did freeze and snow. They were slenderly apparelled, and had no weapons but each one his sickle, nor any victuals. They ranged up and down and could find none of the salvages' habitations. When it drew to night, they were much per-

---

passage, p. 183. Edward Winslow, at the end of his Preface to the Reader in his Good News from New England, says, "some faults have escaped because I could not attend on the press." This probably was also the case with this Relation. It was sent over to George Morton, who not being in London, where it was printed, did not correct the proof sheets. He probably put it into the hands of one of the merchant adventurers, who got it printed. It is not surprising that some mistakes should have been made by the printer in deciphering the MS. See note on page 113. This will account for Morton's name, as well as Carver's, and Williams's being misspelt.

[1] Probably Murdock's Pond, about half a mile from the village, in the rear of Burial hill. It is a deep, round pond. A brook, called Little Brook, issues from it, and crossing the west road, unites with Town brook. See Mass. Hist. Coll. xiii. 181, and Thacher's Plymouth, p. 320.

[2] The fallow deer still run in the extensive woods of Plymouth, a district of country nearly twenty miles square. In Jan. 1831, 160 were killed and 40 taken alive. In Feb. 1839, a deer chased by the dogs, came into the streets of the village, and was caught in the front yard of the Hon. N. M. Davis's house. See Thacher's Plymouth, p. 314.

CHAP. X.
1621.
Jan. 13.

plexed; for they could find neither harbour nor meat; but, in frost and snow, were forced to make the earth their bed and the element their covering. And another thing did very much terrify them; they heard, as they thought, two lions[1] roaring exceedingly for a long time together, and a third that they thought was very near them. So not knowing what to do, they resolved to climb up into a tree, as their safest refuge, though that would prove an intolerable cold lodging. So they stood at the tree's root, that when the lions came, they might take their opportunity of climbing up. The bitch they were fain to hold by the neck, for she would have been gone to the lion. But it pleased God so to dispose, that the wild beasts came not. So they walked up and down under the tree all night. It was an extreme cold night. So soon as it was light, they travelled again, passing by many lakes[2] and brooks

[1] Several of the first settlers of New England supposed that the lion existed here. Higginson, in his New-England's Plantation says, "For beasts, there are some bears, and they say some lions also; for they have been seen at Cape Ann." Wood, in his New-England's Prospect, ch. 6, says, "Concerning lions I will not say that I ever saw any myself; but some affirm that they have seen a lion at Cape Ann. Some likewise being lost in the woods, have heard such terrible roarings, as have made them much aghast; which must be either devils or lions; there being no other creatures which use to roar, saving bears, which have not such a terrible kind of roaring." Josselyn, in his New-England's Rarities, p. 21, says, "The Jackal is a creature that hunts the lion's prey, a shrewd sign that there are lions upon the continent. There are those that are yet living in the country that do constantly affirm, that about 36 or 37 years since, an Indian shot a young lion, sleeping upon the body of an oak blown up by the roots, with an arrow, not far from Cape Ann, and sold the skin to the English." Lechford, too, in his Plain Dealing, p. 47, and Johnson, in his Wonderworking Providence, b. ii. ch. 21, mention the lion among the beasts of New England. Vanderdonck also enumerates lions among the wild animals of New Netherlands. But Morton, in his New English Canaan, ch. 5, remarks, "Lions there are none in New England; it is contrary to the nature of the beast to frequent places accustomed to snow." Dr. Freeman observes, that Goodman and Brown, coming from England, where both the lion and the wolf are unknown, might easily, under the impression of fear, mistake the howling of the one for the roaring of the other.

[2] Plymouth abounds with ponds, that would be called lakes in England. It is supposed that within

and woods, and in one place where the salvages had burnt the space of five miles in length, which is a fine champaign country, and even.¹ In the afternoon, it pleased God from a high hill they discovered the two² isles in the bay, and so that night got to the plantation, being ready to faint with travail and want of victuals, and almost famished with cold. John Goodman was fain to have his shoes cut off his feet, they were so swelled with cold; and it was a long while after ere he was able to go. Those on the shore were much comforted at their return; but they on shipboard were grieved at deeming them lost.

But the next day, being the 14th of January, in the morning about six of the clock, the wind being very great, they on shipboard spied their great new rendezvous on fire; which was to them a new discomfort, fearing, because of the supposed loss of the men, that the salvages had fired them. Neither could they presently go to them for want of water. But after three quarters of an hour they went, as they had purposed the day before to keep the Sabbath on shore,³ because now there was the greater number of people. At their landing they heard good tidings of the return of the two men, and that the house was fired occasionally by a spark that flew into the thatch, which instantly burnt it all up; but the roof stood, and little hurt. The most loss was Master Carver's and William Bradford's,⁴ who

---

the bounds of the town there are more than two hundred. See Mass. Hist. Coll. xiii. 180, and Thacher's Plymouth, p. 320.
¹ A plain commences two miles from the town, and extends six miles southwest. F.
² See note ² on page 163.
³ This seems to be the first sab-
bath which they kept on shore. Prince, p. 169, adduces no authority for his assertion, that "the 31st of Dec. seems to be the first day that any keep the sabbath in the place of their building."
⁴ The omission of Mr. before Bradford's name in this place, and on pages 126, 136, 149, and else-

CHAP. X.
1621.

then lay sick in bed, and if they had not risen with good speed, had been blown up with powder; but, through God's mercy, they had no harm. The house was as full of beds as they could lie one by another, and their muskets charged; but, blessed be God, there was no harm done.

Jan. 15.

Monday, the 15th day, it rained much all day, that they on shipboard could not go on shore, nor they on shore do any labor, but were all wet.

Tuesday, Wednesday, Thursday, were very fair, sunshiny days, as if it had been in April; and our people, so many as were in health, wrought cheerfully.

19.

The 19th day we resolved to make a shed to put our common provision in, of which some were already set on shore; but at noon it rained, that we could not work. This day, in the evening, John Goodman went abroad to use his lame feet, that were pitifully ill with the cold he had got, having a little spaniel with him. A little way from the plantation two great wolves ran after the dog; the dog ran to him and betwixt his legs for succour. He had nothing in his hand, but took up a stick and threw at one of them and hit him, and they presently ran both away, but came again. He got a pale-board in his hand; and they sat both on their tails grinning at him a good while; and went their way and left him.

20.

Saturday, 20th, we made up our shed for our common goods.

21.

Sunday, the 21st, we kept our meeting on land.

22.

Monday, the 22d, was a fair day. We wrought on

where, whilst it is prefixed to the names of persons unquestionably his inferiors, as Mr. Christopher Martin, p. 171, is a strong presumption that this Relation was written by Bradford. If any other person had been the author, he would have prefixed Mr. to Bradford's name.

our houses; and in the afternoon carried up our hogsheads of meal to our common storehouse. The rest of the week we followed our business likewise.

Monday, the 29th, in the morning, cold, frost, and sleet; but after reasonable fair. Both the long-boat and the shallop brought our common goods on shore.[1]

Tuesday and Wednesday, 30th and 31st of January, cold, frosty weather and sleet, that we could not work. In the morning, the master and others saw two savages, that had been on the island near our ship. What they came for we could not tell. They were going[2] so far back again before they were descried, that we could not speak with them.

Sunday, the 4th of February, was very wet and rainy, with the greatest gusts of wind that ever we had since we came forth; that though we rid in a very good harbour, yet we were in danger, because our ship was light, the goods taken out, and she unballasted; and it caused much daubing[3] of our houses to fall down.

Friday, the 9th, still the cold weather continued, that we could do little work. That afternoon, our little house for our sick people was set on fire by a spark that kindled in the roof; but no great harm was done. That evening, the master going ashore, killed five geese, which he friendly distributed among the sick people. He found also a good deer killed. The savages had cut off the horns, and a wolf was eating of him. How he came there we could not conceive.

---

[1] "Jan. 29, dies Rose, the wife of Captain Standish. N. B. This month eight of our number die." Bradford, in Prince, p. 184.

[2] Probably a typographical error for *gone*.

[3] Their houses were probably log-huts, thatched, and the interstices filled with clay.

TWO INDIANS MAKE THEIR APPEARANCE.

CHAP. X.

1621. Feb. 16.

Friday, the 16th, was a fair day; but the northerly wind continued, which continued the frost. This day, after noon, one of our people being a fowling, and having taken a stand by a creek side in the reeds, about a mile and a half from our plantation, there came by him twelve Indians, marching towards our plantation, and in the woods he heard the noise of many more. He lay close till they were passed, and then with what speed he could he went home and gave the alarm. So the people abroad in the woods returned and armed themselves, but saw none of them; only, toward the evening, they made a great fire about the place where they were first discovered. Captain Miles Standish and Francis Cooke being at work in the woods, coming home left their tools behind them; but before they returned, their tools were taken away by the savages. This coming of the savages gave us occasion to keep more strict watch, and to make our pieces and furniture ready, which by the moisture and rain were out of temper.

17. Saturday, the 17th day, in the morning, we called a meeting for the establishing of military orders among ourselves; and we chose Miles Standish our captain, and gave him authority of command in affairs. And as we were in consultation hereabouts, two savages presented themselves upon the top of a hill,[1] over against our plantation, about a quarter of a mile and less, and made signs unto us to come unto them; we likewise made signs unto them to come to us. Whereupon we armed ourselves and stood ready, and sent

---

[1] Watson's Hill, called by the first settlers Strawberry Hill. The Indian name was Cantaugcanteest. When the summit of the hill was levelled in 1814, Indian relics of various kinds were found. See Mass. Hist. Coll. iii. 177.

two over the brook¹ towards them, to wit, Captain Standish and Steven Hopkins,² who went towards them. Only one of them had a musket, which they laid down on the ground in their sight, in sign of peace, and to parley with them. But the savages would not tarry their coming. A noise of a great many more was heard behind the hill; but no more came in sight. This caused us to plant our great ordnances in places most convenient.

Wednesday, the 21st of February,³ the master came on shore, with many of his sailors, and brought with him one of the great pieces, called a minion,⁴ and helped us to draw it up the hill, with another piece that lay on shore, and mounted them, and a saller, and two bases. He brought with him a very fat goose to eat with us, and we had a fat crane and a mallard, and a dried neat's tongue; and so we were kindly and friendly together.

Saturday, the 3d of March, the wind was south, the morning misty, but towards noon warm and fair weather. The birds sang in the woods most pleasantly. At one of the clock it thundered, which was

¹ The Town Brook. See note³ on page 172.
² See note² on page 126.
³ "February 21. Die Mr. William White, Mr. William Mullins, with two more; and the 25th dies Mary, the wife of Mr. Isaac Allerton. N. B. This month seventeen of our number die." Bradford, in Prince, p. 184. Mullins and White were the 10th and 11th signers of the Compact; each of them brought his wife over, and each had three others, probably children, in his family. White was the father of the first child born in New England, as mentioned on page 148. William Mullins is described by Morton, in his Memorial, p. 50, as "a man pious and well deserving, endowed also with a considerable outward estate; and had it been the will of God that he had survived, might have proved a useful instrument in his place."
⁴ The *minion* was a piece of ordnance, the bore of which was 3 1-4 inches diameter. The *saker* (for which saller is probably a misprint,) was a larger gun, the diameter of which at the bore was from 3 1-2 to 4 inches; and the *base* was the smallest sort of artillery, the diameter of whose bore was only 1 1-4 inch. See Crabb's Univ. Tech. Dict.

the first we heard in that country. It was strong and great claps, but short; but after an hour it rained very sadly till midnight.

Wednesday, the 7th of March, the wind was full east, cold, but fair. That day Master Carver, with five others, went to the great ponds,[1] which seem to be excellent fishing places. All the way they went they found it exceedingly beaten, and haunted with deer; but they saw none. Amongst other fowl they saw one, a milk-white fowl, with a very black head. This day some garden seeds were sown.

Friday, the 16th, a fair warm day towards.[2] This morning we determined to conclude of the military orders, which we had begun to consider of before, but were interrupted by the savages, as we mentioned formerly. And whilst we were busied hereabout, we were interrupted again; for there presented himself a savage, which caused an alarm. He very boldly came all alone, and along the houses, straight to the rendezvous; where we intercepted him, not suffering him to go in,[3] as undoubtedly he would out of his boldness. He saluted us in English, and bade us "*Welcome!*" for he had learned some broken English among the Englishmen that came to fish at Monhiggon,[4] and knew by name the most of the captains, commanders, and masters, that usually come.[5] He was a man free in

---

[1] Billington Sea.
[2] Perhaps the word *noon* was here accidentally omitted.
[3] They were unwilling he should see how few and weak they were. They had already lost nearly half of their number, and had the Indians attacked them in their sickly and enfeebled state, they would have fallen an easy prey.

[4] Monhegan, an island on the coast of Maine, between the Kennebec and the Penobscot, and about 12 miles distant from the shore. It was an early and favorite place of resort for the English fishermen. See Williamson's Maine, i. 61.
[5] Seeing the Mayflower in the harbour, he no doubt took her for a fishing-vessel. This explains his

speech, so far as he could express his mind, and of a seemly carriage. We questioned him of many things; he was the first savage we could meet withal. He said he was not of these parts, but of Morattiggon,[1] and one of the sagamores or lords thereof; and had been eight months in these parts, it lying hence a day's sail with a great wind, and five days by land. He discoursed [2] of the whole country, and of every province, and of their sagamores, and their number of men and strength. The wind beginning to rise a little, we cast a horseman's coat about him; for he was stark naked, only a leather about his waist, with a fringe about a span long or little more. He had a bow and two arrows, the one headed, and the other unheaded. He was a tall, straight man, the hair of his head black, long behind, only short before, none on his face at all. He asked some beer, but we gave him strong water, and biscuit, and butter, and cheese, and pudding, and a piece of mallard; all which he liked well, and had been acquainted with such amongst the English. He told us the place where we now live is called Patuxet, and that about four years ago all the inhabitants died of an extraordinary plague,[3] and there is

---

boldness in coming directly to them.

[1] Morattiggon. I know not what part of the country this was meant to designate. Perhaps it is an error for Monhiggon. Samoset evidently was desirous of magnifying his own importance, in giving the Pilgrims to understand that he was a sagamore.

[2] It is difficult to conceive how they could converse together so as to be mutually understood. Edward Winslow, in his Good News from New England, written two years afterwards, when they had had more intercourse with the natives, says, "As for the language, it is very copious, large, and difficult. As yet we cannot attain to any great measure thereof, but can understand them, and explain ourselves to their understanding by the help of those that daily converse with us."

[3] All the early writers on New England agree, that for three or four years previous to the arrival of the Pilgrims, a deadly pestilence had raged all along the seaboard, from the Penobscot to Narraganset Bay. The two tribes dwelling at

CHAP. neither man, woman, nor child remaining, as indeed
X.
we have found none ; so as there is none to hinder our
1621. possession, or to lay claim unto it. All the afternoon
Mar.
16. we spent in communication with him. We would
gladly have been rid of him at night, but he was not
willing to go this night. Then we thought to carry

these extremes, as well as the Nauset Indians, on Cape Cod, escaped, whilst the intermediate inhabitants were almost entirely swept off. Some tribes were nearly extinct; the Massachusetts, in particular, are said to have been reduced from 30,000 to 300 fighting men. Capt. Dermer, who was here in 1619, says, "I passed along the coast where I found some ancient plantations, not long since populous, now utterly void. In other places a remnant remains, but not free of sickness; their disease the plague, for we might perceive the sores of some that had escaped, who described the spots of such as usually die." Higginson, in his New England's Plantation, printed in 1630, says, "Their subjects above twelve years since, were swept away by a great and grievous plague that was amongst them, so that there are very few left to inhabit the country." Morton, in his New English Canaan, b. i. ch. 3, says, "Some few years before the English came to inhabit at New Plymouth, the hand of God fell heavily upon the natives, with such a mortal stroke, that they died on heaps. In a place where many inhabited, there hath been but one left alive to tell what became of the rest ; and the bones and skulls upon the several places of their habitations made such a spectacle after my coming into these parts, that as I travelled in that forest, near the Massachusetts, it seemed to me a new-found Golgotha. This mortality was not ended when the Brownists of New Plymouth were settled at Patuxet, and by all likelihood the sickness that these Indians died of was the plague, as by conference with them since my arrival and habitation in these parts I have learned." Johnson, in his Wonderworking Providence, b. i. ch. 8, says, "About the year 1618, a little before the removal of that church of Christ from Holland to Plymouth in New England, as the ancient Indians report, there befell a great mortality among them, chiefly desolating those places where the English afterwards planted ; their disease being a sore consumption, sweeping away whole families, but chiefly young men and children, the very seeds of increase." "What this disease was," says Gookin, who wrote in 1674, "that so generally and mortally swept away the Indians, I cannot well learn. Doubtless it was some pestilential disease. I have discoursed with some old Indians, that were then youths, who say that the bodies all over were exceeding yellow, describing it by a yellow garment they showed me, both before they died, and afterwards." "There are some old planters," says Increase Mather, writing in 1677, " surviving to this day, who helped to bury the dead Indians, even whole families of them all dead at once." See Purchas, iv. 1778 ; Mass. Hist. Coll. i. 122, 148, xii. 66 ; Hutchinson, i. 34.

In the Great Patent of New England, granted Nov. 3, 1620, the desolating effects of this pestilence are assigned by King James as a reason for granting it. "We have been further given certainly to know, that within these late years there hath, by God's visitation,

him on shipboard, wherewith he was well content, and went into the shallop; but the wind was high and the water scant, that it could not return back. We lodged him that night at Steven Hopkins's house,[1] and watched him.

CHAP. X.

1621.

The next day he went away back to the Masasoits,[2] from whence he said he came, who are our next bordering neighbours. They are sixty strong, as he saith. The Nausites are as near, southeast of them, and are a hundred strong; and those were they of whom our people were encountered, as we before related. They are much incensed and provoked against the English; and about eight months ago slew three Englishmen, and two more hardly escaped by flight to Monhiggon. They were Sir Ferdinando Gorge's[3]

Mar. 17.

---

reigned a wonderful plague amongst the savages there heretofore inhabiting, in a manner to the utter destruction, devastation, and depopulation of that whole territory, so as there is not left, for many leagues together, in a manner, any that do claim or challenge any kind of interest therein; whereby we, in our judgment, are persuaded and satisfied that the appointed time is come in which Almighty God, in his great goodness and bounty towards us and our people, hath thought fit and determined, that these large and goodly territories, deserted as it were by their natural inhabitants, should be possessed and enjoyed by such of our subjects and people as shall by his mercy and favor, and by his powerful arm, be directed and conducted thither." Plymouth Colony Laws, p. 3.

Hutchinson, in his Hist. of Mass. i. 35, remarks, "Our ancestors supposed an immediate interposition of Providence in the great mortality among the Indians, to make room for the settlement of the English.

I am not inclined to credulity, but should not we go into the contrary extreme if we were to take no notice of the extinction of this people in all parts of the continent? In some the English have made use of means the most likely to have prevented it; but all to no purpose. Notwithstanding their frequent ruptures with the English, very few comparatively have perished by wars. They waste, they moulder away, and, as Charlevoix says of the Indians of Canada, they disappear."

[1] See note [2] on page 126.

[2] The English, not understanding Samoset perfectly, supposed that by Massasoit he meant an Indian tribe; but this was the name of the great sagamore, as appears afterwards. F.

[3] See the Life of Sir Ferdinando Gorges in Belknap's Am. Biog. i. 346 — 393, and his Brief Narration, in Mass. Hist. Coll. xxvi. 45 — 93. In this work, p. 63, he mentions an attack that was made in July, 1620, by the Indians of Martha's Vineyard on Capt. Dermer and his com_

CHAP. X.
1621.

men, as this savage told us; as he did likewise of the *huggery*, that is, fight, that our discoverers had with the Nausites, and of our tools that were taken out of the woods, which we willed him should be brought again; otherwise we would right ourselves. These people are ill affected towards the English by reason of one Hunt,[1] a master of a ship, who deceived the people and got them, under color of trucking with them, twenty out of this very place where we inhabit, and seven men from the Nausites, and carried them away, and sold them for slaves, like a wretched man (for twenty pound a man,) that cares not what mischief he doth for his profit.

Mar. 17.

Saturday, in the morning, we dismissed the salvage, and gave him a knife, a bracelet, and a ring. He promised within a night or two to come again and to bring with him some of the Massasoyts, our neighbours, with such beavers' skins as they had to truck with us.

18.

Saturday and Sunday reasonable fair days. On this day came again the savage, and brought with him five other tall, proper men. They had every man a deer's

pany, whom he had sent over to New England. Dermer lost all his men but one, and received fourteen wounds in this encounter; which took place just eight months before; and there can hardly be a doubt that these were the "Sir Ferdinando Gorge's men," mentioned in the text. Dermer had previously been at Nautican, or Nauset. See Prince's Annals, pp. 157, 186.

[1] The name of this Captain Hunt has come down to us loaded with deserved infamy, as the first kidnapper and slave-dealer on the coast of North America. There is a difference in the accounts of the number of the natives which he thus seized and carried off. The President and Council of New England, in their Brief Relation of its Discovery and Plantation, state the number as 24; Gorges mentions 30; whilst Capt. John Smith says 27, agreeing with the number mentioned in the text. Hunt carried these Indians to Spain, where they were humanely rescued and set at liberty by the monks of Malaga. Several of them got over to England, and proved of essential service to Gorges. See Mass. Hist. Coll. xix. 6, xxvi. 58, 61, 132.

skin on him, and the principal of them had a wild cat's skin, or such like, on the one arm. They had most of them long hosen[1] up to their groins, close made, and above their groins to their waist another leather; they were altogether like the Irish trousers.[2] They are of complexion like our English gipseys; no hair or very little on their faces; on their heads long hair to their shoulders, only cut before; some trussed up before with a feather, broad-wise, like a fan; another a fox tail, hanging out. These left (according to our charge given him before) their bows and arrows a quarter of a mile from our town. We gave them entertainment as we thought was fitting them. They did eat liberally of our English victuals. They made semblance unto us of friendship and amity. They sang and danced after their manner, like antics. They brought with them in a thing like a bow-case, (which the principal of them had about his waist,) a little of their corn pounded to powder, which, put to a little water, they eat.[3] He

[1] Leggins.
[2] Morton, in his New English Canaan, b. i. ch. 6, says, "Of such deer's skins as they dress bare, they make stockings, that come within their shoes, like a stirrup stocking, and is fastened above at their belt, which is about their middle. When they have their apparel on, they look like Irish, in their trousers, the stockings join so to their breeches." Wood, in his New England's Prospect, part ii. ch. 5, says, " In the winter time the more aged of them wear leather drawers, in form like Irish trousers, fastened under their girdles with buttons."
[3] " The Indians make a .certain sort of meal of parched maize. This meal they call *nokake*. It is so sweet, toothsome, and hearty, that an Indian will travel many days with no other food but this meal, which he eateth as he needs, and after it drinketh water. And for this end, when they travel a journey, or go a hunting, they carry this nokake in a basket or bag, for their use." Gookin, in Mass. Hist. Coll. i. 150. — " *Nokehick*, parched meal, which is a ready, very wholesome food, which they eat with a little water, hot or cold. I have travelled with near two hundred of them at once, near a hundred miles through the woods, every man carrying a little basket of this at his back, and sometimes in a hollow leather girdle about his middle, sufficient for a man three or four days. With this ready provision, and their bows and arrows, are they ready for war and travel at an hour's warning. With a spoonful of this meal, and a spoon-

had a little tobacco in a bag; but none of them drank[1] but when he liked. Some of them had their faces painted black, from the forehead to the chin, four or five fingers broad; others after other fashions, as they liked. They brought three or four skins; but we

ful of water from the brook, have I made many a good dinner and supper." Roger Williams's Key, in Mass. Hist. Coll. iii. 208. — " If their imperious occasions cause them to travel, the best of their victuals for their journey is *nocake*, (as they call it,) which is nothing but Indian corn parched in the hot ashes. The ashes being sifted from it, it is afterwards beat to powder, and put into a long leathern bag, trussed at their backs like a knapsack, out of which they take thrice three spoonfuls a day, dividing it into three meals. If it be in winter, and snow be on the ground, they can eat when they please, stopping snow after their dusty victuals. In summer they must stay till they meet with a spring or brook, when they may have water to prevent the imminent danger of choking. With this strange *viaticum*, they will travel four or five days together, with loads fitter for elephants than men." Wood's New England's Prospect, part ii. ch. 6.

[1] That is, *smoked*. This was formerly a common expression. Thus Brereton, in his Journal of Gosnold's Voyage, says, " they gave us also of their tobacco, which they *drink* green, but dried into powder, very strong and pleasant." Rosier, in his account of Weymouth's Voyage to New England, in 1605, reprinted in Mass. Hist. Coll. xxviii. 142, says, " We *drank* of their excellent tobacco, as much as we would, with them; but we saw not any great quantity to truck for, and it seemed they had not much left of old, for they spend a great quantity yearly by their continual *drinking*."

Johnson, in his Wonderworking Providence, b. i. ch. 41, mentions a lusty man, (doubtless Underhill,) who held forth to his pastor before the whole congregation, that the spirit of revelation came to him as he was *drinking* a pipe of tobacco." In the Records of Plymouth Colony, under the year 1646, is the following entry. " Anthony Thacher and George Pole were chosen a committee to draw up an order concerning disorderly *drinking* tobacco." — This use of language was probably descriptive of the manner in which the weed was formerly inhaled, and which still prevails in the East. Lane, in his account of the Manners and Customs of the Modern Egyptians, i. 187, says, " In smoking, the people of Egypt, and of other countries of the East, draw in their breath freely, so that much of the smoke descends into the lungs; and the terms which they use to express ' smoking tobacco' signify ' *drinking* smoke,' or ' *drinking* tobacco.' "

Winslow, in his Good News from New England, says, " The men take much tobacco." Roger Williams, in his Key, chs. ii. and xx. says, " They generally all take tobacco, and it is the only plant which men labor in, the women managing all the rest. They say they take tobacco for two causes; first, against the rheum, which causeth the toothache, which they are impatient of; secondly, to revive and refresh them, they drinking nothing but water. Their tobacco bag hangs at their neck, or sticks at their girdle, and is to them instead of an English pocket."

would not truck with them at all that day,¹ but wished them to bring more, and we would truck for all; which they promised within a night or two, and would leave these behind them, though we were not willing they should; and they brought us all our tools again, which were taken in the woods, in our men's absence. So, because of the day, we dismissed them so soon as we could. But Samoset, our first acquaintance, either was sick or feigned himself so, and would not go with them, and stayed with us till Wednesday morning. Then we sent him to them, to know the reason they came not according to their words; and we gave him a hat, a pair of stockings and shoes, a shirt, and a piece of cloth to tie about his waist.

The Sabbath day, when we sent them from us, we gave every one of them some trifles, especially the principal of them. We carried them, along with our arms, to the place where they left their bows and arrows; whereat they were amazed, and two of them began to slink away, but that the other called them. When they took their arrows we bade them farewell, and they were glad; and so, with many thanks given us, they departed, with promise they would come again.

Monday and Tuesday proved fair days. We digged our grounds and sowed our garden seeds.

Wednesday a fine warm day. We sent away Samoset.

That day we had again a meeting to conclude of laws and orders for ourselves, and to confirm those military orders that were formerly propounded, and twice broken off by the savages' coming. But so we were again the third time; for after we had been an

---

¹ It was Sunday.

CHAP. X.
1621.

hour together, on the top of the hill[1] over against us two or three savages presented themselves, that made semblance of daring us, as we thought. So Captain Standish with another, with their muskets, went over to them, with two of the master's mates that follows them without arms,[2] having two muskets with them. They whetted and rubbed their arrows and strings, and made show of defiance; but when our men drew near them, they ran away. Thus were we again interrupted by them. This day, with much ado, we got our carpenter, that had been long sick of the scurvy, to fit our shallop to fetch all from aboard.

Mar. 22.

Thursday, the 22d of March, was a very fair, warm day. About noon we met again about our public business. But we had scarce been an hour together, but Samoset came again, and Squanto,[3] the only native

---

[1] The same hill on which the two Indians appeared, Feb. 17. See note on page 180.

[2] By *arms* must be here meant side arms, swords, &c., as it is stated they had muskets.

[3] Also called Squantum, or Tisquantum. There is some discrepancy in the early accounts of Squanto's captivity. Gorges, in his Brief Narration, ch. 2, says that "there happened to come into the harbour of Plymouth, where I then commanded, one Captain Weymouth, who happened into a river on the coast of America, called Pemmaquid, (the Penobscot,) from whence he brought five of the natives, three of whose names were Manida, Sketwarroes, and Tasquantum, whom I seized upon. They were all of one nation, but of several parts and several families." This was in 1605. But the Governor and Council for New England, in their Relation, printed in 1622, say, "It pleased God to send into our hands Tasquantum, one of those savages that formerly had been betrayed by this unworthy Hunt before named. But this savage being at that time in Newfoundland, Master Dermer, who was there also, found the means to give us intelligence of him, and his opinion of the good use that might be made of his employment." Dermer took Tisquantum with him to England, and on his return to New England in the spring of 1619, brought him back to his native country. In a letter dated Dec. 27, of that year, he says, "When I arrived at my savage's native country, finding all dead, I travelled almost a day's journey westward to a place called Nummastaquyt, (Namasket,) where finding inhabitants, I despatched a messenger a day's journey further west to Poconaokit, which bordereth on the sea; whence came to see me two kings, attended with a guard of fifty armed men, who being well satisfied with that my savage and I discoursed unto them, being de-

of Patuxet, where we now inhabit, who was one of the twenty captives that by Hunt were carried away, and had been in England, and dwelt in Cornhill with Master John Slanie,[1] a merchant, and could speak a little English, with three others; and they brought with them some few skins to truck, and some red herrings, newly taken and dried, but not salted; and signified unto us, that their great sagamore, Masasoyt,[2] was hard by, with Quadequina, his brother, and all their men. They could not express well in English what they would;[3] but after an hour the king came to the top of a hill [4] over against us, and had in his train sixty men, that we could well behold them, and they us. We were not willing to send our governor to them, and they were [5] unwilling to come to us. So

1621.
Mar.
22.

sirous of novelty, gave me content in whatsoever I demanded." These two kings were undoubtedly Massasoit and Quadequina. On going to Virginia, in June, Dermer left Tisquantum at Sawahquatooke, now Saco, whence he probably returned to Patuxet and Namasket. In another letter, dated June 30, 1620, Dermer says, " Squanto cannot deny but that the Pocanokets would have killed me when I was at Namassaket, had he not entreated hard for me." See Mass. Hist. Coll. xxvi. 50, 62, xix. 7, 10, 13 ; Purchas, iv. 1778; Morton's Memorial, pp. 55 — 59.

The beautiful promontory in Quincy, near Thompson's island, will perpetuate the name of this early friend of the Pilgrims. They probably called it after him in their first expedition to the Massachusetts in 1621, when he accompanied them as interpreter. This is probably the same place which is called Squanto's Chapel, by Morton, in his New English Canaan, b. ii. chs. 6 and 8.

" [1] The worshipful John Slany, of London, merchant," was one of the undertakers of the Newfoundland plantation, and treasurer of the Company. He probably sent Squanto to Newfoundland. See Whitebourne's Newfoundland, p. v. and Purchas, iv. 1876, 1888.

[2] Prince says, in his Annals, p. 187, " The printed accounts generally spell him Massasoit ; Gov. Bradford writes him Massasoyt and Massasoyet ; but I find the ancient people, from their fathers in Plymouth Colony, pronounce his name Ma-sas-so-it." It will be seen hereafter that Winslow writes it Massassowat. The sachem, in conformity with a prevailing custom among the Indians, afterwards changed his name, and took that of Owsamequin or Woosamequen. See his Life in B. B. Thatcher's Indian Biography, i. 117 — 140, and in S. G. Drake's Book of the Indians, b. ii. 17 — 29.

[3] See note [2] on page 183.

[4] Watson's hill, mentioned twice before on pages 180 and 190.

[5] The word *were* was accidentally omitted in the original.

CHAP. X.

1621.
Mar. 22.

Squanto went again unto him, who brought word that we should send one to parley with him, which we did, which was Edward Winsloe, to know his mind, and signify the mind and will of our governor, which was to have trading and peace with him. We sent to the king a pair of knives, and a copper chain with a jewel at it. To Quadequina we sent likewise a knife, and a jewel to hang in his ear, and withal a pot of strong water, a good quantity of biscuit, and some butter; which were all willingly accepted.

Our messenger made a speech unto him, that King James saluted him with words of love and peace, and did accept of him as his friend and ally; and that our governor desired to see him and to truck with him, and to confirm a peace with him, as his next neighbour. He liked well of the speech, and heard it attentively, though the interpreters did not well express it. After he had eaten and drunk himself, and given the rest to his company, he looked upon our messenger's sword and armor, which he had on, with intimation of his desire to buy it; but, on the other side, our messenger showed his unwillingness to part with it. In the end, he left him in the custody of Quadequina, his brother, and came over the brook, and some twenty men following him, leaving all their bows and arrows behind them. We kept six or seven as hostages for our messenger. Captain Standish and Master Williamson[1] met the king at the brook, with half a dozen musketeers. They saluted him, and he them; so one

[1] There was a Thomas Williams, but no person of the name of Williamson, among the signers of the Compact. It is probably an error of the press. It is very unlikely that any one of the ship's company would be associated with Standish in this duty. Perhaps it should read Master Allerton, as we find that he went with Standish the next day. See p. 195. See also note on page 113, and note [3] on page 174. Williams was dead before the end of March.

going over, the one on the one side, and the other on the other, conducted him to a house then in building, where we placed a green rug and three or four cushions. Then instantly came our governor, with drum and trumpet after him, and some few musketeers. After salutations, our governor kissing his hand, the king kissed him; and so they sat down. The governor called for some strong water, and drunk to him; and he drunk a great draught, that made him sweat all the while after. He called for a little fresh meat, which the king did eat willingly, and did give his followers. Then they treated of peace, which was:

1. That neither he nor any of his should injure or do hurt to any of our people.

2. And if any of his did hurt to any of ours, he should send the offender, that we might punish him.

3. That if any of our tools were taken away, when our people were at work, he should cause them to be restored; and if ours did any harm to any of his, we would do the like to them.

4. If any did unjustly war against him, we would aid him; if any did war against us, he should aid us.

5. He should send to his neighbour confederates to certify them of this, that they might not wrong us, but might be likewise comprised in the conditions of peace.

6. That when their men came to us, they should leave their bows and arrows behind them, as we should do our pieces when we came to them.

Lastly, that doing thus, King James would esteem of him as his friend and ally.[1]

---

[1] "This treaty," says Belknap, "the work of one day, being honestly intended on both sides, was kept with fidelity as long as Mas-

All which the king seemed to like well, and it was applauded of his followers. All the while he sat by the governor, he trembled for fear. In his person he is a very lusty man, in his best years, an able body, grave of countenance, and spare of speech; in his attire little or nothing differing from the rest of his followers, only in a great chain of white bone beads about his neck; and at it, behind his neck, hangs a little bag of tobacco, which he drank,[1] and gave us to drink. His face was painted with a sad red, like murrey, and oiled both head and face, that he looked greasily. All his followers likewise were in their faces, in part or in whole, painted, some black, some red, some yellow, and some white, some with crosses, and other antic works;[2] some had skins on them, and some naked; all strong, tall men in appearance.

So after all was done, the governor conducted him to the brook, and there they embraced each other, and he departed; we diligently keeping our hostages. We expected our messenger's coming; but anon word was brought us that Quadequina was coming, and our messenger was stayed till his return; who presently came, and a troop with him. So likewise we entertained him, and conveyed him to the place prepared. He was very fearful of our pieces, and made signs of dislike, that they should be carried away; whereupon

---

sasoit lived, but was afterwards, in 1675, broken by Philip, his successor." Am Biog. ii. 214. In Sept. 1639, Massasoit and his eldest son, Mooanam, afterwards called Wamsutta, and in 1662 by the English named Alexander, came into the Court at Plymouth and desired that this ancient league and confederacy might stand and remain inviolable. It was accordingly ratified and confirmed by the government. See Morton's Memorial, p. 210.

[1] See note [1] on page 188.
[2] This description corresponds to the appearance of Black Hawk and Keokuk, and the braves of the Sacs and Foxes, on their visit to Boston in 1837.

commandment was given they should be laid away. He was a very proper, tall young man, of a very modest and seemly countenance, and he did kindly like of our entertainment. So we conveyed him likewise, as we did the king; but divers of their people stayed still. When he was returned, then they dismissed our messenger. Two of his people would have stayed all night; but we would not suffer it. One thing I forgot; the king had in his bosom, hanging in a string, a great long knife. He marvelled much at our trumpet, and some of his men would sound it as well as they could. Samoset and Squanto, they stayed all night with us; and the king and all his men lay all night in the woods, not above half an English mile from us, and all their wives and women with them. They said that within eight or nine days they would come and set corn on the other side of the brook, and dwell there all summer; which is hard by us. That night we kept good watch; but there was no appearance of danger.

The next morning, divers of their people came over to us, hoping to get some victuals, as we imagined. Some of them told us the king would have some of us come see him. Captain Standish and Isaac Alderton [1]

---

[1] Generally spelt ALLERTON. He was the fifth signer of the Compact on board the Mayflower. After the death of his wife Mary, Feb. 25, 1621, he married, in 1626, Fear, a daughter of Elder Brewster. She died in 1633, and he then married a third wife, named Johanna. His son Isaac graduated at Harvard College in 1650. Hutchinson, in his History of Massachusetts, ii. 461, says " Isaac Allerton or Alderton, the first assistant, was employed several times to negotiate matters in England relative to their trade, and at length left them and settled there. His male posterity settled in Maryland. If they be extinct, Point Alderton, at the entrance of Boston harbour, which took his name, will probably preserve it many ages." Judge Davis adds, in his edition of Morton's New England's Memorial, p. 394, " Like the promontory of Palinurus, it is respectfully regarded as the memorial of an ancient worthy; and the appellation, perpetuating the memory of a man of the greatest commercial enterprise in those

went venturously, who were welcomed of him after their manner. He gave them three or four ground-nuts and some tobacco. We cannot yet conceive but that he is willing to have peace with us; for they have seen our people sometimes alone two or three in the woods at work and fowling, whenas they offered them no harm, as they might easily have done; and especially because he hath a potent adversary, the Narowhigansets, that are at war with him, against whom he thinks we may be some strength to him; for our pieces are terrible unto them. This morning they stayed till ten or eleven of the clock; and our governor bid them send the king's kettle, and filled it full of pease, which pleased them well; and so they went their way.

Friday was a very fair day. Samoset and Squanto still remained with us. Squanto went at noon to fish for eels. At night he came home with as many as he could well lift in one hand; which our people were glad of; they were fat and sweet. He trod them out [1] with his feet, and so caught them with his hands, without any other instrument.

This day we proceeded on with our common business, from which we had been so often hindered by the salvages' coming; and concluded both of military

---

early times, is most fitly applied. 'Gaudet cognomine terra.'" — The accurate Hutchinson is for once in an error. Allerton removed to New Haven in Connecticut, previous to the last of March, 1647, and died there in 1659. We are indebted to the Rev. Leonard Bacon, of New Haven, for the discovery of this fact. His conjecture, however, is unfounded that Allerton left no daughter. It appears from Hutchinson, ii. 456, compared with Morton's Memorial, p. 381, that his daughter Mary, who married Thomas Cushman, son of Robert, was alive in 1698, the last survivor of the passengers in the Mayflower. See Mass. Hist. Coll. xxvii. 243 and 301, Professor Kingsley's Historical Discourse, p. 92, and Mitchell's Bridgewater, p. 356.

[1] Of the mud; probably at Eel river, so called from the abundance of eels which are taken there. About 150 barrels are annually caught. See Thacher's Plymouth, p. 322.

orders and of some laws[1] and orders as we thought behooveful for our present estate and condition; and did likewise choose[2] our governor for this year, 1621. which was Master John Carver, a man well approved amongst us.[3]

[March 24. Dies Elizabeth, the wife of Mr. Edward Winslow. N. B. This month thirteen of our number die. And in three months past, dies half our company; the greatest part in the depth of winter,

---

[1] In 1636 a code of laws was made, with a preamble containing an account of the settlement of the Colony. This Code was revised in 1658, and again in 1671, and printed with this title, "The Book of the General Laws of the Inhabitants of the Jurisdiction of New Plymouth." In 1685, a new digest of them was published. In 1836 these several codes were collected and digested into one volume by William Brigham, Esq. Counsellor at Law, agreeably to a Resolve of the Legislature of Massachusetts. It serves to illustrate the condition of the Colony at different periods, the manners, wants, and sentiments of our forefathers, the difficulties with which they struggled, and the remedies provided for their relief. See Mass. Hist. Coll. xxii. 265, 270.

Gov. Hutchinson, with unaccountable carelessness, has asserted, ii. 463, that "they never established any distinct code or body of laws;" grounding his assertion on a passage in Hubbard's Hist. of N. England, which implies no such thing. The quotation, imperfectly given by Hutchinson, is correctly as follows: "The laws they intended to be governed by were the laws of England, the which they were willing to be subject unto, though in a foreign land; and have since that time continued in that mind for the general, adding only some particular municipal laws of their own, suitable to their constitution, in such cases where the common laws and statutes of England could not well reach, or afford them help in emergent difficulties of the place; possibly on the same ground that Pacuvius sometimes advised his neighbours of Capua not to cashier their old magistrates till they could agree upon better to place in their room. So did these choose to abide by the laws of England, till they could be provided of better." Belknap's Am. Biog. ii. 242: Mass Hist. Coll. xv. 62.

[2] "Or rather confirm." Bradford in Prince, p. 188. It will be recollected that Carver had been chosen governor on the 11th of November, the same day on which the Compact was signed. It was now the 23d of March, and the new year beginning on the 25th, according to the calendar then in use, Carver was reëlected for the ensuing year. The question has sometimes been asked, Why was not Brewster chosen? The answer is given by Hutchinson, ii. 460. "He was their ruling elder, which seems to have been the bar to his being their governor, civil and ecclesiastical office in the same person being then deemed incompatible."

[3] Here the daily journal breaks off, and an interval of three months

CHAP. X.
1621.
Mar.

wanting houses and other comforts, being infected with the scurvy and other diseases, which their long voyage and unaccommodate condition brought upon them; so as there die sometimes two or three a day. Of a hundred persons scarce fifty remain; the living scarce able to bury the dead; the well not sufficient to tend the sick, there being, in their time of greatest distress, but six or seven, who spare no pains to help them. Two of the seven were Mr. Brewster, their reverend elder, and Mr. Standish, their captain. The like disease fell also among the sailors, so as almost half their company also die before they sail.[1] But the

occurs before the account of the expedition to Pokanoket, during which nothing is recorded. To fill up this chasm in some measure, I insert the following particulars, which Prince extracts from Gov. Bradford's History, and from his Register, in which he records some of the first deaths, marriages, and punishments at Plymouth.

[1] The exact bill of mortality, as collected by Prince, is as follows.

In December	6
In January	8
In February	17
In March	13
Total	44

Of these were subscribers to the Compact, 21
The wives of Bradford, Standish, Allerton, and Winslow, 4
Also, Edward Thomson, a servant of Mr. White, Jasper Carver, a son of the governor, and Solomon Martin, son of Christopher, 3
Other women, children and servants, whose names are not known, 16
—
44

Before the arrival of the Fortune in Nov. six more died, including Carver and his wife, making the whole number of deaths 50, and leaving the total number of the survivors 50. Of those not named among the survivors, being young men, women, children, and servants, there were 31; amongst whom, as appears from the list of names in the division of the lands in 1623, were Joseph Rogers, probably a son of Thomas, Mary Chilton, probably a daughter of James, Henry Samson, and Humility Cooper. See Baylies' Plymouth, i. 70; Belknap's Am. Biog. ii. 207; Morton's Memorial, p. 376.

Wood, in his New England's Prospect, ch. 2, says, "Whereas many died at the beginning of the plantations, it was not because the country was unhealthful, but because their bodies were corrupted with sea-diet, which was naught, the beef and pork being tainted, their butter and cheese corrupted, their fish rotten, and the voyage long by reason of cross winds, so that winter approaching before they could get warm houses, and the searching sharpness of that purer climate creeping in at the crannies of their crazed bodies, caused death

spring advancing, it pleases God the mortality begins to cease, and the sick and lame recover; which puts new life into the people, though they had borne their sad affliction with as much patience as any could do.

The first offence since our arrival is of John Billington, who came on board at London, and is this month convented before the whole company for his contempt of the Captain's lawful command with opprobrious speeches, for which he is adjudged to have his neck and heels tied together; but upon humbling himself and craving pardon, and it being the first offence, he is forgiven.[1]

April 5. We despatch the ship with Captain Jones, who this day sails from New Plymouth, and May 6 arrives in England.[2]

and sickness." Dudley, too, in his letter to the Countess of Lincoln, in Mass. Hist. Coll. viii. 43, remarks, "Touching the sickness and mortality which every first year hath seized upon us and those of Plymouth, (of which mortality it may be said of us almost as of the Egyptians, that there is not a house where there is not one dead, and in some houses many,) the natural causes seem to be, the want of warm lodging and good diet, to which Englishmen are habituated at home. Those of Plymouth, who landed in winter, died of scurvy, as did our poorer sort, whose housing and bedding kept them not sufficiently warm."

Holmes, in his Annals, i. 168, says, "Tradition gives an affecting picture of the infant colony during this critical and distressing period. The dead were buried on the bank, at a little distance from the rock where the fathers landed; and, lest the Indians should take advantage of the weak and wretched state of the English, the graves were lev-elled, and sown for the purpose of concealment. This information I received at Plymouth from the late Ephraim Spooner, a respectable inhabitant of that town, and deacon of the church, who accompanied me to the spot where those first interments were made. Human bones have been washed out of the bank, within the memory of the present generation. Deacon Spooner, then upwards of 70 years of age, had his information from Mr. Thomas Faunce, who was a ruling elder in the first church in Plymouth, and was well acquainted with several of the first settlers. Elder Faunce knew the rock on which they first landed; and hearing that it was covered in the erection of a wharf, was so affected, that he wept. His tears perhaps saved it from oblivion. He died Feb. 27, 1746, aged 99." See note [1] on page 161.

[1] See note [1] on page 149.

[2] It is a circumstance worthy of notice, that notwithstanding the hardships, privations, and mortality among the Pilgrims, not one of

DEATH OF GOVERNOR CARVER.

CHAP. X.

1621.
April

While we are busy about our seed, our governor, Mr. Carver, comes out of the field very sick, complains greatly of his head. Within a few hours his senses fail, so as he speaks no more, and in a few days after dies, to our great lamentation and heaviness. His care and pains were so great for the common good, as therewith, it is thought, he oppressed himself and shortened his days; of whose loss we cannot sufficiently complain; and his wife deceases about five or six weeks after.[1]

them was induced to abandon the enterprise and return home in the Mayflower. The ship had been detained so long "by reason of the necessity and danger that lay on them, because so many died both of themselves and the ship's company likewise; by which they became so few, as the master durst not put to sea until those that lived recovered of their sickness, and the winter over." Morton's Memorial, p. 67.

[1] "Before I pass on, I may not omit to take notice of the sad loss the church and this infant commonwealth sustained by the death of Mr. JOHN CARVER, who was one of the deacons of the church in Leyden, but now had been and was their first governor. This worthy gentleman was one of singular piety, and rare for humility, which appeared, as otherwise, so by his great condescendency, whenas this miserable people were in great sickness. He shunned not to do very mean services for them, yea, the meanest of them. He bare a share likewise of their labor in his own person, according as their great necessity required. Who being one also of a considerable estate, spent the main part of it in this enterprise, and from first to last approved himself not only as their agent in the first transacting of things, but also all along to the period of his life, to be a pious, faithful, and very beneficial instrument. He deceased in the month of April in the year 1621, and is now reaping the fruit of his labor with the Lord." MS. Records of Plym. Ch. vol. i. p. 27. See also Morton's Memorial, p. 68.

It is supposed that Carver's death was occasioned by a stroke of the sun; and yet, as Baylies observes, "it is not a little remarkable that such an effect should have been produced in this climate in the month of April." Morton says, "he was buried in the best manner they could, with as much solemnity as they were in a capacity to perform, with the discharge of some volleys of shot of all that bare arms."

Nothing is known of Carver previous to his appointment in 1617 as one of the agents of the Church at Leyden. Nor is any thing known of his immediate descendants. It will be seen by the Compact, p. 121, that there were 8 persons in his family. He lost a son Dec. 6, and his daughter Elizabeth married John Howland. See note [2] on page 149. The name of Carver does not appear in the assignment of the lands in 1623, nor in the division of the cattle in 1627; nor does it occur at any subsequent time in the annals of the Colony. "His children attained no civil

Soon after we choose Mr. William Bradford our governor and Mr. Isaac Allerton his assistant, who are by renewed elections continued together sundry years.

May 12. The first marriage in this place is of Mr. Edward Winslow to Mrs. Susanna White, widow of Mr. William White.[1]

June 18. The second offence is the first duel fought in New England, upon a challenge at single combat with sword and dagger, between Edward Doty and Edward Leister, servants of Mr. Hopkins. Both being wounded, the one in the hand, the other in the thigh, they are adjudged by the whole company to have their head and feet tied together, and so to lie for twenty-four hours, without meat or drink; which is begun to be inflicted, but within an hour, because of their great pains, at their own and their master's humble request, upon promise of better carriage, they are released by the governor.]

honors; they rose to no distinction; but less fortunate than the children of the other governors, they remained in obscurity, and were unnoticed by the people." William, the grandson (or nephew) of the governor, died at Marshfield, Oct. 2, 1760, at the age of 102. Not long before his death, this grandson, with his son, his grandson, and great grandson, were all at work together without doors, and the great great grandson was in the house at the same time. Many of the name are still living in various parts of the Old Colony. The town of Carver, in Plymouth County, will help to perpetuate it. Compare Hutchinson's Mass. ii. 456, with Mitchell's Hist. of Bridgewater, pp. 129 and 362; and see Baylies' Plymouth, i. 71, and Belknap's Am. Biog. ii. 179—216.

[1] Wm. White died Feb. 21, and Edward Winslow's first wife, March 24.

CHAPTER XI.

A JOURNEY TO PACKANOKICK, THE HABITATION OF THE GREAT KING MASSASOYT; AS ALSO OUR MESSAGE, THE ANSWER AND ENTERTAINMENT WE HAD OF HIM.[1]

CHAP. XI.

1621. June.

It seemed good to the company, for many considerations, to send some amongst them to Massasoyt, the greatest commander amongst the savages bordering upon us; partly to know where to find them, if occasion served, as also to see their strength, discover the country, prevent abuses in their disorderly coming unto us, make satisfaction for some conceived injuries to be done on our parts, and to continue the league of peace and friendship between them and us. For these and the like ends it pleased the governor to make choice of Steven Hopkins and Edward Winsloe to go unto him; and having a fit opportunity, by reason of a savage called Tisquantum, that could speak English, coming

---

[1] There can hardly be a doubt that the narrative of this expedition was written by Winslow. He and Hopkins were the only persons engaged in it, and of course one of them must have written it. That the author was Winslow, and not Hopkins, is rendered highly probable by the circumstance that Hopkins's name is mentioned first. The peculiar mode in which certain words are spelt corresponds with the manner in which they are spelt in Winslow's Good News from New England. Thus the name of their Indian interpreter is in both papers invariably called Tisquantum, whilst Bradford writes it Squanto. In both narratives too we read Paomet instead of Pamet.

EMBASSY TO MASSASOIT.

CHAP. XI.

1621. June.

unto us, with all expedition provided a horseman's coat of red cotton, and laced with a slight lace, for a present, that both they and their message might be the more acceptable amongst them.

The message was as follows: That forasmuch as his subjects came often and without fear upon all occasions amongst us, so we were now come unto him; and in witness of the love and good-will the English bear unto him, the governor hath sent him a coat, desiring that the peace and amity that was between them and us might be continued; not that we feared them, but because we intended not to injure any, desiring to live peaceably, and as with all men, so especially with them, our nearest neighbours. But whereas his people came very often, and very many together unto us, bringing for the most part their wives and children with them, they were welcome; yet we being but strangers as yet at Patuxet, alias New Plymouth,[1] and not knowing how our corn might prosper, we could no longer give them such entertainment as we had done, and as we desired still to do. Yet if he would be pleased to come himself, or any special friend of his desired to see us, coming from him they should be welcome. And to the end we might know them from others, our governor had sent him a copper chain; desiring if any messenger should come from him to us, we might know him by bringing it with him, and hearken

---

[1] Capt. John Smith, in his map of New England, published in 1616, had given the name of Plymouth to this place. Morton says in his Memorial, p. 56, "The name of Plymouth was so called, not only for the reason here named, but also because Plymouth, in Old England, was the last town they left in their native country; and for that they received many kindnesses from some Christians there." Smith says its Indian name was Accomack, and calls it "an excellent good harbour." The natives also called it Apaum. See Mass. Hist. Coll. xxiii. 1, and xxvi. 97, 119.

and give credit to his message accordingly; also requesting him that such as have skins should bring them to us, and that he would hinder the multitude from oppressing us with them. And whereas, at our first arrival at Paomet,[1] called by us Cape Cod, we found there corn buried in the ground, and finding no inhabitants, but some graves of dead new buried, took the corn, resolving, if ever we could hear of any that had right thereunto, to make satisfaction to the full for it; yet since we understand the owners thereof were fled for fear of us, our desire was either to pay them with the like quantity of corn, English meal, or any other commodities we had, to pleasure them withal; requesting him that some one of his men might signify so much unto them, and we would content him for his pains.[1] And last of all, our governor requested one favor of him, which was that he would exchange some of their corn for seed with us, that we might make trial which best agreed with the soil where we live.

With these presents and message we set forward the 10th June,[3] about nine o'clock in the morning, our guide resolving that night to rest at Namaschet,[4] a town under Massasoyt, and conceived by us to be very near, because the inhabitants flocked so thick upon every slight occasion amongst us; but we found it to be some

---

[1] See note [2] on page 125, and note [1] on page 202.
[2] See note [1] on page 134.
[3] "June 10th being Lord's Day, it is very unlikely that they set out then, and is also inconsistent with the rest of the Journal; whereas July 2d is Monday, when Governor Bradford says, 'We sent Mr. Edward Winslow and Mr. Steven Hopkins to see our new friend Massasoit;' though, to comport with the rest of the Journal, I conclude that on Monday, July 2d, they agreed to send, but set not out till the next morning." Prince, Ann. 191. Morton, in his Memorial, p. 69, says it was July 2.
[4] Namaschet, or Namasket; that part of Middleborough, which the English first began to settle. See Mass. Hist. Coll. iii. 148. Capt. Dermer was at this place in 1619. See note [3] on page 190.

fifteen English miles. On the way we found some ten or twelve men, women, and children, which had pestered us till we were weary of them, perceiving that (as the manner of them all is) where victual is easilest to be got, there they live, especially in the summer; by reason whereof, our bay affording many lobsters, they resort every spring-tide thither; and now returned with us to Namaschet. Thither we came about three o'clock after noon, the inhabitants entertaining us with joy, in the best manner they could, giving us a kind of bread called by them *maizium*,[1] and the spawn of shads, which then they got in abundance, insomuch as they gave us spoons to eat them. With these they boiled musty acorns; but of the shads we eat heartily. After this they desired one of our men to shoot at a crow, complaining what damage they sustained in their corn by them; who shooting some fourscore[2] off and killing, they much admired at it, as other shots on other occasions.

After this, Tisquantum told us we should hardly in one day reach Packanokick, moving us to go some eight miles further, where we should find more store and better victuals than there. Being willing to hasten our journey, we went and came thither at sunsetting, where we found many of the Namascheucks (they so calling the men of Namaschet) fishing upon a wear[3] which they had made on a river which belonged to them, where they caught abundance of bass. These welcomed us also, gave us of their fish, and we

---

[1] Made of *maize*, or Indian corn. See note [1] on page 131.
[2] Paces or yards, understood.
[3] At or near a village now called Titicut, on Taunton river, in the northwest part of Middleborough, adjoining Bridgwater, is a noted place, which was formerly called the Old Indian Wear. Though other wears have been erected on Taunton river, yet this is probably the place intended. F.

them of our victuals, not doubting but we should have enough where'er we came. There we lodged in the open fields, for houses they had none, though they spent the most of the summer there. The head of this river is reported to be not far from the place of our abode.[1] Upon it are and have been many towns, it being a good length. The ground is very good on both sides, it being for the most part cleared. Thousands of men have lived there, which died in a great plague[2] not long since; and pity it was and is to see so many goodly fields, and so well seated, without men to dress and manure the same. Upon this river dwelleth Massasoyt. It cometh into the sea at the Narrohigganset bay, where the Frenchmen so much use. A ship may go many miles up it, as the salvages report, and a shallop to the head of it; but so far as we saw, we are sure a shallop may.[3] But to return to our journey.

July 4.

The next morning we brake our fast, took our leave, and departed; being then accompanied with some six salvages. Having gone about six miles by the river side, at a known shoal place,[4] it being low water, they spake to us to put off our breeches, for we must wade through. Here let me not forget the valor and courage of some of the salvages on the opposite side of the river; for there were remaining alive only two men, both aged, especially the one, being above threescore. These two, espying a company of men entering the river, ran very swiftly, and low in the grass, to meet

---

[1] The Winnatuckset, one of the tributaries of Taunton river, has its source in Carver, seven miles from Plymouth.

[2] See note [3] on page 183.

[3] The river is navigable for sloops as far as Taunton.

[4] About six miles below Old Indian Wear is a noted wading place. The opposite shore of Taunton river is in Raynham. F.—Baylies, says, i. 75, it is "near the new forge on Taunton river, about three miles from the Green.

us at the bank; where, with shrill voices and great courage, standing charged upon us with their bows, they demanded what we were, supposing us to be enemies, and thinking to take advantage on us in the water. But seeing we were friends, they welcomed us with such food as they had, and we bestowed a small bracelet of beads on them. Thus far we are sure the tide ebbs and flows.

Having here again refreshed ourselves, we proceeded in our journey, the weather being very hot for travel; yet the country so well watered, that a man could scarce be dry, but he should have a spring at hand to cool his thirst, beside small rivers in abundance. But the salvages will not willingly drink but at a spring-head. When we came to any small brook, where no bridge was, two of them desired to carry us through of their own accords; also, fearing we were or would be weary, offered to carry our pieces; also, if we would lay off any of our clothes, we should have them carried; and as the one of them had found more special kindness from one of the messengers, and the other salvage from the other, so they showed their thankfulness accordingly in affording us all help and furtherance in the journey.

As we passed along, we observed that there were few places by the river but had been inhabited; by reason whereof much ground was clear, save of weeds, which grew higher than our heads. There is much good timber, both oak, walnut tree, fir, beech, and exceeding great chestnut trees. The country, in respect of the lying of it, is both champaign and hilly, like many places in England. In some places it is very rocky, both above ground and in it; and though

CHAP. XI.

1621.
July 4.

the country be wild and overgrown with woods, yet the trees stand not thick, but a man may well ride a horse amongst them.[1]

Passing on at length, one of the company, an Indian, espied a man, and told the rest of it. We asked them if they feared any. They told us that if they were Narrohigganset men, they would not trust them. Whereat we called for our pieces, and bid them not to fear; for though they were twenty, we two alone would not care for them. But they hailing him, he proved a friend, and had only two women with him. Their baskets were empty; but they fetched water in their bottles, so that we drank with them and departed. After we met another man, with other two women, which had been at rendezvous by the salt water; and their baskets were full of roasted crab fishes and other dried shell fish, of which they gave us; and we eat and drank with them, and gave each of the women a string of beads, and departed.

After we came to a town of Massasoyt's, where we eat oysters and other fish. From thence we went to Packanokick;[2] but Massasoyt was not at home.

---

[1] See note [3] on page 124.

[2] "This was a general name for the northern shore of Narraganset Bay, between Providence and Taunton rivers, and comprehending the present townships of Bristol, Warren, and Barrington, in the State of Rhode Island, and Swanzey, in Massachusetts. Its northern extent is unknown. The principal seats of Massasoit were at Sowams and Kikemuit. The former is a neck of land formed by the confluence of Barrington and Palmer's rivers; the latter is Mount Hope." Belknap's Am. Biog. ii. 221.

Callender, in his Historical Discourse on Rhode Island, says, that "Sowams is the neck since called Phebe's Neck, in Barrington;" but intimates in a note that "perhaps Sowams is properly the name of the river, where the two Swanzey rivers meet and run together for near a mile, when they empty themselves in the Narraganset Bay, or of a small island, where these two rivers meet, at the bottom of New Meadow Neck, so called." See Rhode Island Hist. Coll. iv. 84.

Morton says, p. 69, that "they found his (Massasoit's) place to be about forty miles from New Plymouth."

There we stayed, he being sent for. When news was brought of his coming, our guide Tisquantum requested that at our meeting we would discharge our pieces. But one of us going about to charge his piece, the women and children, through fear to see him take up his piece, ran away, and could not be pacified till he laid it down again; who afterward were better informed by our interpreter. Massasoyt being come, we discharged our pieces and saluted him; who, after their manner, kindly welcomed us, and took us into his house, and set us down by him; where, having delivered our foresaid message and presents, and having put the coat on his back and the chain about his neck, he was not a little proud to behold himself, and his men also to see their king so bravely attired.

For answer to our message, he told us we were welcome, and he would gladly continue that peace and friendship which was between him and us; and, for his men, they should no more pester us as they had done; also, that he would send to Paomet, and would help us with corn for seed, according to our request.

This being done, his men gathered near to him, to whom he turned himself and made a great speech; they sometimes interposing, and, as it were, confirming and applauding him in that he said. The meaning whereof was, as far as we could learn, thus: Was not he, Massasoyt, commander of the country about them? Was not such a town his, and the people of it? And should they not bring their skins unto us? To which they answered, they were his, and would be at peace with us, and bring their skins to us. After this manner he named at least thirty places, and their answer was as aforesaid to every one; so that as it was delightful, it was tedious unto us.

1621. This being ended, he lighted tobacco for us, and fell to discoursing of England and of the King's Majesty, marvelling that he would live without a wife.[1] Also he talked of the Frenchmen, bidding us not to suffer them to come to Narrohiganset, for it was King James's country, and he also was King James's man. Late it grew, but victuals he offered none; for indeed he had not any, being he came so newly home. So we desired to go to rest. He laid us on the bed with himself and his wife, they at the one end and we at the other, it being only planks laid a foot from the ground and a thin mat upon them.[2] Two more of his chief men, for want of room, pressed by and upon us; so that we were worse weary of our lodging than of our journey.

July 5. The next day, being Thursday, many of their *sachims*, or petty governors, came to see us, and many of their men also. There they went to their manner of games for skins and knives. There we challenged them to shoot with them for skins, but they durst not; only they desired to see one of us shoot at a mark, who

---

[1] Anne of Denmark, the wife of James I. of England, died on the 3d of March, 1619, aged 45. See Hume's Hist. of England, ch. xlix.

[2] "In their wigwams," says Gookin, "they make a kind of couch or mattress, firm and strong, raised about a foot high from the earth; first covered with boards that they split out of trees, and upon the boards they spread mats generally, and sometimes bear skins and deer skins. These are large enough for three or four persons to lodge upon; for their mattresses are 6 or 8 feet broad." Morton says, "Their lodging is made in three places of the house about the fire. They lie upon planks, commonly about a foot or eighteen inches above the ground, raised upon rails that are borne up upon forks. They lay mats under them, and coats of deer's skins, otters', beavers', racoons', and of bears' hides, all which they have dressed and converted into good leather, with the hair on, for their coverings; and in this manner they lie as warm as they desire." See Mass. Hist. Coll. i. 150, and New English Canaan, b. i. ch. 4.

shooting with hail-shot, they wondered to see the mark so full of holes.

About one o'clock Massasoyt brought two fishes that he had shot; they were like bream, but three times so big, and better meat.¹ These being boiled, there were at least forty looked for share in them; the most eat of them. This meal only we had in two nights and a day; and had not one of us bought a partridge, we had taken our journey fasting. Very importunate he was to have us stay with them longer. But we desired to keep the Sabbath at home; and feared we should either be light-headed for want of sleep, for what with bad lodging, the savages' barbarous singing, (for they use to sing themselves asleep,) lice and fleas within doors, and mosquitoes without, we could hardly sleep all the time of our being there; we much fearing that if we should stay any longer, we should not be able to recover home for want of strength. So that on the Friday morning, before sunrising, we took our leave and departed, Massasoyt being both grieved and ashamed that he could no better entertain us; and retaining Tisquantum to send from place to place to procure truck for us, and appointing another, called Tokamahamon, in his place, whom we had found faithful before and after upon all occasions.

At this town of Massasoyt's, where we before eat, we were again refreshed with a little fish, and bought about a handful of meal of their parched corn,² which was very precious at that time of the year, and a small string of dried shell-fish, as big as oysters.³ The

---

¹ Probably the fish called tataug. Belknap's Am. Biog. ii. 288.
² See note ³ on page 187.
³ These were probably clams.

latter we gave to the six savages that accompanied us, keeping the meal for ourselves. When we drank, we eat each a spoonful of it with a pipe of tobacco, instead of other victuals; and of this also we could not but give them so long as it lasted. Five miles they led us to a house out of the way in hope of victuals; but we found nobody there, and so were but worse able to return home. That night we reached to the wear[1] where we lay before; but the Namascheucks were returned, so that we had no hope of any thing there. One of the savages had shot a shad in the water, and a small squirrel, as big as a rat, called a *neuxis;* the one half of either he gave us, and after went to the wear to fish. From hence we wrote to Plymouth, and sent Tokamahamon before to Namasket, willing him from thence to send another, that he might meet us with Namasket. Two men now only remained with us; and it pleased God to give them good store of fish, so that we were well refreshed. After supper we went to rest, and they to fishing again. More they gat, and fell to eating afresh, and retained sufficient ready roast for all our breakfasts.

About two o'clock in the morning, arose a great storm of wind, rain, lightning, and thunder, in such violent manner that we could not keep in our fire; and had the savages not roasted fish when we were asleep, we had set forward fasting; for the rain still continued with great violence, even the whole day through, till we came within two miles of home. Being wet and weary, at length we came to Namaschet. There we

---

[1] See note [3] on page 205.

refreshed ourselves, giving gifts to all such as had showed us any kindness. Amongst others, one of the six that came with us from Packanokick, having before this on the way unkindly forsaken us, marvelled we gave him nothing, and told us what he had done for us. We also told him of some discourtesies he offered us, whereby he deserved nothing. Yet we gave him a small trifle; whereupon he offered us tobacco. But the house being full of people, we told them he stole some by the way, and if it were of that, we would not take it; for we would not receive that which was stolen, upon any terms; if we did, our God would be angry with us, and destroy us. This abashed him, and gave the rest great content. But, at our departure, he would needs carry him[1] on his back through a river whom he had formerly in some sort abused. Fain they would have had us to lodge there all night, and wondered we would set forth again in such weather. But, God be praised, we came safe home that night, though wet, weary, and surbated.[2]

CHAP. XI.
1621.
July 7.

[1] Undoubtedly the writer himself, Winslow.
[2] Surbated, with galled feet. They had been absent five days. They started Tuesday morning, and reached Pokanoket on Wednesday, spent Thursday there, left Friday morning before sunrise, and arrived at Plymouth Saturday evening.

CHAPTER XII.

A VOYAGE MADE BY TEN OF OUR MEN TO THE KINGDOM OF NAUSET, TO SEEK A BOY[1] THAT HAD LOST HIMSELF IN THE WOODS; WITH SUCH ACCIDENTS AS BEFELL US IN THAT VOYAGE.

CHAP. XII.
1621. 1st day.

THE 11th of June[2] we set forth, the weather being very fair. But ere we had been long at sea, there arose a storm of wind and rain, with much lightning and thunder, insomuch that a spout arose not far from us. But, God be praised, it dured not long, and we put in that night for harbour at a place called Cummaquid,[3] where we had some hope to find the boy. Two savages were in the boat with us. The one was Tisquantum, our interpreter; the other Tokamahamon, a special

---

[1] The name of this boy was John Billington, according to Bradford, in Prince, p. 192. He was the brother of Francis, who discovered Billington Sea, and the son of John, the first culprit. See note [1] on page 149, and note [2] on page 172. Massasoit had sent word he was at Nauset. See Prince, p. 192.

[2] "This date being inconsistent with several hints in the foregoing and following stories, I keep to Governor Bradford's original manuscript, and place it between the end of July and the 13th of August." Prince, p. 192.

[3] Barnstable harbour; which is formed by a neck of land, about half a mile wide, called Sandy Neck, which projects from Sandwich on the north shore, and runs east almost the length of the town. The harbour is about a mile wide, and four miles long. The tide rises in it from ten to fourteen feet. It has a bar running off northeast from the neck several miles, which prevents the entrance of large ships. Mass. Hist. Coll. iii. 12. See note [3] on page 159.

friend. It being night before we came in, we anchored in the midst of the bay, where we were dry at a low water. In the morning we espied savages seeking lobsters, and sent our two interpreters to speak with them, the channel being between them; where they told them what we were, and for what we were come, willing them not at all to fear us, for we would not hurt them. Their answer was, that the boy was well, but he was at Nauset; yet since we were there, they desired us to come ashore, and eat with them; which, as soon as our boat floated, we did, and went six ashore, having four pledges for them in the boat. They brought us to their sachim, or governor, whom they call Iyanough,[1] a man not exceeding twenty-six years of age, but very personable, gentle, courteous, and fair conditioned, indeed not like a savage, save for his attire. His entertainment was answerable to his parts, and his cheer plentiful and various.

One thing was very grievous unto us at this place. There was an old woman, whom we judged to be no less than a hundred years old, which came to see us, because she never saw English; yet could not behold us without breaking forth into great passion, weeping and crying excessively. We demanding the reason of it, they told us she had three sons, who, when Master Hunt[2] was in these parts, went aboard his ship to trade with him, and he carried them captives into Spain, (for Tisquantum at that time was carried away also,) by which means she was deprived of the comfort of her children in her old age. We told them we

---

[1] Sometimes called Iyanough of Cummaquid, and sometimes Iyanough of Mattakiest, which seems to be the country between Barnstable and Yarmouth harbours. See Prince, p. 193; Mass. Hist. Coll. i. 197, and iii. 15. F.

[2] See pages 186 and 190.

were sorry that any Englishman should give them that offence, that Hunt was a bad man, and that all the English that heard of it condemned him for the same; but for us, we would not offer them any such injury, though it would gain us all the skins in the country. So we gave her some small trifles, which somewhat appeased her.

2d day. After dinner we took boat for Nauset, Iyanough and two of his men accompanying us. Ere we came to Nauset,[1] the day and tide were almost spent, insomuch as we could not go in with our shallop;[2] but the sachim or governor of Cummaquid went ashore, and his men with him. We also sent Tisquantum to tell Aspinet,[3] the sachim of Nauset, wherefore we came. The savages here came very thick amongst us, and were earnest with us to bring in our boat. But we neither well could, nor yet desired to do it, because we had less cause to trust them, being they only had formerly made an assault upon us in the same place,[4] in time of

---

[1] The territory to which the English in 1651 gave the name of Eastham, and the northern part of which still retains the Indian name. The three light-houses, recently erected in that town are called the Nauset Lights. The principal seats of the Nauset Indians were at Namskeket, within the limits of Orleans, and about the cove, which divides this township from Orleans. Captain John Smith mentions twice "the isle Nawset," or "Nausit." See Mass. Hist. Coll. viii. 160, xxvi. 108, 119, and Plym. Col. Laws, p. 94.

[2] The water is very shoal at Nauset, or Eastham. See note [1] on page 152.

[3] "The Indians upon Cape Cod, although not considered a part of the Wamponoags, yet were supposed to be under some kind of subjection to Massasoit. There seem to have been two cantons or sachemdoms of the Cape Indians. One extended from Eel river in Plymouth, to the south shore of the Cape, and comprehended what are now called the Mashpee Indians, and then extended upon the Cape to the eastern part of Barnstable, and as far westward as Wood's Hole; and divers petty sachems or sagamores were comprehended in this division, of which Mashpee was one. The eastern part of the Cape, from Nobscusset, or Yarmouth, made another sachemdom, the capital of which was Nauset, or Eastham. Of these petty tribes the Nauset Indians appear to have been the most important." Hutchinson's Mass. i. 459, and Mass. Hist. Coll. viii. 159.

[4] See page 156.

our winter discovery for habitation. And indeed it was no marvel they did so; for howsoever, through snow or otherwise, we saw no houses, yet we were in the midst of them.

When our boat was aground, they came very thick; but we stood therein upon our guard, not suffering any to enter except two, the one being of Manamoick,[1] and one of those whose corn we had formerly found. We promised him restitution, and desired him either to come to Patuxet for satisfaction, or else we would bring them so much corn again. He promised to come. We used him very kindly for the present. Some few skins we gat there, but not many.

After sunset, Aspinet came with a great train, and brought the boy with him, one bearing him through the water.[2] He had not less than a hundred with him; the half whereof came to the shallop side unarmed with him; the other stood aloof with their bows and arrows. There he delivered us the boy, behung with beads, and made peace with us;[3] we bestowing a knife on him, and likewise on another that first entertained the boy and brought him thither. So they departed from us.

Here we understood that the Narrohiggansets had spoiled some of Massasoyt's men, and taken him. This struck some fear in us, because the colony was so weakly guarded, the strength thereof being abroad.[4]

---

[1] Chatham, the southern extremity of Cape Cod.

[2] "He had wandered five days, lived on berries, then light of an Indian plantation, twenty miles south of us, called Manomet, (Sandwich,) and they conveyed him to the people who first assaulted us." Bradford, in Prince, p. 192.

[3] Bradford adds, "We give them full satisfaction for the corn we had formerly found in their country." Prince, p. 193. See note [1] on page 134.

[4] There were ten men in this expedition. At the same time, according to the dates of this and the previous paper, Winslow and Hop-

But we set forth with resolution to make the best haste home we could; yet the wind being contrary, having scarce any fresh water left, and at least sixteen leagues[1] home, we put in again for the shore. There we met again with Iyanough, the sachim of Cummaquid, and the most of his town, both men, women and children with him. He, being still willing to gratify us, took a runlet,[2] and led our men in the dark a great way for water, but could find none good; yet brought such as there was on his neck with them. In the mean time the women joined hand in hand, singing and dancing before the shallop, the men also showing all the kindness they could, Iyanough himself taking a bracelet from about his neck and hanging it upon one of us.

Again we set out, but to small purpose; for we gat but little homeward. Our water also was very brackish, and not to be drunk. The next morning Iyanough espied us again, and ran after us. We, being resolved to go to Cummaquid again to water, took him into the shallop, whose entertainment was not inferior unto the former.

The soil at Nauset and here is alike, even and sandy, not so good for corn as where we are. Ships may safely ride in either harbour. In the summer they abound with fish. Being now watered, we put forth again, and by God's providence came safely home that night.

---

kins were absent on their expedition to Pokanoket, leaving only seven men at the Plantation, the whole number surviving at this time being nineteen.

[1] The distance from Eastham to Plymouth is not more than twelve leagues. F.
[2] A small barrel.

CHAPTER XIII.

A JOURNEY TO THE KINGDOM OF NAMASCHET, IN DEFENCE OF THE GREAT KING MASSASOYT AGAINST THE NARROHIGGANSETS, AND TO REVENGE THE SUPPOSED DEATH OF OUR INTERPRETER, TISQUANTUM.

AT our return from Nauset we found it true that Massasoyt was put from his country by the Narrohiggansets.[1] Word also was brought unto us that Coubatant,[2] a petty sachim or governor under Massasoyt, whom they ever feared to be too conversant with the Narrohiggansets, was at Namaschet; who sought to draw the hearts of Massasoyt's subjects from him; speaking also disdainfully of us, storming at the peace between Nauset, Cummaquid and us, and at Tisquantum, the worker of it; also at Tokamahamon and one Hobbamock, two Indians, our allies,[3] one of which he would treacherously have murdered a little before, being a special and trusty man of Massasoyt's. Tokamahamon went to him, but the other two would not;

CHAP. XIII.

1621. Aug.

---

[1] Gov. Bradford says nothing of this, nor of Massasoit's being either seized or invaded by the Narragansetts. Prince, p. 193.
[2] Gov. Bradford plainly writes him Corbitant. Prince, p. 194.
[3] In the original " or Lemes," to which no meaning can be attached. It is manifestly an error of the press, and I have given what I consider the true reading. See note [3] on page 174.

CHAP. XIII.

1621.

yet put their lives in their hands, privately went to see if they could hear of their king, and lodging at Namaschet were discovered to Coubatant, who set a guard to beset the house, and took Tisquantum; for he had said if he were dead, the English had lost their tongue. Hobbamock, seeing that Tisquantum was taken, and Coubatant held a knife at his breast, being a strong and stout man, brake from them and came to New Plymouth, full of fear and sorrow for Tisquantum, whom he thought to be slain.

Aug. 13.

Upon this news the company assembled together, and resolved on the morrow to send ten men armed to Namaschet, and Hobbamock for their guide, to revenge the supposed death of Tisquantum on Coubatant, our bitter enemy, and to retain Nepeof,[1] another sachim or governor, who was of this confederacy, till we heard what was become of our friend Massasoyt.

14.

On the morrow we set out ten[2] men, armed, who took their journey as aforesaid; but the day proved very wet. When we supposed we were within three or four miles of Namaschet, we went out of the way, and stayed there till night; because we would not be discovered. There we consulted what to do; and thinking best to beset the house at midnight, each was appointed his task by the Captain,[3] all men encouraging one another to the utmost of their power. By night our guide lost his way, which much discouraged our men, being we were wet, and weary of our arms. But one[4] of our men, having been before at Namaschet, brought us into the way again.

---

[1] This is the only time the name of this chief occurs in the annals of the Colony.

[2] Bradford says, "Captain Standish with 14 men." Prince, p. 194.

[3] Standish.

[4] Either Winslow or Hopkins, who stopped at Namaset in going

Before we came to the town, we sat down and ate such as our knapsacks afforded. That being done, we threw them aside, and all such things as might hinder us, and so went on and beset the house, according to our last resolution. Those that entered demanded if Coubatant were not there; but fear had bereft the savages of speech. We charged them not to stir; for if Coubatant were not there, we would not meddle with them. If he were, we came principally for him, to be avenged on him for the supposed death of Tisquantum, and other matters; but, howsoever, we would not at all hurt their women or children. Notwithstanding, some of them pressed out at a private door and escaped, but with some wounds. At length, perceiving our principal ends, they told us Coubatant was returned with all his train, and that Tisquantum was yet living and in the town; offering some tobacco, other such as they had to eat. In this hurly-burly we discharged two pieces at random, which much terrified all the inhabitants, except Tisquantum and Tokamahamon; who, though they knew not our end in coming, yet assured them of our honesty, that we would not hurt them. Those boys that were in the house, seeing our care of women, often cried *Neen squaes!*[1] that is to say, I am a woman;[2] the women also hanging upon Hobbamock, calling him *towam*, that is,

---

and returning from Pokanoket, in July. If it was Winslow, he may reasonably be considered the writer of this narrative.

[1] This is correct Indian in the Massachusetts and Narragansett dialects. See Eliot's Indian Grammar, in Mass. Hist. Coll. xix. 253; Cotton's Vocabulary of the Massachusetts language, in Mass. Hist. Coll. xxii. 156, 178; Roger Williams's Key to the native language of New England, ch. 5; Wood's Nomenclator, at the end of his New England's Prospect; and Gallatin's Indian Vocabularies, in Coll. Am. Antiq. Soc. ii. 308, 352.

[2] Rather, I am a girl; *squaes* being a diminutive, formed by adding *es* to *squa*. See the Apostle Eliot's Indian Grammar, in Mass. Hist. Coll. xix. 258.

friend.[1] But, to be short, we kept them we had, and made them make a fire, that we might see to search the house. In the mean time, Hobbamock gat on the top of the house, and called Tisquantum and Tokamahamon, which came unto us accompanied with others, some armed, and others naked. Those that had bows and arrows, we took them away, promising them again when it was day. The house we took, for our better safeguard, but released those we had taken, manifesting whom we came for and wherefore.

Aug. 15.

On the next morning, we marched into the midst of the town, and went to the house of Tisquantum to breakfast. Thither came all whose hearts were upright towards us; but all Coubatant's faction were fled away. There, in the midst of them, we manifested again our intendment, assuring them, that although Coubatant had now escaped us, yet there was no place should secure him and his from us, if he continued his threatening us, and provoking others against us, who had kindly entertained him, and never intended evil towards him till he now so justly deserved it. Moreover, if Massasoyt did not return in safety from Narrohigganset, or if hereafter he should make any insurrection against him, or offer violence to Tisquantum, Hobbamock, or any of Massasoyt's subjects, we would revenge it upon him, to the overthrow of him and his. As for those [who] were wounded, we were sorry for it, though themselves procured it in not staying in the house, at our command; yet if they would return home with us, our surgeon[2] should heal them.

---

[1] The most common word for friend, in the Massachusetts and Narragansett dialects was *netop* or *netomp*. See Cotton, in Mass. Hist. Coll. xxii. 165; Wood's Nomenclator; Roger Williams's Key, ch. 1, and Gallatin, in Coll. Am. Antiq. Soc. ii. 321.

[2] Their surgeon and physician was Mr. SAMUEL FULLER, the eighth

At this offer, one man and a woman that were wounded went home with us; Tisquantum and many other known friends accompanying us, and offering all help that might be by carriage of any thing we had, to ease us. So that by God's good providence we safely returned home the morrow night after we set forth.

CHAP. XIII.

1621.
Aug.
15.

signer of the Compact. In 1628, when the scurvy and a malignant distemper broke out among the first settlers at Salem, "Mr. Endicot, understanding that there was one at Plymouth that had skill in such diseases, sent thither for him; at whose request he was sent unto them." He was there again for the same purpose in May, 1629, after the arrival of Higginson's company. We find him also at Dorchester, in June 1630, at the request of Mr. Warham, "to let twenty of these people blood;" again at Salem, in July, and at Charlestown, in August of the same year, after the arrival of Winthrop's colony, whence he writes, "The sad news here is that many are sick, and many are dead. I here but lose time, and long to be at home. I can do them no good, for I want drugs, and things fitting to work with." He died in 1633, of an infectious fever. In the MS. Records of Plymouth Church, vol. i. p. 42, it is stated that "when the church came away out of Holland, they brought with them one deacon, Mr. Samuel Fuller, who officiated amongst them until his death. He was a good man, and full of the holy spirit." Morton says, that "he did much good in his place, being not only useful in his faculty, but otherwise, as he was a godly man, and served Christ in the office of a deacon in the church for many years, and forward to do good in his place, and was much missed after God removed him out of this world." His widow, Bridget, who came in the Anne, in 1623, and his son Samuel gave to the Plymouth church the lot of ground on which the parsonage now stands. See Morton's Memorial, pp. 143 and 173; Mass. Hist. Coll. iii. 66, 74—76, xiii. 186; and Prince's Annals, pp. 253 and 259.

CHAPTER XIV.

A RELATION OF OUR VOYAGE TO THE MASSACHUSETTS,[1] AND WHAT HAPPENED THERE.

CHAP. XIV.

1621.

IT seemed good to the company in general, that though the Massachusets had often threatened us, (as we were informed,) yet we should go amongst them, partly to see the country, partly to make peace with them, and partly to procure their truck. For these ends the governors chose ten men, fit for the purpose, and sent Tisquantum and two other salvages to bring us to speech with the people and interpret for us.

Sept. 18.

We set out about midnight, the tide then serving for us. We supposing it to be nearer than it is, thought to be there the next morning betimes; but it proved well near twenty leagues[2] from New Plymouth. We

---

[1] The territory and tribe probably took their name from the Blue Hills in Milton, which were originally called Massachusetts Mount. Smith speaks of them as "the high mountain of Massachusit." Cotton, in his Vocabulary of the Massachusetts language, gives the following definition: "Mâssa-chusett — a hill in the form of an arrow's head." Roger Williams says, "I had learnt that the Massachusetts was called so from the Blue Hills, a little island thereabout (in Narragansett Bay); and Connonicus's father and ancestors living in those southern parts, transferred and brought their authority and name into those northern parts." See Mass. Hist. Coll. vii. 75, xix. 1; xxvi. 120; R. I. Hist. Coll. iv. 208; and Hutchinson's Mass. i. 460.

[2] The distance from Plymouth to Boston by water is about 40 miles.

THE FIRST LANDING IN BOSTON. 225

came into the bottom of the bay;[1] but being late, we anchored and lay in the shallop, not having seen any of the people. The next morning we put in for the shore. There we found many lobsters, that had been gathered together by the salvages, which we made ready under a cliff.[2] The Captain[3] set two sentinels behind the cliff, to the landward, to secure the shallop, and taking a guide with him and four of our company, went to seek the inhabitants; where they met a woman coming for her lobsters. They told her of them, and contented her for them. She told them where the people were. Tisquantum went to them; the rest returned, having direction which way to bring the shallop to them.

The sachim or governor of this place is called Obbatinewat; and though he lives in the bottom of the Massachuset Bay,[4] yet he is under Massasoyt. He used us very kindly. He told us he durst not then remain in any settled place for fear of the Tarentines.[5] Also the squa sachim,[6] or Massachusets queen, was an enemy to him.

---

[1] By the bay is meant Boston harbour. It extends from Nantasket to Boston, and spreads from Chelsea to Hingham, containing about 75 square miles. See Snow's History of Boston, p. 113.

[2] Supposed to be Copp's hill, at the north end of Boston. At the first settlement of the town, in 1630, this hill, rising to the height of about fifty feet above the sea, presented on its northwest brow an abrupt declivity, long after known as Copp's hill steeps. See Snow's History of Boston, p. 105.

[3] Standish.

[4] By Massachusetts Bay was formerly understood only the inner bay, from Nahant to Point Alderton. Thus Gov. Winthrop speaks of going from Salem to Massachusetts. See Savage's Winthrop, i. 27.

[5] The Tarrateens or Tarrenteens resided on the Kennebec and the other rivers in Maine, and the country east of it. There was great enmity between them and the Indians of Massachusetts Bay, who, although they had formerly been a great people, yet were now so reduced that, upon alarms, they would fly to the English houses as to asylums, where the Tarrenteens durst not pursue them. Hutchinson's Mass. i. 28, 456.

[6] I suppose the widow of Nanepashemet, mentioned on the next page.

CHAP. XIV.
1621.

We told him of divers sachims that had acknowledged themselves to be King James's men,[1] and if he also would submit himself, we would be his safeguard from his enemies; which he did, and went along with us to bring us to the squa sachim. Again we crossed the bay, which is very large, and hath at least fifty islands in it;[2] but the certain number is not known to the inhabitants. Night it was before we came to that side of the bay where this people were. On shore the salvages went, but found nobody. That night also we rid at anchor aboard the shallop.

Sept. 21.

On the morrow we went ashore,[3] all but two men, and marched in arms up in the country. Having gone three miles we came to a place where corn had been newly gathered, a house pulled down, and the people gone. A mile from hence, Nanepashemet, their king, in his life-time had lived. His house was not like others, but a scaffold was largely built, with poles and planks, some six foot from [the] ground, and the house upon that, being situated on the top of a hill.[4]

[1] Of course he could not be, as Prince supposes, the Obbatinnua who, with eight other sachems, on the 13th of the same month, seven days before, had signed a paper, professing their submission to King James; unless his name was affixed subsequently to that date. See Morton's Memorial, p. 67, and Prince's Annals, p. 196.

[2] The number of islands in Boston harbour is not overstated, although several of them, such as Bird Island and Nick's Mate, have been washed away since this Journal was written. A list of them is contained in Snow's Boston, p. 114. Smith, in his Description of New England, says, "The country of the Massachusets is the paradise of all those parts; for here are many isles, all planted with corn, groves, mulberries, and salvage gardens." See Mass. Hist. Coll. iii. 295, and xxvi. 118.

[3] They probably landed at Squantum, in Quincy, which may have been so called by them at this time after their interpreter Tisquantum, who was one of the party. See note on page 191, and Mass. Hist. Coll. ix. 164.

[4] Perhaps Milton Hill, or some one of the Blue Hills. "At Massachusetts, near the mouth of Charles river, there used to be a general rendezvous of Indians. That circle, which now makes the harbours of Boston and Charlestown, round by Malden, Chelsea, Nantasket, Hingham, Weymouth, Braintree, and Dorchester, was the

Not far from hence, in a bottom, we came to a fort, built by their deceased king; the manner thus. There were poles, some thirty or forty feet long, stuck in the ground, as thick as they could be set one by another; and with these they enclosed a ring some forty or fifty foot over;[1] a trench, breast high, was digged on each side; one way there was to go into it with a bridge. In the midst of this palisado stood the frame of a house, wherein, being dead, he lay buried.[2]

About a mile from hence, we came to such another, but seated on the top of a hill. Here Nanepashemet was killed,[3] none dwelling in it since the time of his death. At this place we stayed, and sent two salvages to look [for] the inhabitants, and to inform them of our ends in coming, that they might not be fearful of us. Within a mile of this place they found the women of the place together, with their corn on heaps, whither we supposed them to be fled for fear of us; and the more, because in divers places they had newly pulled down their houses, and for haste in one place had left some of their corn covered with a mat, and nobody with it.

With much fear they entertained us at first; but seeing our gentle carriage towards them, they took heart and entertained us in the best manner they could,

---

capital of a great sachem, much reverenced by all the plantations of Indians round about, and to him belonged Naponset, (Milton,) Punkapog, (Stoughton,) Wessagusset, (Weymouth,) and several places on Charles river, where the natives were seated. The tradition is, that this sachem had his principal seat upon a small hill or rising upland, in the midst of a body of salt marsh in the township of Dorchester, near to a place called Squantum." Hutchinson's Mass. i. 460.

See also Gookin, in Mass. Hist. Coll. i. 148.

[1] This corresponds exactly with the engraving of the Pequot Fort in Underhill's Newes from America, printed in London in 1638, and reprinted in Mass. Hist. Coll. xxvi. 23.

[2] See page 154.

[3] Nanepashemet is supposed to have been killed in 1619, and his widow, the squa sachim, continued in the government. See Lewis's Hist. of Lynn, p. 16.

CHAP. XIV.

1621.
Sept.
21.

boiling cod and such other things as they had for us. At length, with much sending for, came one of their men, shaking and trembling for fear. But when he saw we intended them no hurt, but came to truck, he promised us his skins also. Of him we inquired for their queen; but it seemed she was far from thence;[1] at least we could not see her.

Here Tisquantum would have had us rifle the salvage women, and taken their skins and all such things as might be serviceable for us; for, said he, they are a bad people, and have oft threatened you. But our answer was, Were they never so bad, we would not wrong them, or give them any just occasion against us. For their words, we little weighed them; but if they once attempted any thing against us, then we would deal far worse than he desired.

Having well spent the day, we returned to the shallop, almost all the women accompanying us to truck, who sold their coats from their backs, and tied boughs about them, but with great shamefacedness, for indeed they are more modest than some of our English women are. We promised them to come again to them, and they us to keep their skins.

Within this bay the salvages say there are two rivers;[2] the one whereof we saw, having a fair entrance, but we had no time to discover it. Better harbours for shipping cannot be than here are. At the entrance of the bay are many rocks;[3] and in all likelihood good

---

[1] The residence of the squa sachim of Massachusetts is variously conjectured to have been at Concord, and in the neighbourhood of the Wachusett mountain. There seems, however, no sufficient reason for placing it so remote. See Shattuck's Hist. of Concord, p. 2, and Drake's Book of the Indians, b. ii. p. 40.

[2] The Mystic and the Charles, the former of which they saw.

[3] The Graves and the Brewsters are the principal rocks at the en-

fishing-ground.¹ Many, yea most of the islands have been inhabited, some being cleared from end to end. But the people are all dead,² or removed.

Our victual growing scarce, the wind coming fair, and having a light moon, we set out at evening, and through the goodness of God came safely home before noon the day following.³

trance of Boston bay. It is supposed that in this or some subsequent voyage the three Brewsters were named in honor of their venerable elder, and Point Alderton, the head-land of Nantasket, after Isaac Allerton. See note on page 195.

¹ The neighbourhood of these rocks is excellent fishing-ground.

² They had been swept off by the pestilence mentioned on page 184.

³ Governor Bradford adds, "with a considerable quantity of beaver, and a good report of the place, wishing we had been seated there." Prince, p. 198.

They were absent on this expedition four days. Winslow was probably one of the party, and wrote this account. "All the summer no want. While some were trading, others were fishing cod, bass, &c. We now gather in our harvest; and as cold weather advances, come in store of water fowl, wherewith this place abounds, though afterwards they by degrees decrease; as also abundance of wild turkeys, with venison, &c. Fit our houses against winter, are in health, and have all things in plenty." Bradford, in Prince, p. 198.

CHAPTER XV.

A LETTER SENT FROM NEW ENGLAND TO A FRIEND IN THESE PARTS, SETTING FORTH A BRIEF AND TRUE DECLARATION OF THE WORTH OF THAT PLANTATION; AS ALSO CERTAIN USEFUL DIRECTIONS FOR SUCH AS INTEND A VOYAGE INTO THOSE PARTS.

LOVING AND OLD FRIEND,[1]

ALTHOUGH I received no letter from you by this ship,[2] yet forasmuch as I know you expect the performance of my promise, which was, to write unto you truly and faithfully of all things, I have therefore at this time sent unto you accordingly, referring you for further satisfaction to our more large Relations.[3]

You shall understand that in this little time that a few of us have been here, we have built seven dwelling-houses [4] and four for the use of the plantation, and have made preparation for divers others. We set the last spring some twenty acres of Indian corn,[5] and

---

[1] This letter I think was addressed to George Morton. See note on page 113.

[2] The Fortune, in which this letter and the preceding Journal were sent to England.

[3] The preceding narrative.

[4] See note [2] on page 173.

[5] " Wherein Squanto is a great help, showing us how to set, fish, dress, and tend it." Bradford, in Prince, p. 190. The Indians' season for planting the maize was " when the leaves of the white oak are as big as the ear of a mouse." See Belknap's Hist. of New Hampshire, iii. 70.

THE FIRST THANKSGIVING.

sowed some six acres of barley and pease; and according to the manner of the Indians, we manured our ground with herrings, or rather shads,[1] which we have in great abundance, and take with great ease at our doors. Our corn did prove well; and, God be praised, we had a good increase of Indian corn, and our barley indifferent good, but our pease not worth the gathering, for we feared they were too late sown. They came up very well, and blossomed; but the sun parched them in the blossom.

Our harvest being gotten in, our governor[2] sent four men on fowling, that so we might, after a special manner, rejoice together after we had gathered the fruit of our labors.[3] They four in one day killed as much fowl as, with a little help beside, served the company almost a week. At which time, amongst other recreations, we exercised our arms, many of the Indians coming amongst us, and among the rest their greatest king, Massasoyt, with some ninety men, whom for three days we entertained and feasted; and they went out and killed five deer,[4] which they brought to the plantation, and bestowed on our governor, and upon the captain and others. And although it be not always so plentiful as it was at this time with us, yet by the goodness of God we are so

---

[1] Or rather *alewives*. Morton, in his New English Canaan, b. ii. ch. 7, says, "There is a fish, by some called shads, by some allizes, that at the spring of the year pass up the rivers to spawn in the ponds; and are taken in such multitudes in every river that hath a pond at the end, that the inhabitants dung their ground with them. You may see in one township a hundred acres together set with these fish, every acre taking a thousand of them; and an acre thus dressed will produce and yield so much corn as three acres without fish." The Indians used to put two or three fishes into every corn-hill.

[2] Bradford.

[3] This was the first Thanksgiving, the harvest festival of New England. On this occasion they no doubt feasted on the wild turkey as well as venison. See note [3] on page 229.

[4] See note [2] on page 175.

CHAP. XV.
1621.
Dec. 11.

far from want, that we often wish you partakers of our plenty.[1] We have found the Indians very faithful in their covenant of peace with us, very loving, and ready to pleasure us. We often go to them, and they come to us. Some of us have been fifty miles[2] by land in the country with them, the occasions and relations whereof you shall understand by our general and more full declaration of such things as are worth the noting. Yea, it hath pleased God so to possess the Indians with a fear of us and love unto us, that not only the greatest king amongst them, called Massasoyt, but also all the princes and peoples round about us, have either made suit unto us, or been glad of any occasion to make peace with us; so that seven of them at once have sent their messengers to us to that end.[3] Yea, an isle at sea,[4] which we never saw, hath also, together with the former, yielded willingly to be under the protection and subject to our sovereign lord King James. So that there is now great peace amongst the Indians

---

[1] This representation was rather too encouraging, as will be seen hereafter.

[2] Winslow himself had been to Pokanoket, a distance of forty miles. See page 208.

[3] Morton has preserved in his Memorial, p. 67, the following document.

"*September 13, anno Dom.* 1621.

"Know all men by these presents, that we, whose names are underwritten, do acknowledge ourselves to be the loyal subjects of King James, king of Great Britain, France, and Ireland, Defender of the Faith, &c. In witness whereof, and as a testimonial of the same, we have subscribed our names or marks, as followeth:

Ohquamehud,
Cawnacome,
Obbatinnua,
Nattawahunt,
Caunbatant,
Chikkatabak,
Quadaquina,
Huttmoiden,
Apannow."

Cawnacome was the sachem of Manomet, or Sandwich, Caunbatant of Mattapuyst, or Swanzey, and Chikkatabak, of Neponset. Quadequina was the brother of Massasoit, and Apannow was probably Aspinet, the sachem of Nauset. Obbatinua is supposed to have been the same as Obbatinewat, the sachem of Shawmut, or Boston. But see note on page 225.

[4] Capawack, or Nope, Martha's Vineyard. See Bradford, in Prince, p. 195, and Mass. Hist. Coll. xiii. 89.

themselves, which was not formerly, neither would have been but for us; and we, for our parts, walk as peaceably and safely in the wood as in the highways in England. We entertain them familiarly in our houses, and they as friendly bestowing their venison on us. They are a people without any religion or knowledge of any God,[1] yet very trusty, quick of apprehension, ripe-witted, just. The men and women go naked, only a skin about their middles.

For the temper of the air here, it agreeth well with that in England; and if there be any difference at all, this is somewhat hotter in summer. Some think it to be colder in winter; but I cannot out of experience so say. The air is very clear, and not foggy, as hath been reported. I never in my life remember a more seasonable year than we have here enjoyed; and if we have once but kine,[2] horses, and sheep, I make no question but men might live as contented here as in any part of the world. For fish and fowl, we have great abundance. Fresh cod in the summer is but coarse meat with us. Our bay is full of lobsters[3] all the summer, and affordeth variety of other fish. In September we can take a hogshead of eels in a night, with small labor, and can dig them out of their beds all the winter.[4] We have muscles and othus[5] at our doors. Oysters we have none

---

[1] The writer of this letter, Edward Winslow, afterwards corrected this statement in his Good News from New England. "Whereas," he says, "myself and others in former letters, (which came to the press against my will and knowledge,) wrote that the Indians about us are a people without any religion, or knowledge of any God, therein I erred, though we could then gather no better."

[2] The writer himself was the first to bring over cattle to the plantation, in 1624 — a bull and three heifers. See Prince, p. 225.

[3] See note [4] on page 164, and also page 205.

[4] See note [1] on page 196.

[5] This I think a typographical error for *other* — the word *shell-fish* being accidentally omitted; or perhaps the word in the MS. was *clams*.

near, but we can have them brought by the Indians when we will. All the spring-time the earth sendeth forth naturally very good sallet herbs. Here are grapes,[1] white and red, and very sweet and strong also; strawberries, gooseberries, raspas,[2] &c.; plums[3] of three sorts, white,[4] black, and red, being almost as good as a damson; abundance of roses, white, red and damask; single, but very sweet indeed. The country wanteth only industrious men to employ; for it would grieve your hearts if, as I, you had seen so many miles together by goodly rivers uninhabited;[5] and withal, to consider those parts of the world wherein you live to be even greatly burthened with abundance of people. These things I thought good to let you understand, being the truth of things as near as I could experimentally take knowledge of, and that you might on our behalf give God thanks, who hath dealt so favorably with us.

Our supply of men from you came the 9th of November, 1621, putting in at Cape Cod, some eight or ten leagues from us.[6] The Indians that dwell there-

---

[1] See note [5] on page 165.
[2] Raspas, raspberries.
[3] See note [6] on page 165.
[4] In the original *with* — an error of the press.
[5] Winslow had observed this desolation on the banks of Taunton river. See page 206.
[6] The Fortune, a small vessel of 55 tons, brought over Robert Cushman and 35 persons, a part of whom no doubt were the 20 that put back in the Speedwell. See note [1] on page 99. The Fortune sailed from London the beginning of July, but could not clear the channel till the end of August. She found all the colonists whom the Mayflower had left in April, "lusty and in good health, except six who had died; and she stays a month ere she sails for England." Bradford and Smith, in Prince, p. 198.
The Fortune brought a letter for Mr. Carver from Mr. Weston, dated London, July 6, wherein he writes, "We (the adventurers) have procured you a charter, the best we could, better than your former, and with less limitation." Judge Davis, in a note on Morton's Memorial, p. 73, says, "This intimation refers to a patent from the President and Council of New England to John Pierce and his associates, which was in trust for the company. It was probably brought in this ship, and was a few years since found among the old papers in the Land Office at Boston, by William Smith, Esq. one of the Land Committee. It bears the seals and

about were they who were owners of the corn which we found in caves, for which we have given them full content,[1] and are in great league with them. They sent us word there was a ship near unto them, but thought it to be a Frenchman; and indeed for ourselves we expected not a friend so soon. But when we perceived that she made for our bay, the governor commanded a great piece to be shot off, to call home such as were abroad at work. Whereupon every man, yea boy, that could handle a gun, were ready, with full resolution that, if she were an enemy, we would stand in our just defence, not fearing them. But God provided better for us than we supposed. These came all in health, not any being sick by the way, otherwise than by sea-sickness, and so continue at this time, by the blessing of God.[2] The good-wife

signatures of the Duke of Lenox, the Marquis of Hamilton, the Earl of Warwick, and of Sir Ferdinando Gorges. There is another signature so obscurely written, as to be illegible. It does not appear what use was made of this patent by the Plymouth planters; it was, not long afterwards, superseded by the second patent, surreptitiously obtained by Pierce, for his own benefit, and which, after his misfortunes, was assigned to the adventurers." Judge Davis gives an abstract of this patent in his Appendix, p. 362. I have sought for the original in vain in the archives of the State. It was never printed; and it is to be feared is now lost. The original of the third patent, granted in 1629 to William Bradford and his associates, is preserved in the office of the Register of Deeds at Plymouth. It is on parchment, signed by the Earl of Warwick, and the seal of the Plymouth Company, four inches in diameter, is appended to it. It is prefixed to the printed Laws of Plymouth Colony, p. 21 — 26. See Memorial, p. 95 — 97, and Prince, pp. 204, 217.

[1] See page 217.

[2] The following is an alphabetical list of the persons who came over in the Fortune.

John Adams,	Robert Hickes,
William Bassite,	William Hilton,
William Beale,	Bennet Morgan,
Edward Bompasse,	Thomas Morton,
Jonathan Brewster,	Austin Nicolas,
Clement Brigges,	William Palmer,
John Cannon,	William Pitt,
William Conor,	Thomas Prence,
Robert Cushman,	Moses Simonson,
Thomas Cushman,	Hugh Statie,
Stephen Dean,	James Steward,
Philip De La Noye,	William Tench,
Thomas Flavell	John Winslow,
and son,	William Wright.
Widow Foord,	

Jonathan Brewster was a son of Elder Brewster; Thomas Cushman was a son of Robert; John Winslow was a brother of Edward. Thomas Prence (or Prince) was afterwards governor of the colony.

Ford was delivered of a son the first night she landed, and both of them are very well.

When it pleaseth God we are settled and fitted for the fishing business and other trading, I doubt not but by the blessing of God the gain will give content to all. In the mean time, that we have gotten we have sent by this ship;[1] and though it be not much, yet it will witness for us that we have not been idle, considering the smallness of our number all this summer. We hope the merchants will accept of it, and be encouraged to furnish us with things needful for further employment, which will also encourage us to put forth ourselves to the uttermost.

Now because I expect your coming unto us,[2] with other of our friends, whose company we much desire, I thought good to advertise you of a few things needful. Be careful to have a very good bread-room to put your biscuits in. Let your cask for beer and water be iron-bound, for the first tire, if not more. Let not your

---

De La Noye (or Delano) was, according to Winslow, in his Brief Narration, "born of French parents," and Simonson (or Simmons) was a "child of one that was in communion with the Dutch church at Leyden." The widow Foord brought three children, William, Martha, and John. For a further account of some of these, and the other early settlers, see Farmer's Genealogical Register, Mitchell's Family Register, appended to his Hist. of Bridgewater, and Deane's Family Sketches, in his Hist. of Scituate.

[1] "The Fortune sails Dec. 13, laden with two hogsheads of beaver and other skins, and good clapboards as full as she can hold; the freight estimated near £500. But in her voyage, as she draws near the English coast, is seized by the French, carried into France, kept there fifteen days, and robbed of all she had worth taking; then the people and ship are released, and get to London Feb. 17." Bradford, in Prince, p. 199. Smith, in his New England's Trials, printed in 1622, says she was laden with three hogsheads of beaver skins, clapboard, wainscot, walnut, and some sassafras.

"Upon her departure, the governor and his assistant dispose the late comers into several families, find their provisions will now scarce hold out six months at half allowance, and therefore put them to it, which they bear patiently." Bradford, in Prince, p. 199.

[2] George Morton, to whom I suppose this letter was written, came out in the next ship, the Anne.

meat be dry-salted; none can better do it than the sailors. Let your meal be so hard trod in your cask that you shall need an adz or hatchet to work it out with. Trust not too much on us for corn at this time, for by reason of this last company that came, depending wholly upon us, we shall have little enough till harvest. Be careful to come by some of your meal to spend by the way; it will much refresh you. Build your cabins as open as you can, and bring good store of clothes and bedding with you. Bring every man a musket or fowling-piece. Let your piece be long in the barrel, and fear not the weight of it, for most of our shooting is from stands. Bring juice of lemons, and take it fasting; it is of good use. For hot waters, aniseed water is the best; but use it sparingly. If you bring any thing for comfort in the country, butter or sallet oil, or both, is very good. Our Indian corn, even the coarsest, maketh as pleasant meat as rice; therefore spare that, unless to spend by the way. Bring paper and linseed oil for your windows,[1] with

CHAP. XV.

1621. Dec. 11.

---

[1] Oiled paper to keep out the snow-storms of a New England winter! This serves to give us some idea of the exposures and hardships of the first colonists. It is an indication of progress in domestic comfort when we find Higginson in 1629 writing from Salem to his friends in England, "Be sure to furnish yourselves with glass for windows." See Hutchinson's Collection of Papers, p. 50.

Glass windows were first introduced into England in 1180. They were so rare in the reign of Edward III. that Chaucer, in describing his chamber, mentions particularly that

" with glass
" Were all the windows well y-glazed."

Even in the time of Henry VIII. they were considered a luxury, and yeomen and farmers were perfectly contented with windows of lattice. In the days of Queen Elizabeth they were unknown except in a few lordly mansions, and in them they were regarded as movable furniture. When the dukes of Northumberland left Alnwick castle to come to London for the winter, the few glass windows, which formed one of the luxuries of the castle, were carefully taken out and laid away, perhaps carried to London to adorn the city residence. See Anderson's Hist. of Commerce, i. 90, ed. 1764; Ellis's Specimens of the early English Poets, i. 221, 323; Hallam's Middle Ages, iii. 426, (ed. 1837); Northumberland

CHAP. XV.
1621.
Dec. 11.

cotton yarn for your lamps. Let your shot be most for big fowls, and bring store of powder and shot. I forbear further to write for the present, hoping to see you by the next return. So I take my leave, commending you to the Lord for a safe conduct unto us, resting in him,

Your loving friend,

E. W.[1]

Plymouth, in New England, this 11*th of December*, 1621.

Household Book, Preface, p. 16; E. Everett's Address before the Merc. Lib. Assoc. p. 19.

[1] Edward Winslow, of whom some account will be given hereafter.

THE WINSLOW CHAIR.

CHAPTER XVI.

REASONS AND CONSIDERATIONS TOUCHING THE LAWFULNESS OF REMOVING OUT OF ENGLAND INTO THE PARTS OF AMERICA.

FORASMUCH as many exceptions are daily made against the going into and inhabiting of foreign desert places, to the hindrances of plantations abroad, and the increase of distractions at home; it is not amiss that some which have been ear-witnesses of the exceptions made, and are either agents or abettors of such removals and plantations, do seek to give content to the world, in all things that possibly they can.

And although the most of the opposites are such as either dream of raising their fortunes here to that than which there is nothing more unlike, or such as affecting their home-born country so vehemently, as that they had rather with all their friends, beg, yea, starve in it, than undergo a little difficulty in seeking abroad; yet are there some who, out of doubt in tenderness of conscience, and fear to offend God by running before they are called, are straitened and do straiten others from going to foreign plantations.

For whose cause especially I have been drawn, out of my good affection to them, to publish some reasons

CHAP XVI.

1621.

The Preamble.

CHAP. XVI.
1621.

that might give them content and satisfaction, and also stay and stop the wilful and witty caviller; and herein I trust I shall not be blamed of any godly wise, though through my slender judgment I should miss the mark, and not strike the nail on the head, considering it is the first attempt that hath been made (that I know of) to defend those enterprises. Reason would, therefore, that if any man of deeper reach and better judgment see further or otherwise, that he rather instruct me than deride me.

Cautions.
Gen. xii. 1, 2, & xxxv. 1.
Matth. ii. 19.

Psalm cv. 13.

Heb. i. 1, 2.

Josh. v. 12.

And being studious for brevity, we must first consider, that whereas God of old did call and summon our fathers by predictions, dreams, visions, and certain illuminations, to go from their countries, places and habitations, to reside and dwell here or there, and to wander up and down from city to city, and land to land, according to his will and pleasure; now there is no such calling to be expected for any matter whatsoever, neither must any so much as imagine that there will now be any such thing. God did once so train up his people, but now he doth not, but speaks in another manner, and so we must apply ourselves to God's present dealing, and not to his wonted dealing; and as the miracle of giving manna ceased, when the fruits of the land became plenty, so God having such a plentiful storehouse of directions in his holy word, there must not now any extraordinary revelations be expected. But now the ordinary examples and precepts of the Scriptures, reasonably and rightly understood and applied, must be the voice and word, that must call us, press us, and direct us in every action.

Gen. xvii. 8.

Neither is there any land or possession now, like unto the possession which the Jews had in Canaan, being legally holy and appropriated unto a holy people, the seed of Abraham, in which they dwelt securely, and had their days prolonged, it being by an immediate voice said, that he (the Lord) gave it them as a land of rest after their weary travels, and a type of eternal rest in heaven. But now there is no land of that sanctimony, no land so appropriated, none typical; much less any that can be said to be given of God to any nation, as was Canaan, which they and their seed must dwell in, till God sendeth upon them sword or captivity. But now we are all, in all places, strangers and pilgrims, travellers and sojourners, most properly, having no dwelling but in this earthern tabernacle; our dwelling is but a wandering, and our abiding but as a fleeting, and in a word our home is nowhere but in the heavens,[1] in that house not made with hands, whose maker and builder is God, and to which all ascend that love the coming of our Lord Jesus.

<small>CHAP. XVI.
1621.</small>

<small>2 Cor. v. 1, 2, 3.</small>

Though then there may be reasons to persuade a man to live in this or that land, yet there cannot be the same reasons which the Jews had; but now, as natural, civil and religious bands tie men, so they must be bound, and as good reasons for things terrene and heavenly appear, so they must be led.

And so here falleth in our question, how a man that is here born and bred, and hath lived some years, may remove himself into another country.

<small>Object.</small>

I answer, a man must not respect only to live, and do good to himself, but he should see where he can live to do most good to others; for, as one saith, "He whose living is but for himself, it is time he were dead."

<small>Ans. 1.
What persons may hence remove</small>

---

[1] So were the Jews, but yet their temporal blessings and inheritances were more large than ours. — *Author's Note.*

CHAP. XVI.

1621.

Some men there are who of necessity must here live, as being tied to duties either to church, commonwealth, household, kindred, &c.; but others, and that many, who do no good in none of those, nor can do none, as being not able, or not in favor, or as wanting opportunity, and live as outcasts — nobodies, eyesores, eating but for themselves, teaching but themselves, and doing good to none, either in soul or body, and so pass over days, years and months, yea, so live and so die. Now such should lift up their eyes and see whether there be not some other place and country to which they may go to do good, and have use towards others of that knowledge, wisdom, humanity, reason, strength, skill, faculty, &c. which God hath given them for the service of others and his own glory.

2. Why they should remove.

But not to pass the bounds of modesty so far as to name any, though I confess I know many, who sit here still with their talent in a napkin, having notable endowments both of body and mind, and might do great good if they were in some places, which here do none, nor can do none, and yet through fleshly fear, niceness, straitness of heart, &c. sit still and look on, and will not hazard a drachm of health, nor a day of pleasure, nor an hour of rest to further the knowledge and salvation of the sons of Adam in that new world, where a drop of the knowledge of Christ is most precious, which is here not set by. Now what shall we say to such a profession of Christ, to which is joined no more denial of a man's self?

Luke x.x. 20.

Reas. 1.

Object. But some will say, What right have I to go live in the heathens' country?

Answ. Letting pass the ancient discoveries, contracts and agreements which our Englishmen have long since made in those parts, together with the acknowledgment of the histories and chronicles of other nations, who profess the land of America from the Cape de Florida unto the Bay of Canada [1] (which is south and north three hundred leagues and upwards, and east and west further than yet hath been discovered) is proper to the king of England, yet letting that pass, lest I be thought to meddle further than it concerns me, or further than I have discerning, I will mention such things as are within my reach, knowledge, sight and practice, since I have travailed in these affairs.

And first, seeing we daily pray for the conversion of the heathens, we must consider whether there be not some ordinary means and course for us to take to convert them, or whether prayer for them be only referred to God's extraordinary work from heaven. Now it seemeth unto me that we ought also to endeavour and use the means to convert them; and the means cannot be used unless we go to them, or they come to us. To us they cannot come, our land is full; to them we may go, their land is empty.

This then is sufficient reason to prove our going thither to live, lawful. Their land is spacious and void, and there are few, and do but run over the grass, as do also the foxes and wild beasts. They are not industrious, neither have art, science, skill or faculty to use either the land or the commodities of it; but all spoils, rots, and is marred for want of manuring, gathering, ordering, &c. As the ancient patriarchs, therefore, removed from straiter places into more

---

[1] Jacques Cartier, of St. Malo, in France, discovered the great river of Canada in August, 1534, and in 1535 sailed up as far as Montreal. Florida was discovered by Juan Ponce de Leon, a Spaniard, in 1512. See Holmes's Annals of America, i. 31 and 65.

roomy, where the land lay idle and waste, and none used it, though there dwelt inhabitants by them, as Gen. xiii. 6, 11, 12, and xxxiv. 21, and xli. 20, so is it lawful now to take a land which none useth, and make use of it.

And as it is a common land, or unused and undressed country, so we have it by common consent, composition and agreement;[1] which agreement is double. First, the imperial governor, Massasoit, whose circuits, in likelihood, are larger than England and Scotland, hath acknowledged the King's Majesty of England to be his master and commander, and that once in my hearing, yea, and in writing, under his hand, to Captain Standish, both he and many other kings which are under him, as Pamet, Nauset, Cummaquid, Narrowhiggonset, Namaschet, &c., with divers others that dwell about the bays of Patuxet and Massachuset.[2] Neither hath this been accomplished by threats and blows, or shaking of sword and sound of trumpet; for as our faculty that way is small, and our strength less, so our warring with them is after another manner, namely, by friendly usage, love, peace, honest and just carriages, good counsel, &c., that so we and they may not only live in peace in that land, and they yield subjection to an earthly prince, but that as voluntaries they may be persuaded at length to embrace the Prince of Peace, Christ Jesus, and rest in peace with him forever.

Secondly, this composition is also more particular and applicatory, as touching ourselves there inhabiting.

---

[1] This is to be considered as respecting New England, and the territories about the plantation.—*Author's Note.*

[2] See pages 193 and 232.

The emperor, by a joint consent, hath promised and appointed us to live at peace where we will in all his dominions, taking what place we will, and as much land as we will,[1] and bringing as many people as we will; and that for these two causes. First, because we are the servants of James, king of England, whose the land (as he confesseth) is. Secondly, because he hath found us just, honest, kind and peaceable, and so loves our company. Yea, and that in these things there is no dissimulation on his part, nor fear of breach (except our security engender in them some unthought of treachery, or our uncivility provoke them to anger) is most plain in other Relations,[2] which show that the things they did were more out of love than out of fear.

It being then, first, a vast and empty chaos; secondly, acknowledged the right of our sovereign king; thirdly, by a peaceable composition in part possessed of divers of his loving subjects, I see not who can doubt or call in question the lawfulnesss of inhabiting or dwelling there; but that it may be as lawful for such as are not tied upon some special occasion here, to live there as well as here. Yea, and as the enterprise is weighty and difficult, so the honor is more worthy, to plant a rude wilderness, to enlarge the honor and fame of our

---

[1] In the "Warrantable Grounds and Proceedings of the first Associates of New Plymouth, in their laying the first foundation of this Government, in their making of laws, and disposing of the lands within the same," prefixed to the Code of Laws printed in 1685, it is stated that "by the favor of the Almighty they began the colony in New England (there being then no other within the said continent) at a place called by the natives Apaum, alias Patuxet, but by the English New Plymouth. All which lands being void of inhabitants, we, the said John Carver, William Bradford. Edward Winslow, William Brewster, Isaac Allerton, and the rest of our associates, entering into a league of peace with Massasoit, since called Woosamequin, prince or sachem of those parts, he, the said Massasoit, freely gave them all the lands adjacent, to them and their heirs for ever."

[2] He refers to the preceding Journal.

dread sovereign, but chiefly to display the efficacy and power of the Gospel, both in zealous preaching, professing, and wise walking under it, before the faces of these poor blind infidels.

As for such as object the tediousness of the voyage thither, the danger of pirates' robbery, of the savages' treachery, &c., these are but lions in the way; and it were well for such men if they were in heaven. For who can show them a place in this world where iniquity shall not compass them at the heels, and where they shall have a day without grief, or a lease of life for a moment? And who can tell, but God, what dangers may lie at our doors, even in our native country, or what plots may be abroad, or when God will cause our sun to go down at noon-day, and, in the midst of our peace and security, lay upon us some lasting scourge for our so long neglect and contempt of his most glorious Gospel?

Object. But we have here great peace, plenty of the Gospel, and many sweet delights and variety of comforts.

Answ. True, indeed; and far be it from us to deny and diminish the least of these mercies. But have we rendered unto God thankful obedience for this long peace, whilst other peoples have been at wars? Have we not rather murmured, repined, and fallen at jars amongst ourselves, whilst our peace hath lasted with foreign power? Was there ever more suits in law, more envy, contempt and reproach than nowadays? Abraham and Lot departed asunder when there fell a breach betwixt them, which was occasioned by the straitness of the land; and surely I am persuaded, that howsoever the frailties of men are principal in all contentions, yet the straitness of the place is such, as each man is fain to pluck his means, as it were, out of his neighbour's throat, there is such pressing and oppressing in town and country, about farms, trades, traffick, &c.; so as a man can hardly any where set up a trade, but he shall pull down two of his neighbours.

The towns abound with young tradesmen, and the hospitals are full of the ancient; the country is replenished with new farmers, and the almshouses are filled with old laborers. Many there are who get their living with bearing burdens; but more are fain to burden the land with their whole bodies. Multitudes get their means of life by prating, and so do numbers more by begging. Neither come these straits upon men always through intemperance, ill husbandry, indiscretion, &c., as some think; but even the most wise, sober, and discreet men go often to the wall, when they have done their best; wherein, as God's providence swayeth all, so it is easy to see that the straitness of the place, having in it so many strait hearts, cannot but produce such effects more and more; so as every indifferent minded man should be ready to say with father Abraham, "Take thou the right hand, and I will take the left:" let us not thus oppress, straiten, and afflict one another; but seeing there is a spacious land, the way to which is through the sea, we will end this difference in a day.

That I speak nothing about the bitter contention that hath been about religion, by writing, disputing, and inveighing earnestly one against another, the heat of which zeal, if it were turned against the rude barbarism of the heathens, it might do more good in a day, than it hath done here in many years. Neither of the little love to the Gospel, and profit which is made by the preachers in most places, which might easily drive the zealous to the heathens; who, no doubt, if they had but a drop of that knowledge which here flieth about the streets, would be filled with exceeding great joy and gladness, as that they would even pluck the kingdom of heaven by violence, and take it, as it were, by force.

The last let. The greatest let that is yet behind is the sweet fellowship of friends, and the satiety of bodily delights.

But can there be two nearer friends almost than Abraham and Lot, or than Paul and Barnabas? And yet, upon as little occasions as we have here, they departed asunder, two of them being patriarchs of the church of old, the other the apostles of the church which is new; and their covenants were such as it seemeth might bind as much as any covenant between men at this day; and yet to avoid greater inconveniences, they departed asunder.

Neither must men take so much thought for the flesh, as not to be pleased except they can pamper their bodies with variety of dainties. Nature is content with little, and health is much endangered by mixtures upon the stomach. The delights of the palate *James iii. 6.* do often inflame the vital parts; as the tongue setteth a-fire the whole body. Secondly, varieties here are not common to all, but many good men are glad to snap at a crust. The rent-taker lives on sweet morsels, but the rent-payer eats a dry crust often with watery eyes; and it is nothing to say what some one of a hundred hath, but what the bulk, body and commonalty hath; which I warrant you is short enough.

And they also which now live so sweetly, hardly will their children attain to that privilege; but some circumventor or other will outstrip them, and make them sit in the dust, to which men are brought in one age, but cannot get out of it again in seven generations.

To conclude, without all partiality, the present consumption which groweth upon us here, whilst the land groaneth under so many close-fisted and unmerciful men, being compared with the easiness, plainness and plentifulness in living in those remote places, may quickly persuade any man to a liking of this course, and to practise a removal; which being done by honest, godly and industrious men, they shall there be right heartily welcome; but for other of dissolute and profane life, their rooms are better than their companies. For if here, where the Gospel hath been so long and plentifully taught, they are yet frequent in such vices as the heathen would shame to speak of, what will they be when there is less restraint in word and deed? My only suit to all men is, that whether they live there or here, they would learn to use this world as they used it not, keeping faith and a good conscience, both with God and men, that when the day of account shall come, they may come forth as good and fruitful servants, and freely be received, and enter into the joy of their Master.　　R. C.[1]

---

[1] ROBERT CUSHMAN. It will be recollected that he was twice sent from Leyden to England as the agent of the Pilgrims, and embarked in the Speedwell, in 1620, but was obliged to put back. He came over in the Fortune, and returned in her, as the adventurers had appointed, to give them information of the state of the colony. In 1623, a lot of land was assigned him with those " which came first over in the Mayflower." In a letter to Governor Bradford, dated December 22, 1624, he writes, " I hope the next ships to come to you;" but he was prevented by death. Governor Bradford speaks of him as " our ancient friend, Mr. Cushman, who was our right hand with the adventurers, and for divers years managed all our business with them." He brought his son Thomas with him in the Fortune, whom he

CHAP. XVI.

[*A Letter from New Plymouth.*

1621. LOVING COUSIN,
Nov.

At our arrival at New Plymouth, in New England, we found all our friends and planters in good health, though they were left sick and weak, with very small means; the Indians round about us peaceable and friendly; the country very pleasant and temperate, yielding naturally, of itself, great store of fruits, as vines of divers sorts, in great abundance. There is likewise walnuts, chestnuts, small nuts and plums, with much variety of flowers, roots and herbs, no less pleasant than wholesome and profitable. No place hath more gooseberries and strawberries, nor better. Timber of all sorts you have in England doth cover the land, that affords beasts of divers sorts, and great flocks of turkeys, quails, pigeons and partridges; many great lakes abounding with fish, fowls, beavers, and otters. The sea affords us great plenty of all excellent sorts of sea-fish, as the rivers and isles doth variety of wild fowl of most useful sorts. Mines we find, to our thinking; but neither the goodness nor quality we know. Better grain cannot be than the Indian corn, if we will plant it upon as good ground as a man need desire. We are all freeholders; the rent-day doth not

entrusted to the care of Governor Bradford, and who, after the death of Brewster, was chosen, in 1649, ruling elder of the Plymouth church, in which office he continued till he died in 1691, aged 84. He married Mary, daughter of Isaac Allerton, and his son Isaac, born in 1649, was the first minister of Plympton, and lived to the age of 83. Descendants of this honorable name are numerous in the Old Colony. See Morton's Memorial, pp. 128, 376; Prince, p. 238; Mass. Hist. Coll. iii. 35; Belknap's Am. Biog. ii. 267; Mitchell's History of Bridgewater, p. 372.

trouble us; and all those good blessings we have, of which and what we list in their seasons for taking. Our company are, for most part, very religious, honest people; the word of God sincerely taught us every Sabbath; so that I know not any thing a contented mind can here want. I desire your friendly care to send my wife and children[1] to me, where I wish all the friends I have in England; and so I rest

    Your loving kinsman,
      WILLIAM HILTON.[2]]

---

[1] His wife and two children came in the next ship, the Anne, which arrived at Plymouth in the summer of 1623. See Prince, p. 220, and Morton, p. 379.

[2] I insert this letter, because it was written by one of the passengers in the Fortune. It was first printed in 1622, in Smith's New England's Trials. The writer and his brother Edward, fishmongers of London, commenced, in the spring of 1623, at Dover, the settlement of New Hampshire. Farmer says, "He was at Newbury about 1648, and at Charlestown, Mass. in 1665; and here I suppose he died in 1675, as there is the inventory of William Hilton taken that year in the Probate Records." See Belknap's New Hampshire, p. 4, (Farmer's ed.); Prince, p. 215; Savage's Winthrop, i. 97; Holmes's Annals, i. 183.

CUSHMAN'S DISCOURSE.

CHAPTER XVII.

OF THE STATE OF THE COLONY, AND THE NEED OF PUBLIC SPIRIT IN THE COLONISTS.[1]

NEW ENGLAND, so called not only (to avoid novelties) because Captain Smith hath so entitled it in his Description, but because of the resemblance that is in it of England, the native soil of Englishmen; it being muchwhat the same for heat and cold in summer and winter, it being champaign ground, but not high mountains; somewhat like the soil in Kent and Essex, full of dales and meadow ground, full of rivers and sweet springs, as England is. But principally, so far as we

---

[1] In the course of Robert Cushman's short residence of a month at Plymouth he delivered a discourse to the colonists on the Sin and Danger of Self-Love, from 1 Cor. x. 24, "Let no man seek his own, but every man another's wealth;" which was printed at London in 1622, but without his name. In a tract printed at London in 1644, entitled "A Brief Narration of some Church Courses in New England," I find the following allusion to this discourse; "There is a book printed, called A Sermon preached at Plymouth, in New England, which, as I am certified, was made there by a comber of wool."

Dr. Belknap remarks, that "this discourse may be considered as a specimen of the *prophesyings* of the brethren. The occasion was singular; the exhortations and reproofs are not less so, but were adapted to the existing state of the colony." Judge Davis says that "the late Isaac Lothrop, of Plymouth, often mentioned an intimation, received from an aged relative, as to the spot where this sermon was delivered. It was at the common house of the Plantation, which is understood to have been erected on the southerly side of the bank, where the town brook meets the harbour. Mr. Lothrop died in 1808, aged seventy-three. Not many

CHAP. XVII.
1621.
Dec.

can yet find, it is an island,[1] and near about the quantity of England, being cut out from the main land in America, as England is from the main of Europe, by a great arm of the sea,[2] which entereth in forty degrees, and runneth up northwest and by west, and goeth out either into the South Sea, or else into the Bay of Canada. The certainty whereof, and secrets of which, we have not yet so found as that, as eye-witnesses, we can make narration thereof; but if God give time and means, we shall ere long discover both the extent of that river, together with the secrets thereof; and also try what territories, habitations, or commodities may be found, either in it, or about it.

It pertaineth not to my purpose to speak any thing either in praise or dispraise of the country. So it is, by God's providence, that a few of us are there planted to our content and have with great charge and difficulty attained quiet and competent dwellings there. And thus much I will say for the satisfaction of such as have any thought of going thither to inhabit; that for men which have a large heart, and look after great riches, ease, pleasures, dainties, and jollity in this world, (except they will live by other men's sweat, or have great riches,) I would not advise them to come there, for as yet the country will afford no such mat-

---

years before his death he had the satisfaction of being called to view sundry tools and implements which were dug up at that spot, and which he carefully preserved." See note [4] on page 173; Belknap's Am. Biog. ii. 274; and Morton's Memorial, p. 74.

Prefixed to the discourse is an "Epistle Dedicatory, to his loving friends, the adventurers for New England, together with all well-willers and well-wishers thereunto, grace and peace, &c." The Epistle is here printed entire, and all that is of any general or historical interest in the discourse.

[1] It will be seen hereafter that Winslow too, on the authority of the natives, calls it an island.

[2] Hudson's river.

ters. But if there be any who are content to lay out their estates, spend their time, labors and endeavours, for the benefit of them that shall come after, and in desire to further the Gospel among those poor heathens, quietly contenting themselves with such hardship and difficulties, as by God's providence shall fall upon them, being yet young, and in their strength, such men I would advise and encourage to go, for their ends cannot fail them.

And if it should please God to punish his people in the Christian countries of Europe, for their coldness, carnality, wanton abuse of the Gospel, contention, &c., either by Turkish slavery, or by popish tyranny, (which God forbid,) yet if the time be come, or shall come (as who knoweth?) when Satan shall be let loose to cast out his floods against them, here is a way opened for such as have wings to fly into this wilderness; and as by the dispersion of the Jewish church through persecution, the Lord brought in the fulness of the Gentiles, so who knoweth, whether now by tyranny and affliction, which he suffereth to come upon them, he will not by little and little chase them even amongst the heathens, that so a light may rise up in the dark, and the kingdom of heaven be taken from them which now have it, and given to a people that shall bring forth the fruit of it? This I leave to the judgment of the godly wise, being neither prophet nor son of a prophet. But considering God's dealing of old, and seeing the name of Christian to be very great, but the true nature thereof almost quite lost in all degrees and sects, I cannot think but that there is some judgment not far off, and that God will shortly, even of stones, raise up children unto Abraham.

CHAP. XVII.

1621. Dec.

And whoso rightly considereth what manner of entrance, abiding, and proceedings we have had among these poor heathens since we came hither, will easily think that God hath some great work to do towards them.

They were wont to be the most cruel and treacherous people in all these parts, even like lions; but to us they have been like lambs, so kind, so submissive, and trusty, as a man may truly say, many Christians are not so kind nor sincere.

They were very much wasted of late, by reason of a great mortality[1] that fell amongst them three years since; which, together with their own civil dissensions and bloody wars, hath so wasted them, as I think the twentieth person is scarce left alive; and those that are left, have their courage much abated, and their countenance is dejected, and they seem as a people affrighted. And though when we first came into the country, we were few, and many of us were sick, and many died by reason of the cold and wet, it being the depth of winter, and we having no houses nor shelter, yet when there was not six able persons among us, and that they came daily to us by hundreds, with their sachems or kings, and might in one hour have made a dispatch of us, yet such a fear was upon them, as that they never offered us the least injury in word or deed. And by reason of one Tisquanto,[2] that lives amongst us, that can speak English, we have daily commerce with their kings, and can know what is done or intended towards us among the savages; also we can acquaint them with our courses and purposes, both human and religious. And the greatest commander of

---

[1] See note [3] on page 183. [2] See note [3] on page 190.

THE INDIANS WELL TREATED. 259

the country, called Massasoit,[1] cometh often to visit us, though he lives fifty miles from us, often sends us presents, he having with many other of their governors promised, yea, subscribed obedience to our Sovereign Lord King James, and for his cause to spend both strength and life.[2] And we, for our parts, through God's grace, have with that equity, justice, and compassion carried ourselves towards them, as that they have received much favor, help, and aid from us, but never the least injury or wrong by us.[3] We found the place where we live empty, the people being all dead and gone away,[4] and none living near by eight or ten miles; and though in the time of some hardship, we found, travelling abroad, some eight bushels of corn hid up in a cave, and knew no owners of it, yet afterwards hearing of the owners of it, we gave them (in their estimation) double the value of it.[5] Our care also hath been to maintain peace amongst them, and have always set ourselves against such of them as used any rebellion or treachery against their governors; and not only threatened such, but in some sort paid them their due deserts. And when any of

CHAP. XVII.
1621. Dec.

---

[1] See page 191.
[2] See pages 193 and 232.
[3] They offer us to dwell where we will.—*Cushman's Note.*
 The first planters of Plymouth and Massachusetts invariably purchased of the natives the lands on which they settled, for considerations which were deemed at the time fully equivalent. They followed literally the instructions given by the governor of the New England Company to Gov. Endicott, in 1629: "If any of the salvages pretend right of inheritance to all or any part of the lands granted in our patent, we pray you endeavour to purchase their title, that we may avoid the least scruple of intrusion. Particularly publish that no wrong or injury be offered to the natives." And in 1676, it was as truly as proudly said by Governor Josiah Winslow, of Plymouth, "I think I can clearly say, that before these present troubles broke out, the English did not possess one foot of land in this Colony but what was fairly obtained by honest purchase of the Indian proprietors." See Hutchinson's Mass. ii. 266; Hazard's State Papers, i. 263; Hubbard's Indian Wars, p. 13, (ed. 1677.)
[4] See pages 184 and 206.
[5] See page 217.

them are in want, as often they are in the winter, when their corn is done, we supply them to our power, and have them in our houses eating and drinking, and warming themselves; which thing, though it be something a trouble to us, yet because they should see and take knowledge of our labors, orders and diligence, both for this life and a better, we are content to bear it; and we find in many of them, especially of the younger sort, such a tractable disposition, both to religion and humanity, as that if we had means to apparel them, and wholly to retain them with us, (as their desire is,) they would doubtless in time prove serviceable to God and man; and if ever God send us means, we will bring up hundreds of their children both to labor and learning.

But leaving to speak of them till a further occasion be offered, if any shall marvel at the publishing of this treatise in England, seeing there is no want of good books, but rather want of men to use good books, let them know, that the especial end is, that we may keep those motives in memory for ourselves and those that shall come after, to be a remedy against self-love, the bane of all societies; and that we also might testify to our Christian countrymen, who judge diversely of us, that though we be in a heathen country, yet the grace of Christ is not quenched in us, but we still hold and teach the same points of faith, mortification, and sanctification, which we have heard and learned, in a most ample and large manner, in our own country. If any shall think it too rude and unlearned for this curious age, let them know, that to paint out the Gospel in plain and flat English, amongst a company of plain Englishmen, (as we are,) is the best and most profitable teaching; and we will study plainness, not curiosity, neither in things human nor heavenly. If any error or unsoundness be in it, (as who knoweth?) impute it to that frail man which indited it, which professeth to know nothing as he ought to know it. I have not set down my name, partly because I seek no name, and principally because I would have nothing esteemed by names; for I see a number of evils to arise through names, when the persons are either famous or infamous, and God and man is often injured. If any good or profit arise to thee in the receiving of it, give God the praise and esteem me as a son of Adam, subject to all such frailties as other men are.

And you, my loving friends, the adventurers to this Plantation, as your care has been, first to settle religion[1] here, before either profit or popularity, so I pray you, go on to do it much more, and be careful to send godly men, though they want some of that worldly policy which this world hath in her own generation; and so, though you lose, the Lord shall gain. I rejoice greatly in your free and ready minds to your powers, yea, and beyond your powers to further this work, that you thus honor God with your riches; and I trust you shall be repayed again double and treble in this world, yea, and the memory of this action shall never die. But

[1] "The great and known end of the first comers, in the year of our Lord 1620, leaving their dear native country and all that was dear to them there, transporting themselves over the vast ocean into this remote waste wilderness, and therein willingly conflicting with dangers, losses, hardships and distresses, sore and not a few, was, that without offence, they, under the protection of their native prince, together with the enlargement of his Majesty's dominions, might, with the liberty of a good conscience, enjoy the pure scriptural worship of God, without the mixture of human inventions and impositions; and that their children after them might walk in the holy ways of the Lord." See General Fundamentals, prefixed to the Laws of New Plymouth, published in 1672, and reprinted in Brigham's edition, p. 242.

above all, adding unto this, as I trust you do, like freeness in all other God's services, both at home and abroad, you shall find reward with God, ten thousandfold surpassing all that you do or think. Be not, therefore, discouraged, for no labor is lost nor money spent, which is bestowed for God. Your ends were good, your success is good, and your profit is coming, even in this life, and in the life to come much more. And what shall I say now? A word to men of understanding sufficeth. Pardon, I pray you, my boldness, read over the ensuing treatise, and judge wisely of the poor weakling; and the Lord, the God of sea and land, stretch out his arm of protection to you and us, and over all our lawful and good enterprises, either this, or any other way.

Plymouth, in New England, December 12, 1621.

There is a generation, which think to have more in this world, than Adam's felicity in innocency, being born, as they think, to take their pleasures and their ease. Let the roof of the house drop through, they stir not; let the field be overgrown with weeds, they care not; they must not foul their hand, nor wet their foot. It's enough for them to say, Go you, not, Let us go, though never so much need. Such idle drones are intolerable in a settled commonwealth, much more in a commonwealth which is but as it were in the bud. Of what earth, I pray thee, art thou made? Of any better than the other of the sons of Adam? And canst thou see other of thy brethren toil their hearts out, and thou sit idle at home, or takest thy pleasure abroad?

It is reported that there are many men gone to that other plantation in Virginia, which, whilst they lived in England, seemed very religious, zealous, and conscionable; and have now lost even the sap of grace, and edge to all goodness; and are become mere worldings. This testimony I believe to be partly true, and amongst many causes of it, this self-love is not the least. It is indeed a matter of some commendations for a man to remove himself out of a thronged place into a wide wilderness; to take in hand so long and dangerous a journey, to be an instrument to carry the Gospel and humanity among the brutish heathen; but there may be many goodly shows and glosses, and yet a pad in the straw. Men may make a great appearance of respect unto God, and yet but dissemble with him, having their own lusts carrying them; and, out of doubt, men that have taken in hand hither to come, out of discontentment, in regard to their estates in England, and aiming at great matters here, affecting it to be gentlemen, landed men, or hoping for office, place, dignity, or fleshly liberty. Let the show be what it will, the substance is naught; and that bird of self-love which was hatched at home, if it be not looked to, will eat out the life of all grace and goodness; and though men have escaped the danger of the sea, and that cruel mortality, which swept away so many of our loving friends and brethren, yet except they purge out this self-love, a worse mischief is prepared for them. And who knoweth whether God in mercy have delivered those just men which here departed, from the evils to come, and from unreasonable men, in whom there neither was, nor is, any comfort, but grief, sorrow, affliction, and misery, till they cast out this spawn of self-love?

Now, brethren, I pray you, remember yourselves, and know that you are not in a retired, monastical course, but have given your names and promises one to another, and covenanted here to cleave together in the service of God and the King. What then must you do? May you live as retired hermits, and look after nobody? Nay, you must seek still the wealth of one another, and inquire, as David, How liveth such a man? How is he clad? How is he fed? He is my brother, my associate; we ventured our lives together here, and had a hard brunt of it; and we are in league together. Is his labor harder than mine? Surely I will ease him. Hath he no bed to lie on? Why, I have two; I'll lend him one. Hath he no apparel? Why, I have two suits; I'll give him one of them. Eats he coarse fare, bread and water, and I have better? Why, surely we will part stakes. He is as good a man as I, and we are bound each to other; so that his wants must be my wants, his sorrows my sorrows, his sickness my sickness, and his welfare my welfare; for I am as he is. And such a sweet sympathy were excellent, comfortable, yea, heavenly, and is the only maker and conserver of churches and commonwealths; and where this is wanting, ruin comes on quickly.

It wonderfully encourageth men in their duties, when they see the burthen equally borne; but when some withdraw themselves, and retire to their own particular ease, pleasure, or profit, what heart can men have to go on in their business? When men are come together to lift some weighty piece of timber, or vessel, if one stand still and do not lift, shall not the rest be weakened and disheartened? Will not a few idle drones spoil the whole stock of laborious bees? So one idle belly, one murmurer, one complainer, one self-lover, will weaken and dishearten a whole colony. Great matters have been brought to pass, where men have cheerfully, as with one heart, hand and shoulder, gone about it, both in wars, buildings and plantations; but where every man seeks himself, all cometh to nothing.

The country is yet raw; the land untilled; the cities not builded; the cattle not settled. We are compassed about with a helpless and idle people, the natives of the country, which cannot, in any comely or comfortable manner, help themselves, much less us. We also have been very chargeable to many of our loving friends, which helped us hither, and now again supplied us; so that before we think of gathering riches, we must even in conscience think of requiting their charge, love, and labor; and cursed be that profit and gain which aimeth not at this. Besides, how many of our dear friends did here die at our first entrance; many of them, no doubt, for want of good lodging, shelter, and comfortable things; and many more may go after them quickly, if care be not taken. Is this then a time for men to begin to seek themselves? Paul saith, that men in the *last days* shall be lovers of themselves; but it is here yet but the *first* days, and, as it were, the dawning of this new world. It is now therefore no time for men to look to get riches, brave clothes, dainty fare; but to look to present necessities. It is now no time to pamper the flesh, live at ease, snatch, catch, scrape, and pill, and hoard up; but rather to open the doors, the chests, and vessels, and say, Brother, neighbour, friend, what want ye? any thing that I have? Make bold with it; it is yours to command, to do you good, to comfort and cherish you; and glad I am that I have it for you.

1621. Dec.
Luke xv. 12.

Let there be no prodigal person to come forth and say, Give me the portion of lands and goods that appertaineth to me, and let me shift for myself.[1] It is yet too soon to put men to their shifts. Israel was seven years in Canaan before the land was divided unto tribes, much longer before it was divided unto families; and why wouldest thou have thy particular portion, but because thou thinkest to live better than thy neighbour, and scornest to live so meanly as he? But who, I pray thee, brought this particularizing first into the world? Did not Satan, who was not content to keep that equal state with his fellows, but would set his throne above the stars? Did not he also entice man to despise his general felicity and happiness, and go try particular knowledge of good and evil? And nothing in this world doth more resemble heavenly happiness, than for men to live as one, being of one heart and one soul; neither any thing more resembles hellish horror, than for every man to shift for himself; for if it be a good mind and practice, thus to affect particulars, *mine* and *thine*, then it should be best also for God to provide one heaven for thee, and another for thy neighbour.

Objection. But some will say, If all men will do their endeavours, as I do, I could be content with this

---

[1] Throughout this paragraph there is a manifest reference to the copartnership into which they had been obliged to enter with the merchant adventurers, by which all the property and profits of the Plantation for seven years were to be held as a joint stock, not to be divided till the expiration of that time. The colonists had already become impatient of this arrangement, and were clamorous for a partition of the lands, and the institution of separate property. It was the design of Mr. Cushman to exhort them to be faithful to their engagement, to cherish a public spirit, and to seek the general and ultimate good of the Colony, rather than their personal and immediate interest. See the CONDITIONS on page 81, and note [1] on page 84.

generality; but many are idle and slothful, and eat up others' labors, and therefore it is best to part, and then every man may do his pleasure.

If others be idle and thou diligent, thy fellowship, provocation, and example may well help to cure that malady in them, being together; but being asunder, shall they not be more idle, and shall not gentry and beggary be quickly the glorious ensigns of your commonwealth?

Be not too hasty to say men are idle and slothful. All men have not strength, skill, faculty, spirit, and courage to work alike. It is thy glory and credit, that canst do so well, and his shame and reproach, that can do no better; and are not these sufficient rewards to you both?

If any be idle apparently, you have a law and governors to execute the same, and to follow that rule of the Apostle, to keep back their bread, and let them not eat. Go not therefore whispering to charge men with idleness; but go to the governor and prove them idle, and thou shalt see them have their deserts.

And as you are a body together, so hang not together by skins and gymocks, but labor to be jointed together and knit by flesh and sinews. Away with envy at the good of others, and rejoice in his good, and sorrow for his evil. Let his joy be thy joy, and his sorrow thy sorrow. Let his sickness be thy sickness, his hunger thy hunger, his poverty thy poverty; and if you profess friendship, be friends in adversity, for then a friend is known and tried, and not before.

Lay away all thought of former things and forget them, and think upon the things that are. Look not gapingly one upon other, pleading your goodness, your birth, your life you lived, your means you had and might have had. Here you are by God's providence under difficulties; be thankful to God it is no worse, and take it in good part that which is, and lift not up yourselves because of former privileges. Consider therefore what you are now, and where you are. Say not, I could have lived thus and thus; but say, Thus and thus I must live; for God and natural necessity requireth, if your difficulties be great, you had need to cleave the faster together, and comfort and cheer up one another, laboring to make each other's burden lighter.

There is no grief so tedious as a churlish companion; and nothing makes sorrows easy more than cheerful associates. Bear ye therefore one another's burthen, and be not a burthen one to another. Avoid all factions, frowardness, singularity, and withdrawings, and cleave fast to the Lord and one to another continually; so shall you be a notable precedent to these poor heathens, whose eyes are upon you, and who very brutishly and cruelly do daily eat and consume one another, through their emulations, wars and contentions. Be you, therefore, ashamed of it, and win them to peace, both with yourselves and one another, by your peaceable examples, which will preach louder to them than if you could cry in their barbarous language. So also shall you be an encouragement to many of your Christian friends in your native country, to come to you, when they hear of your peace, love and kindness that is amongst you. But, above all, it shall go well with your souls, when that God of peace and unity shall come to visit you with death, as he hath done many of your associates; you being found of him, not in murmurings, discontent, and jars, but in brotherly love and peace, may be translated from this wandering wilderness unto that joyful and heavenly Canaan.

WINSLOW'S RELATION.

"GOOD NEWES FROM NEW ENGLAND : or a true Relation of things very remarkable at the Plantation of *Plimoth* in New-England.
Shewing the wondrous providence and goodness of GOD, in their preservation and continuance, being delivered from many apparent deaths and dangers.
Together with a Relation of such religious and civill Lawes and Customes, as are in practise amongst the *Indians*, adjoyning to them at this day. As also what Commodities are there to be raysed for the maintenance of that and other Plantations in the said Country.
Written by *E. W.* who hath borne a part in the fore-named troubles, and there lived since their first Arrivall.
Whereunto is added by him a briefe Relation of a credible intelligence of the present Estate of *Virginia*.
LONDON. Printed by *I. D.* for *William Bladen* and *Iohn Bellamie*, and are to be sold at their Shops, at the *Bible* in *Paul's* Church-yard, and at the three Golden Lyons in Corn-hill, neere the *Royall Exchange.* 1624." pp. 66, sm. 4to.

To all well-willers and furtherers of Plantations in New England, especially to such as ever have or desire to assist the people of Plymouth in their just proceedings, grace and peace be multiplied.

RIGHT HONORABLE AND WORSHIPFUL GENTLEMEN, OR WHATSOEVER,

SINCE it hath pleased God to stir you up to be instruments of his glory in so honorable an enterprise as the enlarging of his Majesty's dominions by planting his loyal subjects in so healthful and hopeful a country as New-England is, where the church of God being seated in sincerity, there is no less hope of convincing the heathen of their evil ways, and converting them to the true knowledge and worship of the living God, and so consequently the salvation of their souls by the merits of Jesus Christ, than elsewhere, though it be much talked on and lightly or lamely prosecuted, — I therefore think it but my duty to offer the view of our proceedings to your worthy considerations, having to that end composed them together thus briefly, as you see ; wherein, to your great encouragement, you may behold the good providence of God working with you in our preservation from so many dangerous plots and treacheries as have been intended against us, as also in giving.

his blessing so powerfully upon the weak means we had, enabling us with health and ability beyond expectation in our greatest scarcities, and possessing the hearts of the salvages with astonishment and fear of us; whereas if God had let them loose, they might easily have swallowed us up, scarce being a handful in comparison of those forces they might have gathered together against us; which now, by God's blessing, will be more hard and difficult, in regard our number of men is increased, our town better fortified, and our store better victualled. Blessed therefore be his name, that hath done so great things for us and hath wrought so great a change amongst us.

Accept, I pray you, my weak endeavours, pardon my unskilfulness, and bear with my plainness in the things I have handled. Be not discouraged by our former necessities, but rather encouraged with us, hoping that as God hath wrought with us in our beginning of this worthy work, undertaken in his name and fear, so he will by us accomplish the same to his glory and our comfort, if we neglect not the means. I confess it hath not been much less chargeable to some of you [1] than hard and difficult to us, that have endured the brunt of the battle, and yet small profits returned. Only, by God's mercy, we are safely seated, housed, and fortified, by which means a great step is made unto gain, and a more direct course taken for the same, than if at first we had rashly and covetously fallen upon it.

Indeed three things are the overthrow and bane, as I may term it, of plantations.

---

[1] The merchant adventurers. See pages 67 and 78.

1. The vain expectation of present profit, which too commonly taketh a principal seat in the heart and affection, though God's glory, &c. is preferred before it in the mouth with protestation.

2. Ambition in their governors and commanders, seeking only to make themselves great, and slaves of all that are under them, to maintain a transitory base honor in themselves, which God oft punisheth with contempt.

3. The carelessness of those that send over supplies of men unto them, not caring how they be qualified; so that ofttimes they are rather the image of men endued with bestial, yea, diabolical affections, than the image of God, endued with reason, understanding, and holiness. I praise God I speak not these things experimentally, by way of complaint of our own condition, but having great cause on the contrary part to be thankful to God for his mercies towards us; but rather, if there be any too desirous of gain, to entreat them to moderate their affections, and consider that no man expecteth fruit before the tree be grown; advising all men, that as they tender their own welfare, so to make choice of such to manage and govern their affairs, as are approved not to be seekers of themselves, but the common good of all for whom they are employed; and beseeching such as have the care of transporting men for the supply and furnishing of plantations, to be truly careful in sending such as may further and not hinder so good an action. There is no godly, honest man but will be helpful in his kind, and adorn his profession with an upright life and conversation; which doctrine of manners [1] ought first to be preached by

---

[1] This sentiment shows how little obnoxious the first settlers of New England were to the charge of fanaticism, which has often been alleged against them by persons alike ignorant of their spirit and their history.

THE EPISTLE DEDICATORY.

giving good example to the poor savage heathens amongst whom they live. On the contrary part, what great offence hath been given by many profane men, who being but seeming Christians, have made Christ and Christianity stink in the nostrils of the poor infidels, and so laid a stumbling-block before them. But woe be to them by whom such offences come.

These things I offer to your Christian considerations, beseeching you to make a good construction of my simple meaning, and take in good part this ensuing Relation, dedicating myself and it evermore unto your service; beseeching God to crown our Christian and faithful endeavours with his blessings temporal and eternal.

Yours in this service,
Ever to be commanded,
E. W.[1]

---

[1] EDWARD WINSLOW was, according to Hutchinson, "of a very reputable family and of a very active genius"—"a gentleman of the best family of any of the Plymouth planters, his father, Edward Winslow, Esq., being a person of some figure at Droitwich, in Worcestershire," a town seven miles from Worcester, celebrated for its salt springs. Edward was the eldest of eight children, and was born at Droitwich Oct. 19, 1595, as appears from the following extract from the records of St. Peter's church in that place: "1595, Oct. 20, baptized Edward, son of Edward Winslow, born the previous Friday," which was the 19th. His mother's name was Magdalen; her surname is unknown; she was married Nov. 3, 1594. He was not one of the original band of Pilgrims who escaped to Holland in 1608, but being on his travels, fell in with them at Leyden, in 1617, as we learn from his Brief Narration, where he speaks of "living three years under Mr. Robinson's ministry before we began the work of plantation in New England." His name stands the third among the signers of the Compact on board the Mayflower; and his family consisted at that time of his wife, Elizabeth, George Soule, and two others, perhaps his children, Edward and John, who died young. As has already been seen, and will hereafter appear, he was one of the most energetic and trusted men in the Colony. He went to England in 1623, 1624, 1635 and 1646, as agent of the Plymouth or Massachusetts colonies; and in 1633 he was chosen governor, to which office he was reëlected in 1636 and 1644. He did not return to New England after 1646. In 1655 he was sent by Cromwell as one of three commissioners to superintend the expedition against the Spanish

possessions in the West Indies, and died at sea, near Hispaniola, on the 8th of May of that year, in his 60th year. An interesting letter, written by him at Barbadoes, March 16, and addressed to Secretary Thurloe, is preserved in Thurloe's State Papers, iii. 250. Three letters of his to Gov. Winthrop, one to the Commissioners of the United Colonies, and another to Thurloe from Barbadoes, March 30, are contained in Hutchinson's Collection of Papers, pp. 60, 110, 153, 228, 268.

In 1637 he obtained a grant of a valuable tract of land at Green's harbour, now Marshfield, to which he gave the name of Careswell. This estate continued in the family till a few years since, when it came into possession of Daniel Webster, the late Secretary of State.

Edward Winslow's son, (2) Josiah, born at Plymouth in 1628, was governor of the Colony, from 1673 to his death in 1680, and commanded the New-England forces in Philip's war. (3) Isaac, his only surviving son, sustained the chief civil and military offices in the county of Plymouth after its incorporation with Massachusetts, and was President of the Provincial Council. He died in 1738, aged 68. (4) John, his son, was a captain in the expedition against Cuba in 1740, a colonel at Louisburgh in 1744, and afterwards a major-general in the British service. He died in 1774, aged 71. His son, (5) Isaac, was a physician in Marshfield, and died in 1819, aged 80. His only son, (6) John, was an attorney, and died in 1822, aged 48. His only surviving son, (7) Isaac, and the last surviving male descendant of Gov. Edward, of the name of Winslow, born in 1813, resides in Boston, and possesses original portraits of these his illustrious ancestors. See Mass. Hist. Coll. xxvii. 286.

Edward Winslow had four brothers, all of whom came over to New England. Their names were, John, born in April, 1597; Kenelm, born, April 29, 1599; Gilbert, born in Oct. 1600; and Josiah, born in Feb. 1605. — John came in the Fortune in 1621, married Mary Chilton, who came in the Mayflower, and removed to Boston, in 1655, where he died in 1674, aged 77. He left a numerous posterity, one of whom is Isaac Winslow, Esq., of Roxbury, formerly a merchant in Boston.—Gilbert came in the Mayflower, and soon left the Colony, and it is thought went to Portsmouth, N. H. and died before 1660.—Kenelm and Josiah arrived at Plymouth before 1632, and both settled at Marshfield. The former died whilst on a visit at Salem in 1672, aged 73, and the latter in 1674, aged 69. — Edward Winslow's sisters were Eleanor, born in April, 1598, Elizabeth, born in March, 1601, and Magdalen, born Dec. 26, 1604. Elizabeth died in Jan. 1604, and neither of the other two ever came to New England.

For the copy of the record of St. Peter's Church, Droitwich, containing the births and baptisms of Edward Winslow and his sisters and brothers, excepting Josiah, I am indebted to Isaac Winslow, Esq., of Roxbury, whose son, Isaac, of New York, visited that place for this purpose in Aug 1839. I am also indebted to Mr. Isaac Winslow, of Boston, for the loan of the family bible of the Winslows, containing on one of its covers an ancient register, corresponding nearly with the Droitwich records, with the addition of the birth and baptism of Josiah, the youngest child. See Hutchinson's Mass. i. 187, ii. 457—460; Belknap's Am. Biog. ii. 281—309; Mitchell's Bridgewater, p. 387—390; Deane's Scituate, p. 388—390; Thacher's Plymouth, p. 90—103, 139—144; Morton's Memorial, pp. 178, 235, 259—261, 382, 415; Hazard's Hist. Coll. i. 326.

TO THE READER.

Good Reader,

When I first penned this Discourse, I intended it chiefly for the satisfaction of my private friends; but since that time have been persuaded to publish the same. And the rather, because of a disorderly colony[1] that are dispersed, and most of them returned, to the great prejudice and damage of him[2] that set them forth; who, as they were a stain to Old England that bred them, in respect of their lives and manners amongst the Indians, so, it is to be feared, will be no less to New England, in their vile and clamorous reports, because she would not foster them in their desired idle courses. I would not be understood to think there were no well deserving persons amongst them; for of mine knowledge it was a grief to some that they were so yoked; whose deserts, as they were then suitable to their honest protestations, so I desire still may be in respect of their just and true Relations.

Peradventure thou wilt rather marvel that I deal so

---

[1] At Wessagusset, or Weymouth, of which an ample account will be found in the ensuing Narrative.

[2] Thomas Weston. See note [1] on page 78.

plainly, than any way doubt of the truth of this my Relation; yea, it may be, tax me therewith, as seeming rather to discourage men than any way to further so noble an action. If any honest mind be discouraged, I am sorry. Sure I am I have given no just cause; and am so far from being discouraged myself, as I purpose to return forthwith.[1] And for other light and vain persons, if they stumble hereat, I have my desire, accounting it better for them and us that they keep where they are, as being unfit and unable to perform so great a task.

Some faults have escaped because I could not attend on the press,[2] which I pray thee correct, as thou findest, and I shall account it as a favor unto me.

Thine,

E. W.

---

[1] Winslow returned in the ship Charity, in March, 1624. He had been absent six months, having sailed from Plymouth in the Anne, on the 10th of Sept. previous. See Bradford, in Prince, p. 221, 225.

[2] This serves to confirm the statement of numerous typographical errors in the previous Narrative. See note on page 113, and note [3] on page 174.

A BRIEF RELATION OF A CREDIBLE INTELLIGENCE OF THE
PRESENT ESTATE OF VIRGINIA.

AT the earnest entreaty of some of my much respected friends, I have added to the former Discourse a Relation of such things as were credibly reported at Plymouth, in New England, in September last past, concerning the present estate of Virginia. And because men may doubt how we should have intelligence of their affairs, being we are so far distant, I will therefore satisfy the doubtful therein. Captain Francis West [1] being in New England about the latter end of May past, sailed from thence to Virginia, and returned in August. In September the same ship and company being discharged by him at Damarin's Cove,[2] came to New Plymouth, where, upon our earnest inquiry after the state of Virginia since that bloody slaughter committed by the Indians upon our friends and countrymen,[3] the whole ship's company agreed in this, viz.

---

[1] West had a commission as admiral of New England, to restrain such ships as came to fish and trade without license from the New England Council ; but finding the fishermen stubborn fellows, and too strong for him, he sails for Virginia; and their owners complaining to Parliament, procured an order that fishing should be free. Bradford, in Prince, p. 218, and in Morton, p. 97.

[2] The Damariscove islands, five or six in number, lying west by north from Monhegan, were early resorted to and occupied as fishing-stages. See Williamson's Maine, i. 56.

[3] On the 22d of March, 1622, at mid-day, the Indians, by a precon-

that upon all occasions they chased the Indians to and fro, insomuch as they sued daily unto the English for peace, who for the present would not admit of any; that Sir George Early,[1] &c. was at that present employed upon service against them; that amongst many others, Opachancano,[2] the chief emperor, was supposed to be slain; his son also was killed at the same time. And though, by reason of these forenamed broils in the fore part of the year, the English had undergone great want of food, yet, through God's mercy, there never was more show of plenty, having as much and as good corn on the ground as ever they had. Neither was the hopes of their tobacco crop inferior to that of their corn; so that the planters were never more full of encouragement; which I pray God long to continue, and so to direct both them and us, as his glory may be the principal aim and end of all our actions, and that for his mercy's sake. Amen.

---

certed plan, fell upon the English settlements in Virginia, and massacred 347 persons. A war of extermination immediately ensued. See Smith's Virginia, ii. 64—79, and Stith, p. 208—213.

[1] Yeardley. See note [1] on p. 70.

[2] Opechancanough, as the name is commonly spelt.

CHAPTER XVIII.

OF THEIR BEING MENACED BY THE NARRAGANSETTS, AND
THEIR SECOND VOYAGE TO THE MASSACHUSETTS.

CHAP. XVIII.

1622.

THE good ship called the FORTUNE, which, in the month of November, 1621, (blessed be God,) brought us a new supply of thirty-five persons, was not long departed our coast, ere the great people of Nanohigganset,[1] which are reported to be many thousands strong, began to breathe forth many threats against us, notwithstanding their desired and obtained peace with us in the foregoing summer; insomuch as the common talk of our neighbour Indians on all sides was of the preparation they made to come against us. In reason a man would think they should have now more cause to fear us than before our supply came. But

---

[1] The Narragansetts were a numerous and powerful tribe that occupied nearly the whole of the present territory of the State of Rhode Island, including the islands in Narragansett Bay. They had escaped the pestilence which had depopulated other parts of New England, and their population at this time was estimated at thirty thousand, of whom five thousand were warriors. Roger Williams says they were so populous that a traveller would meet with a dozen Indian towns in twenty miles. They were a martial and formidable race, and were frequently at war with the Pokanokets on the east, the Pequots on the west, and the Massachusetts on the north. See Gookin in Mass. Hist. Coll. i. 147; Callender in R. I. Hist. Coll. iv. 123; Potter's Early History of Narragansett, ibid. iii. 1, and Hutchinson's Mass. i. 457.

though none of them were present, yet understanding by others that they neither brought arms, nor other provisions with them, but wholly relied on us, it occasioned them to slight and brave us with so many threats as they did.[1] At length came one of them to us, who was sent by Conanacus,[2] their chief sachim or king, accompanied with one Tokamahamon, a friendly Indian.[3] This messenger inquired for Tisquantum, our interpreter, who not being at home, seemed rather to be glad than sorry, and leaving for him a bundle of new arrows, lapped in a rattlesnake's skin, desired to depart with all expedition. But our governors not knowing what to make of this strange carriage, and comparing it with that we had formerly heard, committed him to the custody of Captain Standish, hoping now to know some certainty of that we so often heard, either by his own relation to us, or to Tisquantum, at

---

[1] "Since the death of so many Indians, they thought to lord it over the rest, conceive we are a bar in their way, and see Massasoit already take shelter under our wings." Bradford's Hist. quoted by Prince, p. 200. See pages 217 and 219, previous.

[2] Canonicus, the great sachem of the Narragansetts, though hostile to the Plymouth colonists, probably on account of their league with his enemy, Massasoit, showed himself friendly to the first settlers of Rhode Island, who planted themselves within his territory. Roger Williams says that "when the hearts of my countrymen and friends failed me, the Most High stirred up the barbarous heart of Connonicus to love me as his son to the last gasp. Were it not for the favor that God gave me with him, none of these parts, no, not Rhode Island had been purchased or obtained; for I never gat any thing of Connonicus but by gift." In 1636 the Massachusetts Colony sent to him "a solemn embassage," who "observed in the sachem much state, great command over his men, and marvellous wisdom in his answers." Edward Johnson, who probably accompanied the ambassadors, has given in his "Wonderworking Providence," b. ii. ch. vi. a very minute account of their reception and entertainment. He says that "Canonicus was very discreet in his answers." He died June 4th, 1647, according to Winthrop, "a very old man." See his Life in Thatcher's Indian Biography, i. 177—209, and in Drake's Book of the Indians, b. ii. 54—57. See also Mass. Hist. Coll. iii. 215. 229, xiv. 42—44, xvii. 75, 76; Savage's Winthrop, i. 192, ii. 308.

[3] See pages 211, 214, 219.

his return, desiring myself, having special familiarity with the other forenamed Indian, to see if I could learn any thing from him; whose answer was sparingly to this effect, that he could not certainly tell us, but thought they were enemies to us.

That night Captain Standish gave me and another[1] charge of him, and gave us order to use him kindly, and that he should not want any thing he desired, and to take all occasions to talk and inquire of the reasons of those reports we heard, and withal to signify that upon his true relation he should be sure of his own freedom. At first, fear so possessed him that he could scarce say any thing; but in the end became more familiar, and told us that the messenger which his master sent in summer to treat of peace, at his return persuaded him rather to war; and to the end he might provoke him thereunto, (as appeared to him by our reports,) detained many of the things [which] were sent him by our Governor, scorning the meanness of them both in respect of what himself had formerly sent, and also of the greatness of his own person; so that he much blamed the former messenger, saying, that upon the knowledge of this his false carriage, it would cost him his life, but assured us that upon his relation of our speech then with him to his master, he would be friends with us. Of this we informed the Governor and his Assistant[2] and Captain Standish, who, after consultation, considered him howsoever but in the state of a messenger; and it being as well against the law of arms amongst them as us in Europe to lay violent

---

[1] Probably Stephen Hopkins. See note [2] on page 126, and pages 181, 185, and 202.

[2] Isaac Allerton. See note on page 195, and page 201.

hands on any such, set him at liberty; the Governor giving him order to certify his master that he had heard of his large and many threatenings, at which he was much offended; daring him in those respects to the utmost, if he would not be reconciled to live peaceably, as other his neighbours; manifesting withal (as ever) his desire of peace, but his fearless resolution, if he could not so live amongst them. After which he caused meat to be offered him; but he refused to eat, making all speed to return, and giving many thanks for his liberty, but requesting the other Indian again to return. The weather being violent, he used many words to persuade him to stay longer, but could not. Whereupon he left him, and said he was with his friends, and would not take a journey in such extremity.

After this, when Tisquantum returned, and the arrows were delivered, and the manner of the messenger's carriage related, he signified to the Governor that to send the rattlesnake's skin in that manner imported enmity, and that it was no better than a challenge.[1] Hereupon, after some deliberation, the Governor stuffed the skin with powder and shot, and sent it back, returning no less defiance to Conanacus, assuring him if he had shipping now present, thereby to send his men to Nanohigganset, (the place of his abode,) they should not need to come so far by land to us; yet withal showing that they should never come

---

[1] "There is a remarkable coincidence in the form of this challenge with that of the challenge given by the Scythian prince to Darius. Five arrows made a part of the present sent by his herald to the Persian king. The manner of declaring war by the Aracaunian Indians of South America, was by sending from town to town an arrow clenched in a dead man's hand." Holmes, Annals, i. 177. See Rollin, Anc. Hist. b. vi. s. 4; and Mass. Hist. Coll. xv. 69.

unwelcome or unlooked for. This message was sent by an Indian, and delivered in such sort, as it was no small terror to this savage king; insomuch as he would not once touch the powder and shot, or suffer it to stay in his house or country. Whereupon the messenger refusing it, another took it up; and having been posted from place to place a long time, at length came whole back again.

Feb. In the mean time, knowing our own weakness, notwithstanding our high words and lofty looks towards them, and still lying open to all casualty, having as yet (under God) no other defence than our arms, we thought it most needful to impale our town; which with all expedition we accomplished in the month of February, and some few days, taking in the top of the hill under which our town is seated; making four bulwarks or jetties without the ordinary circuit of the pale, from whence we could defend the whole town; in three whereof are gates,[1] and the fourth in time to be. This being done, Captain Standish divided our strength into four squadrons or companies, appointing whom he thought most fit to have command of each; and, at a general muster or training,[2] appointed each his place, gave each his company, giving them charge, upon every alarm, to resort to their leaders to their appointed place, and, in his absence, to be commanded and directed by them. That done according to his order, each drew his company to his appointed place for defence, and there together discharged their muskets. After which they brought their new com-

---

[1] Bradford adds, "Which are locked every night; a watch and ward kept in the day." Prince, p. 200.

[2] This was the first general muster in New England, and the embryo of our present militia system.

AN ATTACK OF THE INDIANS APPREHENDED. 285

manders to their houses, where again they graced them with their shot, and so departed.

Fearing, also, lest the enemy at any time should take any advantage by firing our houses, Captain Standish appointed a certain company, that whensoever they saw or heard fire to be cried in the town, should only betake themselves to their arms, and should enclose the house or place so endangered, and stand aloof on their guard, with their backs towards the fire, to prevent treachery, if any were in that kind intended. If the fire were in any of the houses of this guard, they were then freed from it; but not otherwise, without special command.

Long before this time we promised the people of Massachusets, in the beginning of March to come unto them, and trade for their furs; which being then come, we began to make preparation for that voyage. In the mean time, an Indian, called Hobbamock, who still lived in the town, told us that he feared the Massachusets or Massachuseucks (for so they called the people of that place,) were joined in confederacy with the Nanohigganeucks, or people of Nanohigganset, and that they therefore would take this opportunity to cut off Captain Standish and his company abroad; but, howsoever, in the mean time, it was to be feared that the Nanohigganeucks would assault the town at home; giving many reasons for his jealousy, as also that Tisquantum was in the confederacy, who, we should find, would use many persuasions to draw us from our shallops to the Indians' houses, for their better advantage. To confirm this his jealousy, he told us of many secret passages that passed between him and others, having their meetings ordinarily

CHAP. XVIII.

1622.
Mar.

abroad, in the woods; but if at home, howsoever, he was excluded from their secrecy; saying it was the manner of the Indians, when they meant plainly, to deal openly; but in this his practice there was no show of honesty.

Hereupon the Governor, together with his Assistant and Captain Standish, called together such as by them were thought most meet for advice in so weighty a business; who, after consideration hereof, came to this resolution; that as hitherto, upon all occasions between them and us, we had ever manifested undaunted courage and resolution, so it would not now stand with our safety to mew up ourselves in our new-enclosed town; partly because our store was almost empty, and therefore must seek out for our daily food, without which we could not long subsist; but especially for that thereby they would see us dismayed, and be encouraged to prosecute their malicious purposes with more eagerness than ever they intended. Whereas, on the contrary, by the blessing of God, our fearless carriage might be a means to discourage and weaken their proceedings. And therefore thought best to proceed in our trading voyage, making this use of that we heard, to go the better provided, and use the more carefulness both at home and abroad, leaving the event to the disposing of the Almighty; whose providence, as it had hitherto been over us for good, so we had now no cause (save our sins) to despair of his mercy in our preservation and continuance, where we desired rather to be instruments of good to the heathens about us than to give them the least measure of just offence.

All things being now in readiness, the forenamed

Captain, with ten men, accompanied with Tisquantum and Hobbamock, set forwards for the Massachusets. But we¹ had no sooner turned the point of the harbour, called the Gurnet's Nose,² (where, being becalmed, we let fall our grapnel to set things to right and prepare to row,) but there came an Indian of Tisquantum's family running to certain of our people that were from home with all eagerness, having his face wounded, and the blood still fresh on the same, calling to them to repair home, oft looking behind him, as if some others had him in chase ; saying that at Namaschet³ (a town some fifteen miles from us,) there were many of the Nanohiggansets, Massassowat⁴ our supposed friend, and Conbatant,⁵ our feared enemy, with many others, with a resolution to take advantage on the present opportunity to assault the town in the Captain's absence ; affirming that he received the wound in his face for speaking in our behalf, and by sleight escaped ; looking oft backward, as if he suspected them to be at hand. This he affirmed again to the Governor; where-

CHAP. XVIII.

1622. April.

¹ This indicates that the writer himself, Winslow, was one of the party.
² So early was the name of Gurnet given to this remarkable feature of Plymouth harbour. It is a peninsula or promontory, connected with Marshfield by a beach about six miles long, called Salthouse beach. It contains about twenty-seven acres of excellent soil. On its southern extremity, or nose, are two light-houses. It probably received its name from some headland known to the Pilgrims in the mother country. The late Samuel Davis, of Plymouth, the accurate topographer, and faithful chronicler of the Old Colony, says, " Gurnet is the name of several places on the coast of England ; in the Channel we believe there are at least two." Connected with the Gurnet by a narrow neck, and contiguous to Clark's island, is another headland, called Saquish, containing ten or fourteen acres. See note ² on page 164, Mass. Hist. Coll. xiii. 182, 204, and Thacher's Plymouth, p. 330.
³ See note ⁴ on page 204.
⁴ The sachem of the Wampanoags. See note ² on page 191. It will be observed that Winslow spells many of the Indian words differently from Bradford in the preceding Journal.
⁵ The same as Coubatant or Corbitant. See note ² on page 219.

upon he gave command that three pieces of ordnance should be made ready and discharged, to the end that if we were not out of hearing, we might return thereat; which we no sooner heard, but we repaired homeward with all convenient speed, arming ourselves, and making all in readiness to fight. When we entered the harbour, we saw the town likewise on their guard, whither we hasted with all convenient speed. The news being made known unto us, Hobbamock said flatly that it was false, assuring us of Massassowat's faithfulness. Howsoever, he presumed he would never have undertaken any such act without his privity, himself being a *pinse*,[1] that is, one of his chiefest champions or men of valor; it being the manner amongst them not to undertake such enterprises without the advice and furtherance of men of that rank. To this the Governor answered, he should be sorry that any just and necessary occasions of war should arise between him and any [of] the savages, but especially Massassowat; not that he feared him more than the rest, but because his love more exceeded towards him than any. Whereunto Hobbamock replied, there was no cause wherefore he should distrust him, and therefore should do well to continue his affections.

But to the end things might be made more manifest, the Governor caused Hobbamock to send his wife with all privacy to Puckanokick, the chief place of Massassowat's residence, (pretending other occasions,) there to inform herself, and so us, of the right state of things. When she came thither, and saw all things quiet, and that no such matter was or had been intended, [she] told Massassowat what had happened at Plymouth, (by

---

[1] What is now called a *brave*.

them called Patuxet;[1]) which, when he understood, he was much offended at the carriage of Tisquantum, returning many thanks to the Governor for his good thoughts of him, and assuring him that, according to their first Articles of Peace,[2] he would send word and give warning when any such business was towards.

Thus by degrees we began to discover Tisquantum, whose ends were only to make himself great in the eyes of his countrymen, by means of his nearness and favor with us; not caring who fell, so he stood. In the general, his course was to persuade them he could lead us to peace or war at his pleasure, and would oft threaten the Indians, sending them word in a private manner we were intended shortly to kill them, that thereby he might get gifts to himself, to work their peace; insomuch as they had him in greater esteem than many of their sachims; yea, they themselves sought to him, who promised them peace in respect of us, yea, and protection also, so as they would resort to him; so that whereas divers were wont to rely on Massassowat for protection, and resort to his abode, now they began to leave him and seek after Tisquantum. Now, though he could not make good these his large promises, especially because of the continued peace between Massassowat and us, he therefore raised this false alarm; hoping, whilst things were hot in the heat of blood, to provoke us to march into his country against him, whereby he hoped to kindle such a flame as would not easily be quenched; and hoping if that block were once removed, there were no other between him and honor, which he loved as his life, and

---

[1] See page 183, and note on page 245.   [2] See the Articles on page 193.

preferred before his peace. For these and the like abuses the Governor sharply reproved him; yet was he so necessary and profitable an instrument, as at that time we could not miss him. But when we understood his dealings, we certified all the Indians of our ignorance and innocency therein; assuring them, till they begun with us, they should have no cause to fear; and if any hereafter should raise any such reports, they should punish them as liars and seekers of their and our disturbance; which gave the Indians good satisfaction on all sides.

After this we proceeded in our voyage to the Massachusets; where we had good store of trade,[1] and (blessed be God) returned in safety, though driven from before our town in great danger and extremity of weather.

At our return we found Massassowat at the Plantation; who made his seeming just apology for all former matters of accusation, being much offended and enraged against Tisquantum; whom the Governor pacified as much as he could for the present. But not long after his departure, he sent a messenger to the Governor, entreating him to give way to the death of Tisquantum, who had so much abused him. But the Governor answered, although he had deserved to die, both in respect of him and us, yet for our sakes he desired he would spare him; and the rather, because without him he knew not well how to understand himself or any other the Indians.[2] With this answer the messenger returned, but came again not long after, accompanied with divers others, demanding him from [3]

---

[1] We should like to have known more about this second voyage to Boston harbour. See page 224.
[2] See note [2] on page 183.
[3] On the part of.

Massassowat, their master, as being one of his subjects, whom, by our first Articles of Peace, we could not retain. Yet because he would not willingly do it without the Governor's approbation, offered him many beavers' skins for his consent thereto, saying that, according to their manner, their sachim had sent his own knife, and them therewith, to cut off his head and hands, and bring them to him. To which the Governor answered, It was not the manner of the English to sell men's lives at a price, but when they had deserved justly to die, to give them their reward; and therefore refused their beavers as a gift; but sent for Tisquantum, who, though he knew their intent, yet offered not to fly, but came and accused Hobbamock as the author and worker of his overthrow, yielding himself to the Governor to be sent or not according as he thought meet. But at the instant when our Governor was ready to deliver him into the hands of his executioners, a boat was seen at sea to cross before our town, and fall behind a headland[1] not far off. Whereupon, having heard many rumors of the French, and not knowing whether there were any combination between the savages and them, the Governor told the Indians he would first know what boat that was ere he would deliver them into their custody. But being mad with rage, and impatient at delay, they departed in great heat.

Here let me not omit one notable, though wicked practice of this Tisquantum; who, to the end he might possess his countrymen with the greater fear of us, and so consequently of himself, told them we had

---

[1] This headland is Hither Manomet Point, forming the southern boundary of Plymouth bay. Manomet is the most prominent landmark in Barnstable bay, being visible from all points of its circling shore, from Sandwich to Provincetown. See note [2] on page 148.

the plague buried in our store-house; which, at our pleasure, we could send forth to what place or people we would, and destroy them therewith, though we stirred not from home. Being, upon the forenamed brabbles,[1] sent for by the Governor to this place, where Hobbamock was and some other of us, the ground being broke in the midst of the house, whereunder certain barrels of powder were buried, though unknown to him, Hobbamock asked him what it meant. To whom he readily answered, That was the place wherein the plague was buried, whereof he formerly told him and others. After this Hobbamock asked one of our people, whether such a thing were, and whether we had such command of it; who answered, No; but the God of the English had it in store, and could send it at his pleasure to the destruction of his and our enemies.

This was, as I take it, about the end of May, 1622; at which time our store of victuals was wholly spent, having lived long before with a bare and short allowance. The reason was, that supply of men, before mentioned,[2] which came so unprovided, not landing so much as a barrel of bread or meal for their whole company, but contrariwise received from us for their ship's store homeward. Neither were the setters forth thereof altogether to be blamed therein, but rather certain amongst ourselves, who were too prodigal in their writing and reporting of that plenty we enjoyed.[3] But that I may return.

This boat proved to be a shallop, that belonged to a

---

[1] Brabbles, clamors.
[2] The passengers in the Fortune. See page 234.
[3] Winslow himself had sent home too flattering an account of their condition. See page 232.

fishing ship, called the Sparrow, set forth by Master Thomas Weston, late merchant and citizen of London, which brought six or seven passengers at his charge, that should before have been landed at our Plantation;[1] who also brought no more provision for the present than served the boat's gang for their return to the ship; which made her voyage at a place called Damarin's Cove,[2] near Munhiggen, some forty leagues from us northeastward; about which place there fished about thirty sail of ships, and whither myself was employed by our Governor, with orders to take up such victuals as the ships could spare; where I found kind entertainment and good respect, with a willingness to supply our wants. But being not able to spare that quantity I required, by reason of the necessity of some amongst themselves, whom they supplied before my coming, would not take any bills for the same, but did what they could freely, wishing their store had been such as they might in greater measure have expressed their own love, and supplied our necessities, for which they sorrowed, provoking one another to the utmost of

CHAP. XVIII.

1622. May.

---

[1] "She brings a letter to Mr. Carver from Mr. Weston, of Jan. 17. By his letter we find he has quite deserted us, and is going to settle a plantation of his own. The boat brings us a kind letter from Mr. John Huddleston, a captain of a ship fishing at the eastward, whose name we never heard before, to inform us of a massacre of 400 English by the Indians in Virginia, whence he came. By this boat the Governor returns a grateful answer, and with them sends Mr. Winslow in a boat of ours to get provisions of the fishing ships; whom Captain Huddleston receives kindly, and not only spares what he can, but writes to others to do the like; by which means he gets as much bread as amounts to a quarter of a pound a person per day till harvest; the Governor causing their portion to be daily given them, or some had starved. And by this voyage we not only got a present supply, but also learn the way to those parts for our future benefit." Bradford, in Prince, p. 202. Huddleston's letter, (or Hudston's, as Morton calls him,) may be found in New England's Memorial, p. 80. See note [3] on page 278.

[2] See note [2] on page 278.

CHAP. XVIII.

1622. June.

their abilities; which, although it were not much amongst so many people as were at the Plantation, yet through the provident and discreet care of the governors, recovered and preserved strength till our own crop on the ground was ready.

Having dispatched there, I returned home with all speed convenient, where I found the state of the Colony much weaker than when I left it; for till now we were never without some bread, the want whereof much abated the strength and flesh of some, and swelled others. But here it may be said, if the country abound with fish and fowl in such measure as is reported, how could men undergo such measure of hardness, except through their own negligence? I answer, every thing must be expected in its proper season. No man, as one saith, will go into an orchard in the winter to gather cherries; so he that looks for fowl there in the summer, will be deceived in his expectation. The time they continue in plenty with us, is from the beginning of October to the end of March; but these extremities befell us in May and June. I confess, that as the fowl decrease, so fish increase. And indeed their exceeding abundance was a great cause of increasing our wants. For though our bay and creeks were full of bass and other fish, yet for want of fit and strong seines and other netting, they for the most part brake through, and carried all away before them.[1] And though the sea were full of cod, yet we had neither tackling nor hawsers for our shallops. And indeed had we not been in a place, where divers sort of shell-fish are, that may be taken with the hand, we must have

---

[1] See note [2] on page 171.

perished, unless God had raised some unknown or extraordinary means for our preservation.

In the time of these straits, indeed before my going to Munhiggen, the Indians began again to cast forth many insulting speeches, glorying in our weakness, and giving out how easy it would be ere long to cut us off. Now also Massassowat seemed to frown on us, and neither came or sent to us as formerly. These things occasioned further thoughts of fortification. And whereas we have a hill called the Mount,[1] enclosed within our pale, under which our town is seated, we resolved to erect a fort thereon; from whence a few might easily secure the town from any assault the Indians can make, whilst the rest might be employed as occasion served. This work was begun with great eagerness, and with the approbation of all men, hoping that this being once finished, and a continual guard there kept, it would utterly discourage the savages from having any hopes or thoughts of rising against us. And though it took the greatest part of our strength from dressing our corn, yet, life being continued, we hoped God would raise some means in stead thereof for our further preservation.

---

[1] The burying-hill. See page 168. The intelligence of the massacre in Virginia reached Plymouth in May, and was the immediate incitement to the erection of this fort. See page 279.

" Some traces of the fort are still visible on the eminence called the burying-hill, directly above the meeting-house of the first church in Plymouth. After the fort was used as a place of worship, it is probable they began to bury their dead around it. Before that time the burial-place was on the bank, above the rock on which the landing was made." Judge Davis's note in Morton's Memorial, p. 82. See note [2] on page 168, and page 169 previous.

CHAPTER XIX.

OF THE PLANTING OF MASTER WESTON'S COLONY AT WESSAGUSSET, AND OF SUNDRY EXCURSIONS AFTER CORN.

IN the end of June, or beginning of July, came into our harbour two ships of Master Weston's aforesaid; the one called the Charity,[1] the other the Swan; having in them some fifty or sixty men, sent over at his own charge to plant for him.[2] These we received into our town, affording them whatsoever courtesy our mean condition could afford. There the Charity, being the bigger ship, left them, having many passengers which she was to land in Virginia. In the mean time the body of them refreshed themselves at Plymouth, whilst some most fit sought out a place for

---

[1] By Mr. Weston's ship comes a letter from Mr. John Pierce, in whose name the Plymouth patent is taken, signifying that whom the governor admits into the association, he will approve." Bradford, in Prince, p. 204.

[2] They came upon no religious design, as did the planters of Plymouth; so they were far from being Puritans. Mr. Weston in a letter owns that many of them are rude and profane fellows. Mr. Cushman in another writes, "They are no men for us, and I fear they will hardly deal so well with the savages as they should. I pray you therefore signify to Squanto that they are a distinct body from us, and we have nothing to do with them, nor must be blamed for their faults, much less can warrant their fidelity." And Mr. John Pierce in another writes, " As for Mr. Weston's company they are so base in condition for the most part, as in all appearance not fit for an honest man's company. I wish they prove otherwise." Bradford, in Prince, p. 203.

them. That little store of corn we had was exceedingly wasted by the unjust and dishonest walking of these strangers; who, though they would sometimes seem to help us in our labor about our corn, yet spared not day and night to steal the same, it being then eatable and pleasant to taste, though green and unprofitable; and though they received much kindness, set light both by it and us, not sparing to requite the love we showed them, with secret backbitings, revilings, &c., the chief of them being forestalled and made against us before they came, as after appeared. Nevertheless, for their master's sake, who formerly had deserved well from us,[1] we continued to do them whatsoever good or furtherance we could, attributing these things to the want of conscience and discretion, expecting each day when God in his providence would disburden us of them, sorrowing that their overseers were not of more ability and fitness for their places, and much fearing what would be the issue of such raw and unconscionable beginnings.

At length their coasters returned, having found in their judgment a place fit for plantation, within the bay of the Massachusets[2] at a place called by the Indians Wichaguscusset.[3] To which place the body of them went with all convenient speed, leaving still with us such as were sick and lame, by the Governor's permission, though on their parts undeserved; whom our surgeon,[4] by the help of God, recovered gratis for them, and they fetched home, as occasion served.

They had not been long from us, ere the Indians

---

[1] See note [1] on page 78.
[2] Boston harbour. See notes [1] and [4] on page 225.
[3] Or Wessagusset, now called Weymouth.
[4] Dr. Fuller. See note [2] on p. 222

CHAP. XIX.
1622.

filled our ears with clamors against them, for stealing their corn, and other abuses conceived by them. At which we grieved the more, because the same men,[1] in mine own hearing, had been earnest in persuading Captain Standish, before their coming, to solicit our Governor to send some of his men to plant by them, alleging many reasons how it might be commodious for us. But we knew no means to redress those abuses, save reproof, and advising them to better walking, as occasion served.

Aug.

In the end of August, came other two ships into our harbour. The one, as I take it, was called the Discovery, Captain Jones[2] having the command thereof; the other was that ship of Mr. Weston's, called the Sparrow, which had now made her voyage of fish, and was consorted with the other, being both bound for Virginia.[3] Of Captain Jones we furnished ourselves of such provisions as we most needed, and he could best spare; who, as he used us kindly, so made us pay largely for the things we had. And had not the Almighty, in his all-ordering providence, directed him to us, it would have gone worse with us than ever it had been, or after was; for as we had now but small store of corn for the year following, so, for want of supply, we were worn out of all manner of trucking-stuff, not having any means left to help ourselves by trade; but, through God's good mercy towards us, he had where-

---

[1] That is, the same Indians.

[2] This is supposed to be the same Jones who was captain of the Mayflower. See note [1] on page 102, and note [6] on page 166.

[3] Prince says, p. 205, that "Mr. Winslow seems to mistake in thinking Captain Jones was now bound for Virginia;" and Bradford states that "she was on her way from Virginia homeward, being sent out by some merchants to discover the shoals about Cape Cod, and harbours between this and Virginia."

with, and did supply our wants on that kind competently.[1]

In the end of September, or beginning of October, Mr. Weston's biggest ship, called the Charity, returned for England, and left their colony sufficiently victualled, as some of most credit amongst them reported. The lesser, called the Swan, remained with his colony, for their further help. At which time they desired to join in partnership with us, to trade for corn; to which our Governor and his Assistant[2] agreed, upon such equal conditions, as were drawn and confirmed between them and us. The chief places aimed at were to the southward of Cape Cod; and the more, because Tisquantum, whose peace before this time was wrought with Massassowat, undertook to discover unto us that supposed, and still hoped, passage within the shoals.

Both colonies being thus agreed, and their companies fitted and joined together, we resolved to set forward, but were oft crossed in our purposes. As first Master Richard Greene, brother-in-law to Master Weston, who from him had a charge in the oversight and government of his colony, died suddenly at our Plantation, to whom we gave burial befitting his place, in the best manner we could. Afterward, having further order to proceed by letter from their other Governor at the Massachusets, twice Captain Standish set forth with them, but were driven in again by cross and violent winds; himself the second time being sick

---

[1] "Of her we buy knives and beads, which is now good trade, though at cent. per cent. or more, and yet pay away coat beaver at 3s. a pound, (which a few years after yields 20s.); by which means we are fitted to trade both for corn and beaver." Bradford, in Prince, p. 205, and in Morton's Memorial, p. 83.

[2] Isaac Allerton.

CHAP. XIX.

1622.

Nov.

of a violent fever. By reason whereof (our own wants being like to be now greater than formerly, partly because we were enforced to neglect our corn and spend much time in fortification, but especially because such havock was made of that little we had, through the unjust and dishonest carriage of those people, before mentioned, at our first entertainment of them,) our Governor in his own person supplied the Captain's place; and, in the month of November, again set forth, having Tisquantum for his interpreter and pilot; who affirmed he had twice passed within the shoals of Cape Cod, both with English and French. Nevertheless they went so far with him, as the master of the ship saw no hope of passage; but being, as he thought, in danger, bare up, and according to Tisquantum's directions, made for a harbour not far from them, at a place called Manamoycke;[1] which they found, and sounding it with their shallop, found the channel, though but narrow and crooked; where at length they harboured the ship. Here they perceived that the tide set in and out with more violence at some other place more southerly,[2] which they had not seen nor could discover, by reason of the violence of the season all the time of their abode there. Some judged the entrance thereof might be beyond the shoals; but there is no certainty thereof as yet known.

That night the Governor, accompanied with others, having Tisquantum for his interpreter, went ashore. At first, the inhabitants played least in sight, because none of our people had ever been there before; but understanding the ends of their coming, at length came to them, welcoming our Governor according to their

---

[1] Chatham.   [2] See note [1] on page 103.

savage manner; refreshing them very well with store of venison and other victuals, which they brought them in great abundance; promising to trade with them, with a seeming gladness of the occasion. Yet their joy was mixed with much jealousy, as appeared by their after practices; for at first they were loth their dwellings should be known; but when they saw our Governor's resolution to stay on the shore all night, they brought him to their houses, having first conveyed all their stuff to a remote place, not far from the same; which one of our men, walking forth occasionally, espied. Whereupon, on the sudden, neither it nor they could be found; and so many times after, upon conceived occasions, they would be all gone, bag and baggage. But being afterwards, by Tisquantum's means better persuaded, they left their jealousy, and traded with them; where they got eight hogsheads of corn and beans, though the people were but few. This gave our Governor and the company good encouragement; Tisquantum being still confident in the passage, and the inhabitants affirming they had seen ships of good burthen pass within the shoals aforesaid.

But here, though they had determined to make a second essay, yet God had otherways disposed; who struck Tisquantum with sickness, insomuch as he there died;[1] which crossed their southward trading, and the

---

[1] His disorder was a fever, accompanied with "a bleeding at the nose, which the Indians reckon a fatal symptom." Before his death "he desired the Governor (Bradford) to pray that he might go to the Englishman's God in heaven, bequeathing divers of his things to sundry of his English friends, as remembrances of his love; of whom we had great loss." Bradford, in Prince, p. 206, and in Morton, p. 85. Judge Davis adds in his note, that "Governor Bradford's pen was worthily employed in the tender notice taken of the death of this child of nature. With some aberrations, his conduct was generally irreproachable, and his useful services to the infant settlement entitle him to grateful remembrance."

CHAP.
XIX.

1622.
Nov.

more, because the master's sufficiency was much doubted, and the season very tempestuous, and not fit to go upon discovery, having no guide to direct them.

From thence they departed; and the wind being fair for the Massachusets, went thither, and the rather, because the savages, upon our motion, had planted much corn for us, which they promised not long before that time. When they came thither, they found a great sickness to be amongst the Indians, not unlike the plague, if not the same. They renewed their complaints to our Governor, against that other plantation seated by them, for their injurious walking. But indeed the trade both for furs and corn was overthrown in that place, they giving as much for a quart of corn as we used to do for a beaver's skin; so that little good could be there done.

From thence they returned into the bottom of the bay of Cape Cod, to a place called Nauset; where the sachim[1] used the Governor very kindly, and where they bought eight or ten hogsheads of corn and beans; also at a place called Mattachiest,[2] where they had like kind entertainment and corn also. During the time of their trade in these places, there were so great and violent storms, as the ship was much endangered, and our shallop cast away; so that they had now no means to carry the corn aboard that they had bought, the ship riding by their report well near two leagues from the same, her own boat being small, and so leaky, (having no carpenter with them,) as they durst scarce fetch wood or water in her. Hereupon the Governor caused the corn to be made in a round stack, and bought mats,

---

[1] Aspinet. See page 216.
[2] The country between Barnstable and Yarmouth harbours. See note [1] on page 215.

and cut sedge, to cover it; and gave charge to the Indians not to meddle with it, promising him that dwelt next to it a reward, if he would keep vermin also from it; which he undertook, and the sachim promised to make good. In the mean time, according to the Governor's request, the sachim sent men to seek the shallop; which they found buried almost in sand at a high water mark, having many things remaining in her, but unserviceable for the present; whereof the Governor gave the sachim special charge, that it should not be further broken, promising ere long to fetch both it and the corn; assuring them, if neither were diminished, he would take it as a sign of their honest and true friendship, which they so much made show of; but if they were, they should certainly smart for their unjust and dishonest dealing, and further make good whatsoever they had so taken. So he did likewise at Mattachiest, and took leave of them, being resolved to leave the ship and take his journey home by land with our own company, sending word to the ship that they should take their first opportunity to go for Plymouth, where he determined, by the permission of God, to meet them. And having procured a guide, it being no less than fifty miles to our Plantation,[1] set forward, receiving all respect that could be from the Indians in his journey; and came safely home, though weary and surbated;[2] whither some three days after the ship[3] also came.

The corn being divided, which they had got, Master Weston's company went to their own plantation; it

---

[1] The distance from Eastham to Plymouth by land is about fifty miles.
[2] With galled feet.
[3] The Swan. See page 299.

CHAP. XIX.

1623. Jan.

being further agreed, that they should return with all convenient speed, and bring their carpenter, that they might fetch the rest of the corn, and save the shallop.

At their return, Captain Standish, being recovered and in health, took another shallop, and went with them to the corn, which they found in safety as they left it. Also they mended the other shallop, and got all their corn aboard the ship. This was in January, as I take it, it being very cold and stormy; insomuch as, (the harbour being none of the best,) they were constrained to cut both the shallops from the ship's stern; and so lost them both a second time. But the storm being over, and seeking out, they found them both, not having received any great hurt.

Whilst they were at Nauset, having occasion to lie on the shore, laying their shallop in a creek [1] not far from them, an Indian came into the same, and stole certain beads, scissors, and other trifles, out of the same; which, when the Captain missed, he took certain of his company with him, and went to the sachim, telling him what had happened, and requiring the same again, or the party that stole them, (who was known to certain of the Indians,) or else he would revenge it on them before his departure; and so took leave for that night, being late, refusing whatsoever kindness they offered. On the morrow the sachim came to their rendezvous, accompanied with many men, in a stately manner, who saluted [2] the Captain in this wise. He thrust out his tongue, that one might see the root thereof, and therewith licked his hand

---

[1] Nauset, or Eastham, abounds with creeks. See note [1] on page 156, and Mass. Hist. Coll. viii. 155, 188.

[2] In the original *saluting*; probably a typographical error.

from the wrist to the finger's end, withal bowing the knee, striving to imitate the English gesture, being instructed therein formerly by Tisquantum. His men did the like, but in so rude and savage a manner, as our men could scarce forbear to break out in open laughter. After salutation, he delivered the beads and other things to the Captain, saying he had much beaten the party for doing it; causing the women to make bread, and bring them, according to their desire; seeming to be very sorry for the fact, but glad to be reconciled. So they departed and came home in safety; where the corn was equally divided, as before.

After this the Governor went to two other inland towns, with another company, and bought corn likewise of them. The one is called Namasket,[1] the other Manomet.[2] That from Namasket was brought home partly by Indian women;[3] but a great sickness arising amongst them, our own men were enforced to fetch home the rest. That at Manomet the Governor left in the sachim's custody.

This town lieth from us south, well near twenty miles, and stands upon a fresh river, which runneth into the bay of Nanohigganset,[4] and cannot be less than sixty miles from thence. It will bear a boat of

---

[1] See note 4 on page 204.

[2] The part of Sandwich, which lies on Manomet river. F.

[3] "It is almost incredible," says Roger Williams, "what burthens the poor women carry of corn, of fish, of beans, of mats, and a child besides." Gookin says, "In their removals from place to place, for their fishing and hunting, the women carry the greatest burthen." And Wood says, "In the summer they trudge home two or three miles with a hundred weight of lobsters at their backs; in winter they are their husbands' porters to lug home their venison." See Mass. Hist. Coll. i. 149, iii. 212, and Wood's New England's Prospect, part ii. ch. 20.

[4] This is called Manomet or Buzzard's bay, though Winslow seems to mistake it for Narragansett bay, which is near twenty leagues to the westward. Prince, p. 208.

CHAP. XIX.

1623. Jan.

eight or ten tons to this place. Hither the Dutch or French, or both, use to come. It is from hence to the bay of Cape Cod, about eight miles;[1] out of which bay it floweth into a creek some six miles, almost direct towards the town. The heads of the river and this creek are not far distant. This river yieldeth, thus high, oysters,[2] muscles, clams,[3] and other shellfish; one in shape like a bean,[4] another like a clam; both good meat, and great abundance at all times; besides it aboundeth with divers sorts of fresh fish in their seasons.[5]

---

[1] "This creek runs out easterly into Cape Cod bay at Scussett harbour; and this river runs out westerly into Manomet bay. The distance overland from bay to bay is but six miles. The creek and river nearly meet in a low ground; and this is the place, through which there has been a talk of making a canal, these forty years; which would be a vast advantage to all these countries, by saving the long and dangerous navigation round the Cape, and through the shoals adjoining." Prince, p. 208, (A. D. 1736.) Mass. Hist. Coll. viii. 122.

[2] Oysters are still found in great excellence and plenty in Sandwich, on the shores of Buzzard's bay. See Mass. Hist. Coll. viii. 122.

[3] The common clam, (*mya arenaria,*) or perhaps the quahaug, (*venus mercenaria.*) The English call the former the sand-gaper, the word *clam* not being in use among them, and not to be found in their dictionaries. And yet it is mentioned by Captain Smith, in his Description of New England, printed in 1616. Johnson, whose Wonderworking Providence was published in 1654, speaks of "*clambanks,* a fish as big as horse-muscles." Morton too, in his New English Canaan, (1637) mentions them, and Josselyn, (1672) in his Rarities, p. 96, speaks of "clam, or clamp, a kind of shell-fish, a white muscle." Wood says, ch. ix. "clams or clamps is a shellfish not much unlike a cockle; it lieth under the sand. These fishes be in great plenty. In some places of the country there be clams as big as a penny white-loaf." See Mass. Hist. Col. iii. 224, viii. 193, xiii. 125, xxvi. 121, and Dr. Gould's Report on the Mollusca of Mass. pp. 40—42, and 85, 86.

[4] The razor-shell, (*solen,*) which very much resembles a bean pod, or the haft of a razor, both in size and shape. See Mass. Hist. Coll. viii. 192. Josselyn calls them "*sheath fish,* which are very plentiful, a delicate fish, as good as a prawn, covered with a thin shell like the sheath of a knife, and of the color of a muscle." And Morton says, "*razor fishes* there are." "The animal is cylindrical, and is often used as an article of food under the name of long-clam, razor-fish, knife-handle, &c." See Dr. Gould's Report on the Mollusca of Massachusetts, p. 29.

[5] In Manomet river, as well as in Buzzard's and Buttermilk bays, are found fish of various kinds, such as bass, sheep's head, tautaug, scuppaug, &c. See Mass. Hist. Coll. viii. 122.

The governor, or sachim, of this place was called Canacum;[1] who had formerly, as well as many others, yea all with whom as yet we had to do, acknowledged themselves the subjects of our sovereign lord, the King. This sachim used the Governor very kindly; and it seemed was of good respect and authority amongst the Indians. For whilst the Governor was there, within night, in bitter weather, came two men from Manamoick, before spoken of; and having set aside their bows and quivers, according to their manner, sat down by the fire, and took a pipe of tobacco, not using any words in that time, nor any other to them, but all remained silent, expecting when they would speak. At length they looked toward Canacum; and one of them made a short speech, and delivered a present to him from his sachim, which was a basket of tobacco and many beads, which the other received thankfully. After which he made a long speech to him; the contents hereof was related to us by Hobbamock (who then accompanied the Governor for his guide,) to be as followeth. It happened that two of their men fell out, as they were in game, (for they use gaming as much as any where, and will play away all, even their skin from their backs,[2] yea their wives' skins also, though it may be they are many miles distant from them, as myself have seen,) and growing to great heat, the one killed

---

[1] He was the same as Cawnacome, mentioned in note [3] on page 232.

[2] "In their gamings," says Roger Williams, "they will sometimes stake and lose their money, clothes, house, corn, and themselves, if single persons." Gookin says, "They are addicted to gaming, and will, in that vein, play away all they have." And Wood adds, "They are so bewitched with these two games, that they will lose sometimes all they have, beaver, moose skins, kettles, wampompeage, mowhackies, hatchets, knives, all is confiscate by these two games." See Mass. Hist. Coll. i. 153, iii. 234, and Wood's New England's Prospect, part ii. ch. 14.

the other. The actor of this fact was a *powah*,[1] one of special note amongst them, and such an one as they could not well miss; yet another people greater than themselves threatened them with war, if they would not put him to death. The party offending was in hold; neither would their sachim do one way or other till their return, resting upon him for advice and furtherance in so weighty a matter. After this there was silence a short time. At length, men gave their judgment what they thought best. Amongst others, he asked Hobbamock what he thought; who answered, He was but a stranger to them; but thought it was better that one should die than many, since he had deserved it, and the rest were innocent. Whereupon he passed the sentence of death upon him.

Not long after, having no great quantity of corn left, Captain Standish went again with a shallop to Mattachiest, meeting also with the like extremity of weather, both of wind, snow, and frost; insomuch as they were frozen in the harbour, the first night they entered the same. Here they pretended their wonted love, and spared them a good quantity of corn to confirm the same. Strangers also came to this place, pretending only to see him and his company, whom they never saw before that time, but intending to join with the rest to kill them, as after appeared. But being forced through extremity to lodge in their houses, which they much pressed, God possessed the heart of the Captain with just jealousy, giving strait command, that as one part of his company slept, the rest should wake, declaring some things to them which he understood, whereof he could make no good construction.

[1] *Powow*, a priest and medicine man.

Some of the Indians, spying a fit opportunity, stole some beads also from him; which he no sooner perceived, having not above six men with him, drew them all from the boat, and set them on their guard about the sachim's house, where the most of the people were; threatening to fall upon them without further delay, if they would not forthwith restore them; signifying to the sachim especially, and so to them all, that as he would not offer the least injury, so he would not receive any at their hands, which should escape without punishment or due satisfaction. Hereupon the sachim bestirred him to find out the party; which, when he had done, caused him to return them again to the shallop, and came to the Captain, desiring him to search whether they were not about the boat; who, suspecting their knavery, sent one, who found them lying openly upon the boat's cuddy. Yet to appease his anger, they brought corn afresh to trade; insomuch as he laded his shallop, and so departed. This accident so daunted their courage, as they durst not attempt any thing against him. So that, through the good mercy and providence of God, they returned in safety. At this place the Indians get abundance of bass both summer and winter; for it being now February, they abounded with them.

In the beginning of March, having refreshed himself, he took a shallop, and went to Manomet, to fetch home that which the Governor had formerly bought,[1] hoping also to get more from them; but was deceived in his expectation, not finding that entertainment he found elsewhere, and the Governor had there received.

---

[1] It seems as if the Captain went into Scussett harbour, which goes up westward towards Manomet. Prince, p. 210.

CHAP. XIX.

1623. Mar.

The reason whereof, and of the treachery intended in the place before spoken of, was not then known unto us, but afterwards; wherein may be observed the abundant mercies of God, working with his providence for our good. Captain Standish being now far from the boat, and not above two or three of our men with him, and as many with the shallop, was not long at Canacum, the sachim's house, but in came two of the Massachuset men. The chief of them was called Wituwamat, a notable insulting villain, one who had formerly imbrued his hands in the blood of English and French, and had oft boasted of his own valour, and derided their weakness, especially because, as he said, they died crying, making sour faces, more like children than men.

This villain took a dagger from about his neck, which he had gotten of Master Weston's people, and presented it to the sachim; and after made a long speech in an audacious manner, framing it in such sort, as the Captain, though he be the best linguist amongst us,[1] could not gather any thing from it. The end of it was afterwards discovered to be as followeth. The Massacheuseuks had formerly concluded to ruinate Master Weston's colony; and thought themselves, being about thirty or forty men, strong enough to execute the same. Yet they durst not attempt it, till such time as they had gathered more strength to themselves, to make their party good against us at Plymouth; concluding, that if we remained, though they had no other arguments to use against us, yet we would never leave the death of our countrymen unrevenged; and there-

[1] In the Indian dialects.

fore their safety could not be without the overthrow of both plantations. To this end they had formerly solicited this sachim, as also the other, called Ianough,[1] at Mattachiest, and many others, to assist them, and now again came to prosecute the same; and since there was so fair an opportunity offered by the Captain's presence, they thought best to make sure [of] him and his company.

After this his message was delivered, his entertainment much exceeded the Captain's; insomuch as he scorned at their behaviour, and told them of it. After which they would have persuaded him, because the weather was cold, to have sent to the boat for the rest of his company; but he would not, desiring, according to promise, that the corn might be carried down, and he would content the women[2] for their labor; which they did. At the same time there was a lusty Indian of Paomet,[3] or Cape Cod, then present, who had ever demeaned himself well toward us, being in his general carriage very affable, courteous, and loving, especially towards the Captain. This savage was now entered into confederacy with the rest; yet, to avoid suspicion, made many signs of his continued affections, and would needs bestow a kettle of some six or seven gallons on him, and would not accept of any thing in lieu thereof, saying he was rich and could afford to bestow such favors on his friends whom he loved. Also he would freely help to carry some of the corn, affirming he had never done the like in his life before; and the wind being bad, would needs lodge with

---

[1] Or Iyanough. See note [1] on page 215.
[2] See note [2] on page 305.
[3] Or Pamet, now called Truro. See pages 135 and 139.

him at their rendezvous, having indeed undertaken to kill him before they parted; which done, they intended to fall upon the rest.

The night proved exceeding cold; insomuch as the Captain could not take any rest, but either walked, or turned himself to and fro at the fire. This the other observed, and asked wherefore he did not sleep as at other times; who answered, He knew not well, but had no desire at all to rest. So that he then missed his opportunity.

The wind serving on the next day, they returned home, accompanied with the other Indian; who used many arguments to persuade them to go to Paomet, where himself had much corn, and many other, the most whereof he would procure for us, seeming to sorrow for our wants. Once the Captain put forth with him, and was forced back by contrary wind; which wind serving for the Massachuset, was fitted to go thither. But on a sudden it altered again.

CHAPTER XX.

WINSLOW'S SECOND JOURNEY TO PACKANOKICK, TO VISIT MASSASOIT IN HIS SICKNESS.

DURING the time that the Captain was at Manomet, news came to Plymouth that Massassowat was like to die, and that at the same time there was a Dutch ship driven so high on the shore by stress of weather, right before his dwelling, that till the tides increased, she could not be got off. Now it being a commendable manner of the Indians, when any, especially of note, are dangerously sick, for all that profess friendship to them to visit them in their extremity,[1] either in their persons, or else to send some acceptable persons to them; therefore it was thought meet, being a good and warrantable action, that as we had ever professed friendship, so we should now maintain the same, by observing this their laudable custom; and the rather, because we desired to have some conference with the Dutch, not knowing when we should have so fit an opportunity. To that end, myself having formerly

---

[1] "All their refreshing in their sickness is the visit of friends and neighbours, a poor empty visit and presence; and yet indeed this is very solemn, unless it be in infectious diseases, and then all forsake them and fly." Roger Williams, in Mass. Hist. Coll. iii. 236.

CHAP. XX.
1 6 2 3.
Mar.

been there, and understanding in some measure the Dutch tongue, the Governor again laid this service upon myself, and fitted me with some cordials to administer to him; having one Master John Hamden,[1] a gentleman of London, who then wintered with us, and desired much to see the country, for my consort, and Hobbamock for our guide. So we set forward,

1st day.
and lodged the first night at Namasket, where we had friendly entertainment.

2d day.
The next day, about one of the clock, we came to

[1] It was conjectured by Belknap, Am. Biog. ii. 229, and has since been repeatedly asserted as a fact by other writers, that this person was the celebrated English patriot of the same name. But this is highly improbable. Hampden, who was born in 1594, and married in 1619, was a member of the parliament which assembled in January, 1621, and was dissolved by James in 1622, under circumstances and in a juncture of affairs which rendered it certain that a new parliament must soon be called. It is not at all likely that a person in Hampden's circumstances, a man of family, wealth and consideration, would, merely for the sake of gratifying his curiosity, have left England at this critical period, on a long voyage to another hemisphere, and run the risk of not being at home at the issuing of the writs for a new parliament. For the passage to America was at that time precarious; the vessels were few, and the voyage a long one; so that a person who undertook it could not reasonably calculate upon getting back in much less than a year. Winslow's companion, whoever he was, must have come in the Charity, which brought Weston's colony, unless we adopt the improbable supposition that this " gentleman of London " embarked in one of the fishing vessels that visited the Grand Bank, and took his chance of getting to Plymouth as he could. Now the Charity left London the last of April, 1622, and arrived at Plymouth the last of June. The visit to Massasoit took place in March, 1623, and after this no vessel sailed for England till the Anne, September 10, in which Winslow went home. Of course this " gentleman of London," must have been absent at least eighteen months, which it is altogether improbable that Hampden would have done, running the risk of not being at home to stand for the next parliament, to which he undoubtedly expected to be returned, as we know he actually was.

Besides, had this companion of Winslow been the great English patriot, the silence of the early Plymouth writers on the point is unaccountable. On publishing his "Good News from New England" immediately on his arrival in London, in 1624, one object of which was to recommend the new colony, how gladly would Winslow have appealed for the correctness of his statements to this member of parliament who had passed more than a year in their Plantation. How natural too would it have been for him to have mentioned the fact in his " Brief Narration," published in 1646, only three years after the death of the illustrious patriot. Bradford,

a ferry[1] in Conbatant's country, where, upon discharge of my piece, divers Indians came to us from a house not far off. There they told us that Massassowat was dead, and that day buried; and that the Dutch would be gone before we could get thither, having hove off their ship already. This news struck us blank, but especially Hobbamock, who desired we might return with all speed. I told him I would first think of it. Considering now, that he being dead, Conbatant[2] was the most like to succeed him, and that we were not above three miles from Mattapuyst,[3] his dwelling-place, although he were but a hollow-

also, whose sympathies were all with the popular party in England, in writing an elaborate history of the Colony, would not have failed to record the long residence among them of one who, at the time he wrote, had become so distinguished as the leader of that party in the House of Commons. That his lost history contained no such passage we may be certain; for had it been there, it must have been quoted either by Prince or Morton, who make so free use of it, both of whom too mention this visit to Massasoit, and who would not have omitted a circumstance so honorable to the Colony.

Again. Winslow's companion was "a gentleman of *London.*" Now although John Hampden happened to be born in London, when his father was in parliament in 1594, he was properly of Buckinghamshire. Winslow, who was himself of Worcestershire, if he knew who Hampden was, would not have called him "a gentleman of *London;*" and we cannot suppose that this English gentleman would have spent so many months in the Colony without making himself known to its two leading men, Winslow and Bradford.

Equally unfounded is the statement that has gained so wide a currency and become incorporated with the history of those times, and is repeated in Lord Nugent's Life of Hampden, that John Hampden, in company with Cromwell, Pym, and Hazelrig, had actually embarked for America on board a fleet in the Thames, in 1638, but were detained by an order from the Privy Council. Miss Aikin, in her Memoirs of Charles I., ch. xiii., was the first to detect and expose this error of the historians. — For some of the views in this note I am indebted to the MS. suggestions of the learned editor of Governor Winthrop's History of New England.

[1] Probably the same which is now called Slade's Ferry, in Swanzey. Belknap's Am. Biog. ii. 292.

[2] Conbatant or Corbitant, was the sachem of Pocasset, and was subject to Massasoit. See Baylies' Plymouth, ii. 232.

[3] A neck of land in the township of Swanzey, commonly pronounced Mattapoiset, now Gardner's neck, situated between the Shawomet and Toweset necks. See Belknap's Am. Biog. ii. 292, and Baylies' Plymouth, ii. 232, 234.

hearted friend toward us, I thought no time so fit as this to enter into more friendly terms with him, and the rest of the sachims thereabout; hoping, through the blessing of God, it would be a means, in that unsettled state, to settle their affections towards us; and though it were somewhat dangerous, in respect of our personal safety, because myself and Hobbamock had been employed upon a service against him,[1] which he might now fitly revenge; yet esteeming it the best means, leaving the event to God in his mercy, I resolved to put it in practice, if Master Hamden and Hobbamock durst attempt it with me; whom I found willing to that or any other course might tend to the general good. So we went towards Mattapuyst.

In the way, Hobbamock, manifesting a troubled spirit, brake forth into these speeches: *Neen womasu sagimus, neen womasu sagimus*, &c. "My loving sachim, my loving sachim! Many have I known, but never any like thee." And turning him to me, said, whilst I lived, I should never see his like amongst the Indians; saying, he was no liar, he was not bloody and cruel, like other Indians; in anger and passion he was soon reclaimed; easy to be reconciled towards such as had offended him; ruled by reason in such measure as he would not scorn the advice of mean men; and that he governed his men better with few strokes, than others did with many; truly loving where he loved; yea, he feared we had not a faithful friend left among the Indians; showing, how he ofttimes restrained their malice, &c., continuing a long speech, with such signs of lamentation and unfeigned sorrow, as it would have made the hardest heart relent.

[1] See page 220.

At length we came to Mattapuyst, and went to the sachimo comaco,[1] for so they call the sachim's place, though they call an ordinary house *witeo*;[2] but Conbatant, the sachim, was not at home, but at Puckanokick, which was some five or six miles off. The *squa-sachim*, for so they call the sachim's wife, gave us friendly entertainment. Here we inquired again concerning Massassowat; they thought him dead, but knew no certainty. Whereupon I hired one to go with all expedition to Puckanokick, that we might know the certainty thereof, and withal to acquaint Conbatant with our there being. About half an hour before sun-setting the messenger returned, and told us that he was not yet dead, though there was no hope we should find him living. Upon this we were much revived, and set forward with all speed, though it was late within night ere we got thither. About two of the clock that afternoon, the Dutchmen departed; so that in that respect our journey was frustrate.

When we came thither, we found the house so full of men, as we could scarce get in, though they used their best diligence to make way for us. There were they in the midst of their charms for him, making such a hellish noise, as it distempered us that were well, and therefore unlike to ease him that was sick.[3] About

---

[1] "*Sachimmaacommock*, a prince's house, which, according to their condition, is far different from the other house, both in capacity or receipt, and also the fineness and quality of their mats." Roger Williams's Key, ch. xxii.

[2] *Wetu*, or *wigwam*. See Gallatin's Indian Vocabularies, in Am. Antiq. Soc. Coll. ii. 322.

[3] "There are among them certain men and women, whom they call *powows*. These are partly wizards and witches, holding familiarity with Satan, that evil one; and partly are physicians, and make use, at least in show, of herbs and roots for curing the sick and diseased. These are sent for by the sick and wounded; and by their diabolical spells, mutterings, exorcisms, they seem to do wonders. They use extraordinary strange motions of their bodies, insomuch that they will sweat until they foam; and thus continue for some hours

him were six or eight women, who chafed his arms, legs, and thighs, to keep heat in him. When they had made an end of their charming, one told him that his friends, the English, were come to see him. Having understanding left, but his sight was wholly gone, he asked, Who was come? They told him Winsnow, for they cannot pronounce the letter *l*, but ordinarily *n* in the place thereof.[1] He desired to speak with me. When I came to him, and they told him of it, he put forth his hand to me, which I took. Then he said twice, though very inwardly, *Keen Winsnow?* which is to say, "Art thou Winslow?" I answered, *Ahhe*, that is, Yes. Then he doubled these words; *Matta neen wonckanet namen, Winsnow!* that is to say, "O Winslow, I shall never see thee again."

Then I called Hobbamock, and desired him to tell Massassowat, that the Governor, hearing of his sick-

together, stroking and hovering over the sick." Gookin, in Mass. Hist. Coll. i. 154.

"*Powaws*, priests. These do begin and order their service and invocation of their gods, and all the people follow, and join interchangeably in a laborious bodily service, unto sweating, especially of the priest, who spends himself in strange antic gestures and actions, even unto fainting. In sickness the priest comes close to the sick person, and performs many strange actions about him, and threatens and conjures out the sickness. The poor people commonly die under their hands; for, alas, they administer nothing, but howl and roar and hollow over them, and begin the song to the rest of the people, who all join like a choir in prayer to their gods for them." Roger Williams, in Mass. Hist. Coll. iii. 227, 237.

"The manner of their action in their conjuration is thus. The parties that are sick are brought before them; the powow sitting down, the rest of the Indians give attentive audience to his imprecations and invocations, and after the violent expression of many a hideous bellowing and groaning, he makes a stop, and then all the auditors with one voice utter a short canto. Which done, the powow still proceeds in his invocations, sometimes roaring like a bear, other times groaning like a dying horse, foaming at the mouth like a chafed boar, smiting on his naked breast and thighs with such violence as if he were mad. Thus will he continue sometimes half a day." Wood's New England's Prospect, part ii. ch. 12. See also Hutchinson's Mass. i. 474.

[1] Wood says, ch. 18, "They pronounce *l* and *r* in our English tongue, with much difficulty, calling a lobster a nobstan." Yet

ness, was sorry for the same; and though, by reason of many businesses, he could not come himself, yet he sent me with such things for him as he thought most likely to do him good in this his extremity;[1] and whereof if he pleased to take, I would presently give him; which he desired; and having a confection of many comfortable conserves, &c., on the point of my knife I gave him some, which I could scarce get through his teeth. When it was dissolved in his mouth, he swallowed the juice of it; whereat those that were about him much rejoiced, saying he had not swallowed any thing in two days before. Then I desired to see his mouth, which was exceedingly furred, and his tongue swelled in such a manner, as it was not possible for him to eat such meat as they had, his passage being stopped up. Then I washed his mouth, and scraped his tongue, and got abundance of corruption out of the same. After which I gave him more of the confection, which he swallowed with more readiness. Then he desiring to drink, I dissolved some of it in water, and gave him thereof. Within half an hour this wrought a great alteration in him, in

---

Roger Williams states, that "although some pronounce not *l* nor *r*, yet it is the most proper dialect of other places, contrary to many reports;" and Eliot, in his Indian Grammar, says, "These consonants, *l*, *n*, *r*, have such a natural coincidence, that it is an eminent variation of their dialects. We Massachusetts pronounce the *n*; the Nipmuk Indians pronounce *l*; and the Northern Indians pronounce *r*. As instance:

   We say   *Anum* ⎫
   Nipmuck, *Alum* ⎬ A Dog."
   Northern, *Arum* ⎭

See Mass. Hist. Coll. iii. 223, xix. 248.

[1] "When they are sick, their misery appears, that they have not, but what sometimes they get from the English, a raisin or currant, or any physic, fruit, or spice, or any comfort more than their corn and water, &c. In which bleeding case, wanting all means of recovery or present refreshing, I have been constrained, to and beyond my power, to refresh them, and to save many of them from death, who I am confident perish many millions of them, in that mighty continent, for want of means." Roger Williams, in Mass. Hist. Coll. iii. 236.

the eyes of all that beheld him. Presently after his sight began to come to him, which gave him and us good encouragement. In the mean time I inquired how he slept, and when he went to stool. They said he slept not in two days before, and had not had a stool in five. Then I gave him more, and told him of a mishap we had by the way, in breaking a bottle of drink, which the Governor also sent him, saying if he would send any of his men to Patuxet, I would send for more of the same; also for chickens to make him broth, and for other things, which I knew were good for him; and would stay the return of his messenger, if he desired. This he took marvellous kindly, and appointed some, who were ready to go by two of the clock in the morning; against which time I made ready a letter, declaring therein our good success, the state of his body, &c., desiring to send me such things as I sent for, and such physic as the surgeon durst administer to him.

He requested me, that the day following, I would take my piece, and kill him some fowl, and make him some English pottage, such as he had eaten at Plymouth; which I promised. After, his stomach coming to him, I must needs make him some without fowl, before I went abroad, which somewhat troubled me, being unaccustomed and unacquainted in such businesses, especially having nothing to make it comfortable, my consort being as ignorant as myself; but being we must do somewhat, I caused a woman to bruise some corn, and take the flour from it, and set over the grit, or broken corn, in a pipkin, for they have earthen pots of all sizes.[1] When the day broke, we went out, it

---

[1] See note [3] on page 144.

being now March, to seek herbs, but could not find any but strawberry leaves, of which I gathered a handful, and put into the same; and because I had nothing to relish it, I went forth again, and pulled up a sassafras root, and sliced a piece thereof, and boiled it, till it had a good relish, and then took it out again. The broth being boiled, I strained it through my handkerchief, and gave him at least a pint, which he drank, and liked it very well. After this his sight mended more and more; also he had three moderate stools, and took some rest; insomuch as we with admiration blessed God for giving his blessing to such raw and ignorant means, making no doubt of his recovery, himself and all of them acknowledging us the instruments of his preservation.

That morning he caused me to spend in going from one to another amongst those that were sick in the town, requesting me to wash their mouths also, and give to each of them some of the same I gave him, saying they were good folk. This pains I took with willingness, though it were much offensive to me, not being accustomed with such poisonous savours. After dinner he desired me to get him a goose or duck, and make him some pottage therewith, with as much speed as I could. So I took a man with me, and made a shot at a couple of ducks, some six score paces off, and killed one, at which he wondered. So we returned forthwith and dressed it, making more broth therewith, which he much desired. Never did I see a man so low brought, recover in that measure in so short a time. The fowl being extraordinary fat, I told Hobbamock I must take off the top thereof, saying it would make him very sick again if he did eat it. This he acquainted Massassowat therewith, who would not be persuaded to it, though I pressed it very much, showing the strength thereof, and the weakness of his stomach, which could not possibly bear it. Notwithstanding, he made a gross meal of it, and ate as much as would well have satisfied a man in health. About an hour after he began to be very sick, and straining very much, cast up the broth again; and in overstraining himself, began to bleed at the nose, and so continued the space of four hours. Then they all wished he had been ruled, concluding now he would die, which we much feared also. They asked me what I thought of him. I answered, his case was desperate, yet it might be it would save his life; for if it ceased in time, he would forthwith sleep and take rest, which was the principal thing he wanted. Not long after his blood stayed, and he slept at least six or eight hours. When he awaked, I washed his face, and bathed and suppled his beard and nose with a linen cloth. But on a sudden he chopped his nose in the water, and drew up some therein, and sent it forth again with such violence, as he began to bleed afresh. Then they thought there was no hope; but we perceived it was but the tenderness of his nostril, and therefore told them I thought it would stay presently, as indeed it did.

The messengers were now returned; but finding his stomach come to him, he would not have the chickens killed, but kept them for breed. Neither durst we give him any physic, which was then sent, because his body was so much altered since our instructions; neither saw we any need, not doubting now of his recovery, if he were careful. Many, whilst we were there, came to see him; some, by their report, from a place not less than an hundred miles. To all that came one of his chief men related the manner of his sickness, how near he was spent, how amongst others his friends the English came to see him, and how suddenly they recovered him to this strength they saw, he being now able to sit upright of himself.

The day before our coming, another sachim being there, told him that now he might see how hollow-hearted the English were, saying if we had been such friends in deed, as we were in show, we would have visited him in this his sickness, using many arguments to withdraw his affections, and to persuade him to give way to some things against us, which were motioned to him not long before. But upon this his recovery, he brake forth into these speeches : Now I see the English are my friends and love me ; and whilst I live, I will never forget this kindness they have showed me. Whilst we were there, our entertainment exceeded all other strangers'. Divers other things were worthy the noting ; but I fear I have been too tedious.

At our coming away, he called Hobbamock to him, and privately (none hearing, save two or three other of his pnieses,[1] who are of his council) revealed the plot of the Massacheuseucks, before spoken of, against Master Weston's colony, and so against us ; saying that the people of Nauset, Paomet, Succonet,[2] Mattachiest, Manomet, Agowaywam,[3] and the isle of Capawack,[4] were joined with them ; himself also in his sickness was earnestly solicited, but he would neither join therein, nor give way to any of his. Therefore, as we

---

[1] The same as *pinse*. See page 288.

[2] Sokones, or Succonusset, now called Falmouth.

[3] Or Agawam, part of Wareham.

[4] Martha's Vineyard.

respected the lives of our countrymen, and our own after safety, he advised us to kill the men of Massachuset, who were the authors of this intended mischief. And whereas we were wont to say, we would not strike a stroke till they first began; if, said he, upon this intelligence, they make that answer, tell them, when their countrymen at Wichaguscusset are killed, they being not able to defend themselves, that then it will be too late to recover their lives; nay, through the multitude of adversaries, they shall with great difficulty preserve their own; and therefore he counselled without delay to take away the principals, and then the plot would cease. With this he charged him thoroughly to acquaint me by the way, that I might inform the Governor thereof, at my first coming home. Being fitted for our return, we took our leave of him; who returned many thanks to our Governor, and also to ourselves for our labor and love; the like did all that were about him. So we departed.

That night, through the earnest request of Conbatant, who till now remained at Sawaams,[1] or Puckanokick, we lodged with him at Mattapuyst. By the way I had much conference with him, so likewise at his house, he being a notable politician, yet full of merry jests and squibs, and never better pleased than when the like are returned again upon him. Amongst other things he asked me, if in case he were thus dangerously sick, as Massassowat had been, and should send word thereof to Patuxet for *maskiet*,[2] that is, physic, whether then Mr. Governor would send it; and if he would, whether I would come therewith to him. To

---

[1] See note [2] on page 208.
[2] "*Maskit*, give me some physic." Roger Williams's Key, in R. I. Hist. Coll. i. 159.

both which I answered, Yea; whereat he gave me many joyful thanks. After that, being at his house, he demanded further, how we durst, being but two, come so far into the country. I answered, where was true love, there was no fear; and my heart was so upright towards them, that for mine own part I was fearless to come amongst them. But, said he, if your love be such, and it bring forth such fruits, how cometh it to pass, that when we come to Patuxet, you stand upon your guard, with the mouths of your pieces presented towards us? Whereupon I answered, it was the most honorable and respective entertainment we could give them; it being an order amongst us so to receive our best respected friends; and as it was used on the land, so the ships observed it also at sea, which Hobbamock knew and had seen observed. But shaking the head, he answered, that he liked not such salutations.

Further, observing us to crave a blessing on our meat before we did eat, and after to give thanks for the same, he asked us, what was the meaning of that ordinary custom. Hereupon I took occasion to tell them of God's works of creation and preservation, of his laws and ordinances, especially of the ten commandments; all which they hearkened unto with great attention, and liked well of; only the seventh commandment they excepted against, thinking there were many inconveniences in it, that a man should be tied to one woman; about which we reasoned a good time. Also I told them, that whatsoever good things we had, we received from God, as the author and giver thereof; and therefore craved his blessing upon that we had, and were about to eat, that it might nourish and

CHAP. XX.

1623. Mar.

strengthen our bodies; and having eaten sufficient, being satisfied therewith, we again returned thanks to the same our God, for that our refreshing, &c. This all of them concluded to be very well; and said, they believed almost all the same things, and that the same power that we called God, they called *Kiehtan*.[1] Much profitable conference was occasioned hereby, which would be too tedious to relate, yet was no less delightful to them, than comfortable to us. Here we remained only that night, but never had better entertainment amongst any of them.

5th day.

The day following, in our journey, Hobbamock told me of the private conference he had with Massassowat, and how he charged him perfectly to acquaint me therewith, as I showed before; which having done, he used many arguments himself to move us thereunto. That night we lodged at Namasket; and the

6th day.

day following, about the mid-way between it and home, we met two Indians, who told us, that Captain Standish was that day gone to the Massachusets. But contrary winds again drove him back; so that we found him at home; where the Indian of Paomet still was, being very importunate that the Captain should take the first opportunity of a fair wind to go with him. But their secret and villanous purposes being, through God's mercy, now made known, the Governor caused Captain Standish to send him away, without any distaste or manifestation of anger, that we might the better effect and bring to pass that which should be thought most necessary.

---

[1] "*Ketan* is their good God, to whom they sacrifice after their garners be full with a good crop. Upon this God likewise they invocate for fair weather, for rain in time of drought, and for the recovery of their sick." Wood's New England's Prospect, part ii. ch. 12.

CHAPTER XXI.

OF STANDISH'S EXPEDITION AGAINST THE INDIANS OF WESSA-
GUSSET, AND THE BREAKING UP OF WESTON'S COLONY
AT THAT PLACE.

BEFORE this journey we heard many complaints, both by the Indians, and some others of best desert amongst Master Weston's colony, how exceedingly their company abased themselves by undirect means, to get victuals from the Indians, who dwelt not far from them, fetching them wood and water, &c. and all for a meal's meat; whereas, in the mean time, they might with diligence have gotten enough to have served them three or four times. Other by night brake the earth, and robbed the Indians' store; for which they had been publicly stocked and whipped, and yet was there small amendment. This was about the end of February; at which time they had spent all their bread and corn, not leaving any for seed, neither would the Indians lend or sell them any more upon any terms. Hereupon they had thoughts to take it by violence; and to that spiked up every entrance into their town, being well impaled, save one, with a full resolution to proceed. But some more honestly minded advised John Sanders, their overseer, first to

CHAP. XXI.

1623.

Feb.

write to Plymouth; and if the Governor advised him thereunto, he might the better do it. This course was well liked, and an Indian was sent with all speed with a letter to our Governor, the contents whereof were to this effect; that being in great want, and their people daily falling down, he intended to go to Munhiggen, where was a plantation of Sir Ferdinando Gorges, to buy bread from the ships that came thither a fishing, with the first opportunity of wind; but knew not how the colony would be preserved till his return. He had used all means both to buy and borrow of Indians, whom he knew to be stored, and he thought maliciously withheld it, and therefore was resolved to take it by violence, and only waited the return of the messenger, which he desired should be hastened, craving his advice therein, promising also to make restitution afterward. The Governor, upon the receipt hereof, asked the messenger what store of corn they had, as if he had intended to buy of them; who answered, very little more than that they reserved for seed, having already spared all they could.

Forthwith the Governor and his Assistant sent for many of us to advise with them herein; who, after serious consideration, no way approving of this intended course, the Governor answered his letter, and caused many of us to set our hands thereto; the contents whereof were to this purpose. We altogether disliked their intendment, as being against the law of God and nature, showing how it would cross the worthy ends and proceedings of the King's Majesty, and his honorable Council for this place, both in respect of the peaceable enlarging of his Majesty's dominions, and also of the propagation of the knowledge and law of God, and the glad tidings of salvation, which we and they were bound to seek, and were not to use such means as would breed a distaste in the salvages against our persons and professions, assuring them their master would incur much blame hereby, neither could they answer the same. For our own parts, our case was almost the same with theirs, having but a small quantity of corn left, and were enforced to live on ground-nuts, clams, muscles, and such other things as naturally the country afforded, and which did and would maintain strength, and were easy to be gotten; all which things they had in great abundance, yea, oysters[1] also, which we wanted; and therefore necessity could not be said to constrain them thereunto. Moreover, that they should consider, if they proceeded therein, all they could so get would maintain them but a small time, and then they must perforce seek their food abroad; which, having made the Indians their enemies, would be very difficult for them, and therefore much better to begin a little the sooner, and so continue their peace; upon which course they might with good conscience desire and expect the blessing of God; whereas on the contrary they could not.

Also that they should consider their own weakness, being most swelled, and diseased in their bodies, and therefore the more unlikely to make their party good against them, and that they should not expect help from us in that or any the like unlawful actions. Lastly, that howsoever some of them might escape, yet the

---

[1] Morton says, in his New English Canaan, ch. vii. "There are great store of oysters in the entrance of all rivers. They are not round, as those of England, but excellent fat and all good. I have seen an oyster bank a mile in length. Muscles there are infinite store. I have often gone to Wessaguscus, where were excellent muscles to eat, (for variety,) the fish is so fat and large."

CHAP. XXI.
1623.

principal agents should expect no better than the gallows, whensoever any special officer should be sent over by his Majesty, or his Council for New England, which we expected, and who would undoubtedly call them to account for the same. These were the contents of our answer, which was directed to their whole colony. Another particular letter our Governor sent to John Sanders, showing how dangerous it would be for him above all others, being he was their leader and commander; and therefore in friendly manner advised him to desist.

With these letters we dispatched the messenger; upon the receipt whereof they altered their determination, resolving to shift as they could, till the return of John Sanders from Munhiggen; who first coming to Plymouth, notwithstanding our own necessities, the Governor spared him some corn, to carry them to Munhiggen. But not having sufficient for the ship's store, he took a shallop, and leaving others with instructions to oversee things till his return, set forward

Feb. about the end of February; so that he knew not of this conspiracy of the Indians before his going. Neither was it known to any of us till our return from Sawaams, or Puckanokick; at which time also another sachim, called Wassapinewat, brother to Obtakiest, the sachim of the Massachusets, who had formerly smarted for partaking with Conbatant, and fearing the like again, to purge himself, revealed the same thing.

Mar. 23. The three and twentieth of March being now come, which is a yearly court day, the Governor, having a double testimony, and many circumstances agreeing with the truth thereof, not being[1] to undertake war

[1] The word *inclined* or *disposed* seems to have been accidentally omitted.

without the consent of the body of the company, made known the same in public court, offering it to the consideration of the company, it being high time to come to resolution, how sudden soever it seemed to them, fearing it would be put in execution before we could give any intelligence thereof. This business was no less troublesome than grievous, and the more, because it is so ordinary in these times for men to measure things by the events thereof; but especially for that we knew no means to deliver our countrymen and preserve ourselves, than by returning their malicious and cruel purposes upon their own heads, and causing them to fall into the same pit they had digged for others; though it much grieved us to shed the blood of those whose good we ever intended and aimed at, as a principal in all our proceedings. But in the end we came to this public conclusion, that because it was a matter of such weight as every man was not of sufficiency to judge, nor fitness to know, because of many other Indians, which daily, as occasion serveth, converse with us; therefore the Governor, his Assistant, and the Captain, should take such to themselves as they thought most meet, and conclude thereof. Which done, we came to this conclusion, that Captain Standish should take so many men, as he thought sufficient to make his party good against all the Indians in the Massachuset bay; and because, (as all men know that have to do with them in that kind,) it is impossible to deal with them upon open defiance, but to take them in such traps as they lay for others, therefore he should pretend trade, as at other times; but first go to the English, and acquaint them with the plot, and the end of his own coming; that comparing it with their carriages

CHAP. XXI.

1623.

Mar. 24.

towards them, he might the better judge of the certainty of it, and more fitly take opportunity to revenge the same; but should forbear, if it were possible, till such time as he could make sure [of] Wituwamat, that bloody and bold villain before spoken of; whose head he had order to bring with him, that he might be a warning and terror to all of that disposition.

Upon this Captain Standish made choice of eight men, and would not take more, because he would prevent jealousy, knowing their guilty consciences would soon be provoked thereunto. But on the next day, before he could go, came one [1] of Mr. Weston's company by land unto us, with his pack at his back, who made a pitiful narration of their lamentable and weak estate, and of the Indians' carriages, whose boldness increased abundantly; insomuch as the victuals they got, they would take it out of their pots, and eat before their faces; yea, if in any thing they gainsaid them, they were ready to hold a knife at their breasts; that to give them content, since John Sanders went to Munhiggen, they had hanged [2] one of them that stole

[1] Morton says, "this man's name was Phinehas Prat, who has penned the particulars of his perilous journey, and some other things relating to this tragedy." Hubbard states that he was living in 1677, at the time he was writing his History of New England. In 1662 the General Court of Massachusetts, in answer to a petition of Phinehas Prat, then of Charlestown, which was accompanied "with a narrative of the straits and hardships that the first planters of this Colony underwent in their endeavours to plant themselves at Plymouth, and since, whereof he was one, the Court judgeth it meet to grant him 300 acres of land, where it is to be had, not hindering a plantation." At the Court held May 3, 1665, it was ordered that land be laid out for Prat, "in the wilderness on the east of the Merrimack river, near the upper end of Nacook [Pennacook?] brook, on the southeast of it." Prat married in 1630, at Plymouth, a daughter of Cuthbert Cuthbertson. His heirs had grants of land in Abington subsequent to 1672. Drake says that after long search he has not been able to discover Prat's narrative. It was probably never printed. See Morton's Memorial, p. 90; Drake's Book of the Indians, b. ii. 35; Mass. Hist. Coll. xv. 78, xvii. 122.

[2] The notorious Thomas Morton, of Merry Mount, in his New Eng-

WRETCHED STATE OF WESTON'S COLONY.

CHAP. XXI.

1623. Mar.

their corn, and yet they regarded it not; that another of their company was turned salvage; that their people had most forsaken the town, and made their rendezvous where they got their victuals, because they would not take pains to bring it home; that they had sold their clothes for corn, and were ready to starve both with cold and hunger also, because they could not endure to get victuals by reason of their nakedness; and that they were dispersed into three companies, scarce having any powder and shot left. What would be the

lish Canaan, b. iii. ch. 4, which was published in 1637, is the first writer who mentions a ludicrous fable connected with this execution, which has been made the occasion of some reproach on the first planters of New England. After relating the settlement of Weston's colony at Weymouth, he mentions that one of them stole the corn of an Indian, and upon his complaint was brought before "a parliament of all the people" to consult what punishment should be inflicted on him. It was decided that this offence, which might have been settled by the gift of a knife or a string of beads, "was felony, and by the laws of England, punished with death; and this must be put in execution, for an example, and likewise to appease the salvage. When straightways one arose, moved as it were with some compassion, and said he could not well gainsay the former sentence, yet he had conceived within the compass of his brain an embryon, that was of special consequence to be delivered and cherished. He said that it would most aptly serve to pacify the salvage's complaint, and save the life of one that might, if need should be, stand them in good stead, being young and strong, fit for resistance against an enemy, which might come unexpected, for any thing they knew. The oration made was liked of every one, and he entreated to proceed to show the means how this may be performed. Says he, 'You all agree that one must die; and one shall die. This young man's clothes we will take off, and put upon one that is old and impotent, a sickly person that cannot escape death; such is the disease on him confirmed, that die he must. Put the young man's clothes on this man, and let the sick person be hanged in the other's stead.' 'Amen,' says one, and so say many more. And this had liked to have proved their final sentence; but that one, with a ravenous voice, begun to croak and bellow for revenge, and put by that conclusive motion, alleging such deceits might be a means hereafter to exasperate the minds of the complaining salvages, and that by his death the salvages should see their zeal to justice; and therefore he should die. This was concluded;" and they "hanged him up hard by."

This story of the unscrupulous Morton furnished Butler with the materials out of which he constructed the following fable in his Hudibras, part. ii. canto ii. line 409.

"Our brethren of New England use
Choice malefactors to excuse,
And hang the guiltless in their stead,
Of whom the churches have less need;
As lately happened. In a town,
There lived a cobbler and but one,

CHAP. XXI.

1623.

Mar. 25.

event of these things he said he much feared; and therefore not daring to stay any longer among them, though he knew not the way, yet adventured to come to us; partly to make known their weak and dangerous estate, as he conceived, and partly to desire he might there remain till things were better settled at the other plantation. As this relation was grievous to us, so it gave us good encouragement to proceed in our intendments, for which Captain Standish was now fitted; and the wind coming fair, the next day set forth for the Massachusets.

The Indians at the Massachusets missed this man;

"That out of doctrine could cut use,
And mend men's lives as well as shoes.
This precious brother having slain,
In times of peace, an Indian,
(Not out of malice, but mere zeal,
Because he was an infidel,)
The mighty Tottipotymoy
Sent to our elders an envoy,
Complaining sorely of the breach
Of league, held forth, by brother Patch,
Against the articles in force
Between both churches, his and ours;
For which he craved the saints to render
Into his hands, or hang the offender.
But they, maturely having weighed,
They had no more but him of the trade,
A man that served them in a double
Capacity, to teach and cobble,
Resolved to spare him; yet to do
The Indian Hoghgan Moghgan, too,
Impartial justice, in his stead did
Hang an old weaver, that was bed-rid."

It will be observed that Morton mentions this substitution merely as the suggestion of an individual, which was rejected by the company. Even had it been adopted by them, and carried into execution, it would not have implicated the Plymouth people at all, nor cast the least slur on their characters or principles. For Weston's colony was entirely distinct from theirs, and composed of a very different set of men. Their character, as portrayed by Weston himself, and by Cushman and Pierce, before they came over, may be seen in note [2] on page 296, to which the reader is particularly requested to refer. Morton himself calls "many of them lazy persons, that would use no endeavour to take the benefit of the country." As Belknap says, "they were a set of needy adventurers, intent only on gaining a subsistence." They did not come over from any religious scruples, or with any religious purpose. There is no evidence that they had any church at all; they certainly were not Puritans. Neal says, in his Hist. of New England, i. 102, that Weston obtained a patent under pretence of propagating the discipline of the Church of England in America.

Grahame, i. 198, falls into an error in attributing this execution to Gorges's colony, which settled at the same place in the autumn of the same year; and Drake, b. ii. 34, errs in saying that Morton was one of Weston's company. Morton did not come over till March, 1625, in company with Wollaston, and settled with him not at Weymouth, but in Quincy. See Prince, pp. 221, 231. The accurate Hutchinson, i. 6, should not have made a fact out of the careless Hubbard's supposition, which the latter mentions as barely "possible." See Mass. Hist. Coll. xv. 77.

and suspecting his coming to us, as we conceive, sent one after him, and gave out there that he would never come to Patuxet, but that some wolves or bears would eat him. But we know, both by our own experience, and the reports of others, that though they find a man sleeping, yet so soon as there is life discerned, they fear and shun him. This Indian missed him but very little; and missing him, passed by the town and went to Manomet; whom we hoped to take at his return, as afterward we did. Now was our fort made fit for service, and some ordnance mounted; and though it may seem long work, it being ten months since it begun, yet we must note, that where so great a work is begun with such small means, a little time cannot bring [it] to perfection. Beside, those works which tend to the preservation of man, the enemy of mankind will hinder, what in him lieth, sometimes blinding the judgment, and causing reasonable men to reason against their own safety; as amongst us divers seeing the work prove tedious, would have dissuaded from proceeding, flattering themselves with peace and security, and accounting it rather a work of superfluity and vainglory, than simple necessity. But God, whose providence hath waked, and, as I may say, watched for us whilst we slept, having determined to preserve us from these intended treacheries, undoubtedly ordained this as a special means to advantage us and discourage our adversaries, and therefore so stirred up the hearts of the governors and other forward instruments, as the work was just made serviceable against this needful and dangerous time, though we ignorant of the same.

But that I may proceed, the Indian last mentioned, in his return from Manomet, came through the town,

CHAP. XXI.

1623. Mar.

pretending still friendship and in love to see us; but as formerly others, so his end was to see whether we continued still in health and strength, or fell into weakness, like their neighbours; which they hoped and looked for, (though God in mercy provided better for us,) and he knew would be glad tidings to his countrymen. But here the Governor stayed him; and sending for him to the fort, there gave the guard charge of him as their prisoner; where he told him he must be contented to remain till the return of Captain Standish from the Massachusets. So he was locked in a chain to a staple in the court of guard, and there kept. Thus was our fort hanselled,[1] this being the first day, as I take it, that ever any watch was there kept.

The Captain, being now come to the Massachusets, went first to the ship; but found neither man, or so much as a dog therein. Upon the discharge of a musket, the master and some others of the plantation showed themselves, who were on the shore gathering ground-nuts, and getting other food. After salutation, Captain Standish asked them how they durst so leave the ship, and live in such security; who answered, like men senseless of their own misery, they feared not the Indians, but lived and suffered them to lodge with them, not having sword or gun, or needing the same. To which the Captain answered, if there were no cause, he was the gladder. But, upon further inquiry, understanding that those in whom John Sanders had reposed most special confidence, and left in his stead to govern the rest, were at the plantation, thither he went; and, to be brief, made known the Indians' purpose, and the end of his own coming, as also, (which

[1] Hansel, to use for the first time.

formerly I omitted,) that if afterward they durst not there stay, it was the intendment of the governors and people of Plymouth there to receive them, till they could be better provided; but if they conceived of any other course, that might be more likely for their good, that himself should further them therein to the uttermost of his power. These men, comparing other circumstances with that they now heard, answered, they could expect no better; and it was God's mercy that they were not killed before his coming; desiring therefore that he would neglect no opportunity to proceed. Hereupon he advised them to secrecy, yet withal to send special command to one third of their company, that were farthest off, to come home, and there enjoin them on pain of death to keep the town, himself allowing them a pint of Indian corn to a man for a day, though that store he had was spared out of our seed. The weather proving very wet and stormy, it was the longer before he could do any thing.

In the mean time an Indian came to him, and brought some furs, but rather to gather what he could from the Captain, than coming then for trade; and though the Captain carried things as smoothly as possibly he could, yet at his return he reported he saw by his eyes that he was angry in his heart; and therefore began to suspect themselves discovered. This caused one Pecksuot, who was a pniese,[1] being a man of a notable spirit, to come to Hobbamock, who was then with them, and told him, he understood that the Captain was come to kill himself and the rest of the salvages there. "Tell him," said he, "we know it, but fear him not, neither will we shun him; but let him

[1] The same as *pinse*, on page 288.

CHAP. XXI.

1623. Mar.

begin when he dare, he shall not take us at unawares." Many times after, divers of them severally, or few together, came to the plantation to him; where they would whet and sharpen the points of their knives before his face, and use many other insulting gestures and speeches. Amongst the rest Wituwamat bragged of the excellency of his knife. On the end of the handle there was pictured a woman's face; "but," said he, "I have another at home, wherewith I have killed both French and English, and that hath a man's face on it; and by and by these two must marry." Further he said of that knife he there had, *Hinnaim namen, hinnaim michen, matta cuts;* that is to say, By and by it should see, and by and by it should eat, but not speak. Also Pecksuot, being a man of greater stature than the Captain,[1] told him, though he were a great captain, yet he was but a little man; and, said he, though I be no sachim, yet I am a man of great strength and courage. These things the Captain observed, yet bare with patience for the present.

On the next day, seeing he could not get many of them together at once, and this Pecksuot and Wituwamat both together, with another man, and a youth of some eighteen years of age, which was brother to Wituwamat, and, villain-like, trod in his steps, daily putting many tricks upon the weaker sort of men, and having about as many of his own company in a room with them, gave the word to his men, and the door being fast shut, began himself with Pecksuot, and snatching his own knife from his neck, though with much struggling, killed him therewith, the point where-

---

[1] Standish is said to have been a man of short stature. See note on page 126, and Mass. Hist. Coll. xv. 111, and xviii. 121.

of he had made as sharp as a needle, and ground the back also to an edge. Wituwamat and the other man the rest killed, and took the youth, whom the Captain caused to be hanged. But it is incredible how many wounds these two pineses received before they died, not making any fearful noise, but catching at their weapons and striving to the last. Hobbamock stood by all this time as a spectator, and meddled not, observing how our men demeaned themselves in this action. All being here ended, smiling, he brake forth into these speeches to the Captain: "Yesterday Pecksuot, bragging of his own strength and stature, said, though you were a great captain, yet you were but a little man; but to-day I see you are big enough to lay him on the ground." But to proceed; there being some women at the same time, Captain Standish left them in the custody of Mr. Weston's people at the town, and sent word to another company, that had intelligence of things, to kill those Indian men that were amongst them. These killed two more. Himself also with some of his own men went to another place, where they killed another; and through the negligence of one man, an Indian escaped, who discovered and crossed their proceedings.[1]

---

[1] When the news of the first Indians being killed by Standish at Weymouth reached Mr. Robinson, their pastor, at Leyden, he wrote to the church at Plymouth, December 19, 1623, "to consider the disposition of their Captain, who was of a warm temper. He hoped the Lord had sent him among them for good, if they used him right; but he doubted where there was not wanting that tenderness of the life of man, made after God's image, which was meet;" and he concludes with saying, "O how happy a thing had it been that you had converted some before you killed any!" Prince adds, "It is to be hoped that Squanto was converted." It seems Standish was not of their church at first, and Hubbard says he had more of his education in the school of Mars than in the school of Christ. Judge Davis remarks, "These sentiments are honorable to Mr. Robinson; they indicate a generous philanthropy, which must always gain our affection, and

CHAP. XXI.
1623.
Mar.

Not long before this execution, three of Mr. Weston's men, which more regarded their bellies than any command or commander, having formerly fared well with the Indians for making them canoes, went again to the sachim to offer their service, and had entertainment. The first night they came thither, within night, late came a messenger with all speed, and delivered a sad and short message. Whereupon all the men gathered together, put on their boots and breeches, trussed up themselves, and took their bows and arrows and went forth, telling them they went a hunting, and that at their return they should have venison enough. Being now gone, one being more ancient and wise than the rest, calling former things to mind, especially the Captain's presence, and the strait charge that on pain of death none should go a musket shot from the plantation, and comparing this sudden departure of theirs therewith, began to dislike and wish himself at home again, which was further off than divers other dwelt. Hereupon he moved his fellows to return, but could not persuade them. So there being none but women left, and the other that was turned salvage, about midnight came away, forsaking the paths, lest he should be pursued; and by this means saved his life.

should ever be cherished. Still the transactions to which the strictures relate, are defensible. As to Standish, Belknap places his defence on the rules of duty imposed by his character, as the military servant of the Colony. The government, it is presumed, will be considered as acting under severe necessity, and will require no apology if the reality of the conspiracy be admitted, of which there can be little doubt. It is certain that they were fully persuaded of its existence, and with the terrible example of the Virginia massacre in fresh remembrance, they had solemn duties to discharge. The existence of the whole settlement was at hazard." See Prince, p. 226; Hutchinson's Mass. ii. 461; Belknap's Am. Biog. ii. 330; Morton's Memorial, p. 91.

SKIRMISH WITH THE INDIANS. 341

Captain Standish took the one half of his men, and one or two of Mr. Weston's, and Hobbamock, still seeking to make spoil of them and theirs. At length they espied a file of Indians, which made towards them amain; and there being a small advantage in the ground, by reason of a hill near them, both companies strove for it. Captain Standish got it; whereupon they retreated, and took each man his tree, letting fly their arrows amain, especially at himself and Hobbamock. Whereupon Hobbamock cast off his coat, and being a known pinese, (theirs being now killed,) chased them so fast, as our people were not able to hold way with him; insomuch as our men could have but one certain mark, and then but the arm and half face of a notable villain, as he drew[1] at Captain Standish; who together with another both discharged at once at him, and brake his arm; whereupon they fled into a swamp. When they were in the thicket, they parleyed, but to small purpose, getting nothing but foul language. So our Captain dared the sachim to come out and fight like a man, showing how base and woman-like he was in tonguing it as he did; but he refused, and fled. So the Captain returned to the plantation; where he released the women, and would not take their beaver coats from them, nor suffer the least discourtesy to be offered them.

Now were Mr. Weston's people resolved to leave their plantation, and go for Munhiggen, hoping to get passage and return[2] with the fishing ships. The Captain told them, that for his own part he durst there live with fewer men than they were; yet since they were otherways minded, according to his order from

---

[1] His bow.   [2] To England.

CHAP. XXI.

1623. Mar.

the governors and people of Plymouth, he would help them with corn competent for their provision by the way; which he did, scarce leaving himself more than brought them home. Some of them disliked the choice of the body to go to Munhiggen, and therefore desiring to go with him to Plymouth, he took them into the shallop; and seeing them set sail, and clear of the Massachuset bay,[1] he took leave and returned to Plymouth; whither he came in safety, blessed be God! and brought the head of Wituwamat with him.

Among the rest, there was an Indian youth, that was ever of a courteous and loving disposition towards us. He, notwithstanding the death of his countrymen, came to the Captain without fear, saying, his good conscience and love towards us imboldened him so to do. This youth confessed, that the Indians intended to kill Mr. Weston's people, and not to delay any longer than till they had two more canoes or boats,

---

[1] "Thus this plantation is broken up in a year; and this is the end of those who being all able men, had boasted of their strength and what they would bring to pass, in comparison of the people at Plymouth, who had many women, children, and weak ones with them; and said at their first arrival, when they saw the wants at Plymouth, that they would take another course, and not fall into such a condition as this simple people were come to." Bradford, in Prince, p. 214, and in Morton, p. 92.

"Shortly after Mr. Weston's people went to the eastward, he comes there himself with some of the fishermen, under another name and disguise of a blacksmith; where he hears the ruin of his plantation; and getting a shallop with a man or two comes on to see how things are; but in a storm is cast away in the bottom of the bay between Pascataquak and Merrimak river, and hardly escapes with his life. Afterwards he falls into the hands of the Indians, who pillage him of all he saved from the sea, and strip him of all his clothes to his shirt. At length he gets to Pascataquak, borrows a suit of clothes, finds means to come to Plymouth, and desires to borrow some beaver of us. Notwithstanding our straits, yet in consideration of his necessity, we let him have one hundred and seventy odd pounds of beaver, with which he goes to the eastward, stays his small ship and some of his men, buys provisions and fits himself, which is the foundation of his future courses; and yet never repaid us any thing save reproaches, and becomes our enemy on all occasions." Bradford, in Prince, p. 216. See note[1] on p. 78.

which Mr. Weston's men would have finished by this time, having made them three already, had not the Captain prevented them; and the end of stay for those boats was to take their ship therewith.

Now was the Captain returned and received with joy, the head being brought to the fort, and there set up.[1] The governors and captains with divers others went up the same further, to examine the prisoner, who looked piteously on the head. Being asked whether he knew it, he answered, Yea. Then he confessed the plot, and that all the people provoked Obtakiest, their sachim, thereunto, being drawn to it by their importunity. Five there were, he said, that prosecuted it with more eagerness than the rest. The two principal were killed, being Pecksuot and Wituwamat, whose head was there; the other three were powahs, being yet living, and known unto us, though one of them was wounded, as aforesaid. For himself, he would not acknowledge that he had any hand therein, begging earnestly for his life, saying he was not a Massachuset man, but as a stranger lived with them. Hobbamock also gave a good report of him, and besought for him; but was bribed so to do. Nevertheless, that we might show mercy as well as extremity, the Governor released him, and the rather, because we desired he might carry a message to Obtakiest, his master. No sooner were the irons from his legs, but he would have been gone; but the Gover-

---

[1] "This may excite in some minds an objection to the humanity of our forefathers. The reason assigned for it was that it might prove a terror to others. In matters of war and public justice, they observed the customs and laws of the English nation. As late as the year 1747, the heads of the lords who were concerned in the Scots rebellion were set up over Temple Bar, the most frequented passage between London and Westminster." Belknap's Am. Biog. ii. 326.

nor bid him stay, and fear not, for he should receive no hurt; and by Hobbamock commanded him to deliver this message to his master: That for our parts it never entered into our hearts to take such a course with them, till their own treachery enforced us thereunto, and therefore they might thank themselves for their own overthrow; yet since he had begun, if again by any the like courses he did provoke him, his country should not hold him; for he would never suffer him or his to rest in peace, till he had utterly consumed them; and therefore should take this as a warning; further, that he should send to Patuxet the three Englishmen he had, and not kill them; also that he should not spoil the pale and houses at Wichaguscusset; and that this messenger should either bring the English, or an answer, or both; promising his safe return.

This message was delivered, and the party would have returned with [an] answer, but was at first dissuaded by them, whom afterwards they would, but could not persuade to come to us. At length, though long, a woman came and told us, that Obtakiest was sorry that the English were killed, before he heard from the Governor; otherwise he would have sent them. Also she said, he would fain make his peace again with us, but none of his men durst come to treat about it, having forsaken his dwelling, and daily removed from place to place, expecting when we would take further vengeance on him.

Concerning those other people, that intended to join with the Massacheuseuks against us, though we never went against any of them; yet this sudden and unexpected execution, together with the just judgment of God upon their guilty consciences, hath so terrified and amazed them, as in like manner they forsook their houses, running to and fro like men distracted, living in swamps and other desert places, and so brought manifold diseases amongst themselves, whereof very many are dead; as Canacum, the sachim of Manomet, Aspinet, the sachim of Nauset, and Ianough, sachim of Mattachiest. This sachim in his life, in the midst of these distractions, said the God of the English was offended with them, and would destroy them in his anger; and certainly it is strange to hear how many of late have, and still daily die amongst them. Neither is there any likelihood it will easily cease; because through fear they set little or no corn, which is the staff of life, and without which they cannot long preserve health and strength. From one of these places a boat was sent with presents to the Governor, hoping thereby to work their peace; but the boat was cast away, and three of the persons drowned, not far from our Plantation. Only one escaped, who durst not come to us, but returned; so as none of them dare come amongst us.

I fear I have been too tedious both in this and other things. Yet when I considered how necessary a thing it is that the truth and grounds of this action especially should be made known, and the several dispositions of that dissolved colony, whose reports undoubtedly will be as various, I could not but enlarge myself where I thought to be most brief. Neither durst I be too brief, lest I should eclipse and rob God of that honor, glory, and praise, which belongeth to him for preserving us from falling when we were at the pit's brim, and yet feared nor knew not that we were in danger.

CHAPTER XXII.

OF THE FIRST ALLOTMENT OF LANDS, AND THE DISTRESSED
STATE OF THE COLONY.

CHAP.
XXII.

1623.
April.

The month of April being now come, on all hands we began to prepare for corn. And because there was no corn left before this time, save that was preserved for seed, being also hopeless of relief by supply, we thought best to leave off all other works, and prosecute that as most necessary. And because there was no [1] small hope of doing good, in that common course of labor that formerly we were in;[2] for that the governors, that followed men to their labors, had nothing to give men for their necessities, and therefore could not so well exercise that command over them therein, as formerly they had done; especially considering that self-love wherewith every man, in a measure more or less, loveth and preferreth his own good before his neighbour's, and also the base disposition of some drones, that, as at other times, so now especially would be most burdenous to the rest; it was therefore thought best that every man should use the

---

[1] The word *no* appears to be an error of the press. F.

[2] See note [1] on page 84.

best diligence he could for his own preservation, both in respect of the time present, and to prepare his own corn for the year following; and bring in a competent portion for the maintenance of public officers, fishermen, &c., which could not be freed from their calling without greater inconveniences. This course was to continue till harvest, and then the governors to gather in the appointed portion, for the maintenance of themselves and such others as necessity constrained to exempt from this condition. Only if occasion served, upon any special service they might employ such as they thought most fit to execute the same, during this appointed time, and at the end thereof all men to be employed by them in such service as they thought most necessary for the general good. And because there is great difference in the ground, that therefore a set quantity should be set down for a person, and each man to have his fall by lot,[1] as being most just and equal, and against which no man could except.

At a general meeting of the company, many courses were propounded, but this approved and followed, as being the most likely for the present and future good of the company; and therefore before this month began to prepare our ground against seed-time.

In the midst of April we began to set, the weather being then seasonable, which much encouraged us, giving us good hopes of after plenty. The setting season is good till the latter end of May. But it pleased God, for our further chastisement, to send a great drought; insomuch as in six weeks after the

---

[1] This allotment was only for one year. In the spring of the next year, 1624, "the people requesting the Governor to have some land for continuance, and not by yearly lot, as before, he gives every person an acre of land." Bradford, in Prince, pp. 215 and 226. See this latter allotment in Hazard, i. 100, and in Morton, p. 376.

CHAP. XXII.

1623.
July.

latter setting there scarce fell any rain; so that the stalk of that was first set began to send forth the ear, before it came to half growth, and that which was later not like to yield any at all, both blade and stalk hanging the head, and changing the color in such manner, as we judged it utterly dead. Our beans also ran not up according to their wonted manner, but stood at a stay, many being parched away, as though they had been scorched before the fire. Now were our hopes overthrown, and we discouraged, our joy being turned into mourning.[1]

To add also to this sorrowful estate in which we were, we heard of a supply that was sent unto us many months since, which having two repulses before, was a third time in company of another ship three hundred leagues at sea, and now in three months time heard no further of her; only the signs of a wreck were seen on the coast, which could not be judged to be any other than the same.[2] So that at once God

---

[1] "But by the time our corn is planted, our victuals are spent, not knowing at night where to have a bit in the morning, and have neither bread nor corn for three or four months together, yet bear our wants with cheerfulness and rest on Providence. Having but one boat left, we divide the men into several companies, six or seven in each; who take their turns to go out with a net and fish, and return not till they get some, though they be five or six days out; knowing there is nothing at home, and to return empty would be a great discouragement. When they stay long or get but little, the rest go a digging shell-fish; and thus we live the summer; only sending one or two to range the woods for deer, they now and then get one, which we divide among the company; and in the winter are helped with fowl and ground-nuts." Bradford, in Prince, p. 216.

[2] "At length we receive letters from the adventurers in England of December 22 and April 9 last, wherein they say, 'It rejoiceth us much to hear those good reports that divers have brought home of you;' and give an account, that last fall, a ship, the Paragon, sailed from London with passengers, for New Plymouth; being fitted out by Mr. John Pierce, in whose name our first patent was taken, his name being only used in trust; but when he saw we were here hopefully seated, and by the success God gave us, had obtained favor with the Council for New England, he gets another patent of a larger extent, meaning to keep it to him-

seemed to deprive us of all future hopes. The most courageous were now discouraged, because God, which hitherto had been our only shield and supporter, now seemed in his anger to arm himself against us. And who can withstand the fierceness of his wrath?

These and the like considerations moved not only every good man privately to enter into examination with his own estate between God and his conscience, and so to humiliation before him, but also more solemnly to humble ourselves together before the Lord by fasting and prayer. To that end a day was appointed by public authority, and set apart from all other employments; hoping that the same God, which had stirred us up hereunto, would be moved hereby in mercy to look down upon us, and grant the request of our dejected souls, if our continuance there might any way stand with his glory and our good. But Oh the mercy of our God! who was as ready to hear, as we to ask; for though in the morning, when we assembled together, the heavens were as clear, and the drought as like to continue as ever it was, yet, (our exercise continuing some eight or nine hours,) before

---

self, allow us only what he pleased, hold us as his tenants and sue to his courts as chief lord. But meeting with tempestuous storms in the Downs, the ship is so bruised and leaky that in fourteen days she returned to London, was forced to be put into the dock, £100 laid out to mend her, and lay six or seven weeks to December 22, before she sailed a second time; but being half way over, met with extreme tempestuous weather about the middle of February which held fourteen days, beat off the round house with all her upper works, obliged them to cut her mast and return to Portsmouth, having 109 souls aboard, with Mr. Pierce himself. Upon which great and repeated loss and disappointment, he is prevailed upon for £500 to resign his patent to the Company, which cost him but £50; and the goods with charge of passengers in this ship cost the Company £640, for which they were forced to hire another ship, namely, the Anne, of 140 tons, to transport them, namely, 60 passengers with 60 tons of goods, hoping to sail by the end of April." Bradford, in Prince, pp. 217, 218. See note [6] on pages 234 and 235.

CHAP. XXII.

1623.
July.

our departure, the weather was overcast, the clouds gathered together on all sides, and on the next morning distilled such soft, sweet, and moderate showers of rain, continuing some fourteen days, and mixed with such seasonable weather, as it was hard to say whether our withered corn or drooping affections were most quickened or revived; such was the bounty and goodness of our God. Of this the Indians, by means of Hobbamock,[1] took notice; who being then in the town, and this exercise in the midst of the week, said, It was but three days since Sunday; and therefore demanded of a boy, what was the reason thereof. Which when he knew, and saw what effects followed thereupon, he and all of them admired the goodness of our God towards us, that wrought so great a change in so short a time; showing the difference between their conjuration, and our invocation on the name of God for rain; theirs being mixed with such storms and tempests, as sometimes, instead of doing them good, it layeth the corn flat on the ground, to their prejudice; but ours in so gentle and seasonable a manner, as they never observed the like.

At the same time Captain Standish, being formerly employed by the Governor to buy provisions for the refreshing of the Colony, returned with the same, accompanied with one Mr. David Tomson,[2] a Scotch-

---

[1] This is the last time that Hobbamock's name occurs in the history of the Colony. His services to the infant settlement had been very important, and in the allotment of the land in 1624, mention is made of "Hobbamock's ground." In New England's First Fruits, published in London in 1643, he is described as follows: "As he increased in knowledge, so in affection, and also in his practice, reforming and conforming himself accordingly; and though he was much tempted by enticements, scoffs, and scorns from the Indians, yet could he never be gotten from the English, nor from seeking after their God, but died amongst them, leaving some good hopes in their hearts that his soul went to rest."

[2] David Thomson was sent over

man, who also that spring began a plantation twenty-five leagues northeast from us, near Smith's isles,[1] at a place called Pascatoquack, where he liketh well. Now also heard we of the third repulse that our supply had,[2] of their safe, though dangerous, return into England, and of their preparation to come to us. So that having these many signs of God's favor and acceptation, we thought it would be great ingratitude, if secretly we should smother up the same, or content ourselves with private thanksgiving for that, which by private prayer could not be obtained. And therefore another solemn day was set apart and appointed for that end; wherein we returned glory, honor, and praise, with all thankfulness, to our good God, which dealt so graciously with us; whose name for these and all other his mercies towards his church, and chosen ones, by them be blessed and praised, now and evermore. Amen.

In the latter end of July, and the beginning of August, came two ships with supply unto us; who

---

by Gorges and Mason in the spring of 1623, and commenced a settlement at a place called Little Harbour, on the west side of Piscataqua river, near its mouth. Christopher Levett says he stayed a month at Thomson's plantation in 1623. Afterwards, in 1626, or later, out of dislike of the place or his employers, Thomson removed to Boston harbour, and took possession of "a fruitful island and very desirable neck of land," which were afterwards confirmed to him or his heirs by the government of Massachusetts. This neck of land was Squantum, in Quincy, and the island which is very near it, has ever since been called by his name. It is now the seat of the Farm School. Compare Savage's Winthrop, i. 44, with Hubbard, in Mass. Hist. Coll. xv. 105; and see Adams's Annals of Portsmouth, p. 10, and Levett's voyage into New-England, in Mass. Hist. Coll. xxviii. 164.

[1] So called after himself, by Captain John Smith, who discovered them in 1614. He thus describes them: "Smyth's Isles are a heap together, none near them, against Accominticus." They are eight in number, and are now called the Isles of Shoals. See a description and historical account of them in Mass. Hist. Coll. vii. 242 — 262; xxvi. 120.

[2] "Governor Bradford gives no hint of this third repulse." Prince, p. 219.

CHAP. XXII.

1623.
Aug.

brought all their passengers,[1] except one, in health, who recovered in short time; who, also, notwithstanding all our wants and hardship, blessed be God! found not any one sick person amongst us at the Plan-

[1] The following is an alphabetical list of those who came over in the Anne and Little James.

Anthony Annable,
Edward Bangs,
Robert Bartlett,
Fear Brewster,
Patience Brewster,
Mary Bucket,
Edward Burcher,
Thomas Clark,
Christopher Conant,
Cuthbert Cuthbertson,
Anthony Dix,
John Faunce,
Manasseh Faunce,
Goodwife Flavell,
Edmund Flood,
Bridget Fuller,
Timothy Hatherly,
William Heard,
Margaret Hickes, and her children,
William Hilton's wife and two children,
Edward Holman,
John Jenny,
Robert Long,
Experience Mitchell,
George Morton,
Thomas Morton, jr.
Ellen Newton,
John Oldham,
Frances Palmer,
Christian Penn,
Mr. Perce's two servants,
Joshua Pratt,
James Rand,
Robert Rattliffe,
Nicholas Snow,
Alice Southworth,
Francis Sprague,
Barbara Standish,
Thomas Tilden,
Stephen Tracy,
Ralph Wallen.

This list, as well as that of the passengers in the Fortune, is obtained from the record of the allotment of lands, in 1624, which may be found in Hazard's State Papers, i. 101 — 103, and in the Appendix to Morton's Memorial, pp. 377 — 380. In that list, however, Francis Cooke's and Richard Warren's names are repeated, although they came in the Mayflower; probably because their wives and children came in the Anne, and therefore an additional grant of land was made to them. Many others brought their families in this ship; and Bradford says that "some were the wives and children of such who came before."

Fear and Patience Brewster were daughters of Elder Brewster. John Faunce married Patience, daughter of George Morton, and was father of the venerable Elder Faunce.

Thomas Clark's gravestone is one of the oldest on the Burial hill in Plymouth. See note [2] on page 160. Francis Cooke's wife, Hester, was a Walloon, and Cuthbert Cuthbertson was a Dutchman, as we learn from Winslow's Brief Narration. Anthony Dix is mentioned in Winthrop, i. 287. Goodwife Flavell was probably the wife of Thomas, who came in the Fortune, and Bridget Fuller was the wife of Samuel, the physician. Timothy Hatherly went to England the next winter, and did not return till 1632; he settled in Scituate. Margaret Hicks, was the wife of Robert, who came in the Fortune. William Hilton (see page 251) had sent for his wife and children. George Morton brought his son, Nathaniel, the secretary, and four other children. Thomas Morton, jr. was probably the son of Thomas, who came in the Fortune. John Oldham afterwards became notorious in the history of the Colony. Frances Palmer was the wife of William, who came in the Fortune. Phinehas Pratt had a lot of land assigned him among those who came in the Anne; but he was undoubtedly one of Weston's colony, as appears from page 332. Barbara Standish was the Captain's second wife, whom he married after the arrival of the Anne. Her maiden name is unknown.

Annable afterwards settled in Scituate, Mitchell in Duxbury and Bridgewater, Bangs and Snow in Eastham, and Sprague in Duxbury. John Jenny was a brewer, and in 1636 had "liberty to erect a mill for grinding and beating of corn upon the brook of Plymouth."

Those who came in the first three ships, the Mayflower, the

tation. The bigger ship, called the ANNE,[1] was hired, and there again freighted back;[2] from whence we set sail the 10th of September. The lesser, called the LITTLE JAMES,[3] was built for the company at their charge.[4] She was now also fitted for trade and discovery to the southward of Cape Cod, and almost ready to set sail; whom I pray God to bless in her good and lawful proceedings.

Fortune, and the Anne, are distinctively called the *old comers*, or the *forefathers*. See pages 121 and 235. For further particulars concerning them, see Farmer's Genealogical Register, Mitchell's Bridgewater, and Deane's Scituate.

[1] "Of 140 tons, Mr. William Pierce, master." Bradford, in Prince, pp. 218 and 220.

[2] "Being laden with clapboards, and all the beaver and other furs we have; with whom we send Mr. Winslow, to inform how things are and procure what we want." Bradford, in Prince, p. 221.

[3] "A fine new vessel of 44 tons Mr. Bridges, master." Bradford, in Prince, p. 220.

[4] "They bring about 60 persons, some being very useful and become good members of the body; of whom the principal are Mr. Timothy Hatherly and Mr. George Morton, who came in the Anne, and Mr. John Jenny, who came in the James. Some were the wives and children of such who came before; and some others are so bad we are forced to be at the charge to send them home next year.

"By this ship R. C. [i. e. doubtless Mr. Cushman, their agent,] writes, Some few of your old friends are come; they come dropping to you, and by degrees I hope ere long you shall enjoy them all, &c.

"From the general, [that is, the joint concern, the company] subscribed by thirteen, we have also a letter wherein they say, 'Let it not be grievous to you, that you have been instruments to break the ice for others who come after with less difficulty; the honor shall be yours to the world's end. We bear you always in our breasts, and our hearty affection is towards you all, as are the hearts of hundreds more which never saw your faces, who doubtless pray your safety as their own.'

"When these passengers see our poor and low condition ashore, they are much dismayed and full of sadness; only our old friends rejoice to see us, and that it is no worse, and now hope we shall enjoy better days together. The best dish we could present them with, is a lobster, or piece of fish, without bread, or any thing else but a cup of fair spring water; and the long continuance of this diet, with our labors abroad, has somewhat abated the freshness of our complexion; but God gives us health, &c.

"August 14. The fourth marriage is of Governor Bradford to Mrs. Alice Southworth, widow." Bradford, in Prince, pp. 220, 221. Her maiden name was Carpenter, as appears from the following entry in the records of the Plymouth Church: "1667. Mary Carpenter, (sister of Mrs. Alice Bradford, the wife of Governor Bradford,) a member of the church at Duxbury, died in Plymouth, March 19–20, being newly entered into the 91st year of her age. She was a godly old maid, never married."

CHAPTER XXIII.

OF THE MANNERS, CUSTOMS, RELIGIOUS OPINIONS AND CEREMONIES OF THE INDIANS.

CHAP.
XXIII.
1623.

THUS have I made a true and full narration of the state of our Plantation, and such things as were most remarkable therein since December, 1621. If I have omitted any thing, it is either through weakness of memory, or because I judged it not material. I confess my style rude, and unskilfulness in the task I undertook; being urged thereunto by opportunity, which I knew to be wanting in others, and but for which I would not have undertaken the same. Yet as it is rude, so it is plain, and therefore the easier to be understood; wherein others may see that which we are bound to acknowledge, viz. that if ever any people in these later ages were upheld by the providence of God after a more special manner than others, then we; and therefore are the more bound to celebrate the memory of his goodness with everlasting thankfulness. For in these forenamed straits, such was our state, as in the morning we had often our food to seek for the day, and yet performed the duties of our callings, I mean other daily labors, to provide for after time; and though at some times in some seasons at noon I have seen men stagger by reason of faintness for want of food, yet ere night, by the good providence and blessing of God, we have enjoyed such plenty as though the windows of heaven had been opened unto us. How few, weak, and raw were we at our first beginning, and there settling, and in the midst of barbarous enemies! Yet God wrought our peace for us. How often have we been at the pit's brim, and in danger to be swallowed up, yea, not knowing till afterward that we were in peril! And yet God preserved us; yea, and from how many that we yet know not of, He that knoweth all things can best tell. So that when I seriously consider of things, I cannot but think that God hath a purpose to give that land as an inheritance to our nation, and great pity it were that it should long lie in so desolate a state, considering it agreeth so well with the constitution of our bodies, being both fertile, and so temperate for heat and cold, as in that respect one can scarce distinguish New England from Old.

A few things I thought meet to add hereunto, which I have observed amongst the Indians, both touching their religion and sundry other customs amongst them. And first, whereas myself and others, in former letters, (which came to the press against my will and knowledge,) wrote that the Indians about us are a people without any religion, or knowledge of any God,[1] therein I erred, though we could then gather no better; for as they conceive of many divine powers, so of one, whom they call *Kiehtan*,[2] to be the principal and maker of all the rest, and to be made by none. He, they say, created the heavens, earth, sea and all creatures

---

[1] See page 233.
[2] The meaning of the word Kiehtan, I think, hath reference to antiquity; for *Chise* is an old man, and *Kiehchise* a man that exceedeth in age. — *Winslow's Note.*

contained therein; also that he made one man and one woman, of whom they and we and all mankind came;[1] but how they became so far dispersed, that know they not. At first, they say, there was no sachim or king, but Kiehtan, who dwelleth above in the heavens, whither all good men go when they die, to see their friends, and have their fill of all things. This his habitation lieth far westward in the heavens, they say; thither the bad men go also, and knock at his door, but he bids them *quatchet*, that is to say, walk abroad, for there is no place for such; so that they wander in restless want and penury.[2] Never man saw this Kiehtan; only old men tell them of him, and bid them tell their children, yea to charge them to teach their posterities the same, and lay the like charge upon them. This power they acknowledge to be good; and when they would obtain any great matter, meet together and cry unto him; and so likewise for plenty, victory, &c. sing, dance, feast, give thanks, and hang up garlands and other things in memory of the same.

Another power they worship, whom they call *Hobbamock*, and to the northward of us, *Hobbamoqui*;[3] this, as far as we can conceive, is the devil. Him they call upon to cure their wounds and diseases. When they are curable, he persuades them he sends the same

---

[1] "They relate how they have it from their fathers, that Kautantowwit made one man and woman of a stone, which disliking he broke them in pieces, and made another man and woman of a tree, which were the fountains of all mankind." Roger Williams's Key, ch. xxi.

[2] "*Kautantowwit*, the great southwest God, to whose house all souls go, and from whom came their corn and beans, as they say. They believe that the souls of men and women go to the southwest; their great and good men and women to Kautantowwit's house, where they have hopes, as the Turks have, of carnal joys; murtherers, thieves and liars, their souls, say they, wander restless abroad." Williams's Key, ch. xxi.

[3] Wood, in his New England's Prospect, ch. xix. spells this word *Abamacho*.

THE POWOW, OR MEDICINE MAN.

for some conceived anger against them; but upon their calling upon him, can and doth help them; but when they are mortal and not curable in nature, then he persuades them Kiehtan is angry, and sends them, whom none can cure; insomuch as in that respect only they somewhat doubt whether he be simply good, and therefore in sickness never call upon him. This Hobbamock appears in sundry forms unto them, as in the shape of a man, a deer, a fawn, an eagle, &c. but most ordinarily a snake. He appears not to all, but the chiefest and most judicious amongst them; though all of them strive to attain to that hellish height of honor. He appeareth most ordinary and is most conversant with three sorts of people. One, I confess I neither know by name nor office directly; of these they have few, but esteem highly of them, and think that no weapon can kill them; another they call by the name of *powah;* and the third *pniese.*

The office and duty of the powah is to be exercised principally in calling upon the devil, and curing diseases of the sick or wounded. The common people join with him in the exercise of invocation, but do but only assent, or as we term it, say Amen to that he saith; yet sometime break out into a short musical note with him. The powah is eager and free in speech, fierce in countenance, and joineth many antic and laborious gestures with the same, over the party diseased.[1] If the party be wounded, he will also seem to suck the wound; but if they be curable, (as they say,) he toucheth it not, but *askooke,* that is, the snake, or *wobsacuck,* that is, the eagle, sitteth on his shoulder, and licks the same. This none see but the powah, who tells them he doth it

---

[1] See page 317.

himself. If the party be otherwise diseased, it is accounted sufficient if in any shape he but come into the house, taking it for an undoubted sign of recovery.

And as in former ages Apollo had his temple at Delphos, and Diana at Ephesus, so have I heard them call upon some as if they had their residence in some certain places, or because they appeared in those forms in the same. In the powah's speech, he promiseth to sacrifice many skins of beasts, kettles, hatchets, beads, knives, and other the best things they have to the fiend, if he will come to help the party diseased ; but whether they perform it, I know not. The other practices I have seen, being necessarily called sometimes to be with their sick, and have used the best arguments I could to make them understand against the same. They have told me I should see the devil at those times come to the party ; but I assured myself and them of the contrary, which so proved ; yea, themselves have confessed they never saw him when any of us were present. In desperate and extraordinary hard travail in child-birth, when the party cannot be delivered by the ordinary means, they send for this powah ; though ordinarily their travail is not so extreme as in our parts of the world, they being of a more hardy nature ; for on the third day after child-birth, I have seen the mother with the infant, upon a small occasion, in cold weather, in a boat upon the sea.

Many sacrifices the Indians use, and in some cases kill children. It seemeth they are various in their religious worship in a little distance, and grow more and more cold in their worship to Kiehtan ; saying, in their memory he was much more called upon. The Nanohiggansets exceed in their blind devotion, and have a great spacious house, wherein only some few (that are, as we may term them, priests) come. Thither, at certain known times, resort all their people, and offer almost all the riches they have to their gods, as kettles, skins, hatchets, beads, knives, &c., all which are cast by the priests into a great fire that they make in the midst of the house, and there consumed to ashes. To this offering every man bringeth freely; and the more he is known to bring, hath the better esteem of all men. This the other Indians about us approve of as good, and wish their sachims would appoint the like; and because the plague[1] hath not reigned at Nanohigganset as at other places about them, they attribute to this custom there used.

The pnieses are men of great courage and wisdom, and to those also the devil appeareth more familiarly than to others, and as we conceive, maketh covenant with them to preserve them from death by wounds with arrows, knives, hatchets, &c. or at least both themselves and especially the people think themselves to be freed from the same. And though, against their battles, all of them by painting disfigure themselves, yet they are known by their courage and boldness, by reason whereof one of them will chase almost an hundred men; for they account it death for whomsoever stand in their way. These are highly esteemed of all sorts of people, and are of the sachim's council, without whom they will not war, or undertake any weighty business.[2] In war their sachims, for their more safety, go in the midst of them. They are commonly men of the greatest stature and strength, and such as will endure most hardness, and yet are more discreet, cour-

---

[1] See pages 183 and 206.   [2] See pages 288 and 323.

teous and humane in their carriages than any amongst them, scorning theft, lying, and the like base dealings, and stand as much upon their reputation as any men. And to the end they may have store of these, they train up the most forward and likeliest boys, from their childhood, in great hardness, and make them abstain from dainty meat, observing divers orders prescribed, to the end that when they are of age, the devil may appear to them; causing to drink the juice of sentry [1] and other bitter herbs, till they cast, which they must disgorge into the platter, and drink again and again, till at length through extraordinary oppressing of nature, it will seem to be all blood; and this the boys will do with eagerness at the first, and so continue till by reason of faintness, they can scarce stand on their legs, and then must go forth into the cold. Also they beat their shins with sticks, and cause them to run through bushes, stumps and brambles, to make them hardy and acceptable to the devil, that in time he may appear unto them.

Their sachims cannot be all called kings, but only some few of them, to whom the rest resort for protection, and pay homage unto them; [2] neither may they

---

[1] Or centaury — probably the *sabbatia chloroides*, a plant conspicuous for its beauty, which is found in great abundance on the margin of the ponds in Plymouth. It belongs to the natural order of Gentians, one characteristic of which is an intense bitterness, residing both in the stems and roots. The *gentiana crinita*, or fringed gentian, also grows in this region. See Bigelow's Plants of Boston, pp. 79 and 111.

"The greater centaury is that famous herb wherewith Chiron the *centaur* (as the report goeth) was cured at what time as having entertained Hercules in his cabin, he would needs be handling and tampering with the weapons of his said guest so long until one of the arrows light upon his foot and wounded him dangerously." Holland's Pliny, b. xxv. ch. 6.

[2] "Their government is generally monarchical, their chief sagamore or sachem's will being their law; but yet the sachem hath some chief men that he consults with as his special counsellors. Among some of the Indians their government is mixed, partly monarchical

war without their knowledge and approbation; yet to be commanded by the greater, as occasion serveth. Of this sort is Massassowat, our friend, and Conanacus, of Nanohigganset, our supposed enemy. Every sachim taketh care for the widow and fatherless, also for such as are aged and any way maimed, if their friends be dead, or not able to provide for them. A sachim will not take any to wife, but such an one as is equal to him in birth; otherwise, they say, their seed would in time become ignoble; and though they have many other wives, yet are they no other than concubines or servants, and yield a kind of obedience to the principal, who ordereth the family and them in it. The like their men observe also, and will adhere to the first during their lives; but put away the other at their pleasure. This government is successive, and not by choice. If the father die before the son or daughter be of age, then the child is committed to the protection and tuition of some one amongst them, who ruleth in his stead till he be of age; but when that is, I know not.

Every sachim knoweth how far the bounds and limits of his own country extendeth; and that is his own proper inheritance. Out of that, if any of his men desire land to set their corn, he giveth them as much as they can use, and sets them their bounds. In this circuit whosoever hunteth, if they kill any venison, bring

and partly aristocratical; their sagamore doing not any weighty matter without the consent of his great men or petty sagamores. Their sachems have not their men in such subjection but that very frequently their men will leave them upon distaste or harsh dealing, and go and live under other sachems that can protect them; so that their princes endeavour to carry it obligingly and lovingly unto their people, lest they should desert them, and thereby their strength, power and tribute would be diminished." Gookin in Mass. Hist. Coll. i. 154.

him his fee; which is the fore parts of the same, if it be killed on the land, but if in the water, then the skin thereof. The great sachims or kings know their own bounds or limits of land, as well as the rest. All travellers or strangers for the most part lodge at the sachim's. When they come, they tell them how long they will stay, and to what place they go; during which time they receive entertainment, according to their persons, but want not. Once a year the pnieses use to provoke the people to bestow much corn on the sachim. To that end, they appoint a certain time and place, near the sachim's dwelling, where the people bring many baskets of corn, and make a great stack thereof. There the pnieses stand ready to give thanks to the people, on the sachim's behalf; and after acquaint the sachim therewith, who fetcheth the same, and is no less thankful, bestowing many gifts on them.

When any are visited with sickness, their friends resort unto them for their comfort, and continue with them ofttimes till their death or recovery.[1] If they die, they stay a certain time to mourn for them. Night and morning they perform this duty, many days after the burial, in a most doleful manner, insomuch as though it be ordinary and the note musical, which they take one from another and all together, yet it will draw tears from their eyes, and almost from ours also.[2] But

---

[1] See page 313.
[2] "Upon the death of the sick, the father, or husband, and all his neighbours wear black faces, and lay on soot very thick, which I have often seen clotted with their tears. This blacking and lamenting they observe in most doleful manner divers weeks and months, yea a year, if the person be great and public. — When they come to the grave, they lay the dead by the grave's mouth, and then all sit down, and lament, that I have seen tears run down the cheeks of stoutest captains in abundance; and after the dead is laid in the grave, they have then a second lamentation." Roger Williams's Key, ch. xxxii.

if they recover, then because their sickness was chargeable, they send corn and other gifts unto them, at a certain appointed time, whereat they feast and dance, which they call *commoco*. When they bury the dead, they sow up the corpse in a mat, and so put it in the earth. If the party be a sachim, they cover him with many curious mats, and bury all his riches with him, and enclose the grave with a pale.[1] If it be a child, the father will also put his own most special jewels and ornaments in the earth with it; also will cut his hair, and disfigure himself very much, in token of sorrow. If it be the man or woman of the house, they will pull down the mats, and leave the frame standing, and bury them in or near the same,[2] and either remove their dwelling or give over house-keeping.

The men employ themselves wholly in hunting, and other exercises of the bow, except at some times they take some pains in fishing. The women live a most slavish life; they carry all their burdens,[3] set and dress their corn, gather it in, seek out for much of their food, beat and make ready the corn to eat, and have all household care lying upon them.

The younger sort reverence the elder, and do all mean offices, whilst they are together, although they be strangers. Boys and girls may not wear their hair like men and women, but are distinguished thereby.

A man is not accounted a man till he do some notable act, or show forth such courage and resolution as becometh his place. The men take much tobacco;[4] but for boys so to do, they account it odious.

All their names are significant and variable; for

---

[1] See pages 142, 143 and 154.
[2] See pages 154 and 227.
[3] See note [2] on page 305.
[4] See note [1] on page 188.

when they come to the state of men and women, they alter[1] them according to their deeds or dispositions.

When a maid is taken in marriage, she first cutteth her hair, and after weareth a covering on her head, till her hair be grown out. Their women are diversely disposed; some as modest, as they will scarce talk one with another in the company of men, being very chaste also; yet other some light, lascivious and wanton. If a woman have a bad husband, or cannot affect him, and there be war or opposition between that and any other people, she will run away from him to the contrary party, and there live; where they never come unwelcome, for where are most women, there is greatest plenty.

When a woman hath her monthly terms, she separateth herself from all other company, and liveth certain days in a house alone; after which, she washeth herself, and all that she hath touched or used, and is again received to her husband's bed or family. For adultery, the husband will beat his wife and put her away, if he please. Some common strumpets there are, as well as in other places; but they are such as either never married, or widows, or put away for adultery; for no man will keep such an one to wife.

In matters of unjust and dishonest dealing, the sachim examineth and punisheth the same. In case of thefts, for the first offence, he is disgracefully rebuked; for the second, beaten by the sachim with a cudgel on the naked back; for the third, he is beaten with many strokes, and hath his nose slit upwards, that thereby all men may both know and shun him. If any man kill another, he must likewise die for the same. The

---

[1] See note [2] on page 191.

sachim not only passes the sentence upon malefactors,[1] but executeth the same with his own hands, if the party be then present; if not, sendeth his own knife, in case of death, in the hands of others to perform the same.[2] But if the offender be to receive other punishment, he will not receive the same but from the sachim himself; before whom, being naked, he kneeleth, and will not offer to run away, though he beat him never so much, it being a greater disparagement for a man to cry during the time of his correction, than is his offence and punishment.

As for their apparel, they wear breeches and stockings in one, like some Irish,[3] which is made of deer skins, and have shoes of the same leather. They wear also a deer's skin loose about them, like a cloak, which they will turn to the weather side. In this habit they travel; but when they are at home, or come to their journey's end, presently they pull off their breeches, stockings and shoes, wring out the water, if they be wet, and dry them, and rub or chafe the same. Though these be off, yet have they another small garment that covereth their secrets. The men wear also, when they go abroad in cold weather, an otter or fox skin on their right arm,[4] but only their bracer on the left. Women, and all of that sex, wear strings about their legs, which the men never do.

The people are very ingenious and observative; they

---

[1] See page 308.
[2] "The most usual custom amongst them in executing punishments, is for the sachim either to beat or whip or put to death with his own hand, to which the common sort most quietly submit; though sometimes the sachim sends a secret executioner, one of his chiefest warriors, to fetch off a head by some sudden, unexpected blow of a hatchet, when they have feared mutiny by public execution." Roger Williams's Key, ch. xxii. See also page 291 previous.
[3] See note [2] on page 187.
[4] See page 187.

keep account of time by the moon, and winters or summers; they know divers of the stars by name; in particular they know the north star, and call it *maske*,[1] which is to say, *the bear*;[1] also they have many names for the winds. They will guess very well at the wind and weather beforehand, by observations in the heavens. They report also, that some of them can cause the wind to blow in what part they list — can raise storms and tempests,[2] which they usually do when they intend the death or destruction of other people, that by reason of the unseasonable weather, they may take advantage of their enemies in their houses. At such times they perform their greatest exploits, and in such seasons, when they are at enmity with any, they keep more careful watch than at other times.

As for the language, it is very copious, large, and difficult. As yet we cannot attain to any great measure thereof; but can understand them, and explain ourselves to their understanding, by the help of those that daily converse with us. And though there be difference in a hundred miles' distance of place, both in language and manners, yet not so much but that

---

[1] "*Mosk* or *paukunawaw*, the Great Bear, or Charles's Wain; which words mosk or paukunawaw signifies a bear; which is so much the more observable, because in most languages that sign or constellation is called the Bear." Roger Williams's Key, ch. xii.

[2] "Their powows, by their exorcisms, and necromantic charms, bring to pass strange things, if we may believe the Indians; who report of one Passaconaway, a great sagamore upon Merrimack river, and the most celebrated powow in the country, that he can make the water burn, the rocks move, the trees dance, and metamorphize himself into a flaming man. In winter, when there are no green leaves to be got, he will burn an old one to ashes, and putting these into the water, produce a new green leaf, which you shall not only see, but substantially handle and carry away; and make a dead snake's skin a living snake, both to be seen, felt, and heard." Wood's New England's Prospect, part ii. ch. 12; Hutchinson's Mass. i. 474; Morton's New English Canaan, book i. ch. 9.

INDIAN MEMORIALS.

they very well understand each other.[1] And thus much of their lives and manners.

Instead of records and chronicles, they take this course. Where any remarkable act is done, in memory of it, either in the place, or by some pathway near adjoining, they make a round hole in the ground, about a foot deep, and as much over; which when others passing by behold, they inquire the cause and occasion of the same, which being once known, they are careful to acquaint all men, as occasion serveth, therewith ; and lest such holes should be filled or grown up by any accident, as men pass by, they will oft renew the same; by which means many things of great antiquity are fresh in memory. So that as a man travelleth, if he can understand his guide, his journey will be the less tedious, by reason of the many historical discourses [which] will be related unto him.

---

[1] "There is a mixture of this language north and south, from the place of my abode, about 600 miles; yet within the 200 miles aforementioned, their dialects do exceedingly differ; yet not so but, within that compass, a man may converse with thousands of natives all over the country." Roger Williams's Key, Pref.

"The Indians of the parts of New England, especially upon the sea-coasts, use the same sort of speech and language, only with some difference in the expressions, as they differ in several counties in England, yet so as they can well understand one another." Gookin, in Mass. Hist. Coll. i. 149.

CHAPTER XXIV.

OF THE SITUATION, CLIMATE, SOIL, AND PRODUCTIONS OF NEW ENGLAND.

CHAP. XXIV.
1623.

In all this, it may be said, I have neither praised nor dispraised the country; and since I lived so long therein, my judgment thereof will give no less satisfaction to them that know me, than the relation of our proceedings. To which I answer, that as in one, so of the other, I will speak as sparingly as I can, yet will make known what I conceive thereof.

And first for that continent, on which we are, called New England, although it hath ever been conceived by the English to be a part of the main land adjoining to Virginia, yet by relation of the Indians it should appear to be otherwise; for they affirm confidently that it is an island,[1] and that either the Dutch or French pass through from sea to sea between us and Virginia, and drive a great trade in the same. The name of that inlet of the sea they call Mohegon, which I take to be the same which we call Hudson's river, up which Master Hudson went many leagues, and for want of

[1] See page 256.

means (as I hear) left it undiscovered.[1] For confirmation of this their opinion, is thus much; though Virginia be not above a hundred and fifty leagues from us, yet they never heard of Powhatan, or knew that any English were planted in his country, save only by us and Tisquantum, who went in an English ship thither; and therefore it is the more probable, because the water is not passable for them, who are very adventurous in their boats.

Then for the temperature of the air, in almost three years' experience I can scarce distinguish New England from Old England, in respect of heat and cold, frost, snow, rain, winds, &c. Some object, because our Plantation lieth in the latitude of 42°, it must needs be much hotter. I confess I cannot give the reason of the contrary; only experience teacheth us, that if it do exceed England, it is so little as must require better judgments to discern it. And for the winter, I rather think (if there be difference) it is both sharper and longer in New England than Old; and yet the want of those comforts in the one, which I have enjoyed in the other, may deceive my judgment also. But in my best observation, comparing our own condition with the Relations of other parts of America, I cannot conceive of any to agree better with the constitution of the English, not being oppressed with extremity of heat, nor nipped by biting cold; by which

---

[1] In September, 1609, Hudson ascended the "great river of the mountains," now called by his name, in a small vessel called the Half-Moon, above the city of Hudson, and sent up a boat beyond Albany. Josselyn says, that Hudson "discovered *Mohegan* river, in New England." See Robert Juet's Journal of Hudson's third voyage, in Purchas, iii. 593, and in N. Y. Hist. Coll. i. 139, 140, and 2d series, i. 317—332; Moulton's Hist. of New York, 213, 244—249; Mass. Hist. Coll. xxiii. 372; Belknap's Am. Biog. i. 400.

means, blessed be God, we enjoy our health, notwithstanding those difficulties we have undergone, in such a measure as would have been admired if we had lived in England with the like means. The day is two hours longer than here, when it is at the shortest, and as much shorter there, when it is at the longest.

The soil is variable, in some places mould, in some clay, others, a mixed sand, &c. The chiefest grain is the Indian mays, or Guinea wheat.[1] The seed time beginneth in [the] midst of April,[2] and continueth good till the midst of May. Our harvest beginneth with September. This corn increaseth in great measure, but is inferior in quantity to the same in Virginia; the reason I conceive is because Virginia is far hotter than it is with us, it requiring great heat to ripen. But whereas it is objected against New England, that corn will not grow there except the ground be manured with fish,[3] I answer, that where men set with fish, (as with us,) it is more easy so to do than to clear ground, and set without some five or six years, and so begin anew, as in Virginia and elsewhere. Not but that in some places, where they cannot be taken with ease in such abundance, the Indians set four years together without, and have as good corn or better than we have that set with them; though indeed I think if we had cattle to till the ground, it would be more profitable and better agreeable to the soil to sow wheat, rye, barley, pease and oats, than to set mays, which our Indians call *ewachim*; for we have had experience that they like and thrive well; and the other will not be procured without good labor and diligence,

See note [1] on page 131.   [3] See note [1] on page 231.
See note [5] on page 230.

especially at seed-time, when it must also be watched by night, to keep the wolves from the fish, till it be rotten, which will be in fourteen days. Yet men agreeing together, and taking their turns, it is not much.

Much might be spoken of the benefit that may come to such as shall here plant, by trade with the Indians for furs, if men take a right course for obtaining the same; for I dare presume, upon that small experience I have had, to affirm that the English, Dutch and French return yearly many thousand pounds profit by trade only from that island on which we are seated.

Tobacco may be there planted, but not with that profit as in some other places; neither were it profitable there to follow it, though the increase were equal, because fish is a better and richer commodity, and more necessary, which may be and are there had in as great abundance as in any other part of the world; witness the west-country merchants of England, which return incredible gains yearly from thence. And if they can so do, which here buy their salt at a great charge, and transport more company to make their voyage than will sail their ships, what may the planters expect when once they are seated, and make the most of their salt there, and employ themselves at least eight months in fishing; whereas the other fish but four, and have their ship lie dead in the harbour all the time, whereas such shipping as belong to plantations may take freight of passengers or cattle thither, and have their lading provided against they come? I confess we have come so far short of the means to raise such returns, as with great difficulty we have pre-

CHAP. XXIV.
1623.

served our lives; insomuch as when I look back upon our condition, and weak means to preserve the same, I rather admire at God's mercy and providence in our preservation, than that no greater things have been effected by us. But though our beginning have been thus raw, small and difficult, as thou hast seen, yet the same God that hath hitherto led us through the former, I hope will raise means to accomplish the latter. Not that we altogether, or principally, propound profit to be the main end of that we have undertaken, but the glory of God, and the honor of our country, in the enlarging of his Majesty's dominions. Yet wanting outward means to set things in that forwardness we desire, and to further the latter by the former, I thought meet to offer both to consideration, hoping that where religion and profit jump together (which is rare) in so honorable an action, it will encourage every honest man, either in person or purse, to set forward the same, or at leastwise to commend the welfare thereof in his daily prayers to the blessing of the blessed God.

I will not again speak of the abundance of fowl, store of venison, and variety of fish, in their seasons, which might encourage many to go in their persons. Only I advise all such beforehand to consider, that as they hear of countries that abound with the good creatures of God, so means must be used for the taking of every one in his kind, and therefore not only to content themselves that there is sufficient, but to foresee how they shall be able to obtain the same. Otherwise, as he that walketh London streets, though he be in the midst of plenty, yet if he want means, is not the better, but hath rather his sorrow increased by the sight of that he wanteth, and cannot enjoy it, so also there, if thou want art and other necessaries thereunto belonging, thou mayest see that thou wantest and thy heart desireth, and yet be never the better for the same. Therefore, if thou see thine own insufficiency of thyself, then join to some others, where thou mayest in some measure enjoy the same; otherwise, assure thyself thou art better where thou art. Some there be that thinking altogether of their present wants they enjoy here, and not dreaming of any there, through indiscretion plunge themselves into a deeper sea of misery. As for example, it may be here, rent and firing are so chargeable, as without great difficulty a man cannot accomplish the same; never considering, that as he shall have no rent to pay, so he must build his house before he have it, and peradventure may with more ease pay for his fuel here, than cut and fetch it home, if he have not cattle to draw it there; though there is no scarcity, but rather too great plenty.

I write not these things to dissuade any that shall seriously, upon due examination, set themselves to further the glory of God, and the honor of our country, in so worthy an enterprise, but rather to discourage such as with too great lightness undertake such courses; who peradventure strain themselves and their friends for their passage thither, and are no sooner there, than seeing their foolish imagination made void, are at their wits' end, and would give ten times so much for their return, if they could procure it; and out of such discontented passions and humors, spare not to lay that imputation upon the country, and others, which themselves deserve.

As, for example, I have heard some complain of others for their large reports of New England, and yet because they must drink water and want many delicates they here enjoyed, could presently return with their mouths full of clamors. And can any be so simple as to conceive that the fountains should stream forth wine or beer, or the woods and rivers be like butchers' shops, or fishmongers' stalls, where they might have things taken to their hands? If thou canst not live without such things, and hast no means to procure the one, and wilt not take pains for the other, nor hast ability to employ others for thee, rest where thou art; for as a proud heart, a dainty tooth, a beggar's purse, and an idle hand, be here intolerable, so that person that hath these qualities there, is much more abominable. If therefore God hath given thee a heart to undertake such courses, upon such grounds as bear thee out in all difficulties, viz. his glory as a principal, and all other outward good things but as accessaries, which peradventure thou shalt enjoy, and it may be not, then thou wilt with true comfort and thankfulness receive the least of his mercies; whereas on the contrary, men deprive themselves of much happiness, being senseless of greater blessings, and through prejudice smother up the love and bounty of God; whose name be ever glorified in us, and by us, now and evermore. Amen.

A POSTSCRIPT.

If any man desire a more ample relation of the state of this country, before such time as this present Relation taketh place, I refer them to the two former printed books; the one published by the President and Council for New England, and the other gathered by the inhabitants of this present Plantation at Plymouth in New England: both which books are to be sold by John Bellamy, at his shop at the Three Golden Lions in Cornhill, near the Royal Exchange.[1]

[1] The former of the works here referred to is reprinted in the Mass. Hist. Coll. xix. 1 — 25; the latter is included in the present volume, pp. 109 — 250. See note [1] on page 115.

WINSLOW'S BRIEF NARRATION.

" HYPOCRISIE UNMASKED : By a true Relation of the Proceedings of the Governour and Company of the Massachusets against Samuel Gorton, (and his Accomplices,) a notorious disturber of the Peace and quiet of the severall Governments wherein he lived : With the grounds and reasons thereof, examined and allowed by their Generall Court holden at Boston in New England, in November last, 1646.

Together with a particular Answer to the manifold slanders, and abominable falsehoods which are contained in a Book written by the said Gorton, and entituled *Simplicities Defence against Seven-headed Policy*, &c. Discovering to the view of all whose eyes are open, his manifold Blasphemies ; as also the dangerous agreement which he and his Accomplices made with ambitious and treacherous Indians, who at the same time were deeply engaged in a desperate Conspiracy to cut off all the rest of the English in the other Plantations.

Whereunto is added a Briefe Narration (occasioned by certain aspersions) of the true grounds or cause of the first Planting of New England ; the Precedent of their Churches in the way and worship of God; their Communion with the Reformed Churches ; and their practise towards those that dissent from them in matters of Religion and Church Government. By EDWARD WINSLOW. Psalm cxx. 3, 4. ' What shall be given unto thee, or what shall be done unto thee, thou false tongue ? Sharp arrows of the mighty, with coals of juniper.' Published by Authority.

LONDON. Printed by *Rich. Cotes* for *John Bellamy*, at the Three Golden Lions in Cornhill, neare the Royall Exchange. 1646." sm. 4to, pp. 103.

CHAPTER XXV.

OF THE TRUE GROUNDS OR CAUSE OF THE FIRST PLANTING
OF NEW ENGLAND.

AND now that I have finished what I conceive necessary concerning Mr. Gorton's scandalous and slanderous books,[1] let me briefly answer some objections that I often meet withal against the country of New England.

The first that I meet with is concerning the rise and foundation of our New England Plantations; it being alleged (though upon a great mistake by a late writer)[2]

---

[1] Winslow was sent to England in 1646 as the agent of Massachusetts, to defend that colony against the complaints of Gorton; and for that purpose published the work, the title of which is given on the last page, and of which this Brief Narration constituted an Appendix. No copy of it is known to exist in this country, although it was in the possession both of Morton and Prince; and I have endeavoured in vain to procure it from England. The portion of the volume which I print was copied for me from one in the British Museum. It is very desirable that the whole book should be reprinted here, as Gorton's work, to which it is an answer, has been recently embodied in the Collections of the R. I. Historical Society, and the merits of the case cannot be well understood without reading both sides. Full information about Gorton will be found in Savage's Winthrop, ii. 57, 295 — 299; Hutchinson's Mass. i. 117 — 124, 549; Morton's Memorial, pp. 202 — 206; Mass. Hist. Coll. xvii. 48 — 51; Callender's Historical Discourse, in R. I. Hist. Coll. iv. 89 — 92, and ii. 9 — 20.

[2] This was Robert Baylie, minister at Glasgow, who in 1645 published "A Dissuasive from the Errors of the Time, wherein the tenets of the principal sects, especially of the Independents, are examined."

CHAP. XXV. that division or disagreement in the church of Leyden was the occasion, nay cause, of the first plantation in New England; for, saith the author, or to this effect, when they could no longer agree together, the one part went to New England, and began the Plantation at Plymouth, which he makes the mother, as it were, of the rest of the churches; as if the foundation of our New England plantations had been laid upon division or separation, than which nothing is more untrue.[1] For I persuade myself, never people upon earth lived more lovingly together and parted more sweetly than we, the church at Leyden, did; not rashly, in a distracted humor, but upon joint and serious deliberation, often seeking the mind of God by fasting and prayer; whose gracious presence we not only found with us, but his blessing upon us, from that time to this instant, to the indignation of our adversaries, the admiration of strangers, and the exceeding consolation of ourselves, to see such effects of our prayers and tears before our pil-

---

In this work, page 54, he speaks of "a small company at Leyden, under Master Robinson's ministry, which, partly by divisions among themselves, was well near brought to nought." John Cotton of Boston, who in 1648 wrote his work entitled "The Way of Congregational Churches cleared from the historical aspersions of Mr. Robert Baylie," says, p. 14, "The church at Leyden was in peace, and free from any division, when they took up thoughts of transporting themselves into America with common consent. Themselves do declare it, that the proposition of removal was set on foot and prosecuted by the elders upon just and weighty grounds."

[1] Hutchinson, too, in his Hist. of Mass. ii. 451, says, "During eleven or twelve years' residence in Holland, they had contention among themselves, and divided, and became two congregations." This is a misstatement; they had no contention among themselves. Governor Bradford says in his Dialogue, "They lived together in love and peace all their days, without any considerable differences, or any disturbance that grew thereby, but such as was easily healed in love; and so they continued until with mutual consent they removed into New England." They left Amsterdam for Leyden, as appears from page 34, in order to avoid being drawn into the controversy that was then springing up between Smith's company and Johnson's church.

grimage here be ended. And therefore briefly take notice of the true cause of it.

'Tis true that that poor persecuted flock of Christ, by the malice and power of the late hierarchy, were driven to Leyden in Holland, there to bear witness in their practice to the kingly office of Christ Jesus in his church; and there lived together ten years under the United States, with much peace and liberty. But our reverend pastor, Mr. John Robinson, of late memory, and our grave elder, Mr. William Brewster, (now at rest with the Lord,) considering, amongst many other inconveniences, how hard the country was where we lived, how many spent their estate in it and were forced to return for England, how grievous to live from under the protection of the State of England, how like we were to lose our language and our name of English, how little good we did or were like to do to the Dutch in reforming the sabbath,[1] how unable there to give such education to our children as we ourselves had received, &c., they, I say, out of their Christian care of the flock of Christ committed to them, conceived, if God would be pleased to discover some place unto us, (though in America,) and give us so much favor with the King and State of England as to have their protection there, where we might enjoy the like liberty, and where, the Lord favoring our endeavours by his blessing, we might exemplarily show our tender countrymen by our example, no less burdened than ourselves, where they might live and comfortably subsist, and enjoy the like liberties with us, being freed from antichristian bondage, keep their

---

[1] See note [1] on page 47.

CHAP. XXV.

1617.

names and nation, and not only be a means to enlarge the dominions of our State, but the Church of Christ also, if the Lord have a people amongst the natives whither he should bring us, &c. — hereby, in their great wisdoms, they thought we might more glorify God, do more good to our country, better provide for our posterity, and live to be more refreshed by our labors, than ever we could do in Holland, where we were.[1]

Now these their private thoughts, upon mature deliberation, they imparted to the brethren of the congregation, which after much private discussion came to public agitation, till at the length the Lord was solemnly sought in the congregation by fasting and prayer to direct us; who moving our hearts more and

1618. more to the work, we sent some of good abilities over into England to see what favor or acceptance such a thing might find with the King. These also found God going along with them, and got Sir Edwin Sands, a religious gentleman then living, to stir in it, who procured Sir Robert Naunton, then principal Secretary of State to King James, of famous memory, to move his Majesty by a private motion to give way to such a people (who could not so comfortably live under the government of another State) to enjoy their liberty of conscience under his gracious protection in America, where they would endeavour the advancement of his Majesty's dominions and the enlargement of the Gospel by all due means. This his Majesty said was a good and honest motion, and asking what profits might arise

---

[1] Compare this with Bradford's statement of the reasons and causes of their removal, in Chapter IV. pp. 44—48.

in the part we intended, (for our eye was upon the most northern parts of Virginia,)[1] 'twas answered, Fishing. To which he replied with his ordinary asseveration, "So God have my soul, 'tis an honest trade; t'was the Apostles' own calling," &c. But afterwards he told Sir Robert Naunton (who took all occasions to further it) that we should confer with the bishops of Canterbury and London,[2] &c. Whereupon we were advised to persist upon his first approbation, and not to entangle ourselves with them; which caused our agents to repair to the Virginia Company, who in their court[3] demanded our ends of going; which being related, they said the thing was of God, and granted a large patent, and one of them lent us £300 gratis for three years, which was repaid.

Our agents returning, we further sought the Lord by a public and solemn Fast, for his gracious guidance. And hereupon we came to this resolution, that it was best for one part of the church to go at first, and the other to stay, viz. the youngest and strongest part to go. Secondly, they that went should freely offer themselves. Thirdly, if the major part went, the pastor to go with them; if not, the elder only. Fourthly, if the Lord should frown upon our proceedings, then those that went to return, and the brethren that remained still there, to assist and be helpful to them; but if God should be pleased to favor them that went, then they also should endeavour to help over such as were poor and ancient and willing to come.

---

[1] See note [3] on page 54.
[2] Abbot was at this time archbishop of Canterbury, and John King was bishop of London. See note [2] on page 56, and Fuller's Ch. Hist. iii. 293, and Wood's Athen. Oxon. ii. 294, (ed. Bliss.)
[3] See note [3] on page 67.

These things being agreed, the major part stayed, and the pastor with them, for the present; but all intended (except a very few, who had rather we would have stayed) to follow after. The minor part, with Mr. Brewster, their elder, resolved to enter upon this great work, (but take notice the difference of number was not great.) And when the ship was ready to carry us away, the brethren that stayed having again solemnly sought the Lord with us and for us, and we further engaging ourselves mutually as before, they, I say, that stayed at Leyden feasted us that were to go, at our pastor's house, being large; where we refreshed ourselves, after tears, with singing of psalms, making joyful melody in our hearts, as well as with the voice, there being many of our congregation very expert in music; and indeed it was the sweetest melody that ever mine ears heard. After this they accompanied us to Delph's Haven, where we were to embark, and there feasted us again; and after prayer performed by our pastor, where a flood of tears was poured out, they accompanied us to the ship, but were not able to speak one to another for the abundance of sorrow to part. But we only going aboard, (the ship lying to the quay and ready to set sail, the wind being fair,) we gave them a volley of small shot and three pieces of ordnance, and so lifting up our hands to each other, and our hearts for each other to the Lord our God, we departed, and found his presence with us in the midst of our manifold straits he carried us through. And if any doubt this relation, the Dutch, as I hear, at Delph's Haven preserve the memory of it to this day, and will inform them.

But falling in with Cape Cod, which is in New

England, and standing to the southward for the place we intended,¹ we met with many dangers, and the mariners put back into the harbour of the Cape, which was the 11th of November, 1620; where considering winter was come, the seas dangerous, the season cold, the winds high, and being well furnished for a plantation, we entered upon discovery and settled at Plymouth; where God being pleased to preserve and enable us, we that went were at a thousand pounds charge in sending for our brethren that were behind, and in providing there for them till they could reap a crop of their own labors.

And so, good reader, I have given thee a true and faithful account, though very brief, of our proceedings, wherein thou seest how a late writer,² and those that informed him, have wronged our enterprise. And truly what I have written is far short of what it was, omitting for brevity sake many circumstances; as the large offers the Dutch offered to us, either to have removed into Zealand and there lived with them, or, if we would go on such adventures, to go under them to Hudson's river, (where they have since a great plantation, &c.) and how they would freely have transported us, and furnished every family with cattle, &c.³ Also the English merchants that joined with us in this expedition, whom we since bought out;⁴ which is fitter for a history than an answer to such an objection, and I trust will be accomplished in good time. By all which the reader may see there was no breach between us that went and the brethren that stayed, but such love as indeed is seldom found on earth.

---

[1] See note ¹ on page 102.
[2] Baylie. See note ² on page 379.
[3] See page 42.
[4] See Mass. Hist. Coll. iii. 47.

CHAP. XXV.

1629.

And for the many plantations that came over to us upon notice of God's blessing upon us, whereas 't is falsely said they took Plymouth for their precedent, as fast as they came;[1] 't is true, I confess, that some of the chief of them advised with us, (coming over to be freed from the burthensome ceremonies then imposed in England,) how they should do to fall upon a right platform of worship, and desired to that end, since God had honored us to lay the foundation of a Commonwealth, and to settle a Church in it, to show them whereupon our practice was grounded; and if they found, upon due search, it was built upon the Word, they should be willing to take up what was of God. We accordingly showed them the primitive practice for our warrant, taken out of the Acts of the Apostles, and the Epistles written to the several churches by the said Apostles, together with the commandments of Christ the Lord in the Gospel, and other our warrants

---

[1] "The Dissuader," says Cotton, "is much mistaken when he saith, 'The congregation of Plymouth did incontinently leaven all the vicinity;' seeing for many years there was no vicinity to be leavened. And Salem itself, that was gathered into church order seven or eight years after them, was above forty miles distant from them. And though it be very likely that some of the first comers might help their theory by hearing and discerning their practice at Plymouth, yet therein the Scripture is fulfilled, The kingdom of heaven is like unto leaven, which a woman took and hid in three measures of meal, till all was leavened." Way, &c. p. 16.

Endicott, writing to Governor Bradford from Salem, May 11, 1629, says, "I acknowledge myself much bound to you for your kind love and care in sending Mr. Fuller (the physician) amongst us, and rejoice much that I am by him satisfied touching your judgment of the outward form of God's worship. It is, as far as I can yet gather, no other than is warranted by the evidence of truth, and the same which I have professed and maintained ever since the Lord in mercy revealed himself unto me, being far differing from the common report that hath been spread of you touching that particular." Fuller himself, in a letter dated Massachusetts, June 28, 1630, writes, "Here is a gentleman, one Mr. Coddington, a Boston man, who told me that Mr. Cotton's charge to them at Hampton was, that they should take advice of them at Plymouth, and should do nothing to offend them." Mass. Hist. Coll. iii. 66, 75.

for every particular we did from the book of God. Which being by them well weighed and considered, they also entered into covenant with God and one another to walk in all his ways, revealed or as they should be made known unto them, and to worship him according to his will revealed in his written word only, &c. So that here also thou mayest see they set not the church at Plymouth before them for example, but the primitive churches were and are their and our mutual patterns and examples, which are only worthy to be followed, having the blessed Apostles amongst them, who were sent immediately by Christ himself, and enabled and guided by the unerring spirit of God. And truly this is a pattern fit to be followed of all that fear God, and no man or men to be followed further than they follow Christ and them.

Having thus briefly showed that the foundation of our New England plantations was not laid upon schism, division or separation, but upon love, peace and holiness; yea, such love and mutual care of the church of Leyden for the spreading of the Gospel, the welfare of each other and their posterities to succeeding generations, as is seldom found on earth; and having showed also that the primitive churches are the only pattern which the churches of Christ in New England have in their eye, not following Luther, Calvin, Knox, Ainsworth, Robinson, Ames, or any other, further than they follow Christ and his Apostles, I am earnestly requested to clear up another gross mistake which caused many, and still doth, to judge the harder of New England and the churches there, " because (say they) the Church of Plymouth, which went first from

CHAP. XXV.

Leyden, were schismatics, Brownists, rigid Separatists, &c., having Mr. Robinson for their pastor, who made and to the last professed separation from other the churches of Christ, &c. And the rest of the churches in New England, holding communion with that church, are to be reputed such as they are."

For answer to this aspersion, first, he that knew Mr. Robinson either by his doctrine daily taught, or hath read his Apology, published not long before his death,[1] or knew the practice of that church of Christ under his government, or was acquainted with the wholesome counsel he gave that part of the church which went for New England at their departure and afterward, might easily resolve the doubt and take off the aspersion.

1617. to 1620.

For his doctrine, I living three years[2] under his ministry, before we began the work of plantation in New England, it was always against separation from any the churches of Christ; professing and holding communion both with the French and Dutch churches,[3] yea, tendering it to the Scotch also, as I shall make appear more particularly anon; ever holding forth how wary persons ought to be in separating from a Church,

---

[1] In 1619. Robinson died in 1625.

[2] From 1617 to 1620. Winslow was 22 years old when he united himself to Robinson's church at Leyden. See note on page 274.

[3] Robinson says in his Apology, page 6, " We do profess before God and men, that such is our accord, in the case of religion, with the Dutch Reformed Churches, as that we are ready to subscribe to all and every article of faith in the same Church, as they are laid down in the *Harmony of Confessions of Faith*, published in their name."

Again, on page 8, he says, "Touching the Reformed Churches, what more shall I say? We account them the true churches of Jesus Christ, and both profess and practise communion with them in the holy things of God, what in us lieth. Their sermons such of ours frequent, as understand the Dutch tongue; the sacraments we do administer to their known members, if by occasion any of them be present with us; their distractions and other evils we do seriously bewail; and do desire from the Lord their holy and firm peace."

and that till Christ the Lord departed wholly from it, man ought not to leave it, only to bear witness against the corruption that was in it.

But if any object, he separated from the Church of England and wrote largely against it, but yet let me tell you he allowed hearing the godly ministers preach and pray[1] in the public assemblies; yea, he allowed private communion[2] not only with them, but all that were faithful in Christ Jesus in the kingdom and elsewhere upon all occasions; yea, honored them for the power of godliness, above all other the professors of religion in the world. Nay, I may truly say, his spirit cleaved unto them, being so well acquainted with the integrity of their hearts and care to walk blameless in their lives; which was no small motive to him to persuade us to remove from Holland,[3] where we might probably not only continue English, but have and maintain such sweet communion with the godly of that nation as through God's great mercy we enjoy this day.

'T is true, I confess, he was more rigid in his course and way at first than towards his latter end;[4] for his study was peace and union, so far as might agree with faith and a good conscience; and for schism and divi-

---

[1] Cotton says, "This must not be understood of the Common Prayer Book, but of the prayers conceived by the preacher before and after sermon." Way, p. 8.

[2] "By private communion I suppose he means in opposition to the mixed communion in the public churches; that is, he allowed all of the Church of England who were known to be pious to have communion in his private church. For as Mr. Cotton, writing of Mr. Robinson, says, 'He separated not from any church, but from the world.'" Prince, Annals, p. 174.

[3] The words "to some other place," seem to be here accidentally omitted.

[4] Baylie himself acknowledges that "Master Robinson was the most learned, polished, and modest spirit that ever that sect enjoyed;" and adds, "it had been truly a marvel if such a man had gone on to the end a rigid Separatist." Dissuasive, p. 17.

sion, there was nothing in the world more hateful to him. But for the government of the Church of England, as it was in the Episcopal way, the Liturgy, and stinted prayers of the Church then, yea, the constitution of it as National, and so consequently the corrupt communion of the unworthy with the worthy receivers of the Lord's Supper, these things were never approved of him, but witnessed against to his death, and are by the church over which he was, to this day.[1] And if the Lord would be pleased to stir up the hearts of those in whom (under him) the power of reformation lies to reform that abuse, that a distinction might once be put between the precious and the vile, particular churches might be gathered by the powerful preaching of the Word, those only admitted into communion whose hearts the Lord persuades to submit unto the iron rod of the Gospel, O how sweet then would the communion of the churches be! How thorough the reformation! How easy would the differences be reconciled between the Presbyterian and Independent way! How would the God of peace, who command-

---

[1] "Our faith is not negative, nor consists in the condemning of others, and wiping their names out of the bead-roll of churches, but in the edifying of ourselves; neither require we of any of ours, in the confession of their faith, that they either renounce or in one word contest with the Church of England — whatsoever the world clamors of us in this way. Our faith is founded upon the writings of the Prophets and Apostles, in which no mention of the Church of England is made."

"No man to whom England is known can be ignorant that all the natives there, and subjects of the kingdom, although never such strangers from all show of true piety and goodness, and fraught never so full with many most heinous impieties and vices, are without difference compelled and enforced by most severe laws, civil and ecclesiastical, into the body of that church. And of this confused heap (a few, compared with the rest, godly persons mingled among,) is that national church, commonly called the Church of England, collected and framed. Every subject of the kingdom, dwelling in this or that parish, is bound, will he, nill he, fit or unfit, as with iron bonds, to participate in all holy things, and some unholy also, in that same parish church." Robinson's Apology, pp. 52, 56.

eth love and good agreement, smile upon this nation! How would the subtle underminers of it be disappointed, and the faithful provoked to sing songs of praise and thanksgiving! Nay, how would the God of order be glorified in such orderly walking of the saints! And as they have fought together for the liberties of the kingdom, ecclesiastical and civil,[1] so may they join together in the preservation of them (which otherwise, 't is to be feared, will not long continue) and in the praises of our God, who hath been so good to his poor distressed ones, whom he hath delivered and whom he will deliver out of all their troubles. But I have made too great a digression, and must return.

In the next place I should speak of Mr. Robinson's Apology, wherein he maketh a brief defence against many adversaries, &c. But because it is both in Latin and English,[2] of small price, and easy to be had, I shall forbear to write of it, and only refer the reader to it for the difference between his congregation and other the Reformed Churches.

The next thing I would have the reader take notice of is, that however the church of Leyden differed in some particulars, yet made no schism or separation from the Reformed Churches, but held communion with them occasionally. For we ever placed a large difference between those that grounded their practice upon the word of God, (though differing from us in the exposition or understanding of it) and those that hated such Reformers and Reformation, and went on in antichristian opposition to it and persecution of it, as the

---

[1] This was written and published in England in the time of the civil wars in the reign of Charles I.

[2] See the title of this work, note [3] on page 40.

late Lord Bishops did, who would not in deed and truth (whatever their pretences were) that Christ should rule over them. But as they often stretched out their hands against the saints, so God hath withered the arm of their power, thrown them down from their high and lofty seats, and slain the chief of their persons, as well as the hierarchy, that he might become an example to all those that rise against God in his sabbath, in the preaching of his word, in his saints, in the purity of his ordinances. And I heartily desire that others may hear and fear withal.

As for the Dutch, it was usual for our members that understood the language and lived in or occasionally came over to Leyden, to communicate with them, as one John Jenny,[1] a brewer, long did, his wife and family, &c. and without any offence to the church. So also for any that had occasion to travel into any other part of the Netherlands, they daily did the like. And our pastor, Mr. Robinson, in the time when Arminianism prevailed so much, at the request of the most orthodox divines, as Polyander, Festus Hommius, &c. disputed daily against Episcopius (in the Academy at Leyden) and others, the grand champions of that error, and had as good respect amongst them as any of their own divines.[2] Insomuch as when God took him away from them and us by death, the University and ministers of the city accompanied him to his grave with all their accustomed solemnities, bewailing the great loss that not only that particular church had, whereof he was pastor, but some of the chief of them

---

[1] He was one of the passengers in the Anne. See note on page 352.

[2] See pages 40 — 42.

sadly affirmed that all the churches of Christ sustained a loss by the death of that worthy instrument of the Gospel.[1] I could instance also divers of their members that understood the English tongue, and betook themselves to the communion of our church, went with us to New England, as Godbert Godbertson,[2] &c. Yea, at this very instant, another, called Moses Symonson,[3] because a child of one that was in communion with the Dutch church at Leyden, is admitted into church fellowship at Plymouth in New England, and his children also to baptism, as well as our own, and other Dutch also in communion at Salem, &c.

And for the French churches, that we held and do hold communion with them, take note of our practice at Leyden, viz. that one Samuel Terry was received

---

[1] "Contrary to Mr. Baylie's suggestion, Gov. Bradford and Gov. Winslow tell us that Mr. Robinson and his people always lived in great love and harmony among themselves, as also with the Dutch, with whom they sojourned. And when I was at Leyden in 1714, the most ancient people from their parents told me, that the city had such a value for them, as to let them have one of their churches, in the chancel whereof he lies buried, which the English still enjoy; and that as he was had in high esteem both by the city and university, for his learning, piety, moderation, and excellent accomplishments, the magistrates, ministers, scholars, and most of the gentry mourned his death as a public loss, and followed him to the grave." Prince, p. 238.

Mrs. Adams, the wife of President John Adams, in a letter written Sept. 12, 1786, says, "I would not omit to mention that I visited the church at Leyden, in which our forefathers worshipped, when they fled from hierarchical tyranny and persecution. I felt a respect and veneration upon entering the doors, like what the ancients paid to their Druids."

Robinson was admitted to the privileges of the University of Leyden, Sept. 5, 1615, at the age of 39. The house in which he dwelt was near the Belfry, ("by let Klockhuÿs,") and he was buried March 4, 1625, three days after his death, under the pavement in the aisle of St. Peter's, the oldest church in the city; but no stone marks the spot. These facts were ascertained by Mr. George Sumner, of Boston, who visited Leyden in 1841, and searched the records of the church, the city, and the university.

[2] This name is also spelt Cudbart Cudbartson and Cuthbert Cuthbertson. He came in the Anne, and married Sarah, a sister of Isaac Allerton. See note on page 352.

[3] Symonson came in the Fortune. The name has become changed into Simmons. See note [2] on page 235, and Thacher's Plymouth, p. 72.

from the French church there into communion with us. Also the wife of Francis Cooke,[1] being a Walloon, holds communion with the church at Plymouth, as she came from the French, to this day, by virtue of communion of churches. There is also one Philip Delanoy,[2] born of French parents, came to us from Leyden to New Plymouth, who coming to age of discerning, demanded also communion with us; and proving himself to be come of such parents as were in full communion with the French churches, was hereupon admitted by the church of Plymouth; and after, upon his removal of habitation to Duxburrow,[3] where Mr. Ralph Partridge[4] is pastor of the church, and upon letters of recommen-

---

[1] Francis Cooke came in the Mayflower, and his wife Hester and children in the Anne. See note [3] on page 39.

[2] De la Noye came in the Fortune. This name has become corrupted into Delano.

[3] The church in Duxbury was formed in 1632. "Those that lived on their lots on the other side of the bay, (called Duxburrow,) could no longer bring their wives and children to the public worship and church meetings here (at Plymouth,) but with such burthen, as growing to some competent number, they sued to be dismissed and become a body of themselves; and so they were dismissed about this time, (though very unwillingly,) and some time after being united into one entire body, they procured Reverend Mr. Ralph Partrich to be their pastor." MS. Records Plym. Ch. p. 36. "So that Duxbury seems to be the second town and church in Plymouth Colony, and the next town settled after Newton, that is, Cambridge, in New England." Prince, p. 411. See note on page 126.

[4] Ralph Partridge, "a gracious man of great abilities," arrived at Boston in 1636. He had been a clergyman of the church of England, but "being hunted, by the ecclesiastical setters, like a partridge on the mountains, he had no defence. neither of beak nor claw, but a flight over the ocean." He was a member of the Cambridge Synod, in 1647, and was associated with John Cotton and Increase Mather, in drawing up the Platform of church government and discipline. He continued in the ministry at Duxbury till his death in 1658. Cotton Mather, after playing upon his name through a whole page, concludes his Life of him thus; "Mr. Partridge was, notwithstanding the paucity and poverty of his congregation, so afraid of being any thing that looked like a bird wandering from his nest, that he remained with his poor people, till he took wing to become a bird of paradise, along with the winged seraphim of heaven. *Epitaphium* — AVOLAVIT!" See Morton's Memorial, p. 276; Mather's Magnalia, i. 365; Mitchell's Bridgewater, p. 383.

dation from the church at Plymouth, he was also admitted into fellowship with the church at Duxburrow, being six miles distant from Plymouth; and so, I dare say, if his occasions lead him, may from church to church throughout New England. For the truth is, the Dutch and French churches, either of them being a people distinct from the world, and gathered into a holy communion, and not national churches, — nay so far from it as I verily believe the sixth person is not of the church, — the difference is so small (if moderately pondered between them and us) as we dare not for the world deny communion with them.

And for the Church of Scotland, however we have had least occasion offered to hold communion with them, yet thus much I can and do affirm, that a godly divine coming over to Leyden in Holland, where a book was printed anno 1619, as I take it, showing the nullity of Perth Assembly,[1] whom we judged to be the author of it, and hidden in Holland for a season to avoid the rage of those evil times, (whose name I have forgotten,) this man being very conversant with our pastor, Mr. Robinson, and using to come to hear him on the sabbath, after sermon ended, the church being to partake in the Lord's Supper, this minister stood up and desired he might, without offence, stay and see the manner of his administration and our participation in that ordinance. To whom our pastor answered in these very words, or to this effect, " Reverend Sir, you

---

[1] Sir Dudley Carleton, in a letter to Secretary Naunton, dated at the Hague, July 17, 1619, writes, "I have seen, within these two days, a certain Scottish book, called *Perth Assembly*, written with much scorn and reproach of the proceeding in that kingdom concerning the affairs of the church. It is without name either of author or printer; but I am informed it is printed by a certain English Brownist of Leyden, as are most of the Puritan books sent over of late days into England." Letters, p. 379. See note [1] on page 42.

may not only stay to behold us, but partake with us, if you please; for we acknowledge the churches of Scotland to be the churches of Christ," &c. The minister also replied to this purpose, if not also in the same words, " that for his part he could comfortably partake with the church, and willingly would, but that it is possible some of his brethren of Scotland might take offence at his act; which he desired to avoid in regard of the opinion the English churches, which they held communion withal, had of us." However, he rendered thanks to Mr. Robinson, and desired in that respect to be only a spectator of us.[1] These things I was earnestly requested to publish to the world by some of the godly Presbyterian party, who apprehend the world to be ignorant of our proceedings, conceiving in charity that if they had been known, some late writers and preachers would never have written and spoke of us as they did, and still do as they have occasion. But what they ignorantly judge, write, or speak of us, I trust the Lord in mercy will pass by.

In the next place, for the wholesome counsel Mr. Robinson gave that part of the church whereof he was pastor at their departure from him to begin the great work of plantation in New England, — amongst other wholesome instructions and exhortations he used these expressions, or to the same purpose:

"We are now ere long to part asunder, and the Lord knoweth whether ever he should live to see our faces again. But whether the Lord had appointed it

---

[1] Cotton, in his Way of Congregational Churches Cleared, page 8, says, " I have been given to understand, that when a reverend and godly Scottish minister came that way, (it seemeth to have been Mr. John Tarbes,) he offered him communion at the Lord's table; though the other, for fear of offence to the Scottish churches at home, excused himself."

or not, he charged us before God and his blessed angels, to follow him no further than he followed Christ; and if God should reveal any thing to us by any other instrument of his, to be as ready to receive it as ever we were to receive any truth by his ministry; for he was very confident the Lord had more truth and light yet to break forth out of his holy word. He took occasion also miserably to bewail the state and condition of the Reformed Churches, who were come to a period in religion, and would go no further than the instruments of their Reformation. As, for example, the Lutherans, they could not be drawn to go beyond what Luther saw; for whatever part of God's will he had further imparted and revealed to Calvin, they will rather die than embrace it. And so also, saith he, you see the Calvinists, they stick where he left them; a misery much to be lamented; for though they were precious shining lights in their times, yet God had not revealed his whole will to them; and were they now living, saith he, they would be as ready and willing to embrace further light, as that they had received. Here also he put us in mind of our church covenant,[1] at least that part of it whereby we promise and covenant with God and one with another, to receive whatsoever light or truth shall be made known to us from his written word; but withal exhorted us to take heed what we received for truth, and well to examine and compare it and weigh it with other Scriptures of truth before we received it. For, saith he, it is not possible the Christian world should come so lately out of such

---

[1] See on page 21, the terms of the covenant here alluded to, by which they agree "to walk in all the ways of the Lord, made known or to be made known unto them."

thick antichristian darkness, and that full perfection of knowledge should break forth at once.

"Another thing he commended to us, was that we should use all means to avoid and shake off the name of Brownist,[1] being a mere nickname and brand to make religion odious and the professors of it to the Christian world. And to that end, said he, I should be glad if some godly minister would go over with you before my coming;[2] for, said he, there will be no difference between the unconformable[3] ministers and you, when they come to the practice of the ordinances out of the kingdom.[4] And so advised us by all means

---

[1] In his book on Religious Communion, printed in 1614, Robinson says, p. 45, "He miscalls us Brownists;" and on the title page of his Apology he speaks of "certain Christians, contumeliously called Brownists." See this matter set right by Dr. Holmes, in his Annals, i. 572. Some account of Brown will be given hereafter.

[2] They had engaged a minister to go with them. See page 85.

[3] That is, the nonconforming clergy, who had not separated from the church.

[4] This prediction was remarkably fulfilled in the case of the Massachusetts colonists. Higginson, in 1629, in taking his last look of his native land from the stern of his ship, exclaimed, "We will not say as the Separatists were wont to say at their leaving of England, Farewell, Babylon! Farewell, Rome! But we will say, Farewell, dear England! Farewell, the Church of God in England, and all the Christian friends there! We do not go to New England as separatists from the Church of England." Gov. Winthrop, too, and his company, on their departure in 1630, in their address "to the rest of their brethren in and of the Church of England," say, "We desire you would be pleased to take notice of the principals and body of our company, as those who esteem it our honor to call the Church of England, from whence we rise, our dear mother, and cannot part from our native country, where she specially resideth, without much sadness of heart, and many tears in our eyes, ever acknowledging that such hope and part as we have obtained in the common salvation, we have received in her bosom and sucked it from her breasts. We leave it not therefore as loathing that milk, wherewith we were nourished there, but blessing God for the parentage and education, as members of the same body, shall always rejoice in her good, and unfeignedly grieve for any sorrow that shall ever betide her, and while we have breath, sincerely desire and endeavour the continuance and abundance of her welfare, with the enlargement of her bounds in the kingdom of Christ Jesus; wishing our heads and hearts were fountains of tears for your everlasting welfare, when we shall be in our poor cottages in the wilderness, overshadowed with the spirit of supplication."

to endeavour to close with the godly party of the kingdom of England, and rather to study union than division, viz. how near we might possibly without sin close with them, than in the least measure to affect division or separation from them. And be not loath to take another pastor or teacher, saith he; for that flock that hath two shepherds is not endangered but secured by it."[1]

Many other things there were of great and weighty consequence which he commended to us. But these things I thought good to relate, at the request of some well-willers to the peace and good agreement of the godly, (so distracted at present about the settling of church government in the kingdom of England,) that

These professions were undoubtedly heartfelt and sincere. And yet no sooner were these Nonconformists in a place where they could act for themselves, than they pursued precisely the course taken by the Separatists, adopted their form of ecclesiastical discipline and government, and set up Independent churches. Higginson, though a presbyter of the Church of England, was ordained over again by the members of his own congregation at Salem. Phillips, afterwards the minister of Watertown, who signed the above address with Winthrop, declared soon after his arrival, that if his companions would " have him stand minister by that calling which he received from the prelates in England, he would leave them." And when Mr. Cotton came over in 1633, "by his preaching and practice he did by degrees mould all their church administrations into the very same form which Mr. Phillips labored to introduce into the churches before;" so that after a while there was no perceptible difference between the Puritans of Massachusetts and the Separatists of Plymouth. See Mather's Magnalia, i. 328; Hutchinson's Mass. i. 487; Morton's Memorial, p. 146; Mass. Hist. Coll. iii. 74, xv. 186.

[1] We have here this celebrated farewell discourse of Robinson in its original form. Winslow was present and heard it, and either took it down from memory or from the notes of his pastor. It appeared in print for the first time in 1646. in this work, and all succeeding writers, such as Mather, Prince and Neal, have copied it from Winslow.

" Words," says Prince, speaking of this exhortation, " almost astonishing in that age of low and universal bigotry which then prevailed in the English nation; wherein this truly great and learned man seems to be the only divine who was capable of rising into a noble freedom of thinking and practising in religious matters, and even of urging such an equal liberty on his own people. He labors to take them off from their attachment to him, that they might be more entirely free to search and follow the Scriptures." Annals, p. 176.

CHAP. XXV. so both sides may truly see what this poor despised church of Christ, now at New Plymouth in New England, but formerly at Leyden in Holland, was and is; how far they were and still are from separation from the churches of Christ, especially those that are Reformed.

'T is true we profess and desire to practise a separation from the world, and the works of the world, which are works of the flesh, such as the Apostle speaketh of. And as the churches of Christ are all saints by calling, so we desire to see the grace of God shining forth (at least seemingly, leaving secret things to God) in all we admit into church fellowship with us, and to keep off such as openly wallow in the mire of their sins, that neither the holy things of God nor the communion of the saints may be leavened or polluted thereby. And if any joining to us formerly, either when we lived at Leyden in Holland, or since we came to New England, have with the manifestation of their faith and profession of holiness held forth therewith separation from the Church of England, I have divers times, both in the one place and the other, heard either Mr. Robinson, our pastor, or Mr. Brewster, our elder, stop them forthwith, showing them that we required no such things at their hands,[1] but only to hold forth faith in Christ Jesus, holiness in the fear of God, and submission to every ordinance and appointment of God, leaving the Church of England to themselves and to the Lord, before whom they should stand or fall, and to whom we ought to pray to

Ephes. v. 19—21. 1 Cor. vi. 9—11. Ephes. ii. 11, 12.

---

[1] Cotton too says, "When some Englishmen that offered themselves to become members of his church, would sometimes in their confessions profess their separation from the church of England, Mr. Robinson would bear witness against such profession, avouching they required no such professions of separation from this or that or any church, but only from the world." Way, p. 8.

reform what was amiss amongst them.[1] Now this reformation we have lived to see performed and brought about by the mighty power of God this day in a good measure, and I hope the Lord Jesus will perfect his work of reformation, till all be according to the good pleasure of his will. By all which I desire the reader to take notice of our former and present practice, notwithstanding all the injurious and scandalous taunting reports [that] are passed on us. And if these things will not satisfy, but we must still suffer reproach, and others for our sakes, because they and we thus walk, our practice being, for aught we know, wholly grounded on the written word, without any addition or human invention known to us, taking our pattern from the primitive churches, as they were regulated by the blessed Apostles in their own days, who were taught

---

[1] In 1634, nine years after his death, there was published "A Treatise of the lawfulness of hearing of the ministers in the Church of England; penned by that learned and reverend divine, Mr. John Robinson, late pastor to the English church of God in Leyden; printed according to the copy that was found in his study after his decease." From this rare work I extract the concluding paragraph.

"To conclude. For myself, thus I believe with my heart before God, and profess with my tongue, and have before the world, that I have one and the same faith, hope, spirit, baptism, and Lord, which I had in the Church of England, and none other; that I esteem so many in that Church, of what state or order soever, as are truly partakers of that faith, (as I account many thousands to be,) for my Christian brethren, and myself a fellow member with them of that one mystical body of Christ scattered far and wide throughout the world; that I have always, in spirit and affection, all Christian fellowship and communion with them, and am most ready in all outward actions and exercises of religion, lawful and lawfully done, to express the same; and withal, that I am persuaded the hearing of the word of God there preached, in the manner and upon the grounds formerly mentioned, both lawful, and upon occasion necessary for me and all true Christians, withdrawing from that hierarchical order of church government and ministry, and the appurtenances thereof, and uniting in the order and ordinances instituted by Christ, the only King and Lord of his church, and by all his disciples to be observed; and lastly, that I cannot communicate with or submit unto the said church order and ordinances there established, either in state or act, without being condemned of mine own heart, and therein provoking God, who is greater than my heart, to condemn me much more."

CHAP. XXV. and instructed by the Lord Jesus Christ, and had the unerring and all-knowing spirit of God to bring to their remembrance the things they had heard, — I say if we must still suffer such reproach, notwithstanding our charity towards them who will not be in charity with us, God's will be done.

The next aspersion cast upon us is, that we will not suffer any that differ from us never so little to reside or cohabit with us; no, not the Presbyterian government, which differeth so little from us. To which I answer, our practice witnesseth the contrary. For t' is well known that Mr. Parker and Mr. Noyce,[1] who are ministers of Jesus Christ at Newberry, are in that way, and so known, so far as a single congregation can be exercised in it; yet never had the least molestation or disturbance, and have and find as good respect from magistrates and people as other elders in the Congregational or primitive way. 'T is known also, that Mr. Hubbard,[2] the minister at Hengam, hath declared him-

---

[1] Thomas Parker and James Noyes came to New England in 1634, and were settled in 1635 as pastor and teacher of the church in Newbury, which was the tenth church gathered in Massachusetts. They were cousins, had been pupils and teachers in the same school, came over in the same ship, and lived together in the same house for twenty years, when death separated them. Parker had been a pupil of Archbishop Usher, and Noyes had been a student in the university of Oxford. The celebrated Baxter said "he was a lover of the New England churches according to the New England model, as Mr. Noyes had explained it." We are told by Winthrop that the principal occasion of the synod held at Cambridge in 1643, was because "some of the elders went about to set up some things according to the presbytery, as of Newbury, &c. The assembly concluded against some parts of the presbyterial way, and the Newbury ministers took time to consider the arguments," &c. For further particulars concerning them, see Mather's Magnalia, i. 433 — 441; Savage's Winthrop, ii. 137; Allen's Am. Biog. Dict.; and Eliot's New England Biog. Dict.

[2] Peter Hobart, the first minister of Hingham, was from the town of the same name in Norfolk, England. He was educated at Magdalen College, Cambridge, where he received the degree of A. B. in 1625, and A. M. in 1629. He came to New England in June, 1635. Hubbard says "he was not so fully persuaded of the congregational discipline as some others were; he was reported to be of a presbyterial spirit, and

self for that way; nay, which is more than ever I heard of the other two, he refuseth to baptize no children that are tendered to him, (although this liberty stands not upon a Presbyterian bottom,) and yet the civil state never molested him for it. Only coming to a Synod held in the country the last year, which the magistrates called, requesting the churches to send their elders and such others as might be able to hold forth the light of God from his written word in case of some doubts which did arise in the country, I say he coming the last sitting of the Assembly, which was adjourned to the 8th of June next, was in all meekness and love requested to be present and hold forth his light he went by in baptizing all that were brought to him, hereby waiving the practice of the churches; which he promising to take into consideration, they rested in his answer.

So also 't is well known that before these unhappy troubles arose in England and Scotland, there were divers gentlemen of Scotland that groaned under the heavy pressures of those times, wrote to New England to know whether they might be freely suffered to exercise their Presbyterial government amongst us; and it was answered affirmatively they might. And they sending over a gentleman to take a view of some fit place, a river called Meromeck, near Ipswich and

managed all affairs without advice of the brethren." Some idea of his character may be gathered from the following passage in Winthrop's History; "There was a great marriage to be solemnized at Boston. The bridegroom being of Hingham, Mr. Hubbard's church, he was procured to preach, and came to Boston to that end. But the magistrates, hearing of it, sent to him to forbear. The reasons were, first, for that his spirit had been discovered to be averse to our ecclesiastical and civil government, and *he was a bold man and would speak his mind.*" See more concerning him in Mather's Magnalia, i. 448—452; Lincoln's History of Hingham, pp. 21, 59, 156; Savage's Winthrop, ii. 222, 313; Hubbard, in Mass. Hist. Coll. xv. 192, xvi. 418, xxviii. 248.

Newberry aforesaid, was showed their agent, which he well liked, and where we have since four towns settled, and more may be for aught I know; so that there they might have had a complete Presbytery, and whither they intended to have come. But meeting with manifold crosses, being half seas through, they gave over their intendments; and, as I have heard, these were many of the gentlemen that first fell upon the late Covenant in Scotland. By all which will easily appear how we are here wronged by many, and the harder measure, as we hear, imposed upon our brethren for our sakes, nay pretending our example for their precedent. And last of all, not long before I came away, certain discontented persons in open court of the Massachusets, demanding that liberty, it was freely and as openly tendered to them, showing their former practices by me mentioned, but willed not to expect that we should provide them ministers, &c. for the same; but getting such themselves, they might exercise their Presbyterian government at their liberty, walking peaceably towards us, as we trusted we should do towards them. So that if our brethren here shall be restrained, they walking peaceably, the example must not be taken from us, but arise from some other principle.

But it will be objected, Though you deal thus with the Presbyterian way, yet you have a severe law against Anabaptists;[1] yea, one was whipped at Massachusets for his religion;[2] and your law banisheth them. Answer. 'Tis true the Massachusets

---

[1] This law may be seen in Hazard's State Papers, i. 538. See also Savage's Winthrop, ii. 174.
[2] The name of the person thus punished was Thomas Painter, of Hingham. This was in 1644. See an account of it in Savage's Winthrop, ii. 174.

Government have such a law to banish, but not to whip in that kind. And certain men desiring some mitigation of it, it was answered in my hearing, "'Tis true we have a severe law, but we never did or will execute the rigor of it upon any; and have men living amongst us, nay some in our churches, of that judgment; and as long as they carry themselves peaceably, as hitherto they do, we will leave them to God, ourselves having performed the duty of brethren to them. And whereas there was one whipped amongst us, 't is true we knew his judgment what it was ; but had he not carried himself so contemptuously towards the authority God hath betrusted us with in a high exemplary measure, we had never so censured him ; and therefore he may thank himself, who suffered as an evildoer in that respect. But the reason wherefore we are loath either to repeal or alter the law, is, because we would have it remain in force to bear witness against their judgment and practice, which we conceive them to be erroneous. And yet nevertheless," said the Governor to those [who] preferred the request, " you may tell our friends in England, whither ye are some of you going, since the motion proceedeth from such as we know move it in love to us, we will seriously take it into consideration at our next General Court." So that thou mayest perceive, good reader, that the worst is spoken of things in that kind.

Furthermore, in the Government of Plymouth, to our great grief, not only the pastor [1] of a congregation

[1] The person here referred to was the Rev. Charles Chauncy, at this time minister of Scituate, and afterwards President of Harvard College. It appears, however, that he was willing that the ordinance of baptism should be administered to infants, provided it were done by immersion. He took the degree of A. B. at Trinity College, Cambridge, in 1613, of A. M. in 1617, and of B. D. in 1624. He was also incorporated

waiveth the administration of baptism to infants, but divers of his congregation are fallen with him; and yet all the means the civil power hath taken against him and them is to stir up our elders to give meeting, and see if by godly conference they may be able to convince and reclaim him, as in mercy once before they had done, by God's blessing upon their labors. Only at the foresaid Synod, two were ordered to write to him in the name of the Assembly, and to request his presence at their next meeting aforesaid, to hold forth his light he goeth by in waiving the practice of the churches; with promise if it be light, to walk by it; but if it appear otherwise, then they trust he will return again to the unity of practice with them. And for the other two Governments of Conectacut and Newhaven, if either have any law in force against them, or so much as need of a law in that kind, 't is more than I have heard on.

For our parts (I mean the churches of New England) we are confident, through God's mercy, the way of God in which we walk and according to which we perform our worship and service to Him, concurreth with those rules our blessed Saviour hath left upon record by the Evangelists and Apostles, and is agreeable with the practice of those primitive churches mentioned in the Acts, and regulated by the same Apostles, as appeareth not only in that Evangelical History, but in their Epistles to the several churches there mentioned. Yet nevertheless if any through tenderness of conscience be otherwise minded, to such we never turn a deaf ear, nor become rigorous, though we have

---

A. M. at Oxford, in 1619. See Mather's Magnalia, i. 418—430; Deane's Scituate, pp. 60, 89, 173; Savage's Winthrop, i. 330, ii. 72; Mass. Hist. Coll. iv. 112, x. 30, 174, xxviii. 247; Hutchinson's Mass. i. 227; Wood's Fasti Oxon. First Part, p. 391, (Bliss's ed.)

the stream of authority on our sides. Nay, if in the use of all means we cannot reclaim them, knowing "the wisdom that is from above is first pure, then peaceable, gentle, and easy to be entreated, full of mercy and good fruits, without partiality and without hypocrisy; and the fruit of righteousness is sown in peace of them that make peace," according to James iii. 17, 18; and if any differing from us be answerable to this rule in their lives and conversations, we do not exercise the civil sword against them. But for such as Gorton and his company, whose wisdom seems not to be from above, as appeareth in that it is "full of envying, strife, confusion," being therein such as the Apostle Jude speaks on, viz. "earthly, sensual, devilish," who "despise dominion and speak evil of dignities," these are "murmurers, complainers, walkers after their own lusts, and their mouth speaketh great swelling words, being clouds without water, carried about of winds, trees whose fruit withereth, without fruit, twice dead, plucked up by the roots, raging waves of the sea, foaming out their own shame, wandering stars, to whom, (without repentance, which I much desire to see or hear of in him, if it may stand with the will of God,) is reserved the blackness of darkness forever"—these, I say, are to be proceeded with by another rule, and not to be borne; who suffer as evil-doers, and are a shame to religion, which they profess in word, but deny in their lives and conversations. These every tender conscience abhors, and will justify and assist "the higher powers God hath ordained," against such carnal gospellers, "who bear not the sword in vain," but execute God's vengeance on such; for the civil magistrate is "the minister of God, a revenger to execute wrath on him that doth evil."

CHAP. XXV.

And therefore a broad difference is to be put between such evil-doers and those tender consciences who follow the light of God's word in their own persuasions, (though judged erroneous by the places where they live) so long as their walking is answerable to the rules of the Gospel, by preserving peace and holding forth holiness in their conversations amongst men.

Thus much I thought good to signify, because we of New England are said to be so often propounded for an example. And if any will take us for a precedent, I desire they may really know what we do, rather than what others ignorantly or maliciously report of us, assuring myself that none will ever be losers by following us so far as we follow Christ. Which that we may do, and our posterities after us, the Father of our Lord Jesus Christ and our Father accept in Christ what is according to him; discover, pardon and reform what is amiss amongst us; and guide us and them by the assistance of the Holy Ghost, for time to come, till time shall be no more; that the Lord our God may still delight to dwell amongst his plantations and churches there by his gracious presence, and may go on blessing to bless them with heavenly blessings in these earthly places, that so by his blessing they may not only grow up to a nation, but become exemplary for good unto others. And let all that wish well to Zion say Amen.[1]

---

[1] The work of Winslow, to which this Brief Narration is appended, was afterwards published with a new title-page, as follows: "The danger of tolerating levellers in a civil state; or a historical narration of the dangerous practices and opinions wherewith Samuel Gorton and his levelling accomplices so much disturbed and molested the several plantations in New England. By EDWARD WINSLOW, of Plymouth, in New England. London. 1649." The paging, list of errata, &c. are precisely the same as in the other book, Hypocrisy Unmasked.

Whilst Winslow was in England, he published, in 1649, another book, entitled "*New England's Salamander Discovered* — or a satisfactory answer to many aspersions cast upon New England." This work is reprinted in Mass. Hist. Coll. xxii. 110 — 145.

GOV. BRADFORD'S DIALOGUE.

MORTON'S PREFACE.

Godly and Conscientious Reader,

It is a great part of the happiness of heaven, that the saints in celestial glory are and shall be all of one mind; and it is not unprobably gathered by the learned, that when "the Lord shall be one, and his name one," there shall be a joint concurrence of the saints in and about the matters of God. In the mean time, it is no small grief to every modest, moderate-minded Christian, to see such discord among the best of saints; whereas if the ground of the difference were sometimes well scanned, it would appear to be more in circumstance than in substance, more nominal, or respecting names or abusive names given, than in substantial realities. Rev. Mr. Manton, in his sermon before the honorable House of Commons, saith, "The Devil getteth great advantages by names amongst Christians, as Lutherans, Calvinists, Presbyterians, Independents, inventing," saith he, " either such as may tend to contempt or derision, as of old Christians, of late Puritans, or to tumult and division, as those names amongst us, under which the members of Christ sadly gather into bodies and parties."

Zech. xiv. 9.

Let me add hereunto, that the mischief of this also appeared when light sprung out of [the] darkness of Popery. Then the godly were forced to sustain the name of Puritans and the nickname of Brownists, so as many of the godly in our nation lay in obscurity under contempt of those names;[1] and afterwards, as light appeared, notwithstanding became one in the profession and practice of the truth respecting the kingly office of Christ, wherein they seemingly differed but a little before, both in New England and in Old England; but yet so as some estrangedness remains amongst those, although that in the main and substance of things they are of one mind, and with oneness of heart and mouth do serve the Lord, and do agree in and about the matters of the kingdom of Christ on earth. Yea, and I doubt not but some such of them as were of the eminentest on both sides, who are now departed this life, do agree and have sweet communion with each other in their more nobler part in glory.

I have lately met with a plain, well composed, and useful Dialogue, penned by that honored pattern of piety, William Bradford, Esq. late Governor of the Jurisdiction of New Plymouth Colony, which occasionally treats something of this matter, together with and in defence of such as I may without just offence term martyrs[2] of Jesus, and in defence of the cause they suffered for; it being no other in effect but what our church and the churches of Christ in New England do both profess and practise. I will not defend, neither

---

[1] These differences were partly blown up amongst these Christians by the names of Brownist and Puritans. — *Morton's Note.*

[2] Mr. Henry Barrow, Mr. John Greenwood, Mr. John Penry, Mr. William Dennis, [Mr. John] Coping and Elias [Thacker] and several others that suffered much, though not put to death. — *Morton's Note.*

doth he, all the words that might fall from those blessed souls in defence of the truth, who suffered so bitterly as they did from such as ere while (if I mistake not) were forced to fly into Germany for the cause of God in Queen Mary's days, and returned again in the happy reign of Queen Elizabeth, and turned prelates and bitter persecutors.[1] This thing considered, and other things also, if some passages that fell from them might have been spared, yet in many things we all offend, and "oppression will make a wise man mad," saith Solomon. Such circumstantial weakness will not unsaint a Christian, nor render him no martyr, if his cause be good, as you will find it to be by the perusing of this Dialogue, I doubt not; but let it speak for itself.

Gentle reader, I hope thou wilt obtain a clear resolution about divers things, whereof possibly thou wert in doubt of formerly respecting the premises; in the transcribing whereof I have taken the best care I could to prevent offence and to procure acceptance. If any good comes thereof, let God have all the praise.[2]

---

[1] See pages 9 — 13.
[2] This Preface was written by Secretary Morton, who copied this Dialogue into the records of the Plymouth Church, whence I obtained it. It has never before been printed.

CHAPTER XXVI.

A DIALOGUE, OR THE SUM OF A CONFERENCE BETWEEN SOME YOUNG MEN BORN IN NEW ENGLAND AND SUNDRY ANCIENT MEN THAT CAME OUT OF HOLLAND AND OLD ENGLAND, ANNO DOMINI 1648.[1]

YOUNG MEN.

Gentlemen, you were pleased to appoint us this time to confer with you, and to propound such questions as might give us satisfaction in some things wherein we are ignorant, or at least further light to some things that are more obscure unto us. Our first request therefore is, to know your minds concerning the true and simple meaning of those of *The Separation*, as they are termed, when they say the Church of England is no Church, or no true Church.

ANCIENT MEN.

For answer hereunto, first, you must know that they speak of it as it then was under the hierarchical prelacy, which since have been put down by the State, and not as it is now unsettled.

2. They nowhere say, that we remember, that they

[1] That is, the Dialogue was held or written in 1648.

are no Church. At least, they are not so to be understood; for they often say the contrary.

3. When they say it is no true Church of Christ, they do not at all mean as they are the elect of God, or a part of the Catholic Church, or of the mystical body of Christ, or visible Christians professing faith and holiness, (as most men understand the church); for which purpose hear what Mr. Robinson in his Apology, page 53. "If by the Church," saith he, "be understood the Catholic Church, dispersed upon the face of the whole earth, we do willingly acknowledge that a singular part thereof, and the same visible and conspicuous, is to be found in the land, and with it do profess and practise, what in us lies, communion in all things in themselves lawful, and done in right order."

4. Therefore they mean it is not a true church as it is a National Church, combined together of all in the land promiscuously under the hierarchical government of archbishops, their courts and canons, so far differing from the primitive pattern in the Gospel.

YOUNG MEN.

Wherein do they differ then from the judgment or practice of our churches here in New England?

ANCIENT MEN.

Truly, for matter of practice, nothing at all that is in any thing material; these being rather more strict and rigid in some proceedings about admission of members, and things of such nature, than the other; and for matter of judgment, it is more, as we conceive, in words and terms, than matter of any great substance; for the churches and chief of the ministers

416 BROWNISTS AND SEPARATISTS.

CHAP. XXVI. here hold that the National Church, so constituted and governed as before is said, is not allowable according to the primitive order of the Gospel; but that there are some parish assemblies that are true churches by virtue of an implicit covenant amongst themselves, in which regard the Church of England may be held and called a true church.

Answer. Where any such are evident, we suppose the other will not disagree about an implicit covenant, if they mean by an implicit covenant that which hath the substance of a covenant in it some way discernible, though it be not so formal or orderly as it should be. But such an implicit [covenant] as is no way explicit, is no better than a Popish implicit faith, (as some of us conceive,) and a mere fiction, or as that which should be a marriage covenant which is no way explicit.

YOUNG MEN.

Wherein standeth the difference between the rigid Brownists and Separatists[1] and others, as we observe our ministers in their writings and sermons to distinguish them?

ANCIENT MEN.

The name of Brownists[2] is but a nickname, as

---

[1] The learned and ever-memorable John Hales, of Eton, said of this word Separatist, "Where it may be rightly fixed and deservedly charged, it is certainly a great offence; but in common use now among us, it is no other than a theological scarecrow." Works, i. xv. Foulis, 1765.

[2] James Howell, in one of his letters, aping the style, whilst devoid of the liberal spirit of Sir Thomas Browne, has the following charitable sentiment; "Difference of opinion may work a disaffection in me, but not a detestation. I rather pity than hate Turk and infidel, for they are of the same metal and bear the same stamp as I do, though the inscriptions differ. If I hate any, it is those schismatics that puzzle the sweet peace of our church; so that I could be content to see an Anabaptist go to hell on a Brownist's back." Letters, p. 270, (ed. 1754.)

Puritan[1] and Huguenot,[2] &c., and therefore they do not amiss to decline the odium of it in what they may. But by the rigidness of Separation they do not so much mean the difference, for our churches here in New England do the same thing under the name of *secession* from the corruptions found amongst them, as the other did under the name or term of *separation* from them. Only this declines the odium the better. See Reverend Mr. Cotton's Answer to Mr. Baylie, page the 14th.[3]

That some which were termed Separatists, out of some mistake and heat of zeal, forbore communion in lawful things with other godly persons, as prayer and hearing of the word, may be seen in what that worthy man, Mr. Robinson, hath published in dislike thereof.

YOUNG MEN.

We are well satisfied in what you have said. But they differ also about synods.

---

[1] See note [1] on page 12.

[2] The origin of this word is unknown. Some have thought it was derived from a French and faulty pronunciation of the German word *eidgnossen*, which signifies *confederates*, and which had been originally the name of that valiant part of the city of Geneva, which entered into an alliance with the Swiss cantons in order to maintain their liberties against the tyrannical attempts of Charles III. duke of Savoy. These confederates were called *eignots*, and from thence very probably was derived the word *huguenots*. The Abbé Fleury says, "Ils y furent appelés Huguenots, du nom des Eignots de Genève, un peu autrement prononcé." The term was first applied to the Calvinists of the Cevennes in 1560. See Mosheim's Eccles. Hist. iv. 368; Fleury, Hist. Eccles. xviii. 603. An admirable Memoir of the French Protestants, both in their native country and in America, written by that accurate annalist, Dr. Holmes, is contained in the Mass. Hist. Coll. xxii. 1—84.

[3] " Neither was our departure from the parishional congregations in England a *separation* from them as no churches, but rather a *secession* from the corruptions found amongst them."

CHAP. XXVI.

ANCIENT MEN.

It is true we do not know that ever they had any solemn Synodical Assembly. And the reason may be, that those in England living dispersed and [1] could not meet in their ordinary meetings without danger, much less in synods. Neither in Holland, where they might have more liberty, were they of any considerable number, being but those two churches, that of Amsterdam and that of Leyden. Yet some of us know that the church [of Leyden] sent messengers to those of Amsterdam, at the request of some of the chief of them, both elders and brethren, when in their dissensions they had deposed Mr. Ainsworth and some other both of their elders and brethren, Mr. Robinson being the chief of the messengers sent; which had that good effect, as that they revoked the said deposition, and confessed their rashness and error, and lived together in peace some good time after. But when the churches want neither peace nor light to exercise the power which the Lord hath given them, Christ doth not direct them to gather into synods or classical meetings, for removing of known offences either in doctrine or manners; but only sendeth to the pastors or presbyters of each church to reform within themselves what is amongst them. "A plain pattern," saith Mr. Cotton in his Answer to Mr. Baylie, page 95, "in case of public offences tolerated in neighbour churches, not forthwith to gather into a synod or classical meeting, for redress thereof, but by letters and messengers to admonish one another of what is behooveful; unless

---

[1] Here something seems to have been omitted.

PROPHESYING.

upon such admonition they refuse to hearken to the wholesome counsel of their brethren." And of this matter Mr. Robinson thus writeth in his book, *Just.* page 200,[1] "The officers of one or many churches may meet together to discuss and consider of matters for the good of the church and churches, and so be called a Church Synod, or the like, so they infringe no order of Christ or liberty of the brethren;" not differing herein from Mr. Davenport[2] and the principal of our ministers.

YOUNG MEN.

But they seem to differ about the exercise of prophecy,[3] that is, that men out of office, having gifts,

---

[1] See the title of this book in note [3] on page 40.

[2] John Davenport, born at Coventry in 1597, a graduate of Oxford, and vicar of St. Stephens, in London, came to New England in 1637, with Theophilus Eaton and Edward Hopkins, and with them laid the foundations of the colony of New Haven, in 1638. In 1668, in his 71st year, he removed to Boston, to become the pastor of the First Church, and there died in 1670. See Wood's Athen. Oxon. iii. 889, (ed. Bliss); Mather's Magnalia, i. 292 — 302; Winthrop's N. E. i. 227, 404; Hutchinson's Mass. i. 82, 115, 215; Emerson's History of the First Church in Boston, pp. 110—124. But the most ample and satisfactory account of Davenport will be found in Prof. Kingsley's Centennial Discourse at New Haven, and in Dr. Leonard Bacon's Historical Discourses. These works contain also a noble vindication of the principles and character of the Puritan fathers of New England.

[3] This religious exercise, in which laymen publicly taught and exhorted, was early practised in both the colonies of Plymouth and Massachusetts. As the church of Plymouth was long without a regular pastor, "the ruling elder, when he wanted assistance, used frequently to call upon some of the gifted brethren to pray and give a word of exhortation in their public assemblies; the chief of whom were Gov. Edward Winslow, Gov. Bradford, his son-in-law, Mr. Thomas Southworth, and Secretary Nathaniel Morton; men of superior talents and parts, and of good school-learning." We are told by Gov. Winthrop, in his Journal, March 29, 1631, that "Mr. Coddington and Mr. Wilson and divers of the congregation met at the Governor's, and there Mr. Wilson, praying and exhorting the congregation to love, &c. commended to them the exercise of prophecy in his absence, and designed those whom he thought most fit for it, viz. the governor, Mr. Dudley, and Mr. Nowell, the elder." On the visit of Governor Winthrop and Mr. Wilson to Plymouth in October, 1632, it is related that "on the Lord's day in the afternoon, Mr. Roger Williams (according to their

may upon occasion edify the church publicly and openly, and applying the Scriptures; which seems to be a new practice.

ANCIENT MEN.

It doth but seem so; as many things else do that have by usurpation grown out of use. But that it hath been an ancient practice of the people of God, besides the grounds of Scripture, we will give an instance or two. We find in the ancient Ecclesiastical History of Eusebius, lib. vi. cap. 19, how Demetrius, bishop of Alexandria, being pricked with envy against Origen, complaineth in his letters that there was never such a practice heard of, nor no precedent to be found, that laymen in presence of bishops have taught in the church; but is thus answered by the bishop of Jerusalem and the bishop of Cesarea: "We know not," say they, "why he reporteth a manifest untruth, whenas there may be found such as in open assemblies have taught the people; yea, whenas there were present learned men that could profit the people, and moreover holy bishops, who at that time exhorted them to

---

custom) propounded a question, to which the pastor, Mr. Smith, spake briefly; then Mr. Williams prophesied; and after the governor of Plymouth spake to the question; after him the elder; then two or three more of the congregation. Then the elder desired the governor of Massachusetts and Mr. Wilson to speak to it, which they did." The exercise was grounded on the primitive practice of the Church of Corinth, as described and regulated by the Apostle Paul, in 1 Cor. xii. and xiv. and especially prescribed in the 31st verse of the last named chapter, where he says, "Ye may all prophesy one by one, that all may learn, and all be comforted." It was for encouraging a similar exercising among his clergy, that archbishop Grindal incurred the displeasure of Queen Elizabeth, and was for a time suspended from his see. It should be remembered that this was the scriptural sense of the word *prophesying;* and that prediction is not its only signification, appears from the title of one of Jeremy Taylor's Works, "The Liberty of Prophesying." See Savage's Winthrop, i. 50, 91; Mass. Hist. Coll. iv. 136; Prince's Annals, p. 407; Fuller's Ch. Hist. iii. 6—18; Pierce's Vindication, part i. pp. 92—96.

preach. For example, at Laranda Euelpis was requested of Neon, at Iconium Paulinus was requested by Celsus, at Synada Theodorus was requested by Atticus, who were godly brethren, &c."[1]

The second instance is out of Speed's Cloud of Witnesses, page 71. Saith he, " Rambam or Maymon records, that in the synagogues, first, only a Levite must offer sacrifice; secondly, but any in Israel might expound the law; thirdly, the expounder must be an eminent man, and must have leave from the master of the synagogue; and so contends that Christ, Luke iv. 16, taught as any of Israel might have done as well as the Levites; and the like did Paul and Barnabas, Acts xiii. 15."

If any out of weakness have abused at any time their liberty, it is their personal faulting, as sometimes weak ministers may their office, and yet the ordinance good and lawful.

And the chief of our ministers in New England agree therein. See Mr. Cotton's Answer to Baylie, page the 27th, 2d part. " Though neither all," saith he, " nor most of the brethren of a church have ordinarily received a gift of public prophesying, or preaching, yet in defect of public ministry, it is not an unheard of novelty that God should enlarge private men with public gifts, and[2] to dispense them to edification; for we read that when the church at Jerusalem were all scattered abroad, except the Apostles, yet they that were scattered went every where preaching the word." Acts viii. 4 xi. 19 xx. 21.

---

[1] See Doctor Fulke also on Romans the xi. in answer to the Rhemists. — *Bradford's Note.*

Dr. William Fulke, master of Pembroke Hall, Cambridge, wrote in 1585 a learned confutation of the Rhemish version of the New Testament. See Fuller's Church History, iii. 70.

[2] Some word is here omitted.

Mr. Robinson also, in his Apology, page 45, chapter 8, to take off the aspersion charged on them, as if all the members of a church were to prophesy publicly, answers, "It comes within the compass but of a few of the multitude, haply two or three in a church, so to do; and touching prophecy," saith he, "we think the very same that the Synod held at Embden, 1571, hath decreed in these words: 'First, in all churches, whether but springing up, or grown to some ripeness, let the order of prophecy be observed, according to Paul's institution. Secondly, into the fellowship of this work are to be admitted not only the ministers, but the teachers too, as also of the elders and deacons, yea, even of the multitude, which are willing to confer their gift received of God to the common utility of the church; but so as they first be allowed by the judgment of the ministers and others.' So we believe and practise with the Belgic churches, &c." See more in the immediate following page.

YOUNG MEN.

We cannot but marvel that in so few years there should be so great a change, that they who were so hotly persecuted by the prelates, and also opposed by the better sort of ministers, not only Mr. Gifford, Mr. Bernard, and other such like, but many of the most eminent both for learning and godliness, and yet now not only these famous men and churches in New England so fully to close with them in practice, but all the godly party in the land to stand for the same way, under the new name of Independents, put upon them.

ANCIENT MEN.

CHAP. XXVI.

It is the Lord's doing, and it ought to be marvellous in our eyes; and the rather, because Mr. Bernard, in his book, made their small increase in a few years one and the chief argument against the way itself. To which Mr. Robinson answered, that "Religion is not always sown and reaped in one age; and that John Huss and Jerome of Prague finished their testimony a hundred years before Luther, and Wickliff well nigh as long before them, and yet neither the one nor the other with the like success as Luther. And yet," saith he, "many are already gathered into the kingdom of Christ; and the nearness of many more throughout the whole land, (for the regions are white unto the harvest,) doth promise within less than a hundred years, if our sins and theirs make not us and them unworthy of this mercy, a very plenteous harvest;" (*Justif.* folio 62); as if he had prophesied of these times. Yea, some of us have often heard him say that " even those ministers and other godly persons that did then most sharply oppose them, if they might come to be from under the bishops, and live in a place of rest and peace, where they might comfortably subsist, they would practise the same things which they now did."[1] And truly, many of us have seen this abundantly verified, not only in these latter times, but formerly.

Doctor Ames [2] was estranged from and opposed Mr.

---

[1] See page 45, and note [3] on page 398, and Prince's Annals, p. 305.

[2] William Ames, one of the most acute controversial writers of his age, was educated at Cambridge under the celebrated Perkins, and became fellow of Christ's College. In 1609 he fled from the persecution of archbishop Bancroft, and became minister of the English church at the Hague, whence he was invited by the states of Friesland to the chair of theological professor at Franeker, which he filled

CHAP.
XXVI.

Robinson; and yet afterwards there was loving compliance and near agreement between them; and, which is more strange, Mr. Johnson himself, who was afterwards pastor of the church of God at Amsterdam, was a preacher to the company of English of the Staple at Middleburg, in Zealand, and had great and certain maintenance [1] allowed him by them, and was highly respected of them, and so zealous against this way as that [when] Mr. Barrow's and Mr. Greenwood's Refutation of Gifford [2] was privately in printing in this city, he not only was a means to discover it, but was made the ambassador's instrument to intercept them at the press, and see them burnt; the which charge he did so well perform, as he let them go on until they were wholly finished, and then surprised the whole impression, not suffering any to escape; and then, by the magistrates' authority, caused them all to be openly burnt, himself standing by until they were all consumed to ashes. Only he took up two of them, one to keep in his own study, that he might see their errors, and the other to bestow on a special friend for the like use. But mark the sequel. When he had

with reputation for twelve years. He was a member of the Synod of Dort, and wrote several treatises against the Arminians, besides his famous Medulla Theologiæ. He afterwards removed to Rotterdam, to preach to a congregation of his countrymen there; but the air of Holland not agreeing with his constitution, he determined to remove to New England. This was prevented by his death in 1633. The next spring his widow and children came over, bringing with them his valuable library. Fuller's Hist. of Cambridge, p. 222; Neal's Puritans, i. 436, 578; Belknap's Am. Biog. ii. 161.

[1] £200 per annum. — *Bradford's Note.*

[2] This book was printed in 1591. Its title was "A plain refutation of M. Gifford's book, entitled 'A short treatise against the Donatists of England;' wherein is discovered the forgery of the whole ministry, the confusion, false worship, and antichristian disorder of these parish assemblies, called the Church of England. Here also is prefixed a sum of the causes of our Separation, and of our purposes in practice." A copy of this rare work, reprinted in 1606, is in Prince's New England Library, in the keeping of the Mass. Hist. Society.

JOHNSON'S CONVERSION. 425

done this work, he went home, and being set down in his study, he began to turn over some pages of this book, and superficially to read some things here and there, as his fancy led him. At length he met with something that began to work upon his spirit, which so wrought with him as drew him to this resolution, seriously to read over the whole book; the which he did once and again. In the end he was so taken, and his conscience was troubled so, as he could have no rest in himself until he crossed the seas and came to London to confer with the authors, who were then in prison, and shortly after executed. After which conference he was so satisfied and confirmed in the truth, as he never returned to his place any more at Middleburg, but adjoined himself to their society at London, and was afterwards committed to prison, and then banished; and in conclusion coming to live at Amsterdam, he caused the same books, which he had been an instrument to burn, to be new printed and set out at his own charge. And some of us here present testify this to be a true relation, which we heard from his own mouth before many witnesses.

YOUNG MEN.

We have seen a book of Mr. Robert Baylie's,[1] a Scotchman, wherein he seemeth to take notice of the spreading of the truth under the notion of error, and casts all the disgraces he can on it, and ranks it with others the foulest errors of the time, and endeavours to show how like a small spark it revived out of the ashes, and was brought from Leyden over the seas into New England, and there nourished with much

---

[1] The title of this book is given in note [2] on page 379.

CHAP. XXVI. silence until it spread to other places in the country, and by eminent hands from thence into Old England.

ANCIENT MEN.

As we dare say Mr. Baylie intends no honor to the persons by what he says, either to those here or from whence they came, so are they far from seeking any to themselves, but rather are ashamed that their weak working hath brought no more glory to God; and if in any thing God hath made any of them instruments for the good of his people in any measure, they desire he only may have the glory. And whereas Mr. Baylie affirmeth that, however it was, in a few years the most who settled in the land did agree to model themselves after Mr. Robinson's pattern, we agree with reverend Mr. Cotton, that " there was no agreement by any solemn or common consultation; but that it is true they did, as if they had agreed, by the same spirit of truth and unity, set up, by the help of Christ, the same model of churches, one like to another; and if they of Plymouth have helped any of the first comers in their theory, by hearing and discerning their practices, therein the Scripture is fulfilled that the kingdom of heaven is like unto leaven which a woman took and hid in three measures of meal until all was leavened." Answer to Mr. Baylie, page 17.

_{Matth. xiii. 33.}

YOUNG MEN.

We desire to know how many have been put to death for this cause, and what manner of persons they were, and what occasions were taken against them by bringing them to their end.

ANCIENT MEN.

CHAP. XXVI.

We know certainly of six that were publicly executed, besides such as died in prisons; Mr. Henry Barrow, Mr. Greenwood, (these suffered at Tyburn;) Mr. Penry at St. Thomas Waterings, by London;[1] Mr. William Dennis, at Thetford, in Norfolk; two others at St. Edmund's, in Suffolk, whose names were Copping and Elias [Thacker.][2] These two last mentioned were condemned by cruel Judge Popham,[3] whose countenance and carriage was very rough and severe toward them, with many sharp menaces. But God gave them courage to bear it, and to make this answer:

1594.

1583.

> "My Lord, your face we fear not,
> And for your threats we care not,
> And to come to your read service, we dare not."

These two last named were put to death for dispersing of books.

For Mr. Dennis, he was a godly man, and faithful in his place; but what occasion was taken against him, we know not, more than the common cause.

---

[1] According to Stow's Chronicle, page 765, Henry Barrow and John Greenwood were hung on the 6th of April, 1594. John Penry was executed May 29, 1593. Barrow was a gentleman of Gray's Inn; Greenwood and Penry were clergymen. In 1592, Greenwood was teacher of a church in London, of which Francis Johnson, mentioned in note [1] on page 24, was pastor. See Fuller's Ch. Hist. iii. 136; Hallam's Const. Hist. i. 209, (4th ed.); Prince's Annals, p. 303.

[2] Stow, in his Chronicle, page 697, says, "Elias Thacker was hanged at Saint Edmondsbury on the 4th of June, 1583, and John Coping on the 6th of the same month, for spreading certain books seditiously penned by one Robert Browne, against the Book of Common Prayer established by the laws of this realm. Their books, so many as could be found, were burnt before them." See Strype's Annals, iii. 186; Fuller's Ch. Hist. iii. 66; Neal's Puritans, i. 254, 260, (4to ed.)

[3] This was Lord John Popham, Chief Justice of England, who afterwards took so deep an interest in the colonization of New England, and was foremost in planting the abortive colony at Sagadahoc in 1607. See note [1] on page 50, and note [2] on page 112; and Wood's Athen. Oxon. ii. 20, (Bliss's ed.)

For Mr. Penry, how unjustly he was charged, himself hath made manifest to the world in his books, and that Declaration which he made a little before his suffering; all which are extant in print, with some of his godly letters.[1]

As for Mr. Barrow and Mr. Greenwood, it also appears by their own writings how those statutes formerly made against the Papists were wrested against them, and they condemned thereupon; as may be seen by their Examinations.[2]

YOUNG MEN.

But these were rigid Brownists, and lie under much aspersion, and their names much blemished and beclouded, not only by enemies, but even by godly and very reverend men.

ANCIENT MEN.

They can no more justly be called Brownists, than the disciples might have been called Judasites; for they did as much abhor Brown's apostasy, and profane course, and his defection, as the disciples and other Christians did Judas's treachery.

---

[1] These tracts of Penry are in the Prince Collection, in the Library of the Mass. Hist. Society. Hallam says, "Penry's protestation at his death is in a style of the most affecting and simple eloquence." He was a graduate of Oxford, and was charged with being one of the authors of Martin Mar-Prelate. See Wood's Athen. Oxon. i 591—598, (Bliss's ed.), Hallam's Const. Hist. i. 201, (4th ed.), and Neal's Puritans, i. 374—379.

[2] In the Harleian Miscellany, iv. 340, (Park's ed.) may be seen "The Examinations of Henry Barrowe, John Greenwood, and John Penrie, before the High Commissioners and Lordes of the Counsel; penned by the prisoners themselves before their deathes." "Let any man read the examinations of Barrow and Greenwood, and I am mistaken if he will not perceive a plain-hearted Christian simplicity in their behaviour, and an inhuman spirit of cruelty and tyranny in their persecutors." Peirce's Vindication of the Dissenters, page 146.

And for their rigid and roughness of spirit, as some of them, especially Mr. Barrow, is taxed, it may be considered they were very rigidly and roughly dealt with, not only by the Lord's enemies and their enemies, but by some godly persons of those times, differing in opinions from them; which makes some of us call to mind what one Doctor Taylor hath written in a late book in these stirring times. " Such an eminent man," said he, " hath had the good hap to be reputed orthodox by posterity, and did condemn such a man of such an opinion, and yet himself erred in as considerable matters; but meeting with better neighbours in his life-time, and a more charitable posterity after his death, hath his memory preserved in honor; and the other's name suffers without cause." Of which he gives instances in his book entitled The Liberty of Prophesying, page 33 and following.

We refer you to Mr. Robinson's Answer to Mr. Bernard,[1] where he charges him with blasphemy, railing, scoffing, &c. " For Mr. Barrow," saith Mr. Robinson, " as I say with Mr. Ainsworth, that I will not justify all the words of another man, nor yet mine own, so say I also with Mr. Smith, that because I know not by what particular motion of the Spirit he was guided to write in those phrases, I dare not censure him as you do; especially considering with what fiery zeal the Lord hath furnished such his servants at all times, as he hath stirred up for special reformation. Let the example of Luther alone suffice, whom into what terms his zeal carried, his writings testify; and yet both in him and in Mr. Barrow there might be with

---

[1] See the title of this work in note [3] on page 40.

true spiritual zeal fleshly indignation mingled." Answer to Mr. Bernard, folio 84.

And further in page 86 he saith, that "such harsh terms wherewith he entertains such persons and things in the church as carry with them most appearance of holiness, they are to be interpreted according to his meaning, with this distinction, that Mr. Barrow speaks not of these persons and things simply, but in a respect, and so and so considered; and so no one term given by Mr. Barrow but may, at the least, be tolerated."

YOUNG MEN.

But divers reverend men have expressed concerning this matter that God is not wont to make choice of men infamous for gross sins and vices before their calling, to make them any instruments of reformation after their calling, and proceed to declare that Mr. Barrow was a great gamester and a dicer when he lived in court, and getting much by play, would boast of loose spending it with courtesans, &c.

ANCIENT MEN.

Truly, with due respect to such reverend men be it spoken, those things might well have been spared from putting in print, especially so long after his death, when not only he, but all his friends are taken out of the world, that might vindicate his name. That he was tainted with vices at the court before his conversion and calling, it is not very strange; and if he had lived and died in that condition, it is like he might have gone out of the world without any public brand on his name, and have passed for a tolerable Christian and member of the church. He had hurt enough done him, whilst he lived, by evil and cruel enemies; why should godly men be prejudicated to him after his death in his name? Was not the Apostle Paul a persecutor of God's saints unto death? And doth not the same Apostle, speaking of scandalous and lascivious persons, say, "And such were some of you; but ye are washed, but ye are sanctified, but ye are justified in the name of the Lord Jesus and by the spirit of our God."[1 Cor. vi. 11.]

And if histories deceive us not, was not Cyprian a magician before his conversion, and Augustine a Manichæan? And when it was said unto him in the voice he heard, *Tolle et lege*, he was directed to that place of Scripture, "Not in gluttony and drunkenness, nor in chambering and wantonness, nor in strife and envying; but put ye on the Lord Jesus Christ, and take no thought for the flesh, to fulfil the lusts of it."[Rom. xiii. 13.] [1] By which it may seem that if God do not [2] make choice of such men as have been infamous for gross vices before their calling, yet sometimes he is wont to do it, and is free to choose whom he pleaseth for notable instruments for his own work. As for other things that have been spoken of him and Mr. Greenwood and Mr. Penry, we leave them as they are. But some of us have reason to think there are some mistakes in the relations of those things. Only we shall add other public testimonies concerning them from witnesses of very worthy credit, which are also in print.

First, from Mr. Phillips. A famous and godly

---

[1] This is the Geneva version. See note [3] on page 14.

[2] The word *ordinarily* seems to have been accidentally omitted here.

preacher, having heard and seen Mr. Barrow's holy speeches and preparations for death, said, "Barrow, Barrow, my soul be with thine!" The same author also reports, that Queen Elizabeth asked learned Doctor Reynolds,[1] what he thought of those two men, Mr. Barrow and Mr. Greenwood; and he answered her Majesty that it could not avail any thing to show his judgment concerning them, seeing they were put to death; and being loath to speak his mind further, her Majesty charged him upon his allegiance to speak. Whereupon he answered, that he was persuaded, if they had lived, they would have been two as worthy instruments for the church of God, as have been raised up in this age. Her Majesty sighed and said no more. But after that, riding to a park by the place where they were executed, and being willing to take further information concerning them, demanded of the right honorable the Earl of Cumberland, that was present when they suffered, what end they made. He answered, "a very godly end, and prayed for your Majesty, and the State," &c.[2] We may also add what some of us have heard by credible information, that the Queen demanded of the Archbishop[3] what he thought

---

[1] Dr. John Reynolds, one of the most learned divines of his age, was, according to Anthony Wood, "the pillar of Puritanism, and the grand favorer of Nonconformity." He was born at Devonshire in 1549, and educated in Corpus Christi College, Oxford, of which he was afterwards president. He was the principal champion of the Puritans at the Hampton Court Conference, and was one of the persons appointed by James to make the English version of the Bible now in common use. He had been Dean of Lincoln, and declined a bishopric. He died in 1607. See Wood's Athen. Oxon. ii. 12—19, (Bliss ed.); Prince's Worthies of Devon, pp. 684—692; Fuller's Church History, iii. 172—193, 228, 230.

[2] See Pierce's Vindication of the Dissenters, part. i. 147, and Strype's Life of Bishop Aylmer, p. 247, and Neal's History of New England, i. 71.

[3] Whitgift. He succeeded Grindal in 1584, and held the see till his death in 1604, the second year of James's reign. See Fuller's Ch. Hist. iii. 66, 198.

of them in his conscience. He answered "he thought they were the servants of God, but dangerous to the State." "Alas!" said she, "shall we put the servants of God to death?" And this was the true cause why no more of them were put to death in her days.[1]

YOUNG MEN.

Did any of you know Mr. Barrow? if we may be so bold to ask, for we would willingly know what [was] his life and conversation; because some, we perceive, have him in precious esteem, and others can scarce name him without some note of obloquy and dislike.

ANCIENT MEN.

We have not seen his person; but some of us have been well acquainted with those that knew him familiarly both before and after his conversion; and one of us hath had conference with one that was his domestic servant, and tended upon him both before and some while after the same.

He was a gentleman of good worth, and a flourishing courtier in his time, and, as appears in his own answers to the Archbishop and Doctor Cousens, he was some time a student at Cambridge and the Inns of Court, and accomplished with strong parts.

We have heard his conversion to be on this wise. Walking in London one Lord's day with one of his companions, he heard a preacher at his sermon very loud, as they passed by the church. Upon which Mr.

1586.
Nov. 19.

---

[1] "There be grave professors, who lived near those occurrences, who speak of Queen Elizabeth as ignorant of Barrow's execution and Greenwood's, and displeased at it when she heard of it afterwards." Cotton's Way, page 5. Baylie says, p. 14, that "Queen Elizabeth, by the evil advice of the cruel prelates about her, caused Barrow to be hanged."

Barrow said unto his consort, "Let us go in and hear what this man saith that is thus earnest." "Tush," saith the other, "what! shall we go to hear a man talk?" &c. But in he went and sat down. And the minister was vehement in reproving sin, and sharply applied the judgments of God against the same; and, it should seem, touched him to the quick in such things as he was guilty of, so as God set it home to his soul, and began to work his repentance and conversion thereby. For he was so stricken as he could not be quiet, until by conference with godly men and further hearing of the word, with diligent reading and meditation, God brought peace to his soul and conscience, after much humiliation of heart and reformation of life; so as he left the court, and retired himself to a private life, some time in the country and some time in the city, giving himself to study and reading of the Scriptures and other good works very diligently. And being missed at court by his consorts and acquaintance, it was quickly bruited abroad that Barrow was turned Puritan. What his course was afterwards, his writings show, as also his sufferings and conference with men of all sorts do declare, until his life was taken from him.

And thus much we can further affirm, from those that well knew him, that he was very comfortable to the poor and those in distress in their sufferings; and when he saw he must die, he gave a stock for the relief of the poor of the church, which was a good help to them in their banished condition afterwards. Yea, and that which some will hardly believe, he did much persuade them to peace, and composed many differences that were grown amongst them whilst he lived, and would have, it is like, prevented more that after fell out, if he had continued.

YOUNG MEN.

We thank you for your pains. We hope it will extend further than our satisfaction. We cannot but marvel that such a man should be by so many so aspersed.

ANCIENT MEN.

It is not much to be marvelled at; for he was most plain in discovering the cruelty, fraud, and hypocrisy of the enemies of the truth, and searching into the corruptions of the time, which made him abhorred of them; and peradventure something too harsh against the haltings of divers of the preachers and professors that he had to deal with in those times, who out of fear or weakness did not come so close up to the truth in their practice as their doctrines and grounds seemed to hold forth. Which makes us remember what was the answer of Erasmus to the Duke of Saxony, when he asked his opinion whether Luther had erred. He answered, "his opinions were good, but wished he would moderate his style, which stirred him up the more enemies, no doubt."

YOUNG MEN.

We find in the writings of some such who were very eminent in their times for piety and learning, that those of the Separation[1] found more favor in our native country than those who were reproached by the name of Puritans; and after much discourse thereabouts, come

---

[1] For an account of the difference between the Puritans and the Separatists, see Prince's Annals, pp. 302—305.

CHAP. XXVI. to this conclusion, that no comparison will hold from the Separatists to them in their sufferings but *a minori*; and then they go on and say, what a compulsory banishment has been put upon those blessed and glorious lights, Mr. Cartwright,[1] Mr. Parker,[2] Doctor Ames, &c.

ANCIENT MEN.

Far be it from any of us to detract from or to extenuate the sufferings of any of the servants of God, much less from those worthies forenamed, or any others afterwards mentioned. Yet, under favor, we crave pardon if we cannot consent to the judgment of such eminent ones for piety and learning above hinted. We doubt not, but do easily grant, that the sufferings of those reproached by the name of Puritans were great, especially some of them, and were better known to those pious and learned [men] first above intimated, than the sufferings of those that are reproached by the name of Brownists and Separatists.[3] But we shall

---

[1] Thomas Cartwright, "chief of the Nonconformists," as Fuller calls him, was one of the most learned scholars and skilful disputants of his age. He was born in 1535, and educated at Cambridge; was fellow of Trinity College, and Lady Margaret's professor of divinity. But venturing in some of his lectures to point out the defects in the discipline of the Church, he was expelled from the university. He then went to Geneva, and afterwards became preacher to the English merchants at Antwerp. After his return from Antwerp he was often in trouble by suspensions, deprivations and long imprisonment; till at length the Earl of Leicester made him governor of his hospital at Warwick, where he died in 1603. See Fuller's Ch. Hist. ii. 503, iii. 105, 165, 171; Neal's Puritans, i. 420.

[2] Robert Parker, a Puritan divine of Wiltshire, in consequence of publishing a Treatise on the Cross in Baptism, was obliged in 1607 to fly into Holland. Here he would have been chosen pastor of the English Church at Amsterdam; but the magistrates being afraid of offending King James, he went to Doesburgh, and became minister of the garrison there, where he died in 1630. See Wood's Athen. Oxon. ii. 309, (ed. Bliss); Peirce's Vindication, p. 171; Neal's Puritans, i. 436, 456.

[3] On the occasion of the passage of a law of banishment against the Separatists in 1593, Sir Walter Raleigh said in the House of Commons, "In his conceit the Brownists are worthy to be rooted out of

give you some instances, and leave it to you and some others to consider of.

1. Though no more were publicly executed, yet sundry more were condemned, and brought to the gallows, and ascended the ladder, not knowing but they should die, and have been reprieved, and after banished; some of which we have known and often spoken with.

2. Others have not only been forced into voluntary banishment, by great numbers, to avoid further cruelty, but divers, after long and sore imprisonment, have been forced to abjure the land by oath, never to return without leave. In anno 1604 four persons at once were forced to do so at a public Sessions in London, or else upon refusal they were to be hanged. This their abjuration was done on the statute of the 35 of Queen Elizabeth. Some of these we have also known.

3. We find mention in a printed book of seventeen or eighteen that have died in several prisons in London in six years' time before the year 1592, besides what have been in other parts of the land, and since that time, perishing by cold, hunger, or noisomeness of the prison.

4. In the same year we find a lamentable petition, 1592. now in print, of sixty persons committed unbailably to several prisons in London, as Newgate, the Gatehouse, Clink, &c., being made close prisoners, allowing them neither meat, drink, fire, nor lodging, nor suffering any

---

a commonwealth; but what danger may grow to ourselves if this law passes, it were fit to be considered. If two or three thousand Brownists meet at the seaside, at whose charge shall they be transported? or whither will you send them? I am sorry for it; I am afraid there is near twenty thousand of them in England; and when they are gone, who shall maintain their wives and children?" Simon D'Ewes's Journals, p. 517, and Peirce's Vindication, page 143.

whose hearts the Lord would stir up for their relief, to have any access unto them; so as they complain that no felons, traitors, nor murderers in the land were thus dealt with; and so after many other grievous complaints conclude with these words: "We crave for all of us but the liberty either to die openly or to live openly in the land of our nativity. If we deserve death, it beseemeth the majesty of justice not to see us closely murdered, yea starved to death with hunger and cold, and stifled in loathsome dungeons. If we be guiltless, we crave but the benefit of our innocence, viz. that we may have peace to serve our God and our Prince in the place of the sepulchres of our fathers."[1]

And what numbers, since those times, have been put unto compulsory banishment and other hard sufferings, as loss of goods, friends, and long and hard imprisonments, under which many have died,—it is so well known, that it would make up a volume to rehearse them, and would not only equalize but far exceed the number of those godly called Puritans that have suffered. Suppose they were but few of them ministers that suffered, as above expressed; yet their sorrows might be as great, and their wants more, and their souls as much afflicted, because more contemned and neglected of men.

But some have said *they* were excommunicated; and that was no great matter as excommunications went in those days. So were *these*, not only whilst they were living, but some of them many times after they were dead; and as some of the other were imprisoned, so were more of these. But it is further said, all of them were deprived of their ministry; and so were

---

[1] See Peirce's Vindication of the Dissenters, part. i. p. 144.

these of their livelihood and maintenance, though they had no offices to lose. But those remained still in the land, and were succoured and sheltered by good people in a competent wise, the most of them, and sundry of them lived as well, as may easily be proved, if not better, than if they had enjoyed their benefices; whereas the other were, a great number of them, forced to fly into foreign lands for shelter, or else might have perished in prisons; and these poor creatures endured, many of them, such hardships (as is well known to some of us) as makes our hearts still ache to remember.

We some of us knew Mr. Parker, Doctor Ames, and Mr. Jacob [1] in Holland, when they sojourned for a time at Leyden; and all three boarded together and had their victuals dressed by some of our acquaintance, and then they lived comfortably, and then they were provided for as became their persons. And after Mr. Jacob returned, and Mr. Parker was at Amsterdam,

---

[1] Henry Jacob was born in the county of Kent in 1563, and was educated at Oxford. He became a clergyman of the Church of England, and as Anthony Wood says, "was a person most excellently well read in theological authors, but withal was a most zealous Puritan, or as his son Henry used to say, the first Independent in England." He wrote two treatises against Francis Johnson, the Brownist, in defence of the Church of England's being a true church. But flying from the persecution under Bishop Bancroft in 1604, he fell in with John Robinson at Leyden, and conferring with him embraced his peculiar sentiments of church government. On his return to England, he laid in 1616, the foundation of an Independent or Congregational Church. He continued with his people about eight years, but in 1624 went to Virginia, where he soon after died. From the Library of the American Antiquarian Society, at Worcester, I have obtained the use of a book written by Jacob, entitled "An Attestation of many learned, godly and famous divines, lights of religion and pillars of the gospel, justifying this doctrine, viz. that the church government ought to be always with the people's free consent. Also this, that a true church under the Gospel containeth no more ordinary congregations but one. Anno Dom. 1613." pp. 323. 16mo. This work is not contained in Wood's list of Jacob's writings, nor is it mentioned by Neal. See Wood's Athen. Oxon. iii. 329—333, (Bliss's ed.); Neal's Puritans. i. 438, 476; Mass. Hist. Coll. xi. 164 —167.

(where he printed some of his books,) and Mr. Ames disposed of himself to other places, it was not worse with them; and some of us well know how it fared then with divers precious Christians in those times and places. To speak the truth, the professors in England, though many of them suffered much at the hands of the prelates, yet they had a great advantage of the Separatists; for the Separatists had not only the prelates and their faction to encounter with, (and what harder measure they met with at their hands, above the other, doth sufficiently appear by what is before declared,) but also they must endure the frowns, and many times the sharp invectives, of the forward ministers against them, both in public and private; and what influence they had upon the spirits of the people, is well enough known; also by reason hereof the ministers in foreign countries did look awry at them when they would give help and countenance to the other.

YOUNG MEN.

Indeed, it seems they have sometimes suffered much hardness in the Low Countries, if that be true that is reported of such a man as Mr. Ainsworth, that he should live for some time with nine pence a week. To which is replied by another, that if people suffered him to live on nine pence a week, with roots boiled, either the people were grown extreme low in estate, or the growth of their godliness was come to a very low ebb.

ANCIENT MEN.

The truth is, their condition for the most part was for some time very low and hard. It was with them

SUFFERINGS OF THE SEPARATISTS. 441

as, if it should be related, would hardly be believed. And no marvel. For many of them had lain long in prisons, and then were banished into Newfoundland, where they were abused, and at last came into the Low Countries, and wanting money, trades, friends or acquaintances, and languages to help themselves, how could it be otherwise? The report of Mr. Ainsworth was near those times, when he was newly come out of Ireland with others poor, and being a single young man and very studious, was content with a little. And yet, to take off the aspersion from the people in that particular, the chief and true reason thereof is mistaken; for he was a very modest and bashful man, and concealed his wants from others, until some suspected how it was with him, and pressed him to see how it was; and after it was known, such as were able mended his condition; and when he was married afterwards, he and his family were comfortably provided for. But we have said enough of these things. They had few friends to comfort them, nor any arm of flesh to support them; and if in some things they were too rigid, they are rather to be pitied, considering their times and sufferings, than to be blasted with reproach to posterity.

YOUNG MEN.

Was that Brown,[1] that fell away and made apostasy, the first inventor and beginner of this way?

[1] Robert Brown was descended from an ancient and respectable family in Rutlandshire. His father, Anthony Brown, Esquire, of Tolthorp, sheriff of the county, was nearly related to Cecil, Lord Burleigh. He was educated at Cambridge, and preached some time in Benet. Church, where the vehemence of his delivery gained him reputation with the people. He was first a schoolmaster in Southworth, and then a preacher at Islington, near London. He first separated from the Church of England in 1580, and having been twice imprisoned, at length escaped into Holland, and set up a congregation

CHAP. XXVI.
ANCIENT MEN.

No, verily; for, as one answers this question very well in a printed book, almost forty years ago, that the prophets, apostles, and evangelists have in their authentic writings laid down the ground thereof; and upon that ground is their building reared up and surely settled.[1] Moreover, many of the martyrs, both former and latter, have maintained it, as is to be seen in The Acts and Monuments of the Church. Also, in the days of Queen Elizabeth there was a separated church, whereof Mr. Fitts was pastor,[2] and another before that in the time of Queen Mary, of which Mr. Rough[3] was

---

of his followers at Middleburg. After its dissolution, he returned in 1589 to England, recanted his principles of separation, became reconciled to the established church, and was rewarded with a living in Northamptonshire. Fuller, the church historian, who was born within a mile of his residence, says he often saw him in his youth, and adds that "he had in my time a wife with whom for many years he never lived, and a church wherein he never preached." Being imprisoned for striking the constable of his parish for demanding a church rate of him, he died in Northampton gaol in 1630, in his 81st year. Hornius says, "De eo inter alia ridicula referunt, quod cum frequenter uxorem suam pulsaret, reprehensus propterea responderit, 'Se non verberare eam ut uxorem suam, verum ut nefariam et maledictam vetulam.'" — A good account of this eccentric individual may be found in Bridges's History of Northamptonshire, ii. 366, (Whalley's ed.)

Robinson, in his Justification of Separation, page 54, says, "Now touching Browne, it is true, that as he forsook the Lord, so the Lord forsook him in his way; and so he did his own people Israel many a time. And if the Lord had not forsaken him, he had never so returned back into Egypt, as he did, to live of the spoils of it. And for the wicked things which Mr. Bernard affirmeth he did in this way, it may well be as he saith, and the more wicked things he committed in this course, the less like he was to continue long in it, and the more like to return again to his proper centre, the Church of England, where he should be sure to find companions enough in any wickedness, as it came to pass." See Wood's Athen. Oxon. ii. 17, (ed. Bliss); Fuller's Ch. Hist. iii. 61—65; Strype's Annals, iii. 15; Neal's Puritans, i. 251; Baylie's Dissuasive, p. 13; Hornii Hist. Eccles. p. 231; Hoornbeek, Summa Controv. p. 739.

[1] As for Mr. Robinson's being the author of Independency, Mr. Cotton replies that "the New Testament was the author of it, and it was received in the times of purest, primitive antiquity, many hundreds of years before Mr. Robinson was born." Prince, p. 176. See Cotton's Way, p. 9.

[2] See Prince's Annals, p. 302.

[3] Rough was burnt. See Neal's Puritans, i. 71.

pastor or teacher, and Cudbert Simpson a deacon, who exercised amongst themselves, as other ordinances, so church censures, as excommunication, &c., and professed and practised that cause before Mr. Brown wrote for it. But he being one that afterwards wrote for it, they that first hatched the name of Puritans[1] and bestowed it on the godly professors that desired reformation, they likewise out of the same storehouse would needs bestow this new livery upon others that never would own it, nor had reason so to do. Mr. Cotton, likewise, in his Answer to Mr. Baylie, page fourth, shows how in the year 1567 there were a hundred persons who refused the common liturgy, and the congregations attending thereunto, and used prayers and preaching and the sacraments amongst themselves, whereof fourteen or fifteen were sent to prison, of whom the chiefest were Mr. Smith, Mr. Nixon, James Ireland, Robert Hawkins, Thomas Rowland, and Richard Morecroft; and these pleaded their separation before the Lord Mayor, Bishop Sands, and other commissioners on June 20, 1567, about eighty years ago, being many years before Brown.[2] Divers other instances might be given.

YOUNG MEN.

But if we mistake not, Mr. Brown is accounted by some of good note to be the inventor of that way which is called Brownism, from whom the sect took its name. Moreover, it is said by such of note as aforesaid, that it is not God's usual manner of dealing to leave any of the first publishers or restorers of any truth of his to such fearful apostasy.

[1] In 1564. See note [1] on page 12.

[2] See Fuller's Ch. Hist. ii. 480, and Neal's Puritans, i. 161—164.

ANCIENT MEN.

Possibly this speech might arise from a common received opinion. But reverend Mr. Cotton, in his Answer to Mr. Baylie, saith "the backsliding of Brown from that way of Separation is a just reason why the Separatists may disclaim denomination from him, and refuse to be called Brownists, after his name; and to speak with reason," saith he, " if any be justly to be called Brownists, it is only such as revolt from Separation to formality, and from thence to profaneness." Page 5.

To which we may add, that it is very injurious to call those after his name, whose person they never knew, and whose writings few if any of them ever saw, and whose errors and backslidings they have constantly borne witness against; and what truths they have received have been from the light of God's sacred word, conveyed by other godly instruments unto them; though Brown may sometimes have professed some of the same things, and now fallen from the same, as many others have done.

YOUNG MEN.

Seeing we have presumed thus far to inquire into these ancienter times of you, and of the sufferings of the aforesaid persons, we would likewise entreat you, though never so briefly, to tell us something of the persons and carriages of other eminent men about those times, or immediately after, as Mr. Francis Johnson, Mr. Henry Ainsworth, Mr. John Smith, Mr. John Robinson, Mr. Richard Clifton.

ANCIENT MEN.

Here are some in the company that knew them all familiarly, whom we shall desire to satisfy your request.

Those answered, We shall do it most willingly; for we cannot but honor the memory of the men for the good that not only many others but we ourselves have received by them and their ministry; for we have heard them all, and lived under the ministry of divers of them for some years. We shall therefore speak of them in order briefly.

MR. JOHNSON,

Of whom something was spoken before,[1] was pastor of the church of God at Amsterdam. A very grave man he was, and an able teacher, and was the most solemn in all his administrations that we have seen any, and especially in dispensing the seals of the covenant, both baptism and the Lord's supper. And a good disputant he was. We heard Mr. Smith upon occasion say, that he was persuaded no men living were able to maintain a cause against those two men, meaning Mr. Johnson and Mr. Ainsworth, if they had not the truth on their side. He, by reason of many dissensions that fell out in the church, and the subtilty of one of the elders of the same, came after many years to alter his judgment about the government of the church, and his practice thereupon, which caused a division amongst them. But he lived not many years after, and died at Amsterdam after his return from Embden.

---

[1] On page 424.

YOUNG MEN.

But he is much spoken against for excommunicating his brother[1] and his own father, and maintaining his wife's cause, who was by his brother and others reproved for her pride in apparel.

ANCIENT MEN.

Himself hath often made his own defence, and others for him. The church did, after long patience towards them and much pains taken with them, excommunicate them for their unreasonable and endless opposition, and such things as did accompany the same; and such was the justice thereof, as he could not but consent thereto. In our time his wife was a grave matron, and very modest both in her apparel and all her demeanour, ready to any good works in her place, and helpful to many, especially the poor, and an ornament to his calling. She was a young widow when he married her, and had been a merchant's wife, by whom he had a good estate, and was a godly woman; and because she wore such apparel as she had been formerly used to, which were neither excessive nor immodest, for their chiefest exceptions were against her wearing of some whalebone in the bodice and sleeves of her gown, corked shoes, and other such like things as the citizens of her rank then used to wear. And although, for offence sake, she and he were willing to reform the fashions of them so far as might be without spoiling of their garments, yet it would not content them except they came full up to their size. Such

---

[1] His brother's name was George. See Baylie, p. 15.

was the strictness or rigidness (as now the term goes) of some in those times, as we can by experience and of our own knowledge show in other instances. We shall for brevity sake only show one.

We were in the company of a godly man that had been a long time prisoner at Norwich for this cause, and was by Judge Cooke set at liberty. After going into the country he visited his friends, and returning that way again to go into the Low Countries by ship at Yarmouth, and so desired some of us to turn in with him to the house of an ancient woman in the city, who had been very kind and helpful to him in his sufferings. She knowing his voice made him very welcome, and those with him. But after some time of their entertainment, being ready to depart, she came up to him and felt of his band, (for her eyes were dim with age,) and perceiving it was something stiffened with starch, she was much displeased, and reproved him very sharply, fearing God would not prosper his journey. Yet the man was a plain countryman, clad in gray russet, without either welt or guard, (as the proverb is,) and the band he wore scarce worth threepence, made of their own homespinning; and he was godly and humble as he was plain. What would such professors, if they were now living, say to the excess of our times?[1]

[1] Francis Johnson became a Separatist by reading a book written by Barrow and Greenwood, as related on page 425. In 1592, on the formation of a new congregation of Separatists in London, Johnson was chosen its pastor and Greenwood its teacher. They, with fifty-four of their church, were soon seized by the bishop's officers, and imprisoned. After the execution of Barrow and Greenwood, Johnson escaped from the country, and with some of his people set up a church at Amsterdam. Robinson found him there in 1608, as appears from page 34. On the breaking out of the dissensions among them, Johnson removed to Embden. See note [1] on page 24; Neal's Puritans, pp. 363, 436; Prince Annals, p. 303; Robinson's Justification, p. 55; Baylie's Dissuasive, p. 14; Cotton's Way, p. 6.

CHAP. XXVI.

Mr. Henry Ainsworth,

A man of a thousand, was teacher of this church at Amsterdam at the same time when Mr. Johnson was pastor. Two worthy men they were and of excellent parts. He continued constant in his judgment and practice unto his end in those things about the church government, from which Mr. Johnson swerved and fell. He ever maintained good correspondence with Mr. Robinson at Leyden, and would consult with him in all matters of weight, both in their differences and afterwards. A very learned man he was, and a close student, which much impaired his health. We have heard some, eminent in the knowledge of the tongues, of the university of Leyden, say that they thought he had not his better for the Hebrew tongue in the university, nor scarce in Europe.[1] He was a man very modest, amiable, and sociable in his ordinary course and carriage, of an innocent and unblamable life and conversation, of a meek spirit, and a calm temper, void of passion and not easily provoked. And yet he would be something smart in his style to his opposers in his public writings; at which we that have seen his constant carriage, both in public disputes and the managing of all church affairs, and such like occurrences, have sometimes marvelled. He had an excellent gift of teaching and opening the Scriptures; and things did flow from him with that facility, plainness and sweetness, as did much affect the hearers. He was powerful and profound in doctrine, although his voice was not

---

[1] Cotton, in his Way of Congregational Churches Cleared, page 6, says, "Mr. Ainsworth, a man of a modest and humble spirit, and diligently studious of the Hebrew text, hath not been unuseful to the church in his Exposition of the Pentateuch, especially of Moses his rituals."

strong; and had this excellency above many, that he was most ready and pregnant in the Scriptures, as if the book of God had been written in his heart; being as ready in his quotations, without tossing and turning his book, as if they had laid open before his eyes, and seldom missing a word in the citing of any place, teaching not only the word and doctrine of God, but in the words of God, and for the most part in a continued phrase and words of Scripture. He used great dexterity, and was ready in comparing scripture with scripture, one with another. In a word, the times and place in which he lived were not worthy of such a man.

YOUNG MEN.

But we find that he is taxed, in a book writ by George Johnson, with apostasy and to be a man-pleaser, &c.

ANCIENT MEN.

Who can escape the scourge of tongues? Christ himself could not do it when he was here upon earth, although there was no guile found in his mouth; nor Moses, although he was the meekest man in the earth. For man-pleasing, they that tax him [do it] because he concurred against their violent and endless dissensions about the former matters. And for his apostasy, this was all the matter. When he was a young man, before he came out of England, he at the persuasion of some of his godly friends went once or twice to hear a godly minister preach; and this was the great matter of apostasy, for which those violent men thought him worthy to be deposed from his place, and for which

CHAP. XXVI. they thus charge him. And truly herein they may worthily bear the name of rigid, &c.[1]

Mr. John Smith

Was an eminent man in his time, and a good preacher, and of other good parts; but his inconstancy, and unstable judgment, and being so suddenly carried away with things, did soon overthrow him. Yet we have some of us heard him use this speech: "Truly," said he, "we being now come into a place of liberty, are in great danger, if we look not well to our ways; for we are like men set upon the ice, and therefore may easily slide and fall." But in this example it appears it is an easier matter to give good counsel than to follow it, to foresee danger than to prevent it: which made the prophet to say, "O Lord, the way of man is not in himself, neither is it in man to walk and to direct his steps." He was some time pastor to a company of honest and godly men which came with him out of England, and pitched at Amsterdam. He first fell into some errors about the Scriptures, and so into some opposition with Mr. Johnson, who had been his tutor,

Jere. x. 23.

---

[1] After Johnson's removal to Embden, Ainsworth was the sole pastor of the church at Amsterdam till his death. This "Rabbi of his age," as he was called, "was the author of a very learned commentary on the five books of Moses, in which he shows himself a complete master of the Oriental languages and of Jewish antiquities. His death was sudden, and not without suspicion of violence; for it is reported, that having found a diamond of great value in the streets of Amsterdam, he advertised it in print, and when the owner, who was a Jew, came to demand it, he offered him any acknowledgment he would desire; but Ainsworth, though poor, would accept of nothing but a conference with some of the rabbies upon the prophecies of the Old Testament relating to the Messiah, which the other promised; but not having interest enough to obtain it, and Ainsworth being resolute, it is thought he was poisoned. His congregation remained without a pastor for some years after his death and then chose Mr. Canne, author of the marginal references to the Bible." See Neal's Puritans, i. 363, 386, 437; Baylie's Dissuasive, p. 15; Cotton's Way, p. 6.

and the church there. But he was convinced of them by the pains and faithfulness of Mr. Johnson and Mr. Ainsworth, and revoked them; but afterwards was drawn away by some of the Dutch Anabaptists, who finding him to be a good scholar and unsettled, they easily misled the most of his people, and other of them scattered away. He lived not many years after, but died there of a consumption, to which he was inclined before he came out of England. His and his people's condition may be an object of pity for after times.[1]

Mr. John Robinson

Was pastor of that famous church of Leyden, in Holland; a man not easily to be paralleled for all things, whose singular virtues we shall not take upon us here

---

[1] Smith, who has already been mentioned on pages 22 and 34, was, according to Baylie, p. 15, "a man of right eminent parts." Neal says that he was "a learned man, of good abilities, but of an unsettled head, as appears by the preface to one of his books, in which he desires that his last writing may always be taken for his present judgment. He was for refining upon the Brownists' scheme, and at last declared for the principles of the Baptists; but being at a loss for a proper administrator of the ordinance of baptism, he plunged himself, and then performed the ceremony upon others; which gained him the name of a *Se-baptist*. He afterwards embraced the tenets of Arminius, and published certain conclusions upon those points in the year 1611, which Mr. Robinson answered in 1614; but Smith died soon after, and his congregation dissolved.

"The fall of Mr. Smith," says Cotton, in his Way, p. 6, "and the spirit of errors and instability that fell upon him, was a dreadful warning from heaven against self-fulness and self-pleasing. For though the tyranny of the Ecclesiastical Courts was harsh towards him, and the yokes put upon him in the ministry too grievous to be borne, yet neither was he alone in suffering. Nor were those that suffered with him at that time (Mr. Clifton and Mr. Robinson) such inconsiderable persons that he should affect to go alone from them. He thought he could have gained his tutor, Johnson, [of Amsterdam] from the errors of his rigid separation. But he had promised them not to go over to him without their consents; and they utterly dissuaded him therefrom, as fearing his instability. And yet, contrary to his promise, he went over to him, which led him into manifest temptations and aberrations."

The celebrated Bishop Hall wrote a letter which he addressed "to Mr. Smith and Mr. Robinson, ringleaders of the late Separation, at Amsterdam." See Neal's Puritans, i. 437; Baylie's Dissuasive, pp. 15, 19; Bp. Hall's Epistles, dec. iii. ep. 1.

CHAP. XXVI. to describe. Neither need we, for they so well are known both by friends and enemies. As he was a man learned and of solid judgment, and of a quick and sharp wit, so was he also of a tender conscience, and very sincere in all his ways, a hater of hypocrisy and dissimulation, and would be very plain with his best friends. He was very courteous, affable and sociable in his conversation, and towards his own people especially. He was an acute and expert disputant, very quick and ready, and had much bickering with the Arminians,[1] who stood more in fear of him than any of the university. He was never satisfied in himself until he had searched any cause or argument he had to deal in thoroughly and to the bottom; and we have heard him sometimes say to his familiars that many times, both in writing and disputation, he knew he had sufficiently answered others, but many times not himself; and was ever desirous of any light, and the more able, learned, and holy the persons were, the more he desired to confer and reason with them. He was very profitable in his ministry and comfortable to his people. He was much beloved of them, and as loving was he unto them, and entirely sought their good for soul and body. In a word, he was much esteemed and reverenced of all that knew him, and his abilities [were acknowledged] both of friends and strangers. But we resolved to be brief in this matter, leaving you to better and more large information herein from others.[2]

[1] See pages 41 and 392.
[2] JOHN ROBINSON was born in 1576, but the place of his birth is unknown. He was educated at Emmanuel College, Cambridge, where he entered in 1592, took the degree of Master of Arts in 1600, and Bachelor of Divinity in 1607, the year before he went over to Holland. Before his election as pastor of the Pilgrim Church, mentioned on page 23, he had a benefice near Yarmouth, in Norfolk, where he was often molested by the bishop's officers, and his friends almost ruined in the ecclesiastical

Mr. Richard Clifton

CHAP. XXVI.

Was a grave and fatherly old man when he came first into Holland, having a great white beard ; and pity it was that such a reverend old man should be forced to leave his country, and at those years to go into exile. But it was his lot; and he bore it patiently. Much good had he done in the country where he lived, and converted many to God by his faithful and painful ministry, both in preaching and catechizing. Sound and orthodox he always was, and so continued to his end. He belonged to the church at Leyden; but being settled at Amsterdam, and thus aged, he was loath to remove any more; and so when they removed, he

courts. It is an ungenerous insinuation of Bishop Hall, at the end of his Apology against Brownists, "Neither doubt we to say, that the mastership of the hospital at Norwich, or a lease from that city, (sued for, with repulse,) might have procured that this separation from the communion, government, and worship of the Church of England, should not have been made by John Robinson."

Baylie, that bitter inveigher against the Brownists and Independents, acknowledges that "Robinson was a man of excellent parts, and the most learned, polished and modest spirit that ever separated from the Church of England; that the Apologies and Justifications he wrote were very handsome ; that by Dr. Ames and Mr. Parker he was brought to a greater moderation than he at first expressed; that he ruined the rigid separation, was a principal overthrower of the Brownists, and became the author of *Independency*." As to this last point, however, see Cotton's reply, in note [1] on page 442. The name, however, as Mosheim suggests, may have been derived from an expression of Robinson's in his Apology : " Cœtum quemlibet particularem esse totam, integram et perfectam ecclesiam, ex suis partibus constantem, immediatè et *independenter* quoad alias ecclesias, sub ipso Christo."

As has already been seen, pp. 77 and 384, and will more fully appear hereafter from his Letters, it was Robinson's intention and most earnest desire to come over and settle with his flock at Plymouth ; but he was prevented by the want of means, the opposition of some of the merchant adventurers, and finally by death, which removed him from the world March 1, 1625. The honors paid to his memory at his funeral are recorded in note [1] on page 393. Hoornbeek says, in the work quoted on page 42, " Post obitum ejus, obortâ in cœtu contentione et schismate super communione cum Ecclesiâ Anglicanâ in auditione verbi, D. Robinsoni vidua, liberi, reliquique propinqui et amici in communionem ecclesiæ nostræ recepti fuerunt." Prince says, in his Annals, p. 238, " His son Isaac

CHAP. was dismissed to them there, and there remained until
XXVI. he died.¹ Thus have we briefly satisfied your desire.

YOUNG MEN.

We are very thankful to you for your pains. We perceive God raiseth up excellent instruments in all ages to carry on his own work; and the best of men have their failings sometimes, as we see in these our

came over to Plymouth Colony, lived to above ninety of years, a venerable man, whom I have often seen, and has left male posterity in the county of Barnstable." He lived at Scituate in 1636, and in 1639 removed to Barnstable; he was a highly respectable man, and an Assistant in the government. He married a sister of Elder Faunce, and a son of his, Isaac, was drowned at Barnstable in 1668. See Belknap's Am. Biog. ii. 151—178; Neals Puritans, i. 437; Baylie's Dissuasive, p. 17; Cotton's Way, p. 7; Hoornbeek, Sum. Cont. p. 741; Hornius, Hist. Eccles. p. 232; Mosheim, Eccles. Hist. v. 405; Deane's Scituate, p. 332; Holmes's Annals, i. 191, 575; Prince, 173; Mass. Hist. Coll. xxviii. 248, 249.

In note ³ on page 40 there is a list of the books published by Robinson before the departure of the Pilgrims for America. He afterwards wrote the following works, all of which, with the others, I have had the privilege and pleasure of consulting. 1. "A Defence of the Doctrine propounded by the Synod at Dort, against John Murton and his Associates, with the Refutation of their Answer to a writing touching baptism. By John Robinson. Printed in the year 1624." 4to, pp. 203. 2. "A Treatise of the lawfulness of hearing of the ministers in the Church of England; penned by that learned and reverend divine, John Robinson, late pastor to the English church of God at Leyden. Printed according to the copy that was found in his study after his decease; and now published for the common good. Together with a letter written by the same author, [Leyden, 5 April, 1624] and approved by his Church, which followeth after this Treatise. Anno 1634." pp. 77, 16mo. 3. "Essays, or Observations, divine and moral, collected out of Holy Scriptures, ancient and modern writers, both divine and human, as also out of the great volume of men's manners; tending to the furtherance of knowledge and virtue. By John Robinson. The Second Edition. London. Printed for I. Bellamie. 1638." pp. 556, 4to. In his Preface he speaks of having "diligently observed the great volume of men's manners; having had, in the days of my pilgrimage, special opportunity of conversing with persons of divers nations, estates, and dispositions, in great variety. This kind of study and meditation hath been unto me full sweet and delightful, and that wherein I have often refreshed my soul and spirit, amidst many sad and sorrowful thoughts, unto which God hath called me."

¹ Of course Belknap is in an error, when he says, in his Life of Robinson, Am. Biog. ii. 157, "As nothing more is said of the aged Mr. Clifton, it is probable that he died before this embarkation," i. e. from England to Holland. Baylies, in his Memoir of New Plymouth, i. 11, repeats the error. Yet Prince would have set them right, p. 120.

times, and that there is no new thing under the sun. But before we end this matter, we desire you would say something of those two churches that were so long in exile, of whose guides we have already heard.

ANCIENT MEN.

Truly there were in them many worthy men; and if you had seen them in their beauty and order, as we have done, you would have been much affected therewith, we dare say. At Amsterdam, before their division and breach, they were about three hundred communicants, and they had for their pastor and teacher those two eminent men before named, and in our time four grave men for ruling elders,[1] and three able and godly men for deacons, one ancient widow for a deaconess, who did them service many years, though she was sixty years of age when she was chosen. She honored her place and was an ornament to the congre-

---

[1] The difference between the pastor, or teaching elder, and the ruling elder, as it existed in the churches of the Pilgrims, is thus described by Prince, from their published writings. "1. Pastors, or teaching elders — who have the power of overseeing, teaching, administering the sacraments, and ruling too; and being chiefly to give themselves to studying, teaching, and the spiritual care of the flock, are therefore to be maintained. 2. Mere ruling elders — who are to help the pastors in overseeing and ruling; that their offices be not temporary, as among the Dutch and French churches, but continual; and being also qualified in some degree to teach, they are to teach occasionally, through necessity, or in their pastor's absence or illness; but being not to give themselves to study or teaching, they have no need of maintenance." It appears, from page 65, that they "chose none for governing elders but such as were able to teach." The office of ruling elder also existed in the churches of Massachusetts Bay, at their first planting. Mr. Savage, says, "It was kept up hardly more than fifty years, though in a few churches it continued to the middle of the last century, much reduced, however, in importance, and hardly distinguishable from that of deacon. The title of elders was retained from the beginning as a name for ministers." The office of ruling elder is still kept up in the First Church in Salem, the oldest church in Massachusetts proper, the next after Plymouth. For further particulars concerning the functions and duties of the ruling elder, see Robinson's Apology, ch. iv.; the Cambridge Platform, ch. vii.; Hutchinson's Mass, i. 426; Prince's Annals, p. 177; Savage's Winthrop, i. 31.

gation. She usually sat in a convenient place in the congregation, with a little birchen rod in her hand, and kept little children in great awe from disturbing the congregation. She did frequently visit the sick and weak, especially women, and, as there was need, called out maids and young women to watch and do them other helps as their necessity did require; and if they were poor, she would gather relief for them of those that were able, or acquaint the deacons; and she was obeyed as a mother in Israel and an officer of Christ.

And for the church of Leyden, they were sometimes not much fewer in number, nor at all inferior in able men, though they had not so many officers as the other; for they had but one ruling elder with their pastor, a man well approved and of great integrity; also they had three able men for deacons. And that which was a crown unto them, they lived together in love and peace all their days,[1] without any considerable differences or any disturbance that grew thereby, but such as was easily healed in love; and so they continued until with mutual consent they removed into New England. And what their condition hath been since, some of you that are of their children do see and can tell. Many worthy and able men there were in both places, who lived and died in obscurity in respect of the world, as private Christians, yet were they precious in the eyes of the Lord, and also in the eyes of such as knew them, whose virtues we with such of you as are their children do follow and imitate.

YOUNG MEN.

If we may not be tedious, we would request to know

[1] See pages 34, 36, and 380.

one thing more. It is commonly said that those of the Separation hold none to be true churches but their own, and condemn all the churches in the world besides; which lieth as a foul blot upon them, yea even on some here in New England, except they can remove it.

ANCIENT MEN.

It is a manifest slander laid upon them; for they hold all the Reformed Churches to be true churches, and even the most rigid of them have ever done so, as appears by their Apologies[1] and other writings; and we ourselves some of us know of much intercommunion that divers have held with them reciprocally, not only with the Dutch and French, but even with the Scotch,[2] who are not of the best mould, yea and with the Lutherans also; and we believe they have gone as far herein, both in judgment and practice, as any of the churches in New England do or can do, to deal faithfully and bear witness against their corruptions.

Having thus far satisfied all your demands, we shall here break off this conference for this time, desiring the Lord to make you to grow up in grace and wisdom and the true fear of God, that in all faithfulness and humility you may serve him in your generations.

YOUNG MEN.

Gentlemen, we humbly thank you for your pains with us and respect unto us, and do further crave that upon any fit occasions we may have access unto you for any further information, and herewith do humbly take our leave.[3]

---

[1] See Robinson's Apology, quoted in note [3] on page 388.

[2] See pages 391 — 396.

[3] Bradford continued this Dia-

CHAP. XXVI.

logue in two other parts; one of which I have had in my possession, written with his own hand. The title is as follows: "A Dialogue, or 3d Conference, betweene some yonge men borne in New-England, and some ancient men which came out of Holand and Old England, concerning the Church and the governmente therof." It is longer than the first part which is here printed, and relates chiefly to the "controversyes amongst four sorts of men; The Papists, the Episcopacy, the Presbyterians, and the Independents, as they are called." Being a theological rather than a historical work, I have not deemed it suitable to be inserted in this volume.

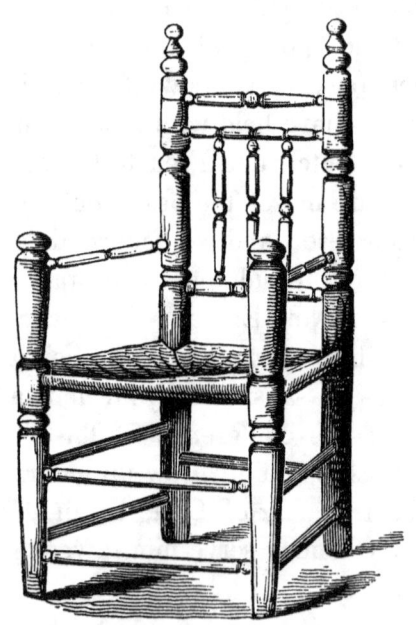

GOVERNOR CARVER'S CHAIR.

GOV. BRADFORD'S MEMOIR

OF

ELDER BREWSTER.

CHAPTER XXVII.

MEMOIR OF ELDER WILLIAM BREWSTER.[1]

Now followeth that which was matter of great sadness and mourning unto this Church. About the 16th of April,[2] in this year, died their reverend Elder,[3] our dear and loving friend, Mr. WILLIAM[4] BREWSTER;. a man that had done and suffered much for the Lord Jesus and the Gospel's sake, and had borne his part in weal and wo with this poor persecuted Church about thirty-six years in England, Holland, and in this wilderness, and done the Lord and them faithful service in his place and calling; and notwithstanding the many troubles and sorrows he passed through, the Lord upheld him to a great age. He was near four-

CHAP. XXVII.

1644. April. 16.

---

[1] From the MS. Records of Plymouth Church, book i. folio 38, into which it was copied by Secretary Morton, from Governor Bradford's MS. History of Plymouth Colony.

[2] Morton, in his Memorial, p. 219, places Brewster's death on the 18th of April, 1643. "Concerning whom," he adds, "I could say much of mine own knowledge; but I shall content myself only to insert the honorable testimony that Mr. William Bradford, deceased, hath left written with his own hand concerning him." He then proceeds to copy a considerable part of the above account. Hutchinson, in his Hist. Mass. ii. 460, inserts about a page of it from Bradford's MS. History. There can be no doubt that the whole Memoir proceeded from the pen of Bradford, and that Morton, in this as in other cases, was a mere copyist.

[3] Burk, in his Hist. of Virginia, i. 214, makes Brewster the military as well as the spiritual leader of the Pilgrims, confounding him with Standish.

[4] Neal, in his Hist. of New England, i. 85, errs in calling him *John;* an error which is repeated by the authors of the Mod. Univ. Hist. xxxix. 271.

score years of age (if not all out) when he died. He had this blessing added by the Lord to all the rest, to die in his bed, in peace, amongst the midst of his friends, who mourned and wept over him, and ministered what help and comfort they could unto him, and he again recomforted them whilst he could. His sickness was not long. Until the last day thereof he did not wholly keep his bed. His speech continued until somewhat more than half a day before his death, and then failed him; and about nine or ten of the clock that evening he died, without any pang at all. A few hours before he drew his breath short, and some few minutes before his last he drew his breath long, as a man fallen into a sound sleep, without any pangs or gaspings, and so sweetly departed this life unto a better.

I would now demand of any what he was the worse for any former sufferings. What do I say? The worse? Nay, surely he was the better, and they now add to his honor. "It is a manifest token," saith the Apostle, "of the righteous judgment of God, that ye may be counted worthy of the kingdom of God, for which ye also suffer; seeing it is a righteous thing with God to recompense tribulation to them that trouble you; and to you who are troubled, rest with us when the Lord Jesus shall be revealed from heaven with his mighty angels;" and "If ye be reproached for the name of Christ, happy are ye; for the spirit of God and of glory resteth upon you." What though he wanted the riches and pleasures of the world in his life, and pompous monuments at his funeral, yet the memorial of the just shall be blessed when the name of the wicked shall rot.

I should say something of his life, if to say a little were not worse than to be silent. But I cannot wholly forbear, though haply more may be done hereafter.

After he had attained some learning, viz. the knowledge of the Latin tongue and some insight into the Greek, and spent some small time at Cambridge, and then being first seasoned with the seeds of grace and virtue, he went to the Court, and served that religious and godly gentleman, Mr. Davison,[1] divers years, when he was Secretary of State; who found him so discreet and faithful, as he trusted him above all other that were about him, and only employed him in matters of greatest trust and secrecy.[2] He esteemed him rather as a son than a servant, and for his wisdom and godliness, in private, he would converse with him more like a familiar than a master. He attended his master when he was sent in ambassage by the Queen into the Low Countries, (in the Earl of Leicester's time,) as for other weighty affairs of State, so to receive possession of the cautionary towns;[3] and in token and sign

1585.

---

[1] The unfortunate William Davison, who fell a victim to Queen Elizabeth's duplicity and statecraft, was a person of great worth and ability. The Earl of Essex, in a letter to King James, April 18, 1587, interceding in his behalf, speaks of him as "beloved of the best and most religious of this land. His sufficiency in council and matters of state is such, as the Queen herself confesseth in her kingdom she hath not such another; his virtue, religion, and worth in all degrees are of the world taken to be so great, as no man in his good fortune hath had more general love than this gentleman in his disgrace;" and Lord Burleigh, in a petition to Queen Elizabeth, February 13, 1586, writes, "I know not a man in the land so furnished universally for the place he had, neither know I any that can come near him." See Supplement to the Cabala, p. 23; Strype's Annals, iii. 373.

[2] Brewster had for a colleague in office under Davison, George Cranmer, the pupil and friend of the judicious Hooker. See Walton's Lives, p. 179, (Major's ed.) Judge Davis justly remarks that "there seems to have been a similarity of character between Mr. Brewster and his patron." Morton's Memorial, p. 221.

[3] In 1584, when Elizabeth entered into a league with the United Provinces, and advanced money to enable them to maintain their independence of Spain, her rival in

thereof the keys of Flushing being delivered to him in her Majesty's name, he kept them some time, and committed them to his servant, who kept them under his pillow on which he slept, the first night. And, at his return, the States honored him with a gold chain, and his master committed it to him, and commanded him to wear it when they arrived in England, as they rode through the country, until they came to the Court. He afterwards remained with him until his troubles, when he was put from his place about the death of the Queen of Scots, and some good time after, doing him many offices of service in the time of his troubles.[1] Afterwards he went and lived in the country, in good

---

power and ambition, she very prudently got consigned into her hands the three important fortresses of Flushing, the Brille, and Rammekins, as pledges for the reimbursement of the money which she advanced in defence of their liberties. They were accordingly called "the cautionary towns." They were surrendered by James in 1616. See Sir Dudley Carleton's Letters, pp. 27—35.

[1] "When Mary, Queen of Scots, had been tried and condemned, and the Parliament of England had petitioned their sovereign for her execution, Elizabeth privately ordered Davison to draw a death-warrant, which she signed, and sent him with it to the Chancellor to have the great seal annexed. Having performed his duty, she pretended to blame him for his precipitancy. Davison acquainted the Council with the whole transaction; they knew the Queen's real sentiments, and persuaded him to send the warrant to the Earls of Kent and Shrewsbury, promising to justify his conduct, and take the blame on themselves. These Earls attended the execution of Mary; but when Elizabeth heard of it, she affected great indignation, threw all the blame on the innocent Secretary, and committed him to the Tower, where he became the subject of raillery from those very counsellors who had promised to countenance and protect him. He was tried in the Star Chamber, and fined £10,000, which being rigorously levied upon him, reduced him to poverty." Belknap's Am. Biog. ii. 253. Camden says, "Thus was Davison, a man of good ingenuity, but not well skilled in court arts, brought upon the court stage of purpose (as most men thought) to act for a time this part in the tragedy; and soon after, the part being acted, and his stage attire laid aside, as if he had failed in the last act, he was thrust down from the stage, and, not without the pity of many, shut up in prison." For a particular account of Davison, and a full vindication of his conduct, see Kippis's Biog. Brit. v. 4—15; and Nicolas's Life of Davison, London, 1823. See also Camden's History of Queen Elizabeth, pp. 389—393; Supplement to the Cabala, pp. 22—25; Strype's Annals, iii. 370—376, 447.

BREWSTER JOINS THE PILGRIMS.

esteem amongst his friends and the good gentlemen of those parts, especially the godly and religious.

CHAP. XXVII.

He did much good in the country where he lived, in promoting and furthering religion; and not only by his practice and example, and provoking and encouraging of others, but by procuring of good preachers to all places thereabouts, and drawing on of others to assist and help to forward in such a work; he himself most commonly deepest in the charge, and sometimes above his ability. And in this state he continued many years, doing the best good he could, and walking according to the light he saw, until the Lord revealed further unto him. And in the end, by the tyranny of the bishops against godly preachers and people, in silencing the one and persecuting the other, he and many more of those times began to look further into particulars, and to see into the unlawfulness of their callings, and the burden of many anti-christian corruptions, which both he and they endeavoured to cast off, as they also did, as in the beginning of this treatise is to be seen.[1]

After they were joined together into communion, he was a special stay and help to them. They ordinarily met at his house on the Lord's day, which was a manor of the bishop's, and with great love he entertained them when they came, making provision for them to his great charge; and continued so to do whilst they could stay in England. And when they were to remove out of the country, he was one of the first in all adventures, and forwardest in any. He was the chief of those that were taken at Boston, in Lincolnshire, and suffered the greatest loss; and

1602.

1607.

---

[1] See page 20.

CHAP. XXVII.
1608.

[one] of the seven that were kept longest in prison, and after bound over to the assizes.[1]

After he came into Holland, he suffered much hardship after he had spent the most of his means, having a great charge and many children; and, in regard of his former breeding and course of life,[2] not so fit for many employments as others were, especially such as were toilsome and laborious. Yet he ever bore his condition with much cheerfulness and contentation. Towards the latter part of those twelve years spent in Holland, his outward condition was mended, and he lived well and plentifully; for he fell into a way, by reason he had the Latin tongue, to teach many students who had a desire to learn the English tongue, to teach them English, and by his method they quickly attained it with great facility; for he drew rules to learn it by, after the Latin manner; and many gentlemen, both Danes and Germans, resorted to him, as they had time from other studies, some of them being great men's sons. He also had means to set up printing,[3] by the help of some friends, and so had employment enough; and by reason of many books which would not be allowed to be printed in England,[4] they might have had more than they could do.

[1] See pages 26 and 27.

[2] The words "of life" I restore from Bradford, in Hutchinson, ii. 460.

[3] Among the books printed by Brewster at Leyden was the following: "Commentarii Succincti et Dilucidi in Proverbia Salomonis. Authore Thomâ Cartwrightio, SS. Theologiæ in Academiâ Cantabrigiensi quondam Professore. Quibus adhibita est Præfatio clarissimi viri Johannis Polyandri, S. Theologiæ Professoris Leidensis. Lugduni Batavorum. Apud Gulielmum Brewsterum, in vico Chorali. 1617." 8vo. pp. 1513. A copy of this work is now in the possession of the Pastor of the First Church in Plymouth, having been presented to that Church in 1828 by the Hon. John Davis, LL.D. the learned editor of Morton's New England's Memorial. Another copy is in the library of the Pilgrim Society at Plymouth. See Thacher's Plymouth, p. 270.

[4] It appears from the following extracts of letters written by Sir Dudley Carleton to Secretary Naun-

But now removing into this country, all these things were laid aside again, and a new course of living must be submitted to ; in which he was no way unwilling to take his part and to bear his burden with the rest, living many times without bread or corn many months together, having many times nothing but fish, and often wanting that also ; and drank nothing but water for many years together, yea, until within five or six years of his death. And yet he lived, by the blessing of God, in health until very old age ; and besides that, he would labor with his hands in the fields as long as he was able. Yet when the Church had no other minister, he taught twice every sabbath, and that both powerfully and profitably, to the great contentment of the hearers, and their comfortable edification. Yea, many were brought to God by his ministry. He did more in their behalf in a year, than many that have their hundreds a year do in all their lives.

ton, from the Hague in 1619, that Brewster was at this time an object of suspicion and pursuit to the English government on account of certain obnoxious books which he had printed.

" July 22. One William Brewster, a Brownist, hath been for some years an inhabitant and printer at Leyden, but is now within three weeks removed from thence and gone back to dwell in London, where he may be found out and examined, not only of this book *De Regimine Ecclesiæ Scoticanæ*, but likewise of *Perth Assembly*, of which if he was not the printer himself, he assuredly knows both the printer and author; for as I am informed, he hath had, whilst he remained here, his hand in all such books as have been sent over into England and Scotland; as particularly a book in folio, entitled *A Confutation of the Rhemists' Translation, Glosses and Annotations of the New Testament*, anno 1618, was printed by him. So was another in 18mo. *De verâ et genuinâ Jesu Christi Domini et Salvatoris nostri Religione*, of which I send your honor herewith the title page ; and if you will compare that, which is underlined therein, with the other, *De Regimine Ecclesiæ Scoticanæ*, of which I send your honor the title-page likewise, you will find it is the same character; and the one being confessed (as that *De verâ et genuinâ Jesu Christi, &c. Religione*, Brewster doth openly avow,) the other cannot well be denied." — " Aug. 20. I have made good inquiry after William Brewster, at Leyden, and am well assured that he is not returned thither ; neither is it likely he will, having removed from thence both his family and goods." — " Sept. 12. In my last I advertised your honor that

CHAP. XXVII.

For his personal abilities, he was qualified above many. He was wise and discreet and well spoken, having a grave, deliberate utterance; of a very cheerful spirit, very sociable and pleasant amongst his friends, of an humble and modest mind, of a peaceable disposition, undervaluing himself and his own abilities, and sometimes overvaluing others; inoffensive and innocent in his life and conversation, which gained him the love of those without as well as those within. Yet he would tell them plainly of their faults and evils, both publicly and privately; but in such a manner as usually was well taken from him. He was tender-hearted, and compassionate of such as were in misery, but especially of such as had been of good estate and rank, and were fallen into want and poverty, either for goodness and religion's sake, or by the injury and oppression of others. He would say, of all men these deserved to be most pitied; and none did more offend

---

Brewster was taken at Leyden; which proved an error, in that the schout, who was employed by the magistrates for his apprehension, being a dull drunken fellow, took one man for another. But Brewer, who set him on work, and being a man of means bare the charge of his printing, is fast in the University's prison; and his printing letters, which were found in his house in a garret, where he had hid them, and his books and papers, are all seized and sealed up. I expect to-morrow to receive his voluntary confession of such books as he hath caused to be printed by Brewster for this year and a half or two years past; and then I intend to send one expressly to visit his books and papers, and to examine him particularly touching *Perth Assembly*, the discourse *De Regimine Ecclesiæ Scoticanæ*, and other Puritan pamphlets, which I have newly recovered." — " Sept. 18. It appears that this Brewer, and Brewster, whom this man set on work, having kept no open shop, nor printed many books fit for public sale in these provinces, their practice was to print prohibited books to be vented underhand in his Majesty's kingdom." — " Jan. 19, 1620. Unless Brewer undertakes to do his uttermost in finding out Brewster, (wherein I will not fail likewise of all other endeavours,) he is not like to be at liberty; the suspicion whereof keeps him from hence, for as yet he appears not in these parts." Carleton's Letters, pp. 380, 386, 389, 390, 437. It appears from page 71, that in May, 1619, Brewster was in England. It is probable he did not return to Leyden, but kept close till the Mayflower sailed.

and displease him, than such as would haughtily and proudly carry and lift up themselves, being risen from nothing, and having little else in them but a few fine clothes or a little riches more than others.

In teaching, he was very stirring, and moving the affections; also very plain and distinct in what he taught; by which means he became the more profitable to the hearers. He had a singular good gift in prayer, both public and private, in ripping up the heart and conscience before God, in the humble confession of sin, and begging the mercies of God in Christ for the pardon thereof. He always thought it were better for ministers to pray oftener, and divide their prayers, than to be long and tedious in the same; except upon solemn and special occasions, as on days of Humiliation and the like. His reason was that the heart and spirits of all, especially the weak, could hardly continue and stand bent (as it were,) so long towards God, as they ought to do in that duty, without flagging and falling off.

For the government of the church, which was most proper to his office, he was careful to preserve good order in the same, and to preserve purity both in the doctrine and communion of the same, and to suppress any error or contention that might begin to arise amongst them; and accordingly God gave good success to his endeavours herein all his days, and he saw the fruit of his labors in that behalf. But I must break off, having thus touched a few heads of things.[1]

---

[1] WILLIAM BREWSTER, the ruling elder of John Robinson's church, and whose name stands fourth among the signers of the Compact, was born in 1564; but the place of his birth is not known. He was probably the oldest of the Pilgrims, being 60 when he arrived at Plymouth. On account of his age and office he probably was not much employed in the civil affairs of the Colony, and consequently his name

CHAP. XXVII. seldom occurs in the preceding History. The reason why he was not chosen governor after the death of Carver in 1621, is stated in note [1] on page 197. It appears from this Memoir that he had "*many* children;" but the exact number has not been ascertained. He brought his wife with him, and four other individuals, who were probably his children. The following are known to have been his children — Jonathan, Love, Wrestling, Patience, and Fear. The last two came in the Anne in 1623; Patience married in 1624 Thomas Prince, who was afterwards governor, and Fear married Isaac Allerton in 1626. It appears from page 173 that the venerable elder had a house lot assigned him in 1621, in Plymouth, on the street now called Leyden-street. In the latter part of his life he built a house in Duxbury, near Captain's Hill, and resided there a short time. His sons Jonathan and Love settled in Duxbury. Love died there, and his son William was deacon of the church in that place. Jonathan, with his family, removed to Connecticut after 1648. There are many descendants of the worthy elder in Plymouth, Duxbury, Kingston, Pembroke, and in Connecticut, and elsewhere. A town on Cape Cod was named after him in 1803, and it is believed that the Brewsters, in Boston harbour, were so called in compliment to him. See note [2] on page 27; Belknap's Am. Biog. ii. 252 — 266; Hutchinson's Mass. ii. 460; Mitchell's Bridgewater, p. 361; Mass. Hist. Coll. x. 73, xx. 57 — 68.

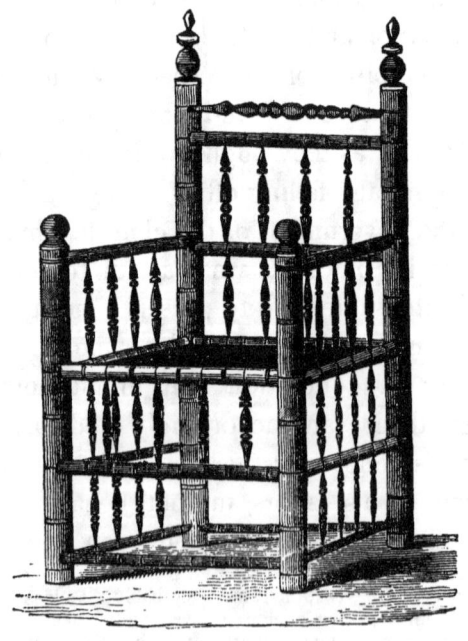

ELDER BREWSTER'S CHAIR.

LETTERS.

"That is the best History, which is collected out of Letters."
                                                        BARONIUS.

"Letters of affairs, from such as manage them, or are privy to them, are of all others the best instructions for history, and to a diligent reader the best histories in themselves."
                                                        LORD BACON.

CHAPTER XXVIII.

ROBINSON TO THE CHURCH.

To the Church of God at Plymouth, in New England.[1]

MUCH BELOVED BRETHREN,

NEITHER the distance of place, nor distinction of body, can at all either dissolve or weaken that bond of true Christian affection in which the Lord by his spirit hath tied us together. My continual prayers are to the Lord for you; my most earnest desire is unto you;[2] from whom I will not longer keep (if God will) than means can be procured to bring with me the wives and children of divers of you and the rest of your brethren, whom I could not leave behind me without great injury both to you and them, and offence to God and all men. The death of so many our dear friends and brethren,[3] oh! how grievous hath it been to you to bear, and to us to take knowledge of; which, if it

---

[1] This and most of the following letters are taken from a fragment of Gov. Bradford's Letter Book, which was rescued about fifty years since from a grocer's shop in Halifax, Nova Scotia. The earlier and more valuable part was unfortunately destroyed, having been put to the most ignoble uses. See Belknap's Am. Biog. ii. 246, and Mass. Hist. Coll. iii. 45.

[2] See note on page 453.

[3] See note [1] on page 198.

CHAP. XXVIII. 1621.

could be mended with lamenting, could not sufficiently be bewailed; but we must go unto them, and they shall not return unto us. And how many even of us God hath taken away here and in England, since your departure, you may elsewhere take knowledge. But the same God has tempered judgment with mercy, as otherwise, so in sparing the rest, especially those by whose godly and wise government you may be and (I know) are so much helped.[1] In a battle it is not looked for but that divers should die ; it is thought well for a side if it get the victory, though with the loss of divers, if not too many or too great. God, I hope, hath given you the victory, after many difficulties, for yourselves and others; though I doubt not but many do and will remain for you and us all to strive with.

Brethren, I hope I need not exhort you to obedience unto those whom God hath set over you in church and commonwealth, and to the Lord in them. It is a Christian's honor to give honor according to men's places ; and his liberty to serve God in faith, and his brethren in love, orderly and with a willing and free heart. God forbid I should need to exhort you to peace, which is the bond of perfection, and by which all good is tied together, and without which it is scattered. Have peace with God first, by faith in his promises, good conscience kept in all things, and oft renewed by repentance ; and so one with another, for his sake who is, though three, one ; and for Christ's sake, who is one, and as you are called by one spirit to one hope.

---

[1] It was certainly a remarkable providence, that out of the 21 men who died the first winter, so few were among the leaders of the expedition. With the exception of Carver, most of the prominent men were spared. How different might have been the fate of the Colony had Bradford, Winslow, Standish and Allerton been cut off.

And the God of peace and grace and all goodness be with you in all the fruits thereof plenteously upon your heads, now and forever.

All your brethren here remember you with great love, a general token whereof they have sent you.

Yours ever in the Lord,
JOHN ROBINSON.

Leyden, (Holland,) June 30, anno 1621.

ROBINSON TO ELDER BREWSTER.

LOVING AND DEAR FRIEND AND BROTHER,[1]

That which I most desired of God in regard of you, namely, the continuance of your life and health, and the safe coming of those sent unto you, that I most gladly hear of, and praise God for the same. And I hope mistress Brewster's weak and decayed state of body will have some repairing by the coming of her daughters,[2] and the provisions in this and other ships sent, which I hear is made for you; which makes us with the more patience bear our languishing state and the deferring of our desired transportation, (which I call desired rather than hoped for,) whatsoever you are borne in hand with by others. For first, there is no hope at all, that I know nor can conceive of, of any new stock to be raised for that end, so that all must depend upon returns from you; in which are so many uncertainties, as that nothing with any certainty can thence be concluded. Besides, howsoever, for the

---

[1] This letter is copied from the records of Plymouth Church, book i. folio 27.

[2] Patience and Fear Brewster, the daughters of the Elder, arrived in the Anne, in 1623. See note on page 352.

present, the adventurers allege nothing but want of money, which is an invincible difficulty; yet if that be taken away by you, others without doubt will be found. For the better clearing of this, we must dispose the adventurers into three parts; and of them some five or six (as I conceive) are absolutely bent for us above others. Other five or six are our bitter professed adversaries. The rest, being the body, I conceive to be honestly minded, and lovingly also towards us; yet such as have others, namely, the forward preachers,[1] nearer unto them than us, and whose course, so far as there is any difference, they would advance rather than ours. Now what a hank[2] these men have over the professors you know; and I persuade myself that for me they of all others are unwilling I should be transported; especially such as have an eye that way themselves, as thinking if I come there, their market will be marred in many regards. And for these adversaries, if they have but half their will to their malice, they will stop my course when they see it intended, for which this delaying serveth them very opportunely;[3] and as one rusty[4] jade can

---

[1] John Lyford, who came over in the spring of 1624, was probably one of those "forward preachers," and John Pemberton, his correspondent, was another. Robert Cushman, in a letter dated Jan. 24, 1624, says "We send a preacher, though not the most eminent, for whose going Mr. Winslow and I gave way to give content to some at London." Bradford speaks of "the minister, Mr. John Lyford, whom a faction of the adventurers send, to hinder Mr. Robinson." See Morton's Memorial, pp. 111, 114, and Prince's Annals, pp. 226, 228.

[2] Hank, influence.

[3] Lyford wrote home to the adverse part of the adventurers, in 1624, counselling them that "the Leyden Company, Mr. Robinson and the rest, must still be kept back, or else all will be spoiled; and lest any of them should be taken in privately on the coast of England, (as it was feared might be done,) they must change the master of the ship, Mr. William Peirce, and put another also in Mr. Winslow's room for merchant, or otherwise it would not be prevented." MS. Records of Plymouth Church, b. i. folio 30.

[4] Rusty, dull, lazy.

hinder by hanging back more than two or three can or will (at least if they be not very free) draw forward, so will it be in this case. A notable experiment of 1623. this they gave in your messenger's presence,¹ constraining the company to promise that none of the money now gathered should be expended or employed to the help of any of us towards you.

Now touching the question propounded by you, I judge it not lawful for you, being a ruling elder, as Rom. xii. 7, 8, and 1 Tim. v. 17, opposed to the elders that teach and exhort and labor in the word and doctrine, to which the sacraments are annexed, to administer them, nor convenient if it were lawful.²

Be you heartily saluted, and you wife with you, both from me and mine. Your God and ours, and the God of all his, bring us together, if it be his will, and keep us in the mean while and always to his glory, and make us serviceable to his majesty, and faithful to the end. Amen.

   Your very loving brother,
       JOHN ROBINSON.³

Leyden, December 20, 1623.

---

¹ This messenger was Edward Winslow, who sailed from Plymouth in the Anne, Sept. 10, 1623, and returned in the Charity in March, 1624. He was the bearer of this letter. See Morton's Memorial, p. 111 ; Prince's Annals, pp. 225, 226. Prince quotes from another letter of Robinson's to Gov. Bradford, brought by the same ship.

² For the difference between a teaching and a ruling elder, see note ¹ on page 455.

³ " By the above written letter it may appear how much the adversary hindered the coming of this blessed servant of Christ into New England, although he so much longed to be with his flock, and his flock with him ; a worthy pattern unto all churches and their ministers to be imitated." — *Bradford's or Morton's Note.*

Morton, in his Memorial, p. 126, says, that " his and their adversaries had been long and continually plotting how they might hinder his coming into New England ; " and Hutchinson, ii. 454, says, that " he was prevented by disappointments from those in England who undertook to provide for the passage of him and his congregation." It appears that " Sir Ferdinando Gorges and others were at this time

CHAP. XXVIII.

1625.

ROGER WHITE TO GOVERNOR BRADFORD.

To his loving friend, Mr. William Bradford, Governor of Plymouth in New England, these be, &c.[1]

LOVING AND KIND FRIENDS, &c.

I know not whether ever this will come to your hands, or miscarry, as other of my letters have done; yet in regard of the Lord's dealing with us here, I have had a great desire to write unto you, knowing your desire to bear a part with us, both in our joys and sorrows, as we do with you.

These therefore are to give you to understand, that it hath pleased the Lord to take out of this vale of tears your and our loving and faithful pastor, and my dear and reverend brother, Mr. John Robinson, who was sick some eight days, beginning first to be sick on a Saturday morning; yet the next day, being the Lord's day, he taught us twice, and the week after grew every day weaker than other, yet felt no pain but weakness, all the time of his sickness. The physic he took wrought kindly, in man's judgment, yet he grew every day weaker than other, feeling little or no

determined that New England should be settled under episcopacy; and though they would allow and encourage people to settle here, they were unwilling that any Puritan ministers should accompany them. The bishops had prevented the crown from granting liberty to the petitioners from Leyden; and it was accounted a great matter, in 1621, to obtain a cautious allowance of indulgence under the authority of the President and Council for the Affairs of New England. But they took great care to obstruct the coming over of so important a man as Mr. Robinson." Sherley, one of the merchant adventurers, incurred the ill-will of his associates, by being in favor of his removal. " The sole cause, he observed, in a letter to the Plymouth people, why the greater part of the adventurers malign me, was that I would not side with them against you and the coming over of the Leyden people." See Holmes's Annals, i. 192, 575.

[1] From the records of Plymouth Church, book i. folio 31, and Gov. Bradford's Letter Book, in Mass. Hist. Coll. iii. 39.

pain, yet sensible, till the very last. He fell sick the 22d of February, and departed this life on the 1st of March. He had a continual inward ague, but, I thank the Lord, was free of the plague, so that all his friends could come freely to him; and if either prayers, tears, or means would have saved his life, he had not gone hence. But he having faithfully finished his course, and performed his work, which the Lord had appointed him here to perform, he now rests with the Lord, in eternal happiness; we wanting him and all church governors, not having one at present that is a governing officer amongst us. Now for ourselves here left, (I mean the whole church,) we still, by the mercy of God, continue and hold close together in peace and quietness, and so I hope we shall do, though we be very weak; wishing (if such were the will of God) that you and we were again together in one, either there or here; but seeing it is the will of the Lord, thus to dispose of things, we must labor with patience to rest contented, till it please the Lord otherwise to dispose of things.[1]

For news, at present here is not much worth the writing; only as in England we have lost our old king, James, who departed this life about a month ago,[2] so here we have lost Grave Maurice,[3] the old prince here,

---

[1] "Until Robinson's death, the congregation at Plymouth had not abandoned the hope of his coming to America with their brethren who remained in Holland. The only solution of the singular fact, that the Plymouth people remained for so many years without a minister, is — that until his death, their affectionate and beloved pastor cherished the desire, and they the expectation, of his coming to America. His death caused the dissolution of his congregation at Leyden, some of whom removed to Amsterdam, and others to New England." Holmes, Ann. i. 191, 575. Dr. Holmes errs in placing Robinson's death in 1626.

[2] King James died March 27, 1625, in his 59th year.

[3] Maurice, the prince of Orange, or landgrave of Holland, died at the Hague April 23, 1625, in his 59th year. He was succeeded by his brother Frederick Henry. See Grattan's Hist. of the Netherlands, p. 250.

who both departed this life since my brother Robinson; and as in England we have a new king, Charles, of whom there is great hope of good, so here likewise we have made Prince Hendrick general, in his brother's place, who is now with the Grave of Mansfield with a great army, close by the enemy, to free Breda, if it be possible, which the enemy hath besieged now some nine or ten months; but how it will fall out at last, is yet uncertain; the Lord give good success, if it be his will. The king is making ready about one hundred sail of ships; the end is not yet certain, but they will be ready to go to sea very shortly; the king himself goes to see them once in fourteen days. And thus fearing lest this will not come to your hands, hoping as soon as I hear of a convenient messenger, to write more at large, and to send you a letter which my brother Robinson sent to London, to have gone to some of you, but coming too late was brought back again; and so for this time I cease further to trouble you, and rest,

Your assured loving friend,
ROGER WHITE.

Leyden, April 28, *anno* 1625.

THOMAS BLOSSOM TO GOVERNOR BRADFORD.

BELOVED SIR,

Kind salutations, &c. I have thought good to write to you, concerning the cause as it standeth both with you and us. We see, alas! what frustrations and disappointments it pleaseth the Lord to send in this our course, good in itself, and according to godliness taken in hand, and for good and lawful ends, who yet pleaseth not to prosper as we are, for reasons best known to himself; and which also nearly concerns us to consider of, whether we have sought the Lord in it as we see, or not. That the Lord hath singularly preserved life in the business to great admiration, giveth me good hope that he will, (if our sins hinder not,) in his appointed time, give a happy end unto it. On the contrary, when I consider how it pleaseth the Lord to cross those means that should bring us together, being now as far off or farther than ever, in our apprehension; as also to take that means away, which would have been so comfortable unto us in that course, both for wisdom of counsel as also for our singular help in our course of godliness; whom the Lord (as it were) took away even as fruit falleth before it was ripe; when neither length of days, nor infirmity of body, did seem to call for his end.[1] The Lord even then took him away, as it were in his anger; whom if tears would have held, he had remained to this day. The loss of his ministry was very great unto me, for I ever counted myself happy in the enjoyment of it, notwithstanding all the crosses and losses otherwise I sustained. Yet indeed the manner of his taking away hath more troubled me, as fearing the Lord's anger in it, that, as I said, in the ordinary course of things, might still have remained, as also, the singular service he might have yet done in the church of God. Alas! dear friends, our state and cause in religion, by his death being wholly destitute of any that may defend our cause as it should against our adversaries; that we may take up that doleful complaint in the Psalm, that there is no prophet left among us, nor

---

[1] "He means Mr. Robinson." — *Bradford's Note.*

any that knoweth how long. Alas! you would fain have had him with you, and he would as fain have come to you. Many letters and much speech hath been about his coming to you, but never any solid course propounded for his going; if the course propounded the last year had appeared to have been certain, he would have gone, though with two or three families. I know no man amongst us knew his mind better than I did, about those things; he was loath to leave the church, yet I know also, that he would have accepted the worst conditions which in the largest extent of a good conscience could be taken, to have come to you. For myself and all such others as have formerly minded coming, it is much what the same, if the Lord afford means. We only know how things are with you by your letters; but how things stand in England we have received no letters of any thing, and it was November before we received yours. If we come at all unto you, the means to enable us so to do must come from you.[1] For the state of our church, and how it is with us, and of our people, it is wrote of by Mr. White. Thus praying you to pardon my boldness with you in writing as I do, I commend you to the keeping of the Lord, desiring, if he see it good, and that I might be serviceable unto the business, that I were with you. God hath taken away my son, that was with me in the

---

[1] "In anno 1629, a considerable number of the brethren of the church, [35, with their families] which were left in Holland, were transported over to us that were of the church in New England; which although it was at about £500 charge, yet it was borne cheerfully by the poor brethren here concerned in it." — Records Plym. Church, book i. folio 33. They arrived in August. Bradford says, "They were shipped at London in May with the ships that came to Salem." Sixty more came in Oct. 1630, in the Handmaid. See Prince's Annals, pp. 264, 322. Grahame, i. 193, wrongs the Leyden congregation, I think, when he says that after the death of Robinson, "very few had the *courage* to proceed to New Plymouth."

ship, when I went back again; I have only two children, which were born since I left you. Fare you well.
Yours to his power,
THOMAS BLOSSOM.[1]

Leyden, December 15, anno 1625.

ROGER WHITE TO GOVERNOR BRADFORD.

To his very loving friend, Mr. William Bradford, Governor of Plymouth in New England, these be, &c.

MY LOVING AND KIND FRIEND, AND BROTHER IN THE LORD,

My own and my wife's true love and hearty salutations to yourself and yours and all the rest of our loving friends with you; hoping in the Lord of your good healths, which I beseech him long to continue for the glory of his name and good of his people. Concerning your kind letter to the church, it was read publicly; whereunto (by the church) I send you here enclosed an answer. Concerning my brother Robinson's sickness and death and our practice, I wrote you at large, some five or six months since; but lest it should miscarry, I have now written to Mr. Brewster thereof, to whom I refer you.

Now concerning your course of choosing your governors yearly, and in special of their choosing yourself year after year, as I conceive they still do, and Mr. Allerton your assistant; howsoever I think it the best way that can be, so long as it please the Lord to con-

---

[1] Thomas Blossom afterwards came over to Plymouth, probably in 1629, and was chosen a deacon of the church. Bradford speaks of him as one of " our ancient friends in Holland." The Church records describe him as " a holy man and experienced saint," and " competently accomplished with abilities " for his place. He died in the summer of 1633. Plym. Ch. Rec. i. 42, and Prince's Annals, p. 437.

tinue your lives, and so good governors offer you, yet, considering man's mortality, whose breath is in his nostrils, and the evils of the times wherein we live, in which it is ordinarily seen that worse follow them that are good, I think it would be a safer course, for after time, the government was sometime removed from one to another; so the assistant one year might be governor next, and a new assistant chosen in his place, either of such as have or have not been in office; sometimes one, sometimes another, as it shall seem most fit to the corporation. My reasons are, 1st, because other officers that come after you, will look (especially if they be ambitiously minded) for the same privileges and continuance you have had; and if he have it not, will take great offence, as though unworthy of the place, and so greatly disgraced, whom to continue, might be very dangerous, and hazard (at least) the overthrow of all; men not looking so much at the reasons why others were so long continued as at the custom. 2dly, because others that are unexperienced in government might learn by experience; and so there might be fit and able men continually, when it pleaseth the Lord to take any away. 3dly, by this means, you may establish the things begun, or done before; for the governor this year, that was assistant last, will in likelihood rather ratify and confirm and go on with that he had a hand in the beginning of, when he was assistant, than otherwise, or persuade the new to it; whereas new governors, especially when there are factions, will many times overthrow that which is done by the former, and so scarcely any thing goeth forward for the general good; neither, that I see, can this be any prejudice to the corporation; for the new may always have the counsel and advice of the old for their direction, though they be out of office. These things I make bold to put to your godly wisdom and discretion, entreating you to pardon my boldness therein, and so leaving it to your discretion to make use of as you see it fitting, not having written the least inkling hereof to any other.

Now I entreat you, at your best leisure to write to me, how you think it will in likelihood go with your civil and church estate; whether there be hope of the continuance of both, or either; or whether you fear any alteration to be attempted in either. The reason of this my request is, the fear of some amongst us, (the which, if that hinder not, I think will come unto you,) occasioned partly by your letter to your father-in-law, Mr. May,[1] wherein you write of the troubles you have had with some, who it is like (having the times and friends on their sides) will work you what mischiefs they can; and that they may do much, many here do fear; and partly by reason of this king's proclamation, dated the 13th of May last, in which he saith that his full resolution is, — to the end that there may be one uniform course of government in and through all his whole monarchy, — that the government of Virginia shall immediately depend on himself, and not be committed to any company or corporation, &c., so that some conceive he will have both the same civil and ecclesiastical government that is in England, which occasioneth their fear. I desire you to write your thoughts of these things, for the satisfying of others; for my own part and some others, we durst rely upon you for that, who, we persuade ourselves, would not be thus earnest for our pastor and church to come to you,

---

[1] The father of his first wife, Dorothy. See note ¹ on page 162.

if you feared the danger of being suppressed. Thus desiring you to pardon my boldness, and remember us in your prayers, I for this time and ever, commit you and all your affairs to the Almighty, and rest

Your assured loving friend
And brother in the Lord,
Roger White.

Leyden, December 1, *anno* 1625.

P. S. The church would entreat you to continue your writing to them, which is very comfortable.

THE LEYDEN PEOPLE TO BRADFORD AND BREWSTER.

To our most dear and entirely beloved brethren, Mr. William Bradford[1] *and Mr. William Brewster, grace, mercy, and true peace be multiplied from God our Father, through our Lord Jesus Christ. Amen.*

Most Dear Christian Friends and Brethren,

As it is no small grief unto you, so it is no less unto us, that we are constrained to live thus disunited each from other, especially considering our affections each unto other, for the mutual edifying and comfort of both, in these evil days wherein we live, if it pleased

---

[1] William Bradford, whose name occurs so frequently in the preceding pages, and whose writings occupy so large a portion of this volume, was born at Austerfield, in Yorkshire, in 1588. His parents died when he was young, and he was trained by his grand-parents and uncles to "the innocent trade of husbandry." His paternal inheritance was considerable; but he had no better education than what falls to the common lot of the children of farmers. Being early interested in religion, and embracing the views of the Separatists, he incurred the displeasure of his relatives and the scoffs of his neighbours; but neither opposition nor scorn could deter him from attending on the ministry of Clifton, and joining Robinson's church. The part which he took in the escape of the Pilgrims to Holland, and in their measures for leaving that country for America, has been related in the preceding narrative. On his arrival at Plymouth he was about 32 years old. We have seen, page 201, that on the death of Carver he was immediately chosen governor of the Colony; and was annually

the Lord to bring us again together; than which as no outward thing could be more comfortable unto us, or is more desired of us, if the Lord see it good, so we no hope of means of accomplishing the same, except it come from you; and therefore must with patience rest in the work and will of God, performing our duties to him and you asunder; whom we are not any way able to help, but by our continual prayers to him for you, and sympathy of affections with you, for the troubles which befall you; till it please the Lord to reunite us again. But, our dearly beloved brethren, concerning your kind and respective letter, howsoever written by one of you, yet as we continue with the consent (at least in affection) of you both, although we cannot answer your desire and expectation, by reason it hath pleased the Lord to take to himself out of this miserable world our dearly beloved pastor, yet for ourselves we are minded, as formerly, to come unto you,

re-elected as long as he lived, excepting three years when Winslow, and two when Prince was chosen — having filled the office 30 years. Though he had not received a learned education, yet he was fond of study and writing, and his attainments were respectable. Cotton Mather says, "the Dutch tongue was almost as vernacular to him as the English; the French tongue he could also manage; the Latin and the Greek he had mastered; but the Hebrew he most of all studied, because, he said, he would see with his own eyes the ancient oracles of God in their native beauty." He died May 9, 1657, in his 69th year, "lamented," as Mather says, "by all the colonies of New England, as a common blessing and father to them all."

Gov. Bradford had one son, John, by his first wife, Dorothy May; and by his second, Alice Southworth, a widow, whose maiden name was Carpenter, and whom he married in 1623, he had two sons, William and Joseph and a daughter, Mercy. John lived in Duxbury; but nothing is known of him after 1662. William was deputy governor of the Colony, and resided in Kingston. Joseph married a daughter of the Rev. Peter Hobart of Hingham. A granddaughter of his married a Waters, of Sharon, and one of her descendants, Asa Waters, of Stoughton, possesses the Governor's bible, printed in 1592, which contains a family record. A marble monument, erected in 1825, on the Burial Hill at Plymouth, marks the spot where Gov. Bradford and his son William are interred. There are many descendants of this excellent man in the Old Colony and elsewhere. See Mather's Magnalia, i. 100—105; Morton's Memorial, pp. 264—270; Hutchinson's Mass. ii. 456; Belknap's Am. Biog. ii. 217 —251; Thacher's Plymouth, p. 106, Mitchell's Bridgewater, p. 358.

when and as the Lord affordeth means; though we see little hope thereof at present, as being unable of ourselves, and that our friends will help us we see little hope. And now, brethren, what shall we say further unto you? Our desires and prayers to God is, (if such were his good will and pleasure,) we might be reunited for the edifying and mutual comfort of both, which, when he sees fit, he will accomplish. In the mean time, we commit you unto him and to the word of his grace; whom we beseech to guide and direct both you and us, in all his ways, according to that his word, and to bless all our lawful endeavours for the glory of his name and good of his people. Salute, we pray you, all the church and brethren with you, to whom we would have sent this letter. If we knew it could not be prejudicial unto you, as we hope it cannot, yet fearing the worst, we thought fit either to direct it to you, our two beloved brethren, leaving it to your goodly wisdom and discretion, to manifest our mind to the rest of our loving friends and brethren, as you see most convenient. And thus entreating you to remember us in your prayers, as we also do you, we for this time commend you and all your affairs to the direction and protection of the Almighty, and rest,

  Your assured loving friends
   And brethren in the Lord,
    FRANCIS JESSOP,
    THOMAS NASH,
    THOMAS BLOSSOM,
    ROGER WHITE,
    RICHARD MAISTERSON.[1]

Leyden, Nov. 30, A. D. 1625.

---

[1] Richard Masterson, afterwards came over to Plymouth, and was a deacon of the church. See note [1] on page 73.

INDEX.

A.

Abbot, George, Archbishop, 56, 383.
Accomack, Plymouth, 203.
Acorns, eaten by the Indians, 145, 205.
Adams, Mrs. John, on Robinson's church at Leyden, 393.
Agawam. See *Ipswich*, and *Wareham*.
Ainsworth, Henry, teacher in the church at Amsterdam, 24, 418. Mentioned, 429, 440, 441, 445. Account of, 448.
Air of New England, 129, 233, 369.
Alden, John, a Pilgrim, 121, 150.
Alderton, Point, 195, 229. See *Allerton*.
Alewives, 172. Used for manure, 231.
Alexander, son of Massasoit, 194.
Allerton, or Alderton, Isaac, 85, 115. Daughter of, last survivor of the Mayflower, 150, 196, 250. Child of, born, 169. Death of his wife, 181. Account of, 195. Point named from, 195, 229. Chosen Assistant, 201. Second wife of, 470.
Allerton, John, a Pilgrim, 116, 122, 150.
Allotment of lands, the first, 346. The second, 347.
America, Reasons and Considerations touching the Lawfulness of removing out of England into the Parts of, 239; cautions respecting it, 240. What persons may remove, 241; why, 242. See *New England*, *Pilgrims*, and *Plymouth*.
Ames, William, account of, 423, 439.
Amsterdam, English church at, 24, 447. Contention of the churches there, 34, 380. Number of communicants at, 36, 455. People from, take leave of the Pilgrims at Delft-Haven, 88. Bradford's account of the church at, 455. Deaconess at, 455. See *Ainsworth*, and *Johnson*.
Anabaptists, law against, 404.
Anne, arrival of the, 351. Passengers in the, 352. Tonnage of the, 353. Return and cargo of the, 353.
Apannow, 232.
Apaum, Plymouth, 203, 245.
Apparel, Indian, 187, 365.
Archer, Gabriel, 103. On sassafras, 130.
Argall, Sir Samuel, Governor of Virginia, 69.
Arminian controversy, in the Low Countries, 40, 392, 452.
Arminius, James, 40.
Armour of the Pilgrims, 134, 156.
Arrows, sent as a challenge, 281.
Aspinet, sachem of Nauset, 216, 244, 302. Meets an embassy, 217. Probably Apannow, 232. Reception of Bradford by, 302. His salutation of Standish, 304. Fate of, 345. See *Indians Nauset*, and *Nauset*.

B.

Bacon, Leonard, Rev., on Alderton, 196. His vindication of the Pilgrims, 419.
Bancroft, Archbishop, persecution by, 423, 439.
Baptism, on the administration of, 64, 65. Views of Hobart respecting, 403; of Chauncy, 405. See *Anabaptists*.
Barnstable, or Cummaquid, error respecting the church in, 77. Everett's Address at, cited, 103. Sachem at, 215. Under Massasoit, 244. See *Iyanough*.
Barnstable bay, 119, 123. Error of Prince respecting, 135. Overshot in the third expedition of the Pilgrims, 159. Entered, in search of a boy, 212. Situation and size of, 214.
Barrington, in the Pokanoket country, 208.
Barrow, Henry, persecuted, 412. Refutation of Gifford by, 424. A martyr, 427. Examination of, 428. Robinson on his al-

490 INDEX.

leged blasphemy, &c., 429. Slanders against, 430. Vindication of, 431. Greenwood and, 432. His character, 433. His conversion, 433. Last acts of, 434.
Baylie, Robert, on the Pilgrims at Leyden, 379, 385. His aspersions, 425. Reply to, by Cotton, 426. On Barrow's death, 433. On Robinson, 453.
Baylies, Francis, errors of, corrected, 56, 75, 99, 134.
Beach grass, on Cape Cod, 123.
Beach point, in Plymouth, 163.
Beaver, among the Massachusetts, 229. Freighted in the Fortune, 236. Loaned to Weston, 342. Freighted in the Anne, 353.
Beaver Dam Brook, in Plymouth, 165.
Belknap, Jeremy, cited, 193, 255, 343, 464.
Bentivoglio, Cardinal, his notice of the Pilgrims, 43.
Bernard, Richard, 422. Robinson's answer to, 40, 429.
Billingsgate Point, in Wellfleet, 151.
Billington, Francis, discovers Billington Sea, 149, 172, 214.
Billington, John, a Pilgrim, 122. First offender, 149, 199. Hung in 1630, 149.
Billington, John, jr., 149. Voyage in search of, 214.
Billington Sea, 149, 167. Discovered and described, 172. Fish and deer there, 182.
Birch bark canoes, 135.
Blackwell, voyage of, to Virginia, 70. Conduct of, 71, 72.
Blossom, Thomas, letter by, to Bradford, 480. Notice of, 483.
Blue Hills, in Milton, called Massachusetts Mount, 224.
Boat Meadow creek, in Eastham, 155.
Boston, England, treatment of Pilgrims at, 26, 465.
Boston, New England, first landing in, 225. Sachem of, 232. See *Obbatinewat.*
Boston harbour, formerly called Massachusetts Bay, 225. Islands in, 226. Second voyage to, 290. Settlement of Thompson there, 351.
Bradford, Dorothy, 148, 162, 485, 487.
Bradford, William, Morton borrowed from, 4, 5. Time of his death, 5, 17, 487. His History, 7. Goes to Holland, 29 ; his employment there, 35. Age of, in 1620, 46, 487. In an excursion up the Cape, 126. Register by, 148. On Billington, 149. In the third exploring party, 149. Sick, 174, 177. Governor of Plymouth, 201, 486. Charter granted to, in 1629, 235. In an expedition for corn, 300. Reception of, at Chatham, 300. Squanto and, 301. Goes to the Massachusetts, 302. Trades at Nauset and Mattachiest, 302. Returns home by land, 303. At Middleborough and Sandwich, 305. Messenger from Weston's colony to, 328. His advice to Weston's company, 328. Holds a general court, 330. Marriage of, 353, 487. His Dialogue, 409. Prophesies, 419, 420. His Memoir of Elder Brewster, 459. His letter-book, 473. Letters to, from Leyden, 478, 480, 483, 486.

Account of, and of his family, 486. His Bible, 487. Monument to, 487.
Bradford, William, jr., 487.
Bradford's and Winslow's Journal, 109. Authorship of it, 115, 126, 128, 150, 158, 170, 177.
Brereton, John, on Cape Cod, 101. On the Elizabeth Islands, 129 ; on sassafras there, 130. On drinking tobacco, 188.
Brewster, Jonathan, 235.
Brewster, William, 22, 23. Bradford's Memoir of, 459—470. Under Secretary Davison, 463. Joins the Pilgrims, 465. Worship at the house of, 24, 465. Imprisonment of, at Boston, England, 27, 465. His library, 27. Goes to Holland, 27, 466. Chosen elder, 36. Becomes a printer, 35, 467. Books printed by, 40, 466. Sent as agent to England, 57. Correspondence of John Robinson and, with Sir Edwin Sandys, 53. Suspected and pursued, 456. Mentioned, 71. Reasons of his going to America, 77, 383. Why not chosen governor, 197, 470. Not a rigid Separatist, 400. His private and official character, 468. Account of his family and descendants, 352, 470. Robinson's letter to, 475. Letter to, from the Leyden people, 486. His sword, 134. His chair, 470. His age, 46, 115. His death, 461.
Brigham, William, edition of the Laws of Plymouth by, 197.
Bristol, in the Pokanoket country, 208.
Brown, Peter, a Pilgrim, 122, 174.
Brown, Robert, the books of, 427. Account of, 441. Separatists before, 442. Backsliding of, 442, 444.
Brownists, some of the principles of the, 66, 416. Dislike of the name, 397, 412, 416, 428, 444. Raleigh on banishing, 436.
Brown's island, in Plymouth harbour, 163.
Burial Hill, in Plymouth, view from, 168. Fortified, 169, 170. Artillery planted on, 181. Fort built on, 295, 335. First burying on, 295.
Burke, Edmund, on the Pilgrims in Holland, 48.
Butler's Hudibras, cited, 333.
Buzzard's Bay, Narraganset mistaken for, 305. French and Dutch trade to, 306. On a canal from, 306.

C.

Callender, John, on Sowams, 208.
Calvin, John, on the liturgy of the Church of England, 11.
Calvinists, Robinson on the, 397.
Cambridge, Platform of, 394.
Cambridge, synod at, 394. Occasion of the, 402. Invitation of Hobart to the, 406; of Chauncy, 406.
Canal, from Buzzard's Bay, 306.
Canacum. See *Cawnacome.*
Canonicus, messenger from, 281. Notice of, 281. Hostile to the Plymouth colonies, 281. Roger Williams, and, 281. Challenge from, 281, 283.

INDEX. 491

Cantaugcanteest, Watson's hill, Plymouth, 130.
Capawack. See *Martha's Vineyard.*
Cape Cod, visited by Captain John Smith, 80, Fallen in with. by the Pilgrims, 101, 117, 384. Historical notice of, 101. Pilgrims put into the harbour of, 102, 117. Edward Everett on, 104. Well wooded, 118, 124. Graham's Survey and Map of, 118. Soil of, 123. Beach grass on, 123. Called Paomet, 125. Indians on, escape pestilence, 184. Particulars as to the Indians on, 216. See *Provincetown.*
Cape Cod Light, 123, 130, 137.
Captain's Hill. in Duxbury, 126.
Careswell, in Marshfield, 275.
Carleton, Sir Dudley, on Sunday in Holland, 47. On the Perth Assembly, 395. His letters to Naunton respecting Brewster, cited, 467.
Carpenter, Mary, "a godly old maid," sister of Gov. Bradford's second wife, 353.
Cartwright, Thomas, the Puritan, 436.
Carver, John, twice an agent to England, 55, 58, 59, 60, 78, 90. Deacon, 60, 200. Sabin Starsmore's letter to, 73. Robinson's letter to, 89. Confidence reposed in, 90. First governor, 122, 200. His sword, 134. Receives the first exploring party, 137. In the third expedition, 149. Seeks lost men, 174. Fishes at Billington Sea, 182. Reception of Massasoit by, 193. Re-elected governor, 197. His and his wife's death, 198, 200. Notice of, and of his family, 200. His chair. 458.
Carver, William, 201.
Cattle, first brought to New England, 233.
Caunbatant, sachem, 232. See *Corbitant.*
Cawnacome, sachem of Manomet, 232, 307. Reception of Bradford by, 307. Standish's visit to, 310. Fate of, 345.
Cedars, on Cape Cod, 118, 124. On Clark's island, 164
Centaury, juice of the, drunk by the Indians, 360.
Chalmers, George, on the Pilgrims' removal from Holland, 48.
Charity, arrival of the, 296. Returns to England. 299.
Charter, second of Plymouth, found in the Land Office in Boston, 234. See *Patents.*
Chatham. See *Manamoick.*
Chauncy Charles, Rev., of Scituate, account of, 405
Chikkatabak, sachem of Neponset, 232.
Chilton, Mary, a Pilgrim, 275.
Church of England, contention about the ceremonies and service book of the, 9, 11, 20. Overthrown, 14, 16. Re-established, 17. Conformity to the, required, 21 ; in the colonization of Virginia, 54. Henry VIII., supreme head of the, 64. Robinson's regard for the, 389, 415, 442. Feelings of Higginson and Winthrop respecting the, 398. Views of the Separatists respecting the, 414. See *Common Prayer, Episcopacy,* and *Liturgy.*

Church of Scotland. See *Presbyterians* and *Communion.*
Churches, the primitive, the only pattern, 387. Robinson's church, modelled according to, 426. See *Communion.*
Clams, at Cape Cod, 119. At Plymouth, 164, 329. Note on, 306.
Clapboards, shipped to England, 353.
Clark, pilot and master's mate of the Mayflower, 85, 112, 150, 155. Clark's island, in Plymouth, named from, 160.
Clark, Thomas, 160, 352.
Clark's Island, arrival of the Pilgrims at, 160. Notices of, 160, 163. The only island in Plymouth harbour, 163. Trees on, 164. The Pilgrims conclude not to settle on, 167.
Clergy, ejectment of the Puritan, 21. Influence of the New England, in civil affairs, 37. On the congregational ordination of, 66. See *Elders* and *Ministry.*
Clifton, Richard, Rev., 22. Bradford's account of, 453.
Climate of New England, 369. See *Air.*
Codfish, at Cape Cod harbour, 119. At Plymouth, 164, 294. Want of means to catch, 171. 294.
Cold Harbour, in Truro, 139.
Columbus, ships of. 86.
Common house at Plymouth, building of the, 169, 173. Burnt, 177. Cushman's Discourse at the, 255. Location of the, 255.
Common Prayer, persecutions for books against the, 427.
Communion, Robinson's doctrine of, 388, 457. Of the Pilgrims with the Dutch and French churches, 392, 457 ; with the Scotch, 394, 395, 457. Bradford on, 457. Robinson on the administration of, by elders, 477.
Community of goods, 84. Qualified, 346.
Compact of the Pilgrims, 120.
Conbatant. See *Corbitant.*
Congregational Church, the first in America, 77.
Congregationalism, 66. An apostolic institution, 401. The primitive church polity, 406. Growth of, 423.
Cooke, Francis, a Pilgrim, and his wife, 122, 352, 394.
Coppin, Robert, second mate of the Mayflower. 112, 148, 150. 155, 159.
Copping. John, a Puritan martyr, 412, 427.
Copp's Hill. in Boston, visited. 225.
Corbitant, hostile to Massasoit and the Pilgrims, 219. Captures Tisquantum, 220. Attempt to take, 221. Escapes, 222. Threatened, 222. Likely to succeed Massasoit, 315. Winslow lodges with, 324 ; their conversation, 325.
Corn. See *Indian corn.*
Cornhill, in Truro, 133, 140.
Cotton, John, of Boston, 5. Error of Cotton Mather, respecting the family of, 30. On the church at Leyden. 380. On the Plymouth church, 386. On Robinson's sentiments, 339. Assists in drawing up the

Cambridge Platform, 394. On Robinson's conduct, 396. Conformity of, with Phillips, 397. On Robinson's separatism, 400. On separation and secession, 417. On public offences in churches, 418. On prophesying, 421. On modelling of different churches, 426. On Elizabeth and the Puritan martyrs, 433. On the author of Independency, 442. On the name Brownists, 444. On Ainsworth, 448. On John Smith, 451.
Cotton, John, jr, minister of Plymouth, 4, 5.
Coubatant. See *Corbitant.*
Court of High Commission, 19.
Cow Yard, in Plymouth harbor, 171.
Crabs, at Plymouth, 164.
Cudbartson, 393. See *Cuthbertson.*
Cummaquid. See *Barnstable.*
Cushman, Isaac, Rev., 250.
Cushman, Mary, last survivor of the Mayflower, 150, 196, 250.
Cushman, Robert, sent twice as agent to England, 55, 57, 78, 249. Letter from, 68. Answers complainants, 84. Correspondence with, 85. Passenger in the Fortune, 99, 116, 249. Letter by, to I. P., 116. His "Reasons, &c." 239. Notice of, 249. Returns in the Fortune, 249. Discourse by, 255. On Weston's company, 296. On the preacher for Plymouth, 476.
Cushman, Thomas, 235, 250. Wife and descendants of, 250.
Cuthbertson, Cuthbert, 352, 393.

D.

Damariscove islands, 278, 293.
Davenport, John, Rev., account of, 419.
Davis, John, his edition of New England's Memorial, 5. Cited, 57, 195, 234, 255, 301, 339.
Davis, Samuel, on the Gurnet, 287.
Davison, William, Secretary, Brewster under, 463, 464. Account of, 463.
Deaconess, at Am terdam, 455.
Deer, near the pond in Truro, 130. In Plymouth, 175, 231. At Billington Sea, 182.
Deer traps, 136.
De la Noye, or Delano, Philip, 235, 236. Admitted to churches of the Pilgrims, 394.
Delft-Haven, 87. Parting at, 88, 384.
Dennis, William, a Puritan martyr, 412, 427.
Dermer, Captain, cited, 184. Attack on, by Indians, 185. Treatment of Squanto by, 190. At Namasket, 190, 204.
De Tocqueville, on the Magnalia, 30. On Plymouth rock, 161.
Dort, Sunday at, 47. Synod of, 47, 424.
Dotey, Edward, a Pilgrim, 116, 122, 127, 150. Punishment of, 201.
Double Brook, in Plymouth, 165.
Douglass, William, on the removal from Holland, 48.
Dover, N. H., settlement at, 251.
Downs, or Dunes, of Holland, 123.
Drake, Sir Francis, vessels of, 86.
Dress, Indian, 185, 365.

Droitwich, birth-place of the Winslow family, 274.
Drought. See *Pilgrims,* and *Plymouth.*
Dudley, Gov. Thomas, 105, 199, 419.
Duelling, punishment of, at Plymouth, 201.
Duxbury, the name, 126. Formation of the church in, 394.
Dwight, Timothy, on Plymouth and the Pilgrims, 161.
Dyer's swamp, in Truro, 129.

E.

Eastham, or Nauset, explored, 151, 153. Expedition to, 214. Corn procured at, 302, 304. See *Nauset.*
East Harbour, in Truro, 120. Pilgrims at, 128, 137, 138. See *Truro.*
East Harbour creek, 128.
East Harbour village, in Truro, 129. Pond village near, 130.
Eel river, in Plymouth, 160, 196, 216.
Elders, remarks on and on their duties, 64, 65, 419, 455. Not chosen to civil offices, 197. Continuance of, 455. At Salem, 455. Robinson on the administration of the sacraments by, 477.
Eliot, John, on the Indian pronunciation of *l, n,* and *r,* 319.
Elizabeth, Queen, favors the Anglican ritual, 12, 21. Suspension of Grindal by, 420. Conduct of, respecting Barrow and Greenwood, 432. Cause of her subsequent toleration, 433. Separatists in the time of, 442. Her duplicity and treatment of Mary and of Davison, 463, 464. Aids Holland against Spain, 464. Fortresses consigned to, 464.
Elizabeth Islands, springs on the, 129. Sassafras exported from, 130.
Embalmed body found, 142.
Embden, synod at, 422. Johnson at, 445.
Endicott, John, sends to Plymouth for a physician, 223, 386. Instructed to purchase the Indians' lands, 259. On the worship at Plymouth, 336.
English, Thomas, a Pilgrim, 116, 122, 150.
Episcopacy, Robinson's dislike of, 390. Attempt to establish, in New England, 478. See *Church.*
Episcopius. Simon, 41.
Everett, Edward, cited, 103.

F.

Fast, the first at Plymouth, 349.
Faunce, Thomas, Elder, 199, 352.
Fire-arms of the Pilgrims, 125, 136, 142, 156, 237.
First Brook, in Plymouth, 165.
Fish, and fishing at Cape Cod, 119, 146. At Plymouth, 164. Want of means to catch, 171, 294. At Monhegan, 182, 278, 293. In Taunton river, 205. At Damariscove islands, 278, 293. At Buzzard's bay, 306. Profits of, in New England, 81, 371, 383.

INDEX. 493

Florida, discovered, 243.
Foord, Goodwife, 235, 236.
Forefathers, first comers so called, 353.
Forefather's Day, 161.
Fortune, arrival of the, 198, 234. Tonnage of the, 234. Names of passengers in the, 235. Return cargo of the, 236. Captured, 236. Passengers in the, 352.
Frankfort, troubles at, 9.
Freeman, James, Rev., of Boston, 120.
Fresh Lake, 172. See *Billington Sea*.
Frobisher, Martin, fleet of, 86.
Froissart, on Wat Tyler and Standysshe, 126.
Fuller, Samuel, the physician of the Pilgrims, 85, 121. Notice of, 222. Heals Weston's sick colonists, 297. Sent for to Salem, 223, 386.
Fuller, Thomas, on Robert Brown, 442.
Furs, trade for, 302, 371. See *Beaver*.

G.

Gambling, among the Indians, 210, 307.
Gardiner, Richard, a Pilgrim, 116, 122.
Gardner's Neck, 315. See *Mattapoiset*.
Geneva Bible, 14.
Gilbert, Sir Humphrey, 87, 155.
Glass windows, history of, 237.
Godbertson, 393. See *Cuthbertson*.
Goodman, John, a Pilgrim, 122. Lost, 174. Encounters wolves, 178.
Gookin, Daniel, cited, 144, 145, 184, 187, 210, 305, 307, 317, 360, 367.
Gorges, Sir Ferdinando, on the Pilgrims, 55. Connected with the family of Lincoln, 75. Men of, attacked by Indians, 185. On Indians carried to England, 190. Error respecting the colony of, 334. Measures by, to establish episcopacy in New England, 478. Thompson sent over by, 351.
Gorton, Samuel, 379.
Gosnold, Bartholomew, error respecting, 75. Discovers Cape Cod, 101, 103, 119. Carries home sassafras, 130.
Graham, J. D., Major, Survey and Map of Cape Cod by, 118.
Grahame, James, in error, 55, 76, 98, 105, 334, 482.
Grapes and grape vines, 130, 132, 165, 234.
Great Bear, the constellation, so called by the Indians, 366.
Great Hollow, in Truro. 131.
Great Meadow creek, in Eastham, 155.
Great Pond, in Eastham, 153.
Green's harbour, in Marshfield, grant to Winslow at, 275.
Greene, Richard, 299.
Greenwood, John, persecuted, 412. Refutation of Gifford by, 424. A preacher in London, 427. A martyr, 427. Examination of, 428. Reynold's and Queen Elizabeth's conversation respecting, 432.
Grimsby, in Lincolnshire, 28.
Grindal, Archbishop, suspended by Elizabeth, 420. Successor of, 432.

Ground-nuts, 329.
Guiana, 52.
Guns of the Pilgrims, 125, 136, 142, 156.
Gurnet, 160, 163, 164, 287.

H.

Hall, Bishop, on Holland, 25. On the Brownists, 451. On Robinson, 453.
Hallam, Henry, cited, 10, 11, 428.
Hampden, John, never in America, 314.
Hampton Court, Conference at, 20, 432.
Hatherly, Timothy, 352, 353.
Higginson, Francis, Rev., cited, 129, 184, 237, 398. Ordained at Salem, 398.
High Head, Truro, soil at, 123.
Highland Light, Cape Cod, 123, 130, 137.
Hilton, William, 235. Letter from New Plymouth by, 250. Settles at Dover, N. H., 251. His wife and children, 251, 352.
Hingham, first minister of, 402.
Hither Manomet Point, in Plymouth, 291.
Hobart, Peter, Rev., of Hingham, 402, 487.
Hobbamock, 219. Flight of, to Plymouth, 220. Expresses fears, 285. Asserts Massasoit's faithfulness, 288. A pinse, 288, 341. Sends his wife to Pokanoket, 288. Guide to Buzzard's Bay, 307. Guide in the visit to Massasoit in his sickness, 314, 315. Lamentations by, for Massasoit, 316. Massasoit reveals a plot to, 323. Interview of Pecksuot with, at Wessagusset, 337. On the death of Pecksuot, 339. Chases Indians, 341. His services, and character, 350.
Hobbamock, and Hobbamoqui, the Indian devil, 356, 357.
Holland. See *Low Countries*.
Holmes, Abiel, in error, 77. Cited, 199, 478, 479.
Hoornbeek, John, on John Robinson and the Arminians, 42, 453.
Hopkins, Oceanus, born, 100, 122, 127.
Hopkins, Stephen, a Pilgrim, 100, 122. Account of, 126, 127. Goes to meet Indians, 181. Samoset lodges with, 185. In the embassy to Pokanoket, 202, 204.
Hopkins's cliff, in Truro, 133.
Hopkins's creek, in Truro, 133, 135.
House lots, laid out at Plymouth, 170, 173.
Houses, building of, commenced at Plymouth, 173. Their probable character, 179.
Howland, John, a Pilgrim, 122, 149. Notice of, and of his family, 150.
Hubbard, William, his history, 58, 79. On the laws of the Pilgrims, 197. On Standish, 339.
Hudson, Henry, at Cape Cod, 101, 103. Explored Hudson's river, 368, 369.
Hudson's river, settlements on, 42. Pilgrims sail for, 101, 117, 385.
Hunt, Captain, the kidnapper, 186, 190, 215.
Hutchinson, Thomas, Gov., cited, 107, 120, 122, 185, 195, 197, 274, 380, 477.

494   INDEX.

I.

Independents and Independency, 422, 442.
Indian Brook, in Wellfleet, 152, 165.
—— burying grounds and graves, 142, 154, 227, 363. In Eastham, 153.
—— challenge, 281, 283.
—— corn, found, 131, 141. A native of America, 131. Indian mode of storing, 133. Taken and afterwards paid for, 134, 140, 204, 235, 259. Parched, 187, 211. Exchanged for seed, 204, 209. Twenty acres of, 230. Aid in planting, from Squanto, 230. Indians' season for planting, 230. Excursion after, 299. Procured, 301, 302, 305, 308, 309. Divided with Weston's company, 303. Want of, at Weston's colony, 328. Allowance of, to Weston's company, 337. Given to the sachems, 362. Account of, 310.
—— hemp, 133, 166.
—— Neck, in Truro, 135
—— priests. See *Powows*.
Indians, burning of underwood by the, 124. First sight of, by the Pilgrims, 127. Their barns, 133. Their baskets, 133, 145. Their mats, 133, 144, 145, 363. Their canoes, 135. Hedges of, to take game, 142. Burials by, 143, 362, 363. Household stuff of the, 144. Seen around a grampus, 151, 153. Their arrows, 158. Fires of, seen at Plymouth, 170, 171. Standish goes in search of, 171. Seen on Clark's island, 179. On Watson's hill, 180, 190, 191. Language of the, 183. Destroyed by pestilence, 183, 206, 229, 234, 258, 259. Treatment of, by Hunt, 186, 190, 215. Apparel of, 187, 365. Use of tobacco by the, 188, 363. Carried away by Weymouth, 190. At Namaschet, 205. Incident of their courage, 206. Submission of, to king James, 210, 226, 232, 244, 259, 307. Their beds, 210. Gamble, 210, 307. General rendezvous of, at Massachusetts, 226. Their forts, 227. Peace produced among the, 232. Their religion, 233, 355. On the right to their soil, 242. Conversion of the, 243, 257, 271. Habits of, 243. Treatment of, 244, 259. Friendly, 258, 272. Lands of, always purchased, 259. Massacre by, in Virginia, 278, 293, 294. Threaten the Pilgrims, 295. Reception of Bradford by, at Chatham, 300. Mode of salutation by, 304. Conspiracy among them, 310. Customs of, in sickness, 313, 317, 362. Effect of Standish's expedition to Wessagusset on the, 345. Decline of the, 345. Notice the fast and the rain, 350. Manners, customs, religious opinions, and ceremonies of the, 354. Their God, 355 ; devil, 356 ; powows, 357 ; sacrifices, 358 ; pniese, 359 ; sachems and sachems' families, 360 ; funerals and mourning, 362. Names among the, 363. Wedlock among the, 364. Crimes and punishments among them, 364. Their apparel, 365 ; language, 366 ; memorials, 367. See *Cape Cod*, *Massasoit*, *Plymouth*, *Samoset*, *Squanto*, and *Squaws*.

Indians, Mashpee, 216.
—— Massachusetts, swept off, by pestilence, 184, 229. Voyage to the, 224. Origin of their name, 224. Squaw sachem of the, 225, 228. Preparations for visiting again, 285. Apprehensions from them. 285. Alarm on the voyage to the, 287. Complaints by the, respecting Weston's company, 298, 302, 327. Bradford's excursion to the, 302. Conspiracy among the, 310, 323, 330, 343. Standish's expedition against the, at Wessagusset, 327, 331. Boldness of, at Wessagusset, 332. Seven, killed in a struggle, 339. Skirmish with, 341. Chased by Hobbamock, 341. Plot of the, confessed, 343. Seat of the sachem of the, 227 ; of the squaw sachem, 228. See *Obbatinewat*, and *Ostakiest*.
—— Namascheucks, 205, 212.
—— Narraganset, suspected of a conspiracy with the Massachusetts, 285. Their devotions, 358.
—— Nauset, encounter with, 156, 185. Steal, 180, 186, 304. Escape the pestilence, 184. Their number, 185. Hostility of the, 185. Treatment of, by Hunt, 186. Their principal seat, 216. Conspiracy by the, 323. See *Aspinet*, and *Nauset*.
—— Penobscot, escape the pestilence, 184.
—— Pequot, 280.
—— —— Tarrateens, 225.
—— Wampanoags, sachem of the, 287.
Infanticide, Indian, 358.
Ipswich, on settling at, 147.
Isles of Shoals, 351.
Iyanough, sachem, 215, 216, 218, 311. Fate of, 345. See *Barnstable*.

J.

Jacob, Henry, 74. Account of, 439.
James I., his dislike of the Geneva Bible, 14. Hostility of, to the Puritans, 20, 56. Influence and acts of, in the Low Countries, 42, 436. Letters patent by, to the Virginia Company, 54. Does not grant an application for freedom in religion, 55, 56, 382. Oath of Allegiance required by, 64. Hates Sir Edwin Sandys, 69. Did not grant letters patent to the Pilgrims, 74. New patent from, 80, 100. On fishing in New England, 81, 383. Reason by, for granting the patent, 184. Wife of, 210. Indian allegiance to, 210, 226, 232, 244, 259, 307. Representation to, in favor of Davison, 463. Death of, 479.
Jenny, John, has leave to build a mill, 172, 352. A passenger in the Anne, 352, 392. Communed with the Dutch, 392.
Johnson, the Lady Arbella, 75.
Johnson, Edward, cited, 23, 158, 184, 188.
Johnson, Francis, Rev., church of, at Amsterdam, 24, 34, 36. Blackwell and, 71, 72. Preacher at Middleburg, 424. Conversion of, 425, 447. Bradford's account of, 445. Excommunications by, 446. His wife, 446. Persecution and flight of, 447.

INDEX. 495

Johnson, George, 446, 449.
Johnson, Isaac, 75. Death of, 76.
Jones, Captain of the Mayflower, 98, 99. Plot wrongly ascribed to, 102, 138. Mentioned, 137, 138, 139, 141, 181. River, in Kingston, named from, 166. Captain of the Discovery, arrives at Plymouth, 278. Furnishes supplies, 298.
Jones's river, in Kingston, 165. Explored, 166.
Josselyn, John, cited, 118, 132, 139, 176, 306.
Juniper trees, 118, 124.

K.

Kautantowwit, Indian god, 356.
Kennebec, Popham's attempt to settle at Sagadahoc, near the, 50, 55, 112, 427.
Kiehtan, the Indian god, 326. Meaning of, 355.
Kikemuit, seat of Massasoit, 208.
Kingston, incorporated, 166. Residence of Wm. Bradford, jr., 487.

L.

Lands, first allotment of, 346; the second, 347.
Language, Indian, 366.
Leister, Edward, a Pilgrim, 122. Punishment of, 201.
Leyden, removal of the Pilgrims to, 35, 380. University of, 35. The congregation in peace at, 36, 380. Arminian controversy there, 40, 392. Influence of James I., at the University of, 42. Pilgrims leave, 87, 384. Baylie and Cotton on the Pilgrims at, 379, 456. Respect there for Robinson, 392, 393. Bradford's account of the church at, 456. Fate of the church there, after Robinson's death, 479, 482. Epistle from the people there to Bradford and Brewster, 486.
Leyden-street, at Plymouth, house-lots laid out on, 170, 173, 174.
Lincoln, Elizabeth, Countess of, 75; Bridget, 76.
Lincoln family, connexion of the, with the New England settlements, 75.
Lions, in New England, 176.
Little James, size of the, 87, 353. Arrival of the, at Plymouth, 87, 150, 351, 352.
Little Namskeket creek, in Orleans, 155.
Liturgy, John Calvin on the, 11. Robinson's dislike of the, 390. See *Church of England.*
Lobsters, at Plymouth, 164, 205, 233. At Boston, 225.
London Company, 55. See *Virginia Company.*
Long Point, Provincetown, 118, 120. Landing at, 123. Diminished, 123. Soil there, 123. Shallop aground on, 150.
Long pond, in Eastham, 153.
Low Countries, religious toleration in the, 23. Influence of James I. there, 42, 436. Reasons and causes of the Pilgrims' removal from the, 44, 381. Sunday there, 47, 381. Two churches of Separatists in the, 418, 453, 455. Sufferings of the Separatists there, 439, 441. Elizabeth's league with the, 463. See *United Provinces.*
Luther, Martin, Robinson's remark on, 423. His zeal, 429. Erasmus on, 435.
Lutherans, Robinson on the, 397.
Lyford, John, 476.

M.

Maize, 131. Meal of parched, 187. See *Indian corn.*
Malaga, monks of, liberate Indians, 186.
Manamoick, Chatham, 217. Bradford at, 300.
Manomet, Point, 148. Bluff of, 159.
Manomet, Sandwich, boy at, 217. Sachem of, 232, 307. Corn procured at, 305. Notice of, 305. See *Cawnacome.*
Manure, fish used for, 231, 370.
Marriages, 94. First, in Plymouth, 201. Indian, 364. Preaching at, 402.
Marshall, John, in error, 84, 100.
Marshfield, grant to Winslow at, 275.
Martha's Vineyard, or Capawack, submission of the Indians of, 232. Conspiracy with the Indians on, 323.
Martin, Christopher, a Pilgrim, 78, 121. Sick, 171. Death and notice of, 172.
Martyr, Peter, cited, 75. On the ships of Columbus, 86.
Martyrs, Puritan, 412, 427. Not Brownists, 428.
Mary, Queen, persecutions and flight of Reformers in the time of, 9, 413. Act of Supremacy of repealed under, 64. Separatists in her time, 442.
Massachusetts Bay, occasion of the settlement of 122. Pilgrims' first visit to, 154. 225. Meaning of, 225. General rendezvous of Indians at, 226. Described, 228. Mission from, to Canonicus, 281. Harmony between the settlers of, and of Plymouth, 398. Law in, against Anabaptists, 404.
Massachusetts Mount, 224.
Massasoit, 127. Samoset's return to, 185, 186. Forces of, 185. Description and entertainment of subjects of, at Plymouth, 186; their return home, 189. Different modes of spelling the word, 191. Visits Plymouth, 191, 259. Winslow's interview with, 192. Reception of, 192, 231. Treaty with, 193, 244, 245. Description of, 194. Treaty with, confirmed in 1662, 194. Withdraws, 194. Reception of Standish and Allerton by, 195. Goes home, 196. Embassy to, 202, 232. Presents to, 203, 209. Message to, and his reply, 203, 209. His territory and principal seats, 208, 225, 244, 288. Sent for and saluted, 209. Speech of, and conference with, 209. Entertainment by, 211. Cape Cod Indians and, 216. Success of the Narragansetts against, 217. Expedition in defence of, 219. Reported hostility of, 287.

Hobbamock's wife sent to, 288. Enraged with Tisquantum, 289, 290. Visits Plymouth, 290. Demands Tisquantum, 291. Seems lukewarm, 295. Sick, 313. Winslow's journey to, 313. Reported death of, 315. Hobbamock's lamentations for, 316. Reception of Winslow by, 318. Tended by Winslow, 319. Convalescent, 320. Reveals a plot, 323. Refuses to join in the conspiracy, 323. See *Pokanoket*.
Masterson, Richard, 73, 488.
Matchlocks, used by the Pilgrims, 125, 136, 142, 156.
Mather, Cotton, on Governor Bradford, 27, 487. Not to be depended on for facts, 30. On Cape Cod, 101. On Ralph Partridge, 394.
Mather, Increase, 5, 30. Charter of Massachusetts obtained by, 37. On the pestilence among the Indians, 184. Assists in making the Cambridge Platform, 394.
Mattakiest, Barnstable, 215.
Mattapoiset, Mattapuyst, or Gardner's Neck, Corbitant at, 232, 315. Visit to, by Winslow, 316. See *Corbitant*.
Maurice, Prince of Orange, 479.
May, Mr., father of Dorothy, wife of Governor Bradford, 485.
Mayflower, 85. Renowned, 99. Birth on board the, at sea, 100, 122, 127. The plotting of the Captain of the, considered, 102. Place of her making Cape Cod, 102. Place of her anchorage, 120, 123. Peregrine White born on board the, 148. Last surviving passenger of the, 150, 196. Tonnage of the, and anchorage, at Plymouth 171. Seen by Samoset, 182. Returns to England, 199. No Pilgrim returns in her, 199. Passengers in the, called old comers, or forefathers, 352.
Meal, of parched maize, 187. See *Indian Corn*.
Medicine men. See *Powows*.
Merchant adventurers, agreement with the, 81. Smith on the, 81. Application by the, for the Plymouth colonists, 114. Cushman's allusions to the, 266. Letters received from the, 348. Robinson on the, 476. Prevent Pilgrims from going to New England, 476, 478.
Merrimack river, settlements on the, 403.
Meyrick, on firelocks and snaphances, 156.
Middleborough. See *Namasket*.
Middleburg, Johnson, preacher at, 424.
Mill, on Town Brook, at Plymouth, 172, 352.
Milman, H. H., Rev., on community of goods, 84.
Milton, Pilgrims in, 227. See *Blue Hills*.
Milton, John, cited, 107.
Mohegan river, the Hudson, 368, 369.
Monardes, on sassafras, 130.
Monhegan, fishing at, 182, 278, 293. Winslow goes to, 293. Voyage to, from Weston's colony, for provisions, 330. Part of Weston's company go to, 341, 342.
Mooanam, son of Massasoit, 194.
Morattigou, 183.
Mortality of the Pilgrims, 100, 111, 148, 168,

169, 181. Table of the, 192. Remarks on the, 197, 265, 474. Robinson on the, 473. See *Indians*.
Morton, George, 113. Bradford's relation sent to, 175. Letter probably sent to, 230. Comes out in the Anne, 236, 352, 353.
Morton, Nathaniel, Secretary, Preface by, 3. His New England's Memorial, 4. Notice of, 6. On the plot to avoid Hudson's river, 102. On Miles Standish, 126. On Namskeket creek, 155. On a shipwreck in Plymouth harbour, 163. Dwelt at Wellingsly Brook, 165. On William Mullins, 181. On the name of Plymouth, 203. On Samuel Fuller, the physician, 223. On Phinehas Prat, 332. Preface by, to Bradford's Dialogue, 411; transcribed it, 413. Takes part in public worship, 419. On Brewster, and Bradford's Memorial of him, 461. On the plotting against Robinson, 477.
Morton, Thomas, on burning underwood, 124. On walnut trees, 132. On grapes, 132. On storing Indian corn, 133. On Indian canoes, 135. On deer traps, 136. On wild geese, 140. On ducks, 140. On planks in Indian graves, 143. On Indian bowls, 144. On Indian hearse cloths, 154. On halibut or turbot, 164. On hemp, 166. On lions in New England, 176. On the pestilence among the Indians, 184. On Indian apparel, 187. On Indian beds, 210. On alewives, 231. On an execution at Weymouth, 332. On Weston's company, 334. Not one of them, 334.
Morton, Thomas, jr., 352.
Mount Hope, residence of Massasoit, 208.
Mourt, G., who he was, 113.
Mullins, William, a Pilgrim, 121. Death of, 181.
Murdock's Pond, in Plymouth, adventure at, 175.
Muscles, at Cape Cod, 119. At Plymouth, 164, 233, 329. At Weymouth, 329.
Mystic river, discovered by the Pilgrims, 228.

N.

Nacook brook, grant on, 332.
Namasket, Middleborough, Dermer at, 190, 204. Under Massasoit, 204. Winslow and Hopkins at, 204, 205, 212. Expedition to, 219. Alarm from, 287. Corn procured at, 305.
Namskeket creek, in Orleans, 155. Seat of the Nauset Indians, 216.
Nanepashemet, grave of, 154, 227. Widow of, 225. House of, 226. Time of his death, 227.
Nash, Thomas, 85, 488.
Naunton, Sir Robert, friendly to the Pilgrims, 55, 56, 382, 383. Carleton's letters to, respecting Brewster, cited, 467.
Nauset, 153. Voyage to, in search of a boy, 214. Sachem of, 216, 244, 302. Expedition to, for corn, 302. See *Eastham*, and *Indians*.

INDEX.

Neal, Daniel, in error, 99, 100. On John Smith, 451. On Brewster, 461.
Nepeof, a sachem, 220.
Neponset, Milton, subject to the Massachusetts sachem, 227. Sachem of, 232.
Netherlands, the battle-ground of Europe, 25. See *Low Countries.*
Nets, want of fishing, 171, 294.
Newbury, church at, 402.
New England, patent for, 80, 100, 184. Visited and named, 80, 255. Attempts to settle, 107, 112. Abandoned as uninhabitable, 112. Grant to the Plymouth Colonists by the President and Council of, 114, 116, 234. Water and air of, 129, 233, 369. First Englishman born in, 148. Pestilence among the Indians in, 183, 206, 229, 234, 258, 259. Supposed to be an island, 256, 368. Cushman on emigration to, 256. Situation, climate, soil, and productions of, 368. Unreasonable expectations respecting, 374. Winslow's Narration of the Grounds of the first Planting of, 377, 379. Measures to establish episcopacy in, 478. See *America, Kennebeck,* and *Plymouth.*
New England's Memorial, Morton's, 4.
Newfoundland, on the discovery of, 155. Separatists banished to, 441.
New Netherlands, 42.
New York, early settlement in, 42.
Nobscusset, Yarmouth, boundary of a sachemdom, 216
Nokake, or nokehich, 187. See *Indian corn.*
Nonconformists, harmony of the Separatists and, 398. See *Puritans.*
North river, in Scituate, 148.
North Star, known to the Indians, 366.
Nowell, Increase, 419.
Noyes, James, Rev., of Newbury, 402.

O.

Oaks, on Cape Cod, 118, 124.
Oaths of Allegiance and Supremacy, 64.
Obbatinewat, a sachem in Massachusetts Bay, 225. Submission of, 226, 232. Probably Obbatinua, 232.
Obtakiest, 343, 344.
Oiled paper, windows made of, 237.
Old comers, first Pilgrims called, 353.
Old Indian Wear, on Taunton river, 205.
Old Tom's hill, in Truro, 135, 139, 147.
Oldmixon, John, errors of, 91, 164.
Opechancanough, a Virginia sachem, 279.
Ordination, remarks on, 66.
Orleans, seat of Nauset Indians, 216. See *Namskeket.*

P.

Painter, Thomas, an Anabaptist, whipped, 404, 405.
Palfrey, John Gorham, cited, 77.
Pamet little river, 133, 135.
Pamet river, in Truro, 118, 125. Notices of, 135. Explored, 139. On settling at, 146.

Paomet, Cape Cod so called, 204.
Paragon, fate of the, 348, 349.
Parker, Robert, Rev., 436, 439.
Parker, Thomas, Rev., of Newbury, 402.
Partridge, Ralph, Rev., of Duxbury, 394.
Partridges, 137.
Passaconaway, magical power of, 366.
Patents, 80. See *James I., New England,* and *Pilgrims.*
Patuxet, Plymouth, 183, 203. Squanto, the only surviving native of, 190.
Pecksuot, conference of, with Hobbamock, 337. His insolence, 338. Killed, 338.
Pemberton, John, Rev., 476.
Penry, John, persecuted, 412. Executed, 427. Unjust charges against, 428. Tracts by, 428.
Perkins, William, Rev., 14.
Persecutions. See *Mary,* and *Pilgrims.*
Perth Assembly, 395, 467.
Pestilence among the Indians, 183, 206, 229, 234, 258, 259. Narragansets escape the, 280.
Philip, the sachem, treaty broken by, 194.
Phillips, George, Rev., of Watertown, 399.
Pierce, John, letter to, 114. Charter taken in the name of, 116, 234, 296, 348. Patent surreptitiously obtained by, 234, 349. On Weston's company, 296. His attempt to come to Plymouth, 348. Resigns his patent, 349.
Pilgrims, used the Geneva Bible, 14. Origin of the, 19. Form a separate church, 21. Their covenant, 21, 397. Two churches of the, 22. Persecuted, 23. Resolve to fly to the Low Countries, 24. Their first attempt prevented, 26. Imprisoned, 27. Their second embarkation, 28. Arrive in the Low Countries, 30. Fate of their wives and children left behind, 31. Result of the persecution of the, 32. In Amsterdam, 34, 455. In Leyden, 35, 380, 456. Trades and employments of the, 35. The number of, 36, 97, 99, 100, 122, 455. Live in peace, 38, 380, 456. Their credit with the Dutch 39, 393. Offers to the, to settle in America or Zealand, 42, 385. Attract the notice of Cardinal Bentivoglio, 43. Reasons and causes for their removal from Holland, 44, 111, 381. Turn their eyes to America, 48, 381; to Guiana, 52. Feelings of the, towards the Spaniards, 53. Conclude for Virginia, 54, 383. Send agents to England, 55, 57, 58, 59, 382. Application by, for freedom in religion, 55, 382. Their correspondence with the Virginia Company, and with their agents in England, 58, 66. Religious principles of the, 64, 65, 387, 388, 395. Obtain a patent from the Virginia Company, 74, 383. Keep a fast, 77, 383. Arrangements of the, for leaving Holland, 78, 383. Meet with discouragements, 81. Their purpose and views in going to America, 81, 261. Their agreement with the merchant adventurers, 81. Did not have all things in common, 84. Vessel and pilot provided for the, 85, 86. Keep a fast, 87. Accompanied to Delft-

63

Haven, 87, 384. The name belongs exclusively to the Plymouth colonists, 88. Their departure, 88, 384. At Southampton, 89. Parting letters to Carver and the, 89, 91, 116. Sail, 97. Put back twice, 98. Plotted against, 99. Dismiss the Speedwell, 99. Imputations on the, 99. Sail again, 100, 117. Voyage, 100. Descry Cape Cod, 101, 117, 384. Stand for Hudson's River, 102, 117, 385. Put back to Cape Cod harbour, 102, 103, 117, 385. Charge against their Captain considered, 102, 138. Nearest plantations to the, 105. Mildness of their first winter, 105, 173. Grant to, by the President and Council of New England, 114, 116, 234. Their compact, and the signing of it, 116, 120. Examinations by the, 122. Choose John Carver, governor, 123. First excursion of the, under Miles Standish, 125. Their first sight of Indians, 127. At East Harbour, in Truro, 128. At the Pond, 130, 136. Find Indian corn, 131, 133; a kettle, 133. At Old Tom's hill, in Truro, 134. At Pamet river, 135. Find canoes, 135; a deer trap, 136. Return, 137. Second expedition of the, 138. Explore Pamet river, 139. Return to Hopkins's cliff, 140. Find more corn, 141; Indian graves, 142; an embalmed body, 142; wigwams, 143. Return, 145. Propose settling at Pamet river, 146. Third expedition of the, under Captain Standish, 149. At Billingsgate Point, 151. In Wellfleet, 152. In Eastham, 153. Find an Indian burying-ground, 153; wigwams, 154. Alarmed by wolves, 155. First encounter of, with Indians, 156. Sail along the coast, 159. On Clark's island, 160. Go on shore, 161. Return to Provincetown harbour, 162. Sail in the Mayflower, and arrive in Plymouth harbour, 163. Conclude to build on the bank at Plymouth, 167. Fortify Burial Hill, 168, 169, 181, 295, 335. Cut timber, 169. Lay out house-lots, 170,173. In want of fish-hooks and nets, 171, 294. Build, 173, 230. Two of the, lost in the woods, 174. Receive Samoset, 182; with other Indians, 187; Squanto, 191; Massasoit, 191, 231. Mortality among the, 197, 265. Burial place of the, 199. Not one of the, return in the Mayflower, 199. Embassy of the, to Massasoit, at Pokanoket, 202. Accessions to the, by the Fortune, 235, 230. Put on short allowance, 236. Their treatment of the Indians, 259. True to their principles, 260. Unjustly charged with fanaticism, 273. Menaced by the Narragansets, 230. Famishing, 294. Supplied by Captain Jones, 298. Advice by the, to Weston's colony, 323. Their wants and means of subsistence, 329. Offer to receive Weston's colony, 337, 342. Aid Weston, 342. Accessions to the, by the Anne and the Little James, 352. Old comers or forefathers among the, 352. Contributions by the first, to bring over and support the others, 385, 482. Not Separatists, 387. Not schismatics, 391. Not exclusionists, 392,

399. Works in vindication of the, 419. See *America, New England, Plymouth*, and *Robinson*.
Pines, on Cape Cod, 118, 124. At Plymouth, 161.
Pinses, braves, 288. Sachems' council, 323, 359. Killed at Weymouth, 339. Account of, 359. Procure corn for the sachems, 362.
Piscataqua, settlement at, commenced, 351.
Plague, Squanto on the, 291. See *Pestilence*.
Plums, at Plymouth, 231.
Plymouth, New England, mildness of the first winter at, 105, 173. Effects of the settlement at, 122. First offence in, 149, 199. Day of the landing at, 161. Rock and place of the landing, 161, 199. Trees and plants of, 164, 165. Soil of, 165. Conclusion to settle there, 167; to fortify Burial Hill, 168, 169. Common house there, 169, 173, 177. House lots laid out in, 170, 173. Mill at, 172, 352. First entry in the records of, 173. Two men lost from, 174. Ponds in, 176. Shed built at, for common goods, 178. Two Indians at, 180. Artillery planted on the hill at, 181. Samoset at, 182. Indian names of, 183, 203, 245. Visit to, by Indians from Masssoit, 186. Garden seeds sown, 189. Savages appear at, 190. Squanto there, 190. Massasoit visits, 191, 259. Treaty at, with Massasoit, 193, 244, 245. Brigham's Digest of the Laws of, 197. Re-election of Carver as governor of, 197. Mortality and burying-place at, 197, 199, 473. Mayflower sails from 199. Death of the governor of, 200. First marriage and duel in, 201. Origin of the name, 203. Embassy from, to Massasoit at Pokanoket, 202. Voyage from, in search of a lost boy, 214. Seven men only at, 218. Expedition from, against the Narragansets, 219. The surgeon and physician at, 222. Voyage from, to the Massachusetts, 224. Arrival of the Fortune at, 235. Things wanted at, 237. Hilton's Letter on, 250. Ship's company arrive at, from Damariscove islands, 278. Impaled, 285. Measures for protecting, 285. Apprehensions there. from the Narragansets, 285, 287. Council held at, 286. Alarmed, 287. Visited by Massasoit, 290. Second voyage from, to Massachusetts, 290. Scarcity of provisions there, 290. Arrival of the Sparrow, 293. Voyage from, to Monhegan, for provisions, 293. Arrival of the Charity and the Swan at, 296. Arrival of the Discovery and Sparrow at, 298. Expeditions from, for corn and to discover a passage round Cape Cod, 300. Winslow's second journey from, to Pokanoket, 313. Expedition from, against the Indians at Weymouth, 327. General Court held at, 331. Indian spy arrested at, 335. Reception of part of Weston's company at, 342. Head set up at, 343. Allotment of lands, 346. Drought and famine at, 348, 354. The first fast at, 349. Thanksgiving, 231, 351. Arrival of the Anne and Little James at, with a list of the passengers, 351, 352. Food for passengers on arriving at, 353. Climate

INDEX. 499

of, 369. Consultation of, by succeeding colonies, 386. White on the government at, 483. See *Burial Hill*, and *Pilgrims*.
Plymouth Church, early records of the, 4. The First Independent or Congregational, in America, 77. Givers of the parsonage ground to the, 223.
Plymouth Company, not applied to by the Pilgrims, 55, 75.
Plymouth harbour, explored, 161. Pilgrims arrive in, 161, 163. Islands in, 161, 163. Fish and fowl in, 164. Includes Kingston and Duxbury harbours, 164. First death in, 168.
Plymouth rock, 161, 199.
Pokanoket, expedition to Massasoit at, 197, 202, 232. Arrival at. 208. Extent of the country, 208. A night at, 210, 211. See *Massasoit*.
Pollock Rip, 102.
Polyander, John, 43.
Pond and Pond village, in Truro, 130, 136. Great Hollow near, 131.
Popham, John, Lord, Colony of, at Sagadahoc, 50, 55, 112, 427. Condemnation of Puritans by, 427.
Portsmouth, settlement at Little Harbour in, 351.
Powows, priests, one sentenced to death, 308. Practices of, among, the sick, 317. With Massasoit, 317. Account of, 357, 366.
Prat, Phinehas, 332, 352.
Prayers, habits of the Pilgrims as to, 156, 167. Brewster on, 469.
Presbyterians, tolerated in New England, 402. See *Communion*.
Priests. See *Powows*.
Prince, Thomas, in error, 57, 58. On attempts to settle New England, 107. Error of, as to Barnstable harbour, 135. On a grant to Peregrine White, 148. Had Bradford's register, 148. On the respect for Robinson at Leyden, 393. On Robinson's Farewell Discourse, 399. On Isaac Robinson, 453. On the difference in elders, 455.
Prince, Thomas, Gov., arrives in the Fortune, 235. Marriage of, 470.
Prophesying, the practice of, 419. Ancient, 420. Liberty of, 421.
Provincetown harbour, Pilgrims at, 102, 117, 385. Survey and Map of, by Major J. D. Graham, 118. Whales and fish there, 119. Notice of, 120. Landing at, 123. Beach grass planted at, 123. Mayflower sails from, 163. Fortune puts into, 234. See *Cape Cod*.
Provisions. See *Indian Corn*, *Pilgrims*, and *Plymouth*.
Punishments, Indian, 365.
Punkapog, Stoughton, 227.
Puritans, the name, 12, 417, 443. Hostility of James I. to the, 20. See *Pilgrims*.

Presents to, 192. Hostage with, 192. Reception of, 194. Described, 195.
Quails, on Cape Cod, 137.
Quincy, Pilgrims at, 226. Supposed residence of the Massachusetts sachems, 227. See *Squantum*.

R.

Race Point, Cape Cod, 119.
Raleigh, Sir Walter, on Guiana, 52. On the law for banishing Separatists, 436.
Rattlesnake's skin, sent with arrows, 281. Returned with powder and shot, 283.
Razor shell, 306.
Reynolds, Captain of the Speedwell, 85. Puts back twice, 98.
Reynolds, John, Rev., 432.
Rhode Island, 281.
Robertson, William, on the removal from Holland, 48. In error, 84, 100.
Robinson, Isaac, 453.
Robinson, John, Rev., 23. Goes over to Holland, 34. Removes from Amsterdam to Leyden, 34. His ministry and character, 36. 452. Time of his death. 393, 479. Books written by, 40, 400, 454. His Apology, 40, 388, 391. Disputes with Episcopius, 41, 392. Age of, in 1620, 46. Correspondence of, with Edwin Sandys, 58; with Sir John Wolstenholme, 63. Preaches a Fast Sermon, 77. Tarries at Leyden, 77, 384. The reason of his not accompanying the Pilgrims, 77, 383, 453. Farewell Fast Sermon by, 87, 396. His parting letter to John Carver, 89; to the whole company, 91, 116. Dies without going to New England, 91, 443. On Standish, 339. His doctrine of communion, 388. His views of and regard for the Church of England, 389, 415, 442. His dislike of Episcopacy and the Liturgy, 390. Respect and funeral honors for, at Leyden, 392, 393, 453. Not a rigid Separatist, 400. His Treatise on the Church of England cited, 400. On Church Synods, 419. On prophesying, 422. His answer to Bernard, 423. His church a model, 426. On Robert Browne, 442. Bradford's account of, 451. Facts respecting, 452. Bp. Hall's insinuation respecting, 453. His intention and desire to settle at Plymouth, 453, 475, 476, 477, 479, 482. Letters from, to the church at Plymouth, 473; to Elder Brewster. 475. Lyford and, 476. Plotting against, 476, 477. On elders, 477. Last days and death of, 393, 478, 481.
Rock harbour creek, in Orleans, 155.
Roses, at Plymouth, 234.
Rowland, Thomas, persecuted, 443.
Ruling elders, difference between teaching and, 455, 477. Still continued in Salem, 455. See *Elders*.

Q.

Quadequina, Massasoit's brother, 191, 232.

S.

Sabbath. See *Sunday*.

INDEX.

Sachems, account of, and of their families, 360. Executioners of the laws, 365.
Sacrifices, Indian, 358.
Sagadahoc. See *Kennebec*.
St. Lawrence river, discovered, 243.
Salem, error respecting the church in, 77. Mission from, to Plymouth, for a physician, 223, 336. Dutch admitted to communion at, 393. Ruling elders in, 455. See *Endicott*, and *Higginson*.
Samoset, description, and reception of, at Plymouth, 182. Lodges with Hopkins, 185. Goes to Massasoit, 185, 186. Returns with others, 186. Remains, 189. Comes again, with Squanto, 190. Tarries, 195, 196.
Sanders, John, overseer of Weston's colony, writes to Plymouth, 327. Bradford replies to, 330. Voyage by, to Monhegan, 330, 332.
Sandwich, Manomet, boy lost at, 217. Sachem at, 232. See *Canonacome*.
Sandy Neck, at Barnstable, 159, 212.
Sandys, Sir Edwin, 55, 56, 382. Correspondence of, with Robinson and Brewster, 58. Notice of, 59. Treasurer and governor of the Virginia Company, 68. Obnoxious to James I., 68.
Saquish, in Plymouth harbour, 160, 164, 287.
Sassafras, on Cape Cod, 118. Medicinal virtues ascribed to, 130. At Plymouth, 164,165.
Savage, James, on Cotton Mather, 30. On Hampden's visit to New England, 315. On ruling elders, 455.
Savins, on Cape Cod, 124.
Scituate, North river in, 148. Chauncy, minister of, 405.
Scussett harbour, in Sandwich, 306.
Sea fowls, at Cape Cod, 119. At Plymouth, 164, 229. Time of the, 294.
Seals, at Plymouth, 172.
Se-baptist, John Smith the, 451.
Self-love, Cushman's discourse on the sin and danger of, 262.
Separatists, 388. Harmony of the Nonconformists and, 398. Views of, respecting the Church of England, 414. Principles of the, 416, 417. No synods among the, 418. On prophesying among the, 419. Law banishing the, 436. Persecution of the, 437. Treatment of in prisons, 437. Excommunicated, 438. Deprived of their livelihood, 439. Banished, 439, 441. Treatment of, by the prelates, 440. Before Robert Brown, 442. See *Pilgrims*.
Shawmut, sachem of, 232. See *Boston*.
Sheath fish, 306.
Shellfish, at Plymouth, 294. At Buzzard's Bay, 306.
Shingle Brook, in Plymouth, 165.
Ships, size and character of, 86.
Sickness, Indian customs in, 317.
Simmons, formerly Symonson, 394.
Simonson, Moses, a Pilgrim, 235, 236, 394.
Skate at Plymouth, 164.
Slade's Ferry, in Swanzey, 315.
Slany, John, 191.
Smallpox. See *Pestilence*.
Smith, John, Rev., and his church at Amsterdam, 22, 34, 429. Persecuted, 443. On Johnson and Ainsworth, 445. Bradford's account of, 450. Facts respecting him, 451.
Smith, John, Captain, surveys and names New England, 80, 101, 255. On the merchant adventurers, 81. On Cape Cod, 101. On New England water, 129. On Indian flax, 166. Names Plymouth, 203. Mentions Nauset, 216. On the country of the Massachusetts, 226. Isles named by, 351.
Smith, Sir Thomas, account of, 68.
Smith's isles, 251.
Snaphances, 156, 157.
Snow's brook, in Eastham. 152.
Soil, English and Indian right to the, 243.
Somer Islands Company, 112.
Southampton, 85. Arrival of the Pilgrims at, 89. Situation of, 89.
Southworth, Thomas, 419.
Sowams, seat of Massasoit, 208.
Spain. See *United Provinces*.
Sparrow, arrival of the, at Plymouth, 291, 293. 298.
Speedwell, 85. Size of the, 86. Unseaworthy, 93. Dismissed, 99.
Spooner, Ephraim, Dea., of Plymouth, 199.
Squa sachem, of the Massachusetts Indians, 225, 229. Of Mattapuyst, 317.
Squanto, or Tisquantum, history of, 190. Place in Quincy, named from, 191. At Plymouth, 195, 196. In an embassy to Massasoit, 202. At Pokanoket, 211. On a voyage in search of a boy, 212. Sent to Aspinet, 216. Expedition against the Narragansetts to revenge the supposed murder of, 219. Captured by Corbitant, 220. Returns to Plymouth, 223. In a voyage to the Massachusetts, 224. Would plunder the Massachusetts, 228. Aid from, about planting Indian corn, 230. Suspicions as to, 285. Double-dealing of, 289. Valuable services of, 290. Demanded by Massasoit, 291. Pilots an expedition for corn, and to discover a passage round Cape Cod, 299, 300. Sickness and death of, 301. Instructs Indians in English salutations, 305.
Squantum, a promontory in Quincy, 191, 226. Taken possession of, by Thompson, 351.
Squaws, modesty of the, 228, 364. Burdens borne by, 305, 311. Treatment of, at Weymouth, 339, 341. Their travail, 358. Servitude of, 363. Particulars respecting, 364.
Standish family, 126.
Standish, Miles, Captain, 115. Leader in an excursion up the Cape, 125. Account of, 125, 338. His coat of mail and sword, 134. In the third expedition, 149. Encounters Nauset Indians, 156, 158. Goes in search of Indians at Plymouth, 171. Death of his wife, 179. Chosen Captain, 180. Sent to meet Indians, 181. Meets Massasoit, 192. Massasoit's reception of, 194. Marches against the Narragansets in defence of Massasoit, 220. In an expedition to the Massachusetts, 225. Secures a messenger from Canonicus, 281. Military preparations of, 284. Sets forward for Massachusetts, 287. Driven back

from an expedition for corn, 299. Goes to Eastham, 304. Salutation of, by Aspinet, 304. Conduct of, at Yarmouth, 308. At Scussett, 309. Treachery against, 311. Returns, 312. Expedition of, against the Indians at Weymouth, 326, 327, 331. Arrives at Weymouth, 336. Trade of, with an Indian spy, 337. Kills Pecksuot in a struggle, 338. Remarks on, by Robinson, Hubbard, and Davis, 339. Skirmishes with Indians, 341. Takes the head of Wituwamat, and returns to Plymouth, 342, 343. Effect of his Expedition, 345. Procures provisions, 350. Second wife of, 352.
Standysshe, John, killed Wat Tyler, 126.
Starsmore, Sabin, 74.
Store house, at Plymouth, 169, 173, 177.
Stout's creek, in Truro, 128.
Strawberry Hill, Watson's hill called, 180.
Sunday, in Holland, 47, 381. On Clark's island, 160. Kept on shore at Plymouth, 177. Refusal of the Pilgrims to traffic on, 189.
Supremacy, oath of, 64.
Swamps, formerly ponds, 130.
Swan, arrival of the, 296. Remains, 298.
Swanzey, 208. See *Corbitant, Gardner's Neck, Mattapoiset*, and *Slade's Ferry*.
Synods, at Dort, 47, 424. At Cambridge, 394, 402. At Embden, 422. None among the Separatists, 408.

T.

Tabor, and Taborites, 38.
Tarbes, John, 396.
Taunton river, 205. Pestilence on, 206, 234. Notice of, 206. Country on, 207.
Thacker, Elias, persecuted, 412. Executed, 427.
Thanksgiving, the first, 231. After a fast, 351.
Theft, Indian punishment of, 364.
Thievish Harbour, 148, 159.
Thompson, David, 350.
Thompson's island, in Boston harbour, 351.
Tilly, Edward, a Pilgrim, 122, 126, 149. Notice of, 151.
Tilly, John, a Pilgrim, 149, 151.
Tisquantum. See *Squanto*.
Titicut, 205, 212.
Tobacco, 188, 194, 363.
Tokamahamon, an Indian guide, 211, 214. Corbitant's hostility to, 219. With a messenger from Canonicus, 281.
Toleration, want of, under James I., 21. Holland reproached for, 23. Application for, by agents from Holland, 55. Of the Pilgrims towards the Dutch and French, 388, 392, 393; towards the Scotch, 394; towards the Presbyterians, 402, 407. Not shown to evil-doers, 407. See *Communion, Pilgrims, Robinson*, and *Separatists*.
Town brook, in Plymouth, Pilgrims settle near, 167. Notice of, 172. Mill on, 172, 352. Crossed to meet Indians, 181. Reception of Massasoit at the, 192.
Training Green in Plymouth, 168.

Trees, on Cape Cod, 118, 124, 132. At Plymouth, 164. In Pokanoket, 207.
Trial, an Indian, 307.
Truro, soil in, 123. Excursions to, 128. Pond in, 130. Second excursion to, 139. See *East harbour*.
Turbot, 164.
Tyburn, persons executed at, 437.
Tyler, Wat, killed, 126.

U.

Uncle Sam's Hill, in Truro, 133.
United Provinces, war between Spain and the, 25; truce between them, 44. Expiration of the truce, 51. See *Low Countries*.
Upham, Charles W., Rev., 77.

V.

Vessels, size and character of, 86.
Virginia, colonization of, 53, 54. Pilgrims conclude for, 54, 383. Settled by Episcopalians, 54. Territorial extent of, 54. Application for religious toleration in, 55. Oaths for emigrants to, 64. Governors of, 69, 70. Blackwell's voyage to, 70. New patent for the northern part of, 80, 100. Effect of the Plymouth settlement on, 122. Winslow on the state of, 278. Indian massacre in, 278, 293, 295. Vessels for, at Plymouth, 298. Proclamation as to the government of, 485. See *New England*.
Virginia Company, 54. Application of the Pilgrims to the 55, 57; their correspondence, 58. Courts held by the, 67. Governors and Treasurers of the, 68. Contentions in the, 69. Patent obtained from the, 74.

W.

Wachusett mountain, 228.
Walloons, 39, 352, 393.
Walnut trees, 132, 164, 165.
Wampom, 143.
Wamsutta, son of Massasoit, 194.
Wareham, conspiracy with the Indians at, 323.
Warren, in the Pokanoket country, 208.
Warren, Richard, a Pilgrim, 121, 150. His widow and descendants, 150.
Wassapinewat, 330.
Water of New England, 129; of Plymouth, 165, 166, 167, 255.
Watertown, minister of, 398.
Watson, Edward, owner of Clark's island, 160.
Watson's hill, two Indians appear on, 180. Names of, 180. Indians again appear there, 190. Massasoit there, 190.
Weavers among the Plymouth settlers, 35.
Wellfleet bay, visited, 151, 152, 153.
Wellingsly Brook, in Plymouth, 165.
Wessagussett, 78. Subject to the Massachusetts sachem, 227. See *Weymouth*.

INDEX.

West, Francis, admiral of New England, 278.
Weston, Thomas, agreement with, 78. Notice of, 78. Inclines to New England, 80. Neglects to provide shipping, 85. On a charter, 234. His people at Weymouth, 276, 296. The Sparrow sent out by, 293. Writes to Mr. Carver, 293. Expedition of his people for corn, 299; their return to Weymouth. 303. His visit and misfortunes, 342. See *Weymouth.*
Weymouth, Captain, carries Indians from Penobscot, 190.
Weymouth, or Wessagusset, 78. Character of Weston's colony at, 276, 296, 334. Account of the planting of, 296. Conduct of the colonists of, at Plymouth, 297, 300. Indians' complaints respecting, 298, 302, 327. Indian conspiracy against, 310, 323. Expedition against the Indians of, 327, 331. Want of provisions at, 328. Too feeble and sick for defence, 329. Wretched state of, 332. Execution at, 332. Standish's arrival there, 336. Carelessness at, 336. Offer to, from the Pilgrims, 337. Seven Indians killed at, 339. Broken up, 341. See *Weston.*
Whales, whaling and, 119, 146.
Whitbourne, Richard, Captain, 155.
White, Roger, letters by, to Bradford, 478, 483.
White, Peregrine, the first born, 148.
White, William, a Pilgrim, 121, 148. Death of, 181, 201.
Whitgift, Archbishop, 432.
Wigwams, discovered, 143. Described, 144. In Eastham, 154. Near Plymouth, 172. Of Nanepashemet, 226.
Wildfowl, at Cape Cod, 119, 137, 139, 140. At Plymouth, 164, 179, 229. Time of the, 294.
Williams, Roger, 132, 133, 142, 187, 280. 305, 317, 318, 319, 356, 365, 366, 367. Prophesying by, at Plymouth, 420.
Williams, Thomas, a Pilgrim, 122. Meets Massasoit, 192.
Wincob, John, patent taken in the name of, 75.
Windows, account of, 237.
Winnatuckset brook, source of, 206.
Winslow chair, cut of the, 238.
Winslow Edward, on John Robinson and Arminianism, 41. Age of, in 1620, 46. Reasons by, for removing from Holland, 47. On Thomas Weston, 78. On the profit from fishing, 81, 383. In the third exploring party, 139. On errors, 175, 277. On the Indian language, 183. On the Indians' use of tobacco, 189. Interview of, with Massasoit, 192. A hostage, 192. Death of his wife, 197, 201. Married again, 201. Probably wrote the narrative of the journey to Pokanoket, 202. In the embassy to Massasoit, 202, 204, 213. Letter from, 230. Cattle brought to Plymouth by, 233. His Relation, 269. Notice of, and of his family and descendants, 274. His return to England, 277, 477. On the state of Virginia, 278. In the second Massachusetts expedition, 287. Goes to Monhegan, 293. Second journey of, to Pokanoket, to visit Massasoit in his sickness, 313. Indian plot revealed to, 324, 326. Lodges with Corbitant, 324. Returns, 326. His brief Narration of the true Grounds for the first Planting of New England, 377, 379, 408. Sent to England in 1646 to defend the colony of Massachusetts against Gorton, 379. Preserves Robinson's Farewell Discourse, 399. Works by, 408. On prophesying by, 419.
Winslow, Gilbert, 275.
Winslow, Isaac, 275.
Winslow, John, 235, 275.
Winslow, Josiah, on the purchase of the Indians' lands, 259. Notice of, 275.
Winslow, Kenelm, 275.
Winter, the first, at Plymouth, 105, 173.
Winthrop, John, Gov., fleet of, rendezvous at Southampton, 89. On a shipwreck on Brown's island, 163. On the Church of England, 398. On the synod at Cambridge, 402. On Rev. Peter Hobart, 402. Takes part in religious services at Plymouth, 419.
Wituwamat, 310, 338. Killed, 339. Head of, taken, 342; stuck up, at Plymouth, 343.
Wives of sachems, 361. See *Squa*, and *Squaws.*
Wolstenholme, Sir John, 55, 63, 66.
Wolves, alarms from, 155. Encountered, 178.
Wood, Anthony, cited, 59, 432, 439.
Wood, William, 118, 124, 129, 132, 133, 135, 136, 140, 142, 143, 164, 166, 176, 187, 188, 198, 305, 306, 307, 318, 366.
Wood End, on Cape Cod, 118, 119.
Wood-gaile, 129.
Woosamequin, or Massasoit, 245.

Y.

Yarmouth, Mattachiest, 216. Corn procured at, 302, 303. Valor of Standish at, 309.
Yeardley, Sir George, Governor of Virginia, 70, 279.

Z.

Ziska, John, 38.

THE END.